Roger C. Sullivan and
the Triumph of the Chicago
Democratic Machine, 1908–1920

Roger C. Sullivan and the Triumph of the Chicago Democratic Machine, 1908–1920

RICHARD ALLEN MORTON

Foreword by FRANK SULLIVAN

McFarland & Company, Inc., Publishers

Jefferson, North Carolina

Portions of Chapter 5 first appeared in Richard Allen Morton,
"'It Was Bryan and Sullivan Who Did the Trick': How William Jennings Bryan
and Illinois' Roger C. Sullivan Brought the Nomination to
Woodrow Wilson in 1912," *Journal of the Illinois State Historical
Society* (summer 2015). Portions of Chapter 6 first appeared
in Richard Allen Morton, "Man of Belial: Roger C. Sullivan,
the Progressive Democracy, and the Senatorial Elections of 1914,"
Journal of the Illinois State Historical Society (winter 1999).

LIBRARY OF CONGRESS CATALOGUING-IN-PUBLICATION DATA

Names: Morton, Richard Allen, 1951– author.
Title: Roger C. Sullivan and the triumph of the Chicago Democratic machine,
1908/1920 / Richard Allen Morton ; foreword by Frank Sullivan.
Description: Jefferson, North Carolina : McFarland & Company, Inc.,
Publishers, 2019 | Includes bibliographical references and index.
Identifiers: LCCN 2018054638 | ISBN 9781476675015
(softcover : acid free paper) ∞
Subjects: LCSH: Sullivan, Roger C. (Roger Charles), 1861–1920. |
Politicians—Illinois—Chicago—Biography. | Chicago (Ill.)—Biography. |
Democratic Party (Chicago, Ill.)—History—20th century. | Democratic
Party (Ill.)—History—20th century. | Chicago (Ill.)—Politics and
government—20th century. | Cook County (Ill.)—Politics and
government—20th century.
Classification: LCC F548.45.S88 M675 2019 | DDC 324.2092 [B] —dc23
LC record available at https://lccn.loc.gov/2018054638

BRITISH LIBRARY CATALOGUING DATA ARE AVAILABLE

ISBN (print) 978-1-4766-7501-5
ISBN (ebook) 978-1-4766-3450-0

Front cover image: Roger Sullivan, June 1912 (Library of Congress)

Printed in the United States of America

*McFarland & Company, Inc., Publishers
Box 611, Jefferson, North Carolina 28640
www.mcfarlandpub.com*

For J. Leonard Bates and
Aaron David Neal

Acknowledgments

In a project such as this, there are many dozens of people who have made a contribution. There is always the challenge of balancing those who have been especially important with all those others who also served without surrendering to the temptation of creating a massive list. Please accept my apologies in advance if you are not mentioned.

Of course I must give credit to the interest and tolerance of my historical colleagues and peers, Robert McColley and John Andrick. They have been there always there to mentor, to encourage, and to assist.

The several members of the Sullivan family, who know who they are, deserve my heartiest thanks for standing with me through the long years of research and writing. To them belongs so much of the credit here. Their support and friendship have meant everything.

My wife, Sharon, my sisters, Julie Hepler and Rebecca Morton, and my brother, David Neal, as well as Jeff and Doris Dunlap with Buffy, Willow, Winnie, and Tillie Morton have all given me the strength to press on.

Added to the list must be the good folks at McFarland, whose professionalism and accessibility have greatly facilitated an inevitably difficult process. Thank you!

Table of Contents

Foreword

by Frank Sullivan

In 1954, when I ran for state representative, an old timer asked me why I had never mentioned my distant relationship to Roger C. Sullivan in my campaign. I told him that my great-uncle had died so long ago—more than three decades before—that I didn't think anyone would remember him. The old timer disagreed. "Ah," he said, "there's magic in that name!" Another time, I met a Mr. O'Shea, who recounted a story about the death of his father, a precinct captain. Accompanying his mother with the body to the Illinois Central Railroad Station for burial downstate, they were met by Sullivan himself, the head of the whole Democratic organization, who came to offer his condolences and to assist the family financially. I believe that many other examples of Sullivan's unique personality and humanity could be cited and that it was this distinguishing aspect of the man that was at the heart of his leadership and political success. Richard J. Daley, for whom I served for a time as press secretary, was a basically good man—warm, friendly, but not very outgoing in the sense that we picture someone like "Boss" Frank Skeffington as played by Spencer Tracey in the *Last Hurrah* (1958), one of the great and more accurate motion pictures about urban machine politics. Roger Sullivan was such a man.

The popular support upon which Sullivan was to build a political machine could also be measured in a way familiar to some writers of history—by the population turnout for Sullivan's funeral (April 17, 1920), which the Republican *Chicago Tribune* described as "The largest in Chicago history." My father, one of Sullivan's nephews, a 15-year-old in 1920, was riding with his parent in the third car of the funeral procession. He told me that the crowds on both sides of the streets on the 10 blocks through downtown Chicago were "four to five deep." The *Tribune* upped my father's observation and reported that the crowds were "Twenty-deep."

According to the newspaper the funeral cortege included an amazing 684 automobiles along with 500 marching Chicago policemen and 500 marching Chicago firemen. There was no organizing of the crowds, and among their numbers were hundreds, thousands even, for whom Roger Sullivan must have done favors and who called him "friend." If there was one thing that he recognized, it was that politics is first and last about people.

Richard Allen Morton has produced a volume that manages to fit in among all the accounts of politicking the real person who successfully built the organization that was to dominate local politics and play a highly significant role on the national scene from Woodrow Wilson in 1912 to John Kennedy and Lyndon Johnson in the 1960s. Without

Sullivan's "people skills," it is difficult to imagine his being able to join together the many interests and groups to create his "Democracy."

Chicago was and still is a city of neighborhoods of people of differing backgrounds. The largest number of immigrants came from Germany, Ireland, Italy, Russia and Bohemia. The number of German immigrants was so large that the German language was once taught in most of the city's public elementary schools. The large number of immigrants from Ireland included Sullivan's father-to-be when he was 17 and Sullivan's mother-to-be when she was 16. Both parents settled in Belvidere, Illinois, where Sullivan grew up. The flow of immigrants from Bohemia was to be reflected in the mayoral election of Anton Cermak, eleven years after Sullivan's death in 1920.

One of Roger Sullivan's accomplishments was in creating a common ground in the Democratic Party for so many of these groups. The Irish were the most active, but Sullivan turned no one away and in building his organization managed to find a place for everyone. He harbored no prejudices and showed no favoritisms. His was not an "Irish machine."

Even those who were not Democrats merited his respect and concern, including African Americans, who during his lifetime were only at most about 4 percent of Chicago's population and overwhelmingly Republican. Julian Taylor, editor of the African-American *Broadax* (Chicago), wrote of what he described as the many ways Sullivan had always spoken out and acted on behalf of racial harmony in the city: "Mr. Sullivan and his family believed in rights and justice for all men." Other examples cited by Taylor as to how Sullivan generated the political enthusiasm to bolster the political machine was his stance during the 1908 Democratic National Convention in Denver where he blocked the efforts of some Southern senators to disavow two constitutional amendments protecting black rights stemming from the aftermath of the Civil War. Added to this was Sullivan's refusal to bow to public pressure, after his election as clerk of the Cook County probate court in 1893, to fire his personal secretary, William G. Anderson, an African American, who would later become a prominent attorney. According to editor Taylor, Sullivan stated that he "did not care one thing about the color of the skin of Mr. Anderson … as long as he discharged his duties properly." Mr. Anderson stayed on the job. Race riots in East St. Louis Illinois in 1917 and in Chicago in 1919 were occasions for Sullivan to appeal for law and order and to insist publicly that both "white and colored races can and must live together in harmony."

I believe that these public stances and the precedents they created went a long way toward cementing the population components that were to bind together the Democratic machine of Chicago for so many decades. This was Roger C. Sullivan, and this is very much who this book is about.

Frank Sullivan is Roger Sullivan's grandnephew. He was the press secretary for Richard J. Daley, and is a retired reporter for the Chicago Sun-Times *and the author of* Legend: The Only Inside Story About Mayor Richard J. Daley *(1989).*

Preface

I have known Roger Sullivan for decades. I met him while working on my dissertation, which concerned Edward F. Dunne, the only man to have served as both mayor of Chicago and governor of Illinois. Their careers were virtually simultaneous, and during my research, Sullivan kept reappearing. This otherwise unknown man seemed be at the heart of every internal issue of the Chicago and Illinois Democratic parties. Before long, it became clear that Sullivan was probably the party's single most important leader in Chicago during the period and that most of the elected officials, like Dunne, while never mere myrmidons, were relatively less significant in terms of actual brokering of power and policy.

I also became aware of a lengthy and divisive factional feud within the Party between those adhering to Sullivan and his growing web of alliances and associations on one side and the personal "city hall crowd" of five-time mayor Carter H. Harrison II on the other. Gradually, it became apparent that the "Sullivan Democracy" represented something different from the personal machine clustered around Harrison and built upon his patronage; that Sullivan, in fact, envisioned and strived for an enduring structure of party control within a diverse and fractious party leadership that would be built upon the mutual self-interest for achieving order.

The greatest epiphany came with the realization that Sullivan's ultimate success in cornering power as paramount leader within the state and metropolitan Democratic Party, and then in passing along both the leadership and the organization to his successor, George Brennan, was the true beginning of the famous Chicago Democratic Machine. Others, like Brennan, Anton Cermak, Pat Nash, and, of course, that stellar practitioner of urban politics, Mayor Richard J. Daley, I knew, built and adapted the organization over succeeding decades, but it was Sullivan (and his allies) who put it together. While not entirely unrealized, especially within the Cook County Democratic Party itself, Sullivan's decisive role had been largely overlooked by the historians.

Accordingly, I began to focus my research upon Roger Sullivan. The first outcome was an article about his 1914 Senate run in which he easily defeated the candidate of William Jennings Bryan (Sullivan's most vehement and enduring political enemy), then Secretary of State, who was backed up by the sitting Democratic senator, governor, and mayor of Chicago. He lost narrowly to a Republican opponent, but his primary victory virtually guaranteed his final success as head of the party.

After this, I concentrated upon Roger Sullivan's early rise to prominence and his later successes. What emerged was an increasingly fascinating chronology of an extraordinary politician and his brilliant maneuvering within a political culture so complicated as to be repeatedly described as byzantine. Without any useful papers available—either for Sullivan or for any other major player—the research challenges were considerable, requiring careful perusal of newspapers, periodicals, and government records as well as of the scattered collection of existing autobiographies, biographies and historical monographs that touched upon the subject.

A major breakthrough was achieved through contact with the Sullivan family. Not only were they willing, and even eager, to assist my research, but they were collectively highly knowledgeable about the personal details of my subject's life. Their assistance added immeasurably to the scope of my work. With their information and insights, my understanding of Roger C. Sullivan took on the added dimension of his humanity. The man that so excited my interest (and admiration) as a political actor was also revealed as a unique personality.

I knew about his success as an entrepreneur—indeed most of his generation of politicos in Chicago combined business with politics—but I was unaware of the scope of his commercial accomplishments, which alone would have guaranteed him a place, at least as a footnote, in his city's histories. I also knew that he was widely respected by virtually everyone with whom he came in contact (even by those who opposed him politically), but I did not fully comprehend the degree of charisma, benevolence, and frank likability that he commanded. Most importantly, I learned that, for all of his political and business accomplishments, it was his family that was at the center of his life—and for Roger Sullivan the concept of family was one that was vastly extended to include even distant cousins in Ireland that he had never met. A very direct and logical person, he was also profoundly spiritual in his attachment to his Christian faith and the teachings of his church. He was, in sum, very distant from the bawdy stereotypes of the cynical big city boss.

The first fruit of all of this was a book concerned with Sullivan's early career, *Roger C. Sullivan and the Making of the Chicago Democratic Machine, 1881–1908* (McFarland, 2016). This traced his rise within the context of the changing city and state political culture as a politician, businessman, and pater familias from his birth through his election as Illinois' national committeeman. It includes detailed discussion of his feud with William Jennings Bryan, and his success outmaneuvering and temporarily driving Mayor Harrison out of politics.

This is the second volume about Roger Sullivan and the development of his organization. It covers the time when he was in ascendency, including his major moment in the national spotlight as a decisive player in the nomination of Woodrow Wilson in 1912. Also chronicled is his nearly successful run for the United States Senate. But most important is the discussion of the finalization of his "Democracy" and its transformation into the Chicago machine. However, no account would be complete without further exploration of the man and his personal life, and this too has merited inclusion.

The immediate purpose of these studies is to shed light into one of history's many dim corners to seek a further understanding of the realities of political power. Machine politics as practiced by Sullivan and his successors were uniquely American, and speak to the vast and unfolding experience of the world's greatest experiment in representative government. Beyond this is the goal of uncovering meaningful and relevant information about one of the nation's great metropolises. But closest to my heart, and also an important measure of success, is the resurrection of the life and career of an extraordinary human being.

Introduction:
"The Benevolent Boss"
(April 1920)

"He was wiser than most of the children of light."

"Roger C. Sullivan Dead," proclaimed the *Chicago Tribune's* bold headline on April 15, 1920. The news was as unexpected as it was momentous. For weeks the public had been assured of his imminent recovery from a serious case of bronchitis; and being but fifty-nine years of age, and usually a model of vigor, he hardly seemed to be an immediate candidate for the grave. As someone who had come to be a familiar, even beloved, figure, his passing inspired real shock and grief. A predictable torrent of sadness, sympathy, and reflection burst forth in the editorial pages of the local press, which, in this age before sophisticated electronic communication, were focal points in the expression and creation of public sentiment.

With considerable feeling, the *Chicago Tribune,* which had always opposed him politically, now proclaimed Sullivan as the "benevolent 'boss' of the Illinois Democracy," widely beloved for both himself and his charitable activities, and to whom at least some of the credit for important reform measures like civil service, direct primaries, woman's suffrage, and reorganization of the state government was due. The paper editorially extolled him as "one of the very few men in public life whose death would find so many people with a sense of loss."[1]

The *Chicago Herald-Examiner* wrote of him as a "towering figure in national, state, and municipal politics," whose genius was in his understanding of the "human factor in politics" and his recognition that "patronage, friendship, and helpfulness were the cornerstones" for public success. Almost everyone credited him for the nomination of Woodrow Wilson in 1912, while also admitting that his career was not untainted by controversy.

Others in the press were equally flattering. *The Chicago Evening Post,* never on his side, celebrated his personality as "of a kind that inspires affection," even if he "played the game of politics by such rules as circumstances demanded." Still it could not be denied that "thousands of people thruout [sic] the country" had lost "a kindly friend." The *Chicago Daily News,* the mouthpiece of the often sternly progressive Victor Lawson, more bluntly identified Roger Sullivan as a "boss" who used the "tools that came to hand." However, it also praised him as "instrumental in providing [Chicago] with much progressive legislation," and for being "conscientious in his selection of men to receive his organization's support for positions on the bench." Moreover, while there might be "commonly an unsound premise in his reasoning that led him astray," it could not be denied that "the faults of his political leadership were the faults of American democracy as interpreted in a great metropolitan center of mixed population." His death was a "distinct loss to the Chicago public" of a "practical yet conscientious leader."[2]

The national media, too, noted his passing with reflection. Most newspapers referenced his importance at the 1912 Democratic convention, as well as his success in a decade-long feud with William Jennings Bryan. Almost all resorted to an overstated rags-to-riches cliché based on his rise from a $1.25 a day job in the machine shops to his exalted status as a multimillionaire businessman and powerful political leader. Some discussed his epic factional battles with former Mayor Carter H. Harrison II. Much more insightful and revelatory of the curious ambiguity with which he was viewed by so many was a rambling editorial from the ultra-liberal *Baltimore Sun*. Unable to deny Sullivan's positive achievement in enabling its hero, Wilson, to become president, or his importance in local, state, and national affairs, the writer also struggled with the fact that Sullivan was also an adroit practitioner of urban politics of the type widely despised by some progressives:

> In his day and generation, he was wiser than most of the children of the light … he understood the value as well as the justice of recognizing popular sentiment…. He may have failed to make the world better; but in his way, he often helped it from getting worse…. There was so much natural good in him that critics often forgot how bad he was, considered from the stern moralist's lofty perch … he makes us wonder why bad men often have such an excess of good qualities, and why good men are so frequently lacking in them.[3]

Roger Charles Sullivan (Sullivan family collection).

Among his political and business peers, there was far less conflicted moral angst. President Wilson, now in his sickbed following a series of strokes, approved a message that labeled Sullivan a "good friend" and that extended his "deepest and warmest sympathies." Illinois Senator Medill McCormick, though a Republican, had remained in anxious contact with the family throughout the illness. He now described him as "a brave and loyal man." Representative John W. Rainey introduced a resolution in the House of Representatives that spoke of Roger's ability to "do good quietly and unselfishly." The sitting mayor of Chicago, Republican William Hale Thompson, called him a "fine man." However, displaying characteristic gaucherie, he also noted that the Democratic leader had not been looking "so good" lately. Former Governor Charles Deneen celebrated Sullivan as a "born leader," and credited him for helping make "many good laws" in Chicago and Illinois, while Governor Frank O. Lowden sent a message praising his "friend" with whom he long had been on a first name basis and had regularly exchanged Christmas greetings. State's Attorney Maclay Hoyne also claimed a close attachment unaffected by their political rivalries with the man he now recognized as "one of Chicago's most useful citizens."

Robert Sweitzer, Cook County Treasurer and Sullivan's candidate for mayor in 1911 and 1919, was in despair over the loss of his "closest friend," noting the departed's "big heartedness" and his habit of "always trying to help somebody." Samuel Insull, public utility baron of the city, was also one of the multitudes who laid claim to Roger Sullivan as his best chum. Just prior to breaking down unable to speak further, he tearfully described the departed to reporters as "one of the real big men of Chicago." Dudley Field Malone, former collector of the port of New York, pronounced him "the most honorable man I ever met in politics." Carter H. Harrison II was predictably more restrained and merely extended to Helen Sullivan the "deepest sympathies of Mrs. Harrison and myself in your great bereavement." At the constitutional convention, meeting in Springfield, a memorial resolution was ratified praising Sullivan for being "the foremost citizen of Illinois" and "a financial leader, and philanthropic citizen, statesman and patriot." Even delegates from the GOP articulated their respect for a man who retained the "common touch" and always kept his word.[4]

And the telegrams poured in from across the political and social spectrum, from prominent office-holders like A. Mitchell Palmer, Attorney General of the United States, Franklin Lane, Secretary of the Interior, from fellow "bosses," past and present, like Thomas Taggart of Indiana and James Guffey of Pennsylvania, from the former and current chairs of the Democratic party Norman E. Mack and Vance McCormick, from businessmen and financiers like Bernard Baruch, Oscar Foreman, founder of the Foreman Bank, C. H. Markham, president of the Illinois Central Railroad, and Michael Girten head of the Marquette Life Insurance Company, from the mayors of Joliet, Danville, and Litchfield, Illinois, from educators like President James Burns of Notre Dame University, and from prominent private citizens like Joseph and Rose Kennedy, parents of a sickly John Fitzgerald Kennedy, who was not quite three years old. And so it went to include missives from the many less exalted private citizens who felt a need to express their sorrow at the passing of Roger C. Sullivan, a man whose only elective office was a two-year term as clerk of the Cook County probate court.[5]

The morning following his death, Sullivan's home was filled with of dozens of elaborate floral wreaths and other constructions, including one sent by President Wilson, as well as scores of visitors who came to pay their respects and to view the body. It was a mixed crowd of "rich and poor, unknown and influential rubbing elbows." There were "old men totter[ing] thru [sic] the flower-laden room in which the body reposed, and parents carrying children in their arms, [who] stopped that the little ones might look upon the mortal remains of Roger Sullivan." Some old friends hung around to recount stories. Original members of the Nectar Club, Sullivan's first political organization, like coal man Frank Stuyvesant Peabody (who Roger wanted to run in 1920 for the United States Senate) and William Legner (who named a son Roger), reminisced about the old days when they were young and hungry, when "R.C." or "Roge" was just starting out in politics. White-haired gentlemen, who were not so prominent, spoke of knowing Roger during his youth in the car shops and about what a comer he had been.[6]

The arrangements were made by the Great Man's lieutenants, George Brennan, Dennis

Outside the church (Sullivan family collection).

Egan, and Sullivan's old friend and public relations expert, Bernard "B. J." Mullaney. It was to be the largest funeral in Chicago's history, eclipsing that of assassinated Mayor Carter H. Harrison I in 1893. The procession to take the body of Roger Sullivan to his last service was scheduled to leave the house at 9:00 a.m. However, because of the unexpected size of the surrounding crowd, it was not until approximately 10:00 a.m. that the solemn parade of from 7,000 to 8,000, riding in cars or marching, at last got under way. Moving slowly through the streets, it took an hour for the procession to arrive at the Holy Name Cathedral, the seat of the Catholic Archdiocese of Chicago. The large casket was carried in by the pallbearers who included some of the late leader's oldest friends like Stephen D. Griffin, William G. Legner, Patrick Nash, John F. O'Malley, Frank S. Peabody, Frank J. Quinn of Peoria, and Robert Sweitzer. They were preceded by Father Michael Sullivan (one of Roger's Irish immigrant cousins), deacon of the church, and followed by Roger's wife, Helen, who, accompanied by her children, maintained a studied dignity throughout.[7]

The cathedral, located on North State Street at Superior was a majestic setting, appropriate for a man so widely esteemed and who esteemed so strongly his religion. The massive edifice was dedicated in 1875, costing the then huge sum of $250,000, featuring an awe-inspiring marble altar and specially cast bronze doors. The building was 233 feet long, 126 feet wide, while boasting a soaring ceiling 150 feet high, it was designed to seat about 2,000. However, according to newspaper reports, as many as 15,000 mourners

Pallbearers (Sullivan family collection).

crowded in, while further thousands stood respectfully outside. The casket was placed upon a catafalque at the head of the center aisle. Upon it lay a carpet of flowers in company of but a few of the other floral arrangements from the house. On the altar throne sat Archbishop George Cardinal Mundelein, dressed in purple regalia, with four other priests, also in purple, seated nearby. Twenty priests were listed as celebrants, while over a hundred others were in chairs on both sides of the altar. Father James Callahan, of Mount Carmel parish, presided over the requiem mass. The choir of the Quigley Memorial Seminary provided vocal music.[8]

Old friend Bishop Peter J. Muldoon delivered the eulogy in which he spoke of a young boy from rural Illinois "unendowed with family position or wealth" who was now mourned by the president of the United States. Roger Sullivan's life was a realization of the American promise, he told his listeners: "Where else, outside of America, could this happen?" And it was not the vagaries of fortune to which his life's achievements could be credited. No, it was "hard work" and his willingness "to love mankind" and "to work for mankind." Guiding him always in his rise in the world, according to the good bishop, were "the principles of Jesus Christ," upon which "our constitution is fashioned" and to which Roger dedicated himself as a young man while working as a driver for a priest in Belvedere, Illinois. Though he was a public man who made a great contribution, and who

The funeral procession (Sullivan family collection).

was known for his willingness to forego rancor against his opponents, it was through his good works as "a private citizen towards his fellow man that the real Roger Sullivan revealed himself." At the heart of his life was his family—"all that he strove for was that blessed place"—which gave him that "one protected spot" where he could always seek refuge from the turmoil of life. Now, he was gone, but he deserved to be remembered as the "true and faithful son of the Church, the true and loyal citizen, the constructive agent for so much that was good for the government of his state and of the nation," and as one who was "ever faithful to every friend," whose "word was like unto his bond," and who was a "faithful husband and loving father." At about noon Cardinal Mundelein closed the ceremony with the benediction.[9]

The casket was carried to the waiting hearse, and the procession reorganized with 684 automobiles accompanied by 10,000 or more marchers in a cortege that included two forty-piece bands playing dirges, over 600 mounted, marching, and motorcycle-riding policemen, and 500 firemen. Mayor Thompson was there with the city council, a set of county officials, the Cook County Democratic Committee, the state committee, members of the national committee, numerous congressmen and state legislators, judges from the municipal, superior, and circuit courts, and contingents from every civic division including one representing the sanitation workers dressed in spotless white uniforms. All displayed the same melancholy aspect. Joseph Tumulty, Wilson's political secretary, was present representing the president, and the honorary pallbearers were a pantheon of state and local leaders and other prominent men including Governor Lowden, Senator McCormick, Mayor Thompson, Samuel Insull, J. Ogden Amour, Victor Olander, Victor F. Lawson, Julius Rosenwald, William Wrigley, Charles Boeschenstein, Henry T. Rainey, Urey Woodson, Arthur W. Charles, Charles Deneen, Ernest Hoover, James Dailey, George Brennan, Dennis Egan, and (future senator) Frank Smith. The procession crawled down State Street to the Loop, then moved west on Washington Avenue into the Fourteenth Ward, Sullivan's political base. A newsreel—a testament in itself in 1920 to the importance of the event—shows well-dressed citizens standing in respectful silence five and six deep on the sidewalks. The crowds were estimated to exceed 200,000. At Halsted Street, the foot marchers dropped out, while those in the automobiles drove on to Mount Carmel Cemetery where the mortal remains of Roger C. Sullivan were laid to rest.[10]

1

Before
(1861–1908)

"In the beginning this organization was known as the Sullivan Democracy."—Fletcher Dobyns, *The Underworld of American Politics* (New York: Fletcher Dobyns, 1932), p. 36.

By 1908, Roger C. Sullivan had achieved an unparalleled degree of power in the Illinois, Cook County, and Chicago Democratic parties; by the end of his career in 1920, he could claim the perfection and finalization of the control structure known to history as the Chicago Democratic Machine. His triumph and that of his organization required overcoming myriad obstacles, not least of which were the centrifugal forces always present in Chicago's often fragmented political culture. Powerful opposition also emerged and re-emerged in Mayor Carter H. Harrison II, whose own body of loyalists enjoyed the succor of William Jennings Bryan and William Randolph Hearst. This fomented what would prove to be one of the greatest rivalries in the chronicle of American politics, raging for years until "Boss" Sullivan and his organization achieved a final victory in 1916.

Along the way and afterwards, Roger Sullivan would make a president, run for the United States Senate, and somehow manage to bring a kind of benign consistency to the apparent contradiction between his fundamental decency, human compassion, belief in what used to be known as the American Dream, and the ethos of the Progressive Era that deplored his skill in making organizational politics more efficient and effective. In Sullivan's personal complexities, insights common to all sharing the human predicament may well be found, but even more tellingly, the evolution of his career and that of his organization between 1908 and 1920 speak beyond the inner world of American politics of his time and place to the innate limitations, and challenges of representative government.

But before there could be the Boss, there had to be the politician, and before the politician, an ambitious young man hungry for success and place. Roger Charles Sullivan's saga begins in Belvidere, a diminutive burg in northern Illinois. With 2,500 residences, 40 stores, nine churches, and a brewery, it was typical of hundreds of other small towns in the upper Midwest that found prosperity from the railroad. It was there that he was born on February 3, 1861, as the second child and son of Eugene and Mary (O'Sullivan) Sullivan. The couple had emigrated separately from Ireland in the 1850s, then met and wed in America. They set up household and raised a family of nine children. Eugene engaged in a number of businesses over the years including a peddling route north into Wisconsin and a notions store that also sold spirits over which the family for a time lived.[1]

Roger Sullivan's Irish heritage would be a defining element of his life. Like many from the Emerald Isle, he retained an intense clannish attachment that extended even to relatives across the ocean that he did not know. When he became successful, his home would often serve as the place of first residence for his kin arriving in America. Also like many Irish Americans, he was always a devoted Roman Catholic. As a youth, he boarded and worked for the local priest, and this experience, no doubt, enhanced significantly his otherwise basic education. The evidence suggests strongly that he always spoke with a brogue, and later as a prominent man, he would sometimes speak for the cause of Irish independence. Moreover, in an era when the Irish were predominate players in American urban governance, his ancestry was, no doubt, one factor in his decision to enter political life. This was to begin soon after his move to Chicago at the age of seventeen.

He secured board and employment from a former neighbor, training as a machinist in the repair shops of the West Side Street Car Company. More importantly, he soon made the acquaintance of John Patrick Hopkins. Like Sullivan, Hopkins was the child of Irish immigrant. An extremely personable and competent young man who hailed from Buffalo, New York, he went to work immediately after his arrival in the Windy City for the Pullman Company, known for manufacturing Palace sleeper railroad cars. In a quick succession of promotions, he went from being a machinist to the position of timekeeper for the entire local operation.

The pair became fast and best friends, as well as permanent political partners. Hopkins by this time enjoyed some small stature in the local Democratic Party, but he and Sullivan first attracted attention with the 1889 campaign to annex the large suburb of Hyde Park to Chicago. Included within its boundaries was the town of Pullman, the private fiefdom of John's now former employer; Hopkins had broken with the manufacturer, and gone into the grocery business, eventually owning a chain of stores around the city. The annexation campaign was successful, and Hopkins and Sullivan's stock rose considerably.

They would soon have their own small but increasingly powerful factionette of friends initially known as the Nectar Club. It derived its moniker from a brand of beer brewed by one of its number likened to the nectar of the gods. There were several dozen members, all of whom were young men of mostly first generation immigrant stock. Many were Irish but also many who were not. However, all found in politics both excitement and entrepreneurial advantage.

Like the others, Roger Sullivan could now claim his own measure of capitalist achievement. He became involved in a number of enterprises including a small coal carting company and that universal route to wealth in this period of extraordinary expansion, real estate speculation. When reasonably secure, he brought his younger siblings and his parents (his father dying soon afterwards) to live in Chicago. On February 11, 1885, he married Helen Quinlan, with whom he would have a son and four daughters. His family would be the enduring center of his life and always his first priority.

Politically, he prospered as well. Hopkins enjoyed a special relationship with Grover Cleveland (John's family lived in Cleveland's ward in Buffalo, where Hopkins senior was a policeman and a saloon keeper, both of which suggested political involvement). This was one factor in Roger's appointments to a series of patronage positions that began with a job as Custodian of the Cook County Hospital, where he performed administrative duties, followed by terms as a federal gauger regulating the production and quality of liquor, and as a federal deputy tax collector.

But it was at the unruly Democratic Cook County Convention of 1890 where Roger Sullivan achieved his first notable political success. Hopkins was a serious candidate for the nomination for sheriff, an immensely powerful and patronage-rich office. This was in itself a measure of the growing importance of their faction. Hopkins narrowly lost, but Sullivan as compensation was chosen for clerk of the Probate Clerk. He proved to be an effective and energetic campaigner, and served his two year term honorably and well.

Sullivan and Hopkins' meteoric ascendance reflected the opportunities present for those with ambition, ability, and luck in the remarkable environment that was Chicago in the latter part of the nineteenth century. For

John Patrick Hopkins (*Illinois Political Directory, 1899*).

decades, population exploded at the rate of eight percent a year driven by massive economic development in virtually all aspects of manufacturing—though the city's "crown jewel" was the seemingly endless and odiferous stockyard that provided the nation with most of its meat. In considerably less than a lifetime, the Windy City became the metropolis for virtually the entire center of the developing nation. It soon could claim responsibility for six percent of all industrial production in what was becoming the world's largest economy.

Filling the factories and wards were immigrants and their children, adding a rich ethnic diversity; Poles, Bohemians (Czechs), Italians, Russians, Swedes, Norwegians, Hungarians, and Austrians, among others, joined with those of German and Irish origins to add their share to the vital but increasingly unmanageable metropolitan community. Chicago was becoming the embodiment of the promises, as well as the unprecedented challenges, of the new industrial society that was coming to define America.[2]

Not least of the challenges was a governmental structure inadequate for the escalating need for order and basic services. This was met with hurried improvisation that brought a staggeringly complex division of power among township, ward, city, suburban town, county, state, and federal authorities augmented by a growing set of independent boards and a large and elected judiciary. Virtually incomprehensible (one expert judged that Cook County had at one point as many as 300 "governments") and characterized by overlapping and ill-defined responsibilities, the situation made for an increasingly dysfunctional political culture. With literally hundreds of governmental niches, each with their own patronage and possibilities for power, politics within the parties became ever more factional. Gone were the days when Chicago as the large town could be dominated by a relatively few Republican and Democratic ward leaders. Nor could the "old" elites, who predominated in the years after the Civil War, avoid being overwhelmed and their

Roger C. Sullivan

Candidate for County Clerk and Clerk of County Court

REGISTRATION DAYS
TUESDAY, OCT. 16
TUESDAY, OCT. 23

EVERYBODY MUST REGISTER
AGAIN FOR THIS ELECTION

OVER

Top: **Roger and Helen Sullivan (Sullivan family collection).** *Bottom:* **Campaign card.**

considerable influence diminished to something like irrelevance. Adding further to the difficulties was the proliferation of often competitive saloon rings, each jealous of their local turf, and ravenous in their competition to exchange votes for public money.[3]

Perhaps not surprisingly, the solution to this threat of political anarchy was to emerge from within the very entrepreneurial culture that was driving growth. A new generation of politicos began to make their presence felt in the late 1880s. Marrying commercial instincts with political influence, these businessman politicians, who included the members of the Nectar Club like Sullivan and Hopkins, were unabashed in their quest for business advantage through the pursuit of political power. However, they also eschewed the illegality associated with the saloon rings. Instead, echoing the unfettered and predatory capitalism of their era, they looked for benefit from "legal graft" like patronage, advantage in securing government contracts, and insider information. Their influence would bring into politics the business values of order and efficiency (and ruthless competition), as well as an ethos similar to that in the contemporary impetus towards monopolistic consolidation in the economy. It was this and they (and Roger C. Sullivan and his allies in particular) that were to build what was first known as the Sullivan Democracy, and then as the Chicago Machine.

And already by the 1880s, such men were beginning the drive for consolidation of power within the Democratic Party. The early steps were slow and halting. In 1881, the Iroquois Club, its name evocative of a federation of different tribes, was created as a central organization for Democratic leaders. Its principal founder was Erskine M. Phelps, a prosperous shoe manufacturer. Although it never became more than a social center, it would endure well into the twentieth century. A more direct attempt was tried in 1890 with the incorporation of the Wah-na-ton (supposedly a Lakota name that meant "one who chases foes"). The use of an Indian moniker was in emulation of New York City's Tammany Hall, suggesting the new club's ultimate purpose. Hopkins and Sullivan were among the founders, and it boasted an elaborate organizational hierarchy with ward commissioners, a bevy of vice presidents, a president, and a board of directors. However, it only lasted a few years before fading away, as did an actual Tammany Club of Chicago organized somewhat later.

A more significant effort was made in December 1892, in a supposedly secret meeting at the Great Northern Hotel. Over a hundred Democratic leaders attended, representing most of the important factions. Hopkins was among those issuing the invitations. It was hoped to build upon recent victories in the November elections to bring about some kind of permanent coordination within the party. Perhaps predictably, there was much talk, but less agreement. In the end, the only outcome was a committee to study the matter further.[4]

However, the meeting underscored the growing potency of the idea of greater centralization within the Democratic Party as the scramble for perquisites and the lack of order were becoming prohibitively dysfunctional. But the inability to find workable compromises was not the only source of immediate failure. By this point, no scheme could succeed without the approval of former Mayor Carter H. Harrison I, and he declined to participate.

In 1891, Harrison was already a legendary figure in the history of Chicago. Born in Kentucky, he arrived just before the Civil War, made a fortune, and then entered politics in the 1870s. In 1879, he won the first of four successive two-year terms as mayor. In 1891, he came out of retirement to challenge the sitting Democratic mayor, Dewitt C. Cregier. However, he lost the race for delegates in the ward conventions. Crying foul, he ran an independent candidacy, splitting his party's vote down the middle and electing the Republican. Even as the meeting was convening at the Great Northern Hotel, Harrison was preparing for another mayoral bid in 1893. This proved stunningly successful, and he swept all before him to win the nomination and the election by substantial margins.

Known as the "Eagle," Harrison was the object of a genuine cult of personality. He soon organized his own "city hall crowd" that proved irresistible to any opposition; even Hopkins and Sullivan reluctantly entered his camp, as did virtually every other factional leader. For a brief moment, it appeared that Carter H. Harrison though force of personality and his undeniable political appeal would achieve the elusive goal of a durable and centralized authority within the local party. More than this, there was every expectation that in 1896, he would be a viable candidate for a presidential or vice presidential nomination. But everything changed on October 23, 1893, when he was shot to death by in his own front hall a deranged office-seeker.[5]

Harrison's assassination proved to be a watershed moment for Sullivan, Hopkins, and their faction. When the smoke cleared, John P. Hopkins was the party's nominee to complete Harrison's term. Decisive in his selection was the backing of the president of the United States, Grover Cleveland, for whom both he and Roger had worked diligently in 1892. Just after becoming mayor, John traveled to Washington, D.C., and returned with Chicago's federal patronage in hand. With control of the distribution of the highly desirable federal plums, Hopkins, Sullivan and their allies were able to build upon the longing for order within the party to create a brief period of unprecedented peace and harmony. For the first time, the local press began consistently referencing a Democratic Machine. This, however, was not the disciplined, highly centralized organization of future decades. Instead, it was an exercise in a kind of democratic centralism by the leaders of the sundry factions as presided over by the mayor. It was only held together by a general satisfaction with the distribution of benefits. In the years ahead, when the party was being rendered by violent internal rivalries, this would be recalled nostalgically, which would legitimize Hopkins and Sullivan's claims for leadership.

But it could not last; external stresses soon weakened the fragile unity. In 1893, the worst depression to date fell with an ever more suffocating weight upon the nation, and particularly upon Chicago, where so many jobs were in manufacturing. Growing unemployment undercut enthusiasm among the workers who generally voted Democratic, striking at the roots of the party's base. Worse still, the Pullman Strike broke out in Chicago in late spring 1894 as a reaction to wage cutting and habits of intimidation and retaliation against dissident employees. Like most of the city, including its elites, Mayor Hopkins backed the strikers against George Pullman, who in his indifference to human suffering personified a contemporary melodramatic villain. The mayor made his sympathies clear and assured fair policing, even as his grocery company distributed food. Sullivan, the evidence suggests, later did his best to find employment for blacklisted strikers.

What began locally quickly became a national conflict when Eugene Debs' American Railway Union voted its support. Soon there was open warfare between union men and the railroad employers' association across the country. Although the strikers strived to avoid interfering with trains carrying the mails, President Cleveland used this excuse to send in troops to break the strike. Hopkins opposed the intervention, but did not break formally with the White House.

By late summer 1894, the economic conditions and a general revulsion against Cleveland evoked dread and apprehension among Democrats about the coming spring elections. Mayor Hopkins announced his decision not to seek another term. However, if Democratic victories in Chicago were now unlikely, they were made impossible during the last months of his administration by a major public scandal that centered upon the issuance of two public utility franchises.

Natural gas for lighting and heat in Chicago was under the control of a "Gas Trust," an association of companies that divided territories and coordinated services and prices. This had been recently found to be illegal in federal court, but it continued to function informally as (ultimately successful) appeals were made. The circumstances were ripe for a quick profit if the city council could be induced to authorize new companies to begin service. These franchises could then be sold to the Trust, which would be compelled to buy them to keep its monopoly. No plant construction or other actual capital outlay would be necessary, and a tidy return was guaranteed. This was tried repeatedly in the city council, and Mayor Hopkins had responded with vetoes.

Thus when the council suspended its usual procedures on February 25, 1895, to cram through two ordinances with extremely generous terms creating the Ogden Gas and Cosmopolitan Electric companies, the city confidently expected Hopkins to block the measures. To intense general outrage, he signed them, arguing that the new firms provided competition that would benefit consumers. Mass meetings were held, scathing editorials were written, and during the storm the Civic Federation and the subsequently created Municipal Voters' League achieved a new prominence in city politics, providing ongoing scrutiny and pressure for structural reforms (that never really occurred).

There was nothing illegal in the franchises, although there were charges, never proved, that some aldermen were bribed, nor did the ordinances originate with Hopkins, Sullivan, or their circle. But it is equally clear that Sullivan at some point became involved, probably in convincing his friend to forego the use of the veto. The details are elusive, but Roger C. Sullivan not too many years afterwards became effectively chief executive officer of both companies (eventually succeeding by 1905 to the titles of secretary and president), unquestionably reaping a substantial remuneration. In return, he and Hopkins were to endure ever after the stigma of being "gas kings," a charge that was trotted out by their opposition whenever convenient.

The companies did build plants and actually began operation, and the Ogden did manage to lower prices in a section of Chicago for a time. However, the two firms were for the most part privately purchased over the years by the owners of the Gas Trust, and in 1913, they were integrated into Samuel Insull's utility empire. However, they would be only part of Sullivan's expanding personal business empire. In 1893, Hopkins and Sullivan partnered with John D. Hurley to form Aurora Automatic Machine and Independent Pneumatic Tool companies which eventually evolved into Thor Power Tool before being absorbed into Stewart-Warner in the 1960s. Also Sullivan invested with his brother Mark and Charles Sawyer in the capitalization of the Sawyer Biscuit Company. In 1915, Roger became its president. It sold crackers, cookies, and other baked goods, and became a major brand in the northeastern United States, eventually constructing a second plant in New York City. Years after Sullivan's passing, it became part of the Kellogg Corporation. In 1904 Hopkins and Sullivan joined with Hopkins' nephew William Lydon to reorganize his marine engineering company Lydon & Drews into the Great Lakes Dredge & Dock Company which Sullivan was pressed into running after the untimely deaths of Lydon and Hopkins within two weeks of each other in 1918.

As widely expected, the Republicans won everywhere in 1895, including Chicago's municipal elections. Sullivan had accepted the nomination for Cook County Clerk, proffered as a sop to the departing mayor, and though he ran well, even he lost. With greatly reduced access to city patronage (although even the party out of power was by custom allotted some share), the lingering aftereffects of the Ogden Scandal, and the opprobrium being heaped upon the Cleveland administration, the bonds of the machine began to unravel. It was a desperate time for Democrats.

It was in this context of dislocation and despair that Democrats, virtually en masse, embraced the Silver Issue that would come to dominate party politics in the years ahead. Subsumed from the platform of the People's or Populist Party, organized in 1892, a policy of coining prodigious numbers of silver dollars at the rate of sixteen to one of gold held the promise for true believers of increasing the supply of money, reducing interest rates, relieving the burden of debtors like farmers, and generally stimulating the economy. For others, less concerned about economic theory, silver offered a chance to redefine the Democratic Party as something other than the creature of Grover Cleveland and his failed policies. Even Sullivan and Hopkins flirted with the movement; Roger served as a delegate, and John was represented by proxy (being in Europe for his health) at the Illinois Currency Convention called by Democratic Governor John P. Altgeld. Inviting himself to speak was a former congressman from Nebraska, William Jennings Bryan, who was becoming a leading spokesman for the cause. A year later, his ability to mesmerize would secure his nomination for the presidency at the Democratic National Convention held in Chicago.

By that point, Hopkins and Sullivan, obeying the blandishments of President Cleveland, and being less than enthralled with Bryan, had become leaders of Illinois' Sound Money League created to oppose the free coinage of silver. They now argued that changing to a bimetallic standard without parallel action by the other major economic powers of the world would simply result in draining the nation of the yellow metal (as silver would be dumped in the United States in exchange for the more desirable metal) creating a de facto silver standard and great economic dislocation.

Following Bryan's nomination in July 1896, the pair helped organize the National Democratic Party, which ran Illinois' John M. Palmer for president. Hopkins served on the national committee and as national campaign manager, while Sullivan was instrumental in the state operation. Palmer polled few votes, but Bryan always blamed the Gold Democrats for killing his momentum for victory in 1896; he never forgot.

Accordingly, John and Roger, with myriad other leaders, were read out of the party. However, they retained much of their local influence. Sullivan, in particular, continued as boss of the Thirteenth (subsequently redefined as the Fourteenth) Ward, but neither was now included in the inner circles of leadership. Hopkins even endured the indignity of his photograph being removed from the walls of party headquarters. The machine they had nurtured was dismantled, and the Chicago Democracy reverted to its usual factional discord. John P. Altgeld, although losing the governorship in 1896, made a bid for party leadership, but he was checked by a new force that developed seemingly *Ex nihilo* in the vacuum left by Hopkins and Sullivan.

In the years after his father's assassination, Carter H. Harrison II was little more than a fringe player. Certainly there seemed no important interest in resurrecting his father's legacy. With the exit or expulsion of so many Gold Democrats, however, Harrison found his opportunity with an appointment to a seat on the Democratic State Committee to replace one of the heretics. In 1897, he began a mayoral campaign under the tutelage of the "Little Dutchman," Robert "Bobby" Emmett Burke. Burke was a former printer and union activist, who, though lacking business experience, was a skilled political strategist. Building upon the tattered remnants of the Eagles' organization, and adding many of the old style saloon rings, including that of the First Ward's notorious aldermen, "Hinky

Dink" Michael Kenna, and "Bathhouse" John Coughlin, he cobbled together a coalition that swept Harrison first to the nomination, and then to a close electoral victory.[6]

Winning reelection in 1901 and 1903 (narrowly), Harrison built his own "city hall crowd." However, his organization remained personal with limited impact outside of the city limits. Entirely dependent upon municipal patronage and the retention of the mayor's office, the Harrison faction was never able to control the party in downstate Illinois, while even within the great metropolis there remained significant resistance. In part this was due to the understandable reluctance of downstate Democrats to allow a sitting mayor of Chicago to control their future, a concern Hopkins, Sullivan, and company would assuage through an emphasis on mutual interests and benefits. Not unimportant, either, were Burke and Harrison's clumsy and usually heavy-handed efforts to assert power that offended just about everyone concerned. These were met with repeated rebuffs, as was demonstrated in 1900 by their unsuccessful attempt to compel the gubernatorial nomination of one of their "boys."[7]

The situation presaged resurgence for Hopkins and Sullivan, who had retained the respect of the other leaders and the rank and file, and who were coming increasingly to personify the possibility of a return to a semblance of party unity. Moreover, William Jennings Bryan, concerned about avoiding the opposition of the former Gold Democrats as he began preparing for his second try at the presidency, was signaling his willingness to accept the apostates back into the party. So it was that Roger Sullivan at the 1898 gathering of state Democrats in Peoria was elevated without controversy to the state committee.

Hopkins restoration was delayed for almost another two years, but once begun it moved forward rapidly. In January 1900, he announced his intention to become a delegate to the national convention. Despite the opposition of Carter Harrison, he was duly selected, as was Sullivan, to represent the state. More significantly, Hopkins joined his partner on the state committee. Both went through the motions of supporting Bryan's presidential campaign, but his loss actually enhanced their status.

With a party now deflated by defeat, temporarily disillusioned with William Jennings Bryan and his crusades, and heartily tired of factional discord—most recently exemplified by a bitter and ongoing feud between Mayor Harrison and former Governor Altgeld—there was a strong momentum for a return to the now fabled days of harmony and the benign leadership of Hopkins (and Sullivan). It was in this spirit that John was elected chair of the Illinois state committee, which would hereafter remain a key element in their coalition of alliances.

With Altgeld's death in 1902 and the scattering to the winds of the reform elements he had gathered together, the configuration of power within the Illinois party became essentially dichotomous. The Harrisonites, now exclusively led by the mayor after a break in 1901 with Burke, were mostly based in Chicago among those dependent upon municipal patronage, while the Hopkins/Sullivan organization controlled the state committee, commanded wide downstate support, and found further strength in Republican wards that were otherwise ignored by city hall. The lines were not absolute, and much of the "warfare" between the two factions was centered upon nothing more than attracting leaders to cross over—something that happened with great regularity in this volatile political environment.

In 1903, Mayor Harrison and his cohorts achieved a major success in electing the chair of the Cook County Democratic Committee. But it was at the state and national conventions of 1904 that the strength of the Hopkins/Sullivan alliance was fully revealed. They exercised a bit of political ruthlessness in the state committee by assigning to themselves the responsibility for making up the slates for state candidates and the national delegation. These were subject only to ratification by the state conclave, which they correctly expected to dominate. This was not the usual practice, but within the rules. Harrison, unable to interfere, admitted that "the other crowd is in control," but nonetheless filled fourteen rail coaches with his men to try to pack the galleries of the Springfield gathering. However, the other crowd sent twenty-seven. Hopkins and Sullivan's choices were approved (typically, to underscore their desire to unify the party, they included some of Harrison's men and others). Prominent in the convention was their new lieutenant, George Brennan, who would eventually succeed Sullivan as boss.[8]

A week later, Harrison used similar steamroller tactics to rule the Cook County Convention. Moreover, William Jennings Bryan at the national gathering of Democrats took up the mayor's cause by challenging the Illinois delegation. Striving mightily to stir the delegates, he spoke against the "machine" (meaning Hopkins and Sullivan) with his usual skill and drama. No longer in favor, Bryan's appeals were in vain. The two Chicago leaders went on to join the other "reorganizers" (or those seeking to remove the influence of the Nebraskan and Bryanism) to help nominate Alton Parker for the presidency.

Even more significantly, Roger C. Sullivan was elected by the Illinois caucus as the state's new national committeeman. This symbolized his elevation as sole head of the faction. Hopkins, tired of the political game and beset by ill-health, was determined to withdraw and retire from active politics. Sullivan, already a popular and powerful figure, was selected without significant opposition. However, he was to inherit not only the mantle of leadership, but also the enmities of Bryan and Harrison.

Fortuitously, within months after the general election, Carter Harrison was precipitously removed from the field of political combat by the only completely reformist upsurge in modern Chicago history. For decades the issue of public transportation and the foibles of the streetcar companies had festered in the public consciousness. In the fall of 1904, it burst forth in a torrent that compelled the mayor to end (temporarily as it proved) his political career. He was replaced by Judge Edward F. Dunne, a political tyro and vociferous proponent of immediate municipal ownership of the street railways, who, in the spring 1905, swept to the Democratic nomination and to the mayor's office by substantial margins of victory. Harrison left for California, and his organization disintegrated.

Sullivan and Hopkins cynically endorsed Dunne, correctly judging that the new mayor was more of an idealist than a politico, who would show little aptitude in organizing his own city hall crowd. They were right; Mayor Dunne soon managed to alienate most regular Democrats, regardless of faction, with ill-advised distributions of municipal patronage and perquisites. Worse, he also failed to transform his popular mandate into successful transportation reform. All of this only served to strengthen Sullivan's power, and if he did not as yet completely dominate the Chicago and Illinois Democracies, he was by now unquestionably the most powerful figure in the city and state parties. His position would be tested almost immediately by a formable challenge from a resurgent William Jennings Bryan.

With Parker attracting even fewer votes in 1904 than he had in 1896 and 1900, the Nebraskan, virtually overnight, again became the bride of his party. Moreover, Dunne was Bryan's loyal liegeman, and the his election as mayor in 1905 appeared to offer opportunities for exacting revenge on Sullivan and Hopkins as former Gold Democrats, while transforming the Illinois party into a Bryan fiefdom. Accordingly, he began a nationally publicized campaign in 1906 to force Sullivan's removal from the national committee. First, he directed his operatives, led by Millard Fillmore "M.F." Dunlap of Jacksonville, who had been his school chum, to organize the Majority Rule League (after the supposed minority rule of the 1904 state convention) to be his instrument of local influence. This was followed by an imperious diktat demanding the Chicago leader's resignation, and, if that were not forthcoming, his removal. Failing to follow his orders, the Great Commoner warned, would result in his refusal to campaign in the next Illinois elections. Later he even urged Democrats to forego voting for their own state ticket should Sullivan remain (this was an unthinkable political heresy in a time when many were born into their political affiliations).

Carter Henry Harrison II (*Illinois Political Directory, 1899***).**

However, William Jennings Bryan's ultimatum, probably to his surprise, failed to evoke the desired response. Sullivan adroitly fought back, strategically concentrating his attack as much as possible upon his local opponents, while striving at first to avoid a direct confrontation with the popular Bryan. When they brought up the Ogden Gas scandal, he responded with a scathing and detailed critique of their own use of government for personal gain. Eventually, even Bryan's wealth, accumulated during years of "public service," proved fit fodder for defensive fire. When it became clear that he was not succeeding, the Man from Nebraska allowed the matter to fade. Sullivan's success in fending off the attacks of the most powerful Democrat in America would prove to be a rite of passage solidifying his prestige and power.

Meanwhile, Bryan's imagined dominance of the Sucker State was further undercut with Mayor Dunne's decisive defeat for reelection in April 1907. Being unable to bring about his solution to the problems of public transportation, and being equally unable either to build an organization or work with the professionals of his party, Dunne stood little chance. He was replaced by Fred Busse, head of the city's Republican federal faction, and a politician of the old school (whose administration would prove to be among the more corrupt in Chicago's history).

With Altgeld dead, Harrison in exile, Bryan frustrated, and Dunne out of office, it was Sullivan who remained standing. Widely recognized as the "boss" (an epithet he hated), he now dominated the State Committee, the Cook County Committee, and the Democratic share of city patronage. But Roger C. Sullivan's paramountcy and that of his organization was neither secure nor absolute. There were to be years of struggle ahead before he and what would become known as the Chicago Machine were to achieve their final triumph.

2

The "most vilified man in public life in Chicago" (1908)

"Let the battle now begin, Illinois, Illinois."—chant for Roger Sullivan

William Jennings Bryan was nothing if not tenacious. He was never discouraged by defeat. Although losing the presidency in 1896 and 1900, and repudiated at the convention in 1904, his enduring commitment to what he conceived as his historical mission, married to his uncommon ability to inspire faith in himself and his causes, had served to make him the only viable candidate for his party's 1908 nomination. This was a troubling development for Roger Sullivan, especially as the Nebraskan retained hopes of dominating the Illinois Democratic Party.

As before, an alliance of local Bryan operatives began to coalesce. In mid-summer 1907, Millard Fillmore Dunlap, took charge of organizing in the state. This was not an unexpected development—but less anticipated was the designation of Bobby Burke as the Nebraskan's point man in Chicago. Given that former mayor Harrison was back in California, and former mayor Dunne was out of office and favor, there was probably no one else available of sufficient stature in the county and city. Nonetheless, Bryan's reliance on Burke, a professional politician with a questionable reputation among reformers, seemed to suggest a degree of pragmatism previously absent from the Nebraskan's earlier offensives.[1]

Sullivan, understandably, was not eager to embrace the man who had wished for his political ruin. Moreover, as one of the leading sachems of the national party, now counted with men like Charles Murphy of New York, and Tom Taggart of Indiana, he, like them, was apprehensive about another Bryan candidacy with its "radical" associations and probability of defeat. Even worse was the possibility, however unlikely, of victory, which would elevate his sworn enemy into the White House. On the other hand, their candidate in 1904, Alton Parker, had done poorly, undercutting any argument about electability. Most importantly, there was no resistance possible against the rising tide for the Commoner among the rank and file.

There was some discussion about trotting out an aging Grover Cleveland, something that held no interest for the former president, who, in any case, died on June 24, 1908. Eventually Sullivan and the national Democratic leadership reluctantly accepted the inevitable. With grace, but little enthusiasm, the Chicago leader endorsed the decision

William Jennings Bryan (Library of Congress, LC-USZC2-6372).

of a Cook County caucus of leaders (from which he was pointedly absent) to back Bryan. John P. Hopkins, who despised the Nebraskan, was less gracious, refusing even to be interviewed on the subject.[2]

However, both soon made a symbolic gesture of buying tickets to a Bryan "harmony" banquet held on January 8, 1908–though they probably did not attend. Meanwhile, the

Commoner was advised by the national committee to forget his feud with Roger, and reports appeared that in return for Illinois' votes at the national convention, the Nebraskan would stay out of the state's factional disputes. For a while, he did just that, refusing all comment on the Illinois situation. Even more dramatically, the two antagonists happened to meet in late January on a Lincoln, Nebraska railroad platform (Sullivan was traveling to Denver, the convention site, in his capacity as chair of the subcommittee to oversee the arrangements), where Bryan greeted Sullivan politely. As the newspapers breathlessly reported, they even shook hands—for only the second time ever (apparently). Both denied any deeper meaning to the encounter beyond simple courtesy, but it looked as though a détente had been achieved. Some found this apparent reconciliation a source of amusement. The *Chicago Tribune,* for example, was sardonic in its joy that "Mr. Bryan and Mr. Sullivan are [now] walking hand in hand down the flowery paths of harmony while the tutelary genius of democracy hovers overhead and blesses them."[3]

Well might the *Tribune* have been cynical. Bryan's continued hostility and determination to oust Sullivan—perhaps stoked by his Illinois base—become apparent when Bobby Burke, in the mantle of a Bryan purist, temporarily renamed his County Democracy (marching club and now political organization) as the County Democracy Bryan League. Even more portentously, Carter H. Harrison II arrived in Chicago to join in what was shaping up as a new offensive against the "boss."[4]

This opened in late February 1908, when the Commoner traveled to Jacksonville, Illinois to strategize with M. F. Dunlap and Judge Owen Thompson, another reliable ally. From there, he went to Springfield to address a gathering of the State League of Bryan Clubs. His speech was a scathing excoriation of Sullivan. [I want] "my enemies in front of me and not behind my back," he proclaimed emphatically, and if nominated, he promised he would insist upon a national committee that was genuinely on his side and not just going through the motions. Sullivan was simply "not the right sort!" Otherwise, the meeting accomplished little more than to elect officers (with former Vice President Adlai Stevenson selected as president). But to Bryan's surprise, his clarion call to throw the rascal out again fell flat. With virtually everyone supporting him for the nomination, whether for reasons of principle or expediency, there was simply no broad desire to resume the factional battles that had been so crippling to the party in the past—certainly not for the benefit of Messrs. Burke, Harrison, Dunlap, and Thompson.[5]

Moreover, as Bryan should have understood, Sullivan's position was buttressed by the growing support and esteem of his political peers around the country. This was illustrated when Mr. and Mrs. Roger Sullivan on March 10, hosted a distinguished company at the Colonial Theatre in Chicago that included Mr. and Mrs. Thomas Taggart and family (Taggart was now serving as national chairman), and other political figures like the mayor of Omaha, Nebraska, the governor of Wyoming, and the powerful Georgia politician and national committeeman, Clark Howell. No one, it seems, except the Commoner and his most dedicated Illinois myrmidons, wanted to tear the party apart in an election year. Nor, for that matter, were the professionals comfortable with the idea of endowing Bryan with the kind of absolute authority that would be implied should he be able to ruin Roger Sullivan.[6]

Bryan finally got the message. Within weeks, it was being reported that he had met with state chair and Sullivan man, Charles Boeschenstein, in Chicago and agreed (again?) that in return for an endorsement by the state convention, he would at last agree to an armistice with the boss. "The contest between Mr. Sullivan and myself is a thing of the past, and I do not intend to revive it," he now proclaimed publicly. The choice of the state's national committeeman, he graciously conceded, belonged to "the [state] delegates [to the national convention] selected by the people." For a time even Dunlap and Thompson became quiet.[7]

However, this did not stop Burke and Harrison, who now were working together (though the former mayor would not go to Denver, but returned to California). In the weeks before the Democrats gathered in Springfield, Burke held meetings of his organization at which plans were laid to call rival ward caucuses in Chicago with an eye towards the possibility of a counter-state convention. Sullivan responded angrily that Burke and company were nothing less than "four flushers" for going back on what he believed were agreements from the previous fall not to break ranks. He was also dismissive: "If one wanted to dignify them with comment, a good deal could be said. But what's the use? Carter Harrison is dead politically and why revive him with criticism? Everyone understands Bobby Burke!" Apparently they did. Burke's and Harrison's obstructive and elaborate schemes attracted almost no backing, especially as Bryan was no longer involved.[8]

Accordingly, the state Democratic convention was an unmitigated affirmation of Roger Sullivan and his Democracy. In 1904, everyone knew he was in charge, but in 1908, he was visibly so. His now rotund figure—there had been recently some humorous comments to the effect that the narrow doors of the new party headquarters in Chicago would have to be widened for his benefit—was the center of all attention. His every frown and smile was noted, while the actual transmission of orders was left to George Brennan, who slowly hobbled the aisles assuring conformity.

In contrast, John Hopkins, while for the last time a delegate, was conspicuously quiet. He had recently returned from a European trip (possibly for his health) and was doubtlessly fatigued. Moreover, although still very much in the inner circle, he was now semi-retired, at least as far as public office and activity were concerned. He would even decline to represent Illinois at the national convention. He explained: "I am going to Denver as a private citizen and to enjoy myself." Moreover, he saw no need for his official presence as "it will be a quiet and unanimous affair." This did not mean that he did not still have his own point of view, and he let be known that he disagreed with Sullivan about endorsing Bryan. After years of antagonism and attack, Hopkins was not inclined to forgive and forget, and he argued that the state party would gain more from backing Governor John A. Johnson of Minnesota. He was unwilling, however, to disrupt friend Roger's plans for the state conclave.[9]

And these came off with only two minor disruptions. First, a conflict emerged over the inclusion in the platform of a plank endorsing "personal liberty," a reference to the issue of liquor prohibition. Its source was the United Societies for Local Self-Government, an organization representing the liquor interests, which was particularly influential among Chicago's Germans and Bohemians. Their leading spokesman at the convention was their secretary, a young Czech state legislator and future mayor (and ultimately a political heir to Sullivan), named Anton Cermak.

Cermak was to have a singular role in Chicago's politics in the era of Roger Sullivan and beyond. Unlike so many other Democratic leaders, he was not Irish but Czech. He came from the Austrian-Hungarian town of Kladno (now in the Czech Republic) where he was born in 1873, and from which in 1889, his family immigrated to Braidwood, Illinois. There he began a long relationship with his schoolteacher and mentor, George Brennan, Sullivan's future lieutenant and successor. Coming first to Chicago in 1890, he remained but a few months when, pressed for funds, he returned home to work in the mines. Fired for leading his fellow workers in a demand for pay raises, he migrated back to the Windy City and began a wood distribution service. Later, he branched out into a successful trucking business. Under the tutelage of Brennan, he also became involved in grass roots Democratic politics, serving first as a precinct captain. In 1902, with the backing of the Sullivan Democracy, he was elected to the Illinois state legislature. By 1906, he was instrumental in the dry United Societies, of which he served as secretary. He was, by that point, a powerful player in his own right with his own base in the Bohemian community.[10]

Unlike Cermak and most Chicago Democrats, many downstaters followed their hero, William Jennings Bryan, in jumping on the wagons of the Illinois Anti-Saloon League and the Women's Christian Temperance Union by backing their goal of complete state prohibition. Consequently, during the convention there was briefly noise and disruption. But the "personal liberty" plank passed handily.[11]

A much more serious challenge emerged when the delegates turned their attention to the remainder of the platform. This had been written by Brennan and, at Sullivan's instructions, it included a general endorsement of Bryan for the presidential nomination. Judge Owen Thompson wanted it amended to require voting for Bryan as long as he was a candidate. This was clearly a last-minute maneuver, and the chair of the convention, Watseka's Free P. Morris, refused to recognize Thompson, who thereupon stood on his chair, waving his arms, and shouting. To quiet him, Morris made an inquiry, but then ruled Thompson's demand to have his resolution put before the body as out of order. Consternation abounded around Sullivan, whose "scowl increased in depth" as Brennan and others rushed to his side to seek instructions. Meanwhile, Thompson continued his disruption until an eager sergeant-at-arms bodily pulled him down to the floor—probably at the order of the boss. Morris quickly called the roll, and the platform was hurriedly adopted. Instantly, Brennan was on his feet calling for adjournment, which was granted, and the delegates began filing out.[12]

Sullivan was more generous to those outside of his organization in the distribution of delegate-at-large seats. Harrison and Burke were naturally excluded. Former Vice President Adlai Stevenson had been originally slated, but he had been a bit too willing to deal with Thompson. On the other hand, former mayor Edward F. Dunne was included with those going to Denver. William Jennings Bryan, in Chicago for a banquet at the Iroquois Club, professed that he was "well satisfied with the results." Bobby Burke, on the other hand, was not, and he announced his intention to challenge the regulars at the national convention with his own slate.[13]

Burke's scheming aside; the state gathering was a convincing demonstration of Sullivan's preeminence. Even in downstate bastions of Bryan support, Roger's allies almost universally prevailed. There were a few exceptions, such as the Twenty-First congressional district, where the delegates of Christian county attempted to foment a rebellion. However, these were minor and insignificant.[14]

Events in Illinois were paralleled nationally as Bryan also began making deals to secure his nomination with other previously disdained political figures like Tom Taggart of Indiana. Engaged in what would prove to be his last (in public anyway) desperate grasp for the presidency, for Bryan, unlike for Henry Clay in 1839, becoming president was more important than being righteous. Victory could only be secured if he were able, as he had failed to do in 1896 and 1900, to attract the votes of Eastern workers. Unable

Chicago Tribune, **April 23, 1908.**

to replace or overawe the entrenched organizational leaders, he had come to accept the need for an accommodation.

The irony of all this became clear when George Brennan and John P. Hopkins introduced an element of humor by initiating a short-lived campaign to promote Roger Sullivan as Bryan's running mate. Brennan started it all in May 1908, with strong statements calling for his friend and leader's nomination. Sullivan, while professing to be flattered, was predictably noncommittal, if not somewhat incredulous. A few weeks later, Hopkins actually organized the Roger C. Sullivan Club of Chicago "to promote [his] candidacy ... for vice president ... [based upon his] great force of character, fine executive ability, [and because he] is a man of ... rugged honesty." The roster of the new organization was a predictable collection of allies and friends, with scores of downstate men joining with the legions from Cook County. Making the whole affair even more surreal was Brennan's contention that Bryan, if he "survives the first shock," would eventually see the wisdom of Sullivan becoming his vice president. In fact, the Nebraskan let the matter pass without significant comment. On the other hand, the press did treat the matter seriously, and there have been similarly odd parings in the history of American presidential politics. In the end, probably at Sullivan's urging, the "movement" would fade away. However, there was at least the satisfaction of having made the anti–Sullivan Illinois Democrats "shudder" at the thought of the "B&S" ticket, which may have been the point in the first place.[15]

Though he was not actually a viable candidate for the vice presidency, and quite possibly would not have been interested if he had been (subordination of any kind to Bryan holding no appeal), Roger Sullivan was very much the important personage before and during the convention. As chair of the subcommittee overseeing arrangements in Denver and as one of the preeminent king-makers of the party, his opinions and activities were eagerly followed by the press. He also deliberately courted national interest with a creative publicity stunt.

On Tuesday, June 20, at 11:00 o'clock in the morning, a caravan of four leased Studebaker automobiles and a truck (to carry baggage and to serve as a commissary) left downtown Chicago for the Mile High City or bust. Roger was not along. His duties required a more immediate presence in Denver, but his brother and political confidant, Eugene Sullivan, was in charge of the party of fifteen other delegates and friends. The projected trip was a real adventure in 1908. Given the distance involved of approximately 1,200 miles, the generally poor state of the roads, and the fact that the West was just a few decades removed from the wilder days of the frontier, the journey took on the character of an African safari—not unlike those so popular among the rich and famous in the period. Along the way, the party was succored by indigenous Democrats, and the newspapers followed the progress of the intrepid explorers with interest.

It took nearly a week for the caravan to make camp in Des Moines, Iowa, having been waylaid in Colo, Iowa by an aged woman planted in the middle of the road, energetically waving a large American flag. She was Julia Sullivan Daily, (Roger and Eugene Sullivan's aunt—their father's younger sister), and she warned the party that they could only proceed over her dead body unless they stopped for cake and lemonade on her front lawn. One of the travelers referred to the episode as the "Barbara Frietchie interlude" (after the legendary flag-waving heroine memorialized in John Greenleaf Whittier's Civil War ballad for supposedly refusing to take down the American flag in the presence of General Robert E. Lee and Confederate forces). A fine time was had by all. Afterwards, the travelers resumed their sojourn to their next destination, distant and exotic Omaha. However, a sudden storm and tornado compelled them to seek shelter in Missouri Valley, Nebraska. They found refuge with an 81 year old, farmer, who claimed to be the only Democrat in the county, and entertained them with stories of the picturesque local customs.

Adding to their discomfiture, a number of their vehicles thereupon almost immediately broke down. Despite all, they were twelve hours ahead of schedule, when, on the June 28, they arrived in Lincoln, Nebraska. Here they were greeted by the mayor and the 400 members of a cheering and waving crowd. This was followed by a brief pilgrimage to William Jennings Bryan at his nearby mansion, Fairview, where he posed for photographs in one of the cars and humorously asked for their support in Denver for a good roads plank in the Democratic platform. Soon they were on their way again, arriving at last in Denver on the Glorious Fourth, exhausted but exalted by their adventures. They had a right to be proud, and Roger to be pleased by all the positive news coverage.[16]

Other Illinois Democrats also poured into Denver, though by more conventional means. These included Bobby Burke's County Democracy Bryan Club, who moved with military precision in their traditional silk hats. They were purposely matched in appearance and discipline by Alderman Johnny Power's County Democracy, which was created originally as a splinter of Burke's group. In between changing trains in Lincoln, Nebraska, Power's boys used the occasion to chant their devotion to Sullivan and his as yet unrepudiated vice presidential candidacy. Bryan was present at the station to greet former Mayor Edward F. Dunne, and both were compelled to endure the hymn of praise:

> Let the battle now begin, Illinois, Illinois,
> We know we sure can win, Illinois, Illinois,
> For with Bryan the candidate,
> Roger his running mate,
> You can sweep the worker state, Illinois, Illinois.

Neither Bryan nor Dunne's response was recorded.[17]

Sullivan brought along his own large party on the train, including much of his family. They were met in Denver by Alderman "Bathhouse John" Coughlin. The Bath, who designated himself an unofficial greeter, was profuse in his welcome to "our beautiful state" (he owned an elaborate summer home in Colorado Springs, complete with zoo), which he claimed was "the most important geographical location of the known world outside of the first ward [sic] of Chicago." Roger delighted in the attention and also was impressed with Denver finery for the convention. The streets around the Auditorium were wired with a forest of electric lights—quite striking in 1908—as well as arches, flags, and columns for all of the forty-six states. Each of the columns was surmounted by a two foot square celluloid photo of a prominent local Democrat. However, Illinois' was unadorned initially as there was uncertainty as to whether Burke or Sullivan should be memorialized. This was immediately rectified in Roger's favor.[18]

Sullivan doubtlessly observed the street adornments with more than a casual eye. As the chair of the subcommittee charged with the preparations for the convention, he helped oversee the decorations inside the Auditorium, and these reflected his own ornate Edwardian sensibilities. From top to bottom, the walls were embellished with palm trees, flags, banners, and the stars and stripes. These adornments were relieved only by irregular sized portraits of important Democrats and Americans of the past, with the likeness of George Washington suggesting to many William Jennings Bryan in a powdered wig. The ceiling was embellished with five pointed stars, but most striking was a flock of five oversized eagles suspended by wires in the front of the hall. The largest and most impressive bird was poised directly over the speaker's podium—a symbolism subject at the time to

Convention Hall interior (Library of Congress, LC-USZ-87245).

varying interpretations. The consensus of opinion, however, found it all highly attractive and inspirational. Of greater political moment were Sullivan's placement of the Nebraska delegation in the "place of honor" front and center, and the appointment of his brother, Eugene Sullivan, as chief doorkeeper supervising 112 assistants.[19]

For all of his part in the planning, Roger's most important moment actually came during a pre-convention caucus of the Illinois delegation. This was held to elect members of convention committees, and to select the state's national committeeman for the next four years. Sullivan was the incumbent, but for months he had made clear his determination to retire in favor of State Chair Charles Boeschenstein. Serving since 1904, Roger had been a very active member. However, the job required frequent trips, usually to New York and Washington, D.C., and he was eager to lay down this burden. Retirement also made political sense as well. Assumption of the office had helped propel him into a publicly recognized position as leader of the state party. Now, despite William Jennings Bryan, his position was more secure, and he was among the most widely known political figures in the country. He, therefore, no longer needed the job for either power or prominence. Of course, too, it was good politics to reward an important downstate Democrat like Boeschenstein.[20]

To his apparent surprise, he found himself thwarted in this intention, not by his enemies, but by his friends. At the heart of the rebellion, for such it was, were widely circulating rumors that Roger was stepping down to propitiate Bryan. Dismayed and angered, Sullivan's men in the delegation were seized with a collective determination to disprove this humiliating and widely held assumption, and to protect the reputation and standing of their leader—even against his will. When the caucus met on July 6, things began routinely enough. There was some discussion concerning who to elect to the credentials committee, with M.F. Dunlap claiming Bryan had been assured they would choose a friendly Democrat, meaning former mayor Edward F. Dunne. Sullivan gently disagreed that any binding deal had been reached, and he was backed up by Cook County chair William O'Connell. George Brennan was chosen instead in a test vote of 43½ to 10½ (half votes were from delegates-at-large).[21]

Next up was the selection of the state's national committeeman. Instantly, Alderman Johnny Powers, in an apparently prearranged move, rose to nominate Roger Sullivan. The object of his endorsement, just as quickly attempted to stifle things. "I ask the privilege of not returning to the national committee," he requested, and while he admitted that years earlier his "right to be on the committee was questioned and I wanted it," he now asked "the delegates to vote for my friend, Charles Boeschenstein." Powers was having none of it, and called for a vote by acclamation, but was ruled out of order by the presiding officer, Fred Kern. Sullivan now formally nominated Boeschenstein, stating as explicitly as possible: "I do not want the place. Charles Boeschenstein is my friend and I want you to elect him to the national committee."[22]

Voices clamored. Thomas J. Webb managed to be recognized and emotionally proclaimed his absolute commitment to Roger, explaining that as Sullivan had become unfairly the "most vilified man in public life in Chicago," his friends were bent upon sparing him further humiliation—"whether he was willing to endure it or not." Now Dunlap unintentionally fanned the flames by chiming that Bryan had been told an "acceptable man" would be chosen. This angered even Sullivan a little, who demanded specifically which man Dunlap meant (he meant, of course, himself). Before Dunlap could reply, Boeschenstein announced that he would refuse election and called upon "every friend of mine" to vote for Roger, who was pleading "it is impossible for me to accept!"[23]

Edward F. Dunne vainly asked for the caucus to respect Sullivan's decision. Sullivan stood to try one more time, but George Brennan was heard to threaten softly to "loose on his jaw" if he spoke again. A vote was hurriedly called and Sullivan was reelected by a margin of 47½ to 6½ votes. He could not be angry, and he confessed that while he was "proud and grateful … it was a mistake," and that they "should have elected Boeschenstein." Such was the nature of the relationships among the leaders of the organization, such was the nature of Roger Sullivan's authority, and such was the nature of the personal affection and respect he inspired.[24]

Bryan was not happy about the reelection of Sullivan, but he let it pass in the spirit of the fragile harmony prevailing at the convention (there was little else he could do if he expected to unite the party behind his candidacy). Adding to the relative tranquility was Bryan's decision to stay home at Fairview. However, he maintained a close watch over events through his brother Charles. He virtually dictated the platform (an endorsement of good roads not being included), but this time there was no reference to the now moribund silver issue that had stirred controversy in every previous convention since 1896. The only conflict came with his insistence upon the inclusion of a plank addressing the judicial injunctions that were so despised by the unions as a tool of their oppression.

The more conservative party spirits were concerned about a section that would have contempt citations for activities outside of the courtroom tried before someone other than the issuing judge. In the end, this was deleted without protest. Partially in return, Sullivan and the other party sachems reluctantly accepted Bryan's choice of Theodore Bell as temporary chair.[25]

The Denver convention was remarkably sedate with only a few fireworks. The first relatively feeble bursts, however, were not long in coming. By the time the national chair, Tom Taggart, called things to order on July 7, 1908, at about half past noon, it had become the general understanding that Alton Parker would introduce a controversial resolution praising Grover Cleveland, who had died just weeks before. There was a real fear that he would include some kind of offensive reference to the late president's valiant stand against "radicalism," meaning Bryan and Bryanism. The New York delegation, of which Parker was a member, and its leader, Tammany boss Charles Murphy, refused, again in the spirit of harmony, to endorse his action, compelling him to act as an individual delegate. However, even this was thwarted by the chair, who chose simply to ignore Parker's frantic calls and gesticulations. He was allowed subsequently as a point of personal privilege and respect to read his declaration aloud (it was actually quite inoffensive), but there the matter ended. Instead, Cleveland was honored with a general statement of praise, and, thanks to Sullivan, a portrait of the late president draped in black cloth graced the hall. This was the first time since 1892 that his image was displayed at a Democratic national convention. Still, though Parker, with Bryan's permission, was elected chair of the Platform Committee, it was a bitter humiliation for the party's titular leader.[26]

The reception accorded Bobby Burke's much vaunted challenge to the Illinois delegation was also summary. As Bryan, in a meeting at Fairview, had advised Judge Owen Thompson and the other loyalists to avoid further "combat" against Sullivan, there were only Burke and his men to challenge the legality of Illinois' representation. His efforts proved to be insignificant. The matter was first taken up by a subcommittee of the national committee specially appointed to review the situation and to make recommendations. Burke and Prentiss, together with John J. Coburn and Dan Jesse showed up at about 11:00 a.m. outside the national committee room where the hearings were to be held. Here they were confronted by the convention's chief doorkeeper, Roger's brother, Gene Sullivan, who making a few sarcastic remarks, called for the backup of a Denver police officer, and under the implied threat of this extra muscle, compelled the little group to wait elsewhere until they were needed. Others who were to testify were allowed immediate entry, and this enforced exile to a waiting room was a deliberate humiliation. It was also exactly the kind of gamesmanship common in Chicago politics, which sometimes suggested a schoolyard.[27]

Once summoned, the quartet made their case: (1) the state convention itself was illegal because it was based upon primary elections founded upon a law since ruled unconstitutional by the Illinois supreme court, and; (2) the meetings of the state's congressional districts to select delegates to the national convention were fraudulently conducted. Roger Sullivan appeared in rebuttal. It was true, he admitted, that the state's highest court had thrown out the primary law. However, the law in question only applied to the selections for the state convention, not to the process of selecting national delegates. As far as alleged irregularities were concerned, Burke and company had little moral ground upon which to stand as the twenty "delegates" they brought to Denver had been selected by such clandestine and unorthodox means as to be characterized by the press as the "occult democracy" [sic]. The subcommittee voted by a margin of 3 to 2 (underscoring the importance of Bryan's decision not to become involved) to seat the regular delegation, a decision subsequently upheld by the Committee on Resolutions. Bobby Burke found no support to take the issue before the entire convention, and there the matter died.[28]

The convention now moved on to nominating William Jennings Bryan. Some in the press speculated that there might be a real contest, and two candidates, George Gray of Delaware and Governor John A. Johnson of Minnesota diligently sought support. Their efforts were all for naught; by a margin of 892½ votes to Gray's 59½ and Johnson's 46, Bryan easily won his third bid for the Democratic presidential nomination. Sullivan kept his word, and Illinois' votes were included among his total, as were those of Indiana and New York.[29]

The vice presidential nomination was far less certain. Bryan provided no instructions. There was a long list of forty or so possibilities including Theodore Bell of California, Edward F. Dunne of Illinois, Governor Joseph Folk of Missouri, William Randolph Hearst of New York, Tom L. Johnson of Ohio, Charles Towne of New York, and even Roger Sullivan (to name just a few of the more prominent of those attracting speculation), but no clear frontrunner. Added to the muddle was the fact that many on the list were not especially interested. Sullivan's choice was John A. Mitchell of Illinois. As one of the founders and first presidents of the United Mine Workers, and as a vice president of the American Federation of Labor, he was an important union man. In addition, Mitchell helped organize the National Civic Federation, and he was currently the head of its Trade Agreement Division. He would have brought to the ticket considerable credibility among Eastern workers, and Sullivan did his best over a period of months to convince him to seek the honor. For once, his powers of persuasion failed him. Mitchell declined because he did "not care for the turmoil of public life," and because he preferred to focus upon an ongoing personal crusade against child labor.[30]

It was Tom Taggart who, in the end, supplied the nominee. John Kern was a relatively minor Indiana politician, whose last public position was as city solicitor for the city of Indianapolis. Most recently, his career had been marked by two defeats for his state's governorship. Still, he could boast a good record on labor issues, and he was identified with neither the more committed elements of the silver men, nor with the Gold Democrats. The Indiana boss lined up support in a three-hour meeting with Sullivan and other leaders. As no one else generally deemed suitable wanted the office, and as Kern pleased the conservatives of the party without alarming the radicals, Bryan accepted their decision, and the inoffensive Hoosier was duly nominated by acclamation.[31]

Roger Sullivan could be well pleased with the outcome of the 1908 Democratic national convention. He was, it was true, going back to the national committee against his wishes, but under circumstances that were highly gratifying. He also, no doubt, basked in the acclaim he received for contributing to the convention preparations. More importantly, the tenuous and even unnatural détente between Bryan and the party regulars had held. The rank and file was placated by the Nebraskan's nomination, while the conservatives had a platform they could support. The chasm that had so divided and crippled the party for over a decade seemed to be at last bridged. The apparent good feeling this engendered towards the nominee was not entirely feigned; George Brennan, who was inclined towards dramatic overstatement, even went so far as to suggest going ahead and nominating the Commoner for the 1912 elections (presumably he meant for reelection).[32]

On the last day of the convention Roger Sullivan took some time to relax, spending an hour or so leading the brass band associated with Power's contingent around Denver. This was followed by a quick sightseeing trip to the nearby Rocky Mountains. Two days after adjournment (Sullivan made the motion), he joined Norman E. Mack, the new chair of the national committee, with his own family and others for a visit to the local amusement park, Lakeside. There John P. Hopkins always the ladies man, and in Denver as a private citizen, treated the assembled company and reporters to a demonstration of his ability to trip the light fantastic. This excited admiration, but there were even more comments about his choice of partner, Bryan's daughter, Mrs. Ruth Bryan Leavitt. When questioned by some of the incredulous reporters, Mrs. Leavitt responded tersely that "my friends are my father's friends." Earlier, there had been an even more unlikely distaff association; during the first days of the convention, Alice Roosevelt Longworth, the daughter of President Theodore Roosevelt wearing an "ecru linen suit, three-fourths coat, [and a] hat of [a] contrasting shade of brown," (Mrs. Longworth was a major celebrity of her generation, whose every activity was eagerly followed) shared Box 4 with Roger's wife, Helen, and other members of his party.[33]

With all official and unofficial duties completed, Sullivan now treated himself, his family, and companions to a brief vacation in his chauffeur-driven touring cars (both having been shipped to Denver by train). Their itinerary included Colorado Springs, Glenwood Springs, Yellowstone National Park, and other points of interest. Also coming along was Hopkins, whose low opinion of Bryan was revealed to be unaffected by the charms of the Commoner's daughter; his sole public comment about events being that at least "the tail end of [the ticket] is all right."[34]

For his part, Bryan showed an almost desperate concern to maintain the Chicago leader's good will. Not long after adjournment, the Commoner sent Richard Pettigrew, a former United States Senator from South Dakota, to visit Sullivan, Charles Murphy, and a few others, to assure them that appropriate rewards would be forthcoming once he entered the White House.[35]

Well may Bryan have worried; some long-time supporters and allies were abandoning him because of his rapprochement with the regulars. In Illinois, to general surprise, Judge William Prentiss, long a devotee of the Nebraskan but angered by the Commoner's refusal to back Burke's challenge, announced he was now rejecting his former hero. The Nebraskan was no longer "the ideal Bryan of the past," he bitterly complained, and had betrayed his idealism by embracing machine politicians because he "was crazy for the presidency." Prentiss decided to back the Republican nominee, William Howard Taft, in large part because of his admiration for the incumbent Republican president, Theodore Roosevelt.[36]

Less idealistic, but conceivably more damaging, were the actions of New York media magnate and the great political pretender of the age, William Randolph Hearst. Despite his protestations to the contrary, Hearst had still harbored hopes for the Democratic nomination. When that was not forthcoming, and when it became clear that Bryan was treating with Charles Murphy, head of New York's Tammany Hall and a Hearst nemesis, the publisher moved forward to create his own ticket on his own dime. A convention of the Independence Party was held in Chicago between 27 and 28 July, and the unknown Thomas L. Hisgen of Massachusetts was nominated for president on a platform that included an endorsement of the initiative and referendum as well as a strong plank in favor of protecting labor from federal injunctions. Both were issues that Bryan had either forgone or had compromised to placate conservative opinion. This "party" managed to get on the ballot in thirty-three states, but it would poll almost nothing. However, the Hearst newspapers in Chicago and elsewhere initiated a vicious attack against Bryan, which featured scathing editorial cartoons of the man they had lauded for years as a hero.[37]

At Bryan's request, "Roger"—he was increasingly identified by his first name or as "Roger C." in the Chicago press—was initially focused upon the Bryan campaign. Throughout the late summer and fall of 1908, he made frequent excursions east to work with the national committee. Moreover, as national campaign headquarters was located in the annex of the Auditorium in Chicago, he met regularly with Bryan during his candidate's frequent visits to the city. This left little time initially for the state contests, which he delegated to his lieutenants.[38]

In the governor's primary, George Brennan and most especially, coal magnate Francis Stuyvesant Peabody, long a close Sullivan-Hopkins associate, had backed Bloomington's Adlai Stevenson, Cleveland's former vice president and Bryan's running mate in 1900. Stevenson had apparently made amends for his wavering support of Sullivan in the past, and he seemed to be the strongest candidate available against the Republican incumbent, Charles Deneen. His principal opponent in the Democratic primary was James Hamilton "Ham" Lewis. He was Edward F. Dunne's corporation counsel between 1905 and 1907, and would become a major political actor in the state into the 1930s.[39]

The race for the important job as Cook County State's Attorney was another of special interest for Sullivan's men. Republican Governor Charles Deneen once served in the office, and. with the power to solicit indictments from a grand jury, it was potentially a position of great power in a political culture where the courts were sometimes just another arena for the factional wars. It was John P. Hopkins, in one of his last political acts, who arranged for the nomination of Jacob Kern, who held the job

George Brennan (Library of Congress, LC-DIG-ggbain-37240).

previously between 1892 and 1896. His chief opponent was Maclay Hoyne, a rising star on the horizon, who in 1903, had been appointed by Mayor Carter Harrison as assistant corporation counsel.[40]

Both contests were to be decided under a new law that set the primaries in August 1908 (and in years thereafter in April). It was an extremely complicated and lengthy statute that dictated that candidates for all political offices except for presidential and vice presidential electors, members of the board of trustees of the University of Illinois, and those in township and school elections were to be selected by elected delegates meeting in state, county, congressional district, and state senatorial district conventions. Moreover, it provided for the direct selection by voters of all party committees from the state level down to the precincts to include the managing boards for congressional districts, state senatorial districts, counties, cities, and villages. Each member of a state committee was to be selected in primaries in one of the state's congressional districts. Congressional committees were composed (with certain exceptions in cases where counties were divided among congressional districts) of the county chairs. County committees were to be made up of the chairs of inclusive precinct committees, which were to be directly elected, and. senatorial district committees of three or more counties were to be comprised of one elected representative per county. In districts of only two counties, two of the three members of the committee were to be chosen from the county that had polled most recently the highest total for the party concerned. This was the third primary statute enacted in as many years, and each had become more complex and incomprehensible. This was largely because they were ruled successively unconstitutional by the Illinois Supreme Court based upon some technicality. Nor would the act of 1908 settle the matter; during Sullivan's lifetime, court rulings mandated new laws in 1909, 1910, 1911, 1912, 1913, 1916, and 1919; all of which would fail the test of judicial review.[41]

The August primaries were another impressive demonstration of the strength of the Sullivan Democracy. Stevenson won handily, although Lewis ran unexpectedly well in Chicago where he was especially popular. Sullivan greeted the former-vice president's victory with enthusiasm, calling him "an ideal candidate." Similarly, in the hotly contested fight for the nomination for state's attorney in Cook County, Jacob Kern was victorious, much to the satisfaction of John Hopkins. But it was in the races that affected party governance where Roger Sullivan's influence was most immediately apparent. The new state committee was now comprised of a Sullivan majority of twenty-three of twenty five members, including brother Gene Sullivan. Similarly, in Cook County the new central committee was overwhelmingly friendly, and it, acting as the county convention, would choose both a managing and executive committee that closely reflected Sullivan's wishes. He was included on both, and representing the Chicago wards was a list that was mostly comprised of such familiar names as George Brennan, Thomas Little (from Sullivan's home Fourteenth Ward), and William O'Connell, who after a new party constitution for Cook County was implemented in accordance with the new law, would be reelected as county chair. Included among the two representatives for Sullivan's Fourteenth Ward was his rising protégé, Patrick Nash, who in the 1930s was party boss.[42]

Though the primary determined the party's candidates for state office, nonetheless, the law required a state convention. This met in Springfield September 9, 1908, essentially as a campaign rally. Its leading attraction was an appearance by William Jennings Bryan himself. Regardless of all controversy and defeat, he remained the party's greatest attraction. Special trains were scheduled to bring the crowds in from Chicago and elsewhere.

Upon his arrival, he could not forgo the opportunity to speak extemporaneously at the National Hotel in the city to the crowd of about 1,000. Later that day, he delivered two short, but well-received addresses before the convention that expounded upon his Jeffersonian principles. That afternoon, 5,000 filled the courthouse square for yet another acclaimed speech. It was a joyous day for the vociferous Commoner, one of applause and cheers.[43]

Sullivan remained in the background, and surrendered the platform to Bryan and Adlai Stevenson, who, with the other primary victors, was duly nominated by the convention. But even the rapturous nature of Bryan's welcome could not disguise the power of Sullivan. Just days before, as the presidential nominee lectured a crowd of mostly Democratic political operatives in Chicago on party loyalty, a member of the audience, "with either a malicious memory or too many drinks" shouted out: "What about Roger Sullivan? Hurray for Roger Sullivan!" William Jennings Bryan, three time presidential nominee of the Democratic Party and one of the most powerful and acclaimed personalities of the age, could only stand quietly and wait for the general applause and laughter to fade. Sullivan sitting on the podium made no indication that he had heard, but it was clear who was "the real boss now."[44]

Bryan's fear about the sincerity of Sullivan and the Illinois party fealty was not unfounded. The Chicago leader, to be sure, was closely involved in the national campaign, and he appeared with Bryan at the State's Fair and other venues. Both Sullivan and John P. Hopkins each also very publicly donated $1,000 (M.F. Dunlap only contributed $500). However, as early as September, the press was reporting a decision of the state committee to focus mainly upon the state races. Moreover, observers noted that on those rare occasions when Sullivan's talks with his political troops were recorded—as they were during an East St. Louis visit—they included ample expressions of support for Stevenson, but hardly a mention of William Jennings Bryan.[45]

And by now the boss was doing everything possible for his gubernatorial candidate, at one point threatening each of the state's precinct captains with replacement by "a better man" should they lag in enthusiasm and energy. Adlai Stevenson seemed to have a real chance at victory. His Republican incumbent Governor Charles S. Deneen was, it was true, a skilled politician with his own faction, and he could cite a generally positive record in Springfield. The Democratic nominee, however, had a real claim to being a national statesman. Moreover, Deneen enemies were legion in his own party, and some of them, Congressman William Lorimer in particular, were quietly backing the Democrat.[46]

There was nothing in Stevenson's immediate past that made him vulnerable, so the Republicans and their allies in the press evolved a two-fold strategy of misdirection. First, they went after his Civil War record uncovering Stevenson's supposed Copperhead or pro–Confederate (or at least anti–Lincoln) sympathies. At one point, the Democrat felt the need to assure the voters that, contrary to Republicans were claims, their candidate had in fact not been pleased by Lincoln's assassination. One Jennie Starkey of Waynesville, Illinois, basked in a brief moment of public attention when she swore to her personal knowledge of Stevenson's membership in the Knights of the Golden Circle, a notorious anti-war and anti–Lincoln organization. All of this was a revival of the hallowed G.O.P. practice of "waving the bloody shirt," presenting themselves as the party of the Union victory and of patriotism, and their opponents as the party of treason and rebellion. It was a hoary tactic, once effective in the decades after the Civil War and still so among some of the older generation, but now almost meaningless to younger voters.[47]

But the primary target of the Republican assaults was Roger Sullivan, portrayed as the actual candidate. The offensive began with a barrage of press accusations that a Democratic victory would guarantee "Roger will be the regent of Illinois." The Republican state committee then picked up the theme, followed by Deneen, who added a new twist in claiming that the Chicago leader wanted to establish a joint-dictatorship with the governor's factional rival, William Lorimer. In fact, Sullivan did have growing ties with Lorimer. The largely irrelevant and ignored Hearst Independence Party also got into the act at their one large rally in the Chicago, where Thomas L. Hisgen hit a new height (or low) in grandiloquence in portraying Roger as "a political pariah, one time an Ishmaelite, formerly a disowned democrat [sic], and the Siamese twin of John P. Hopkins!"[48]

In the closing weeks before the elections, there were signs that all might not be going well for the Democrats. Especially portentous was the fiasco of what was supposed to be the grand climax of their campaign in Illinois, one meant to seize the interest of the national press. It did, but not for the intended reasons. William Jennings Bryan was scheduled to arrive by train at 7:00 p.m. on October 31. Sullivan and the County Party planned a series of massive rallies featuring the Commoner around the city with elaborate parades between the sites. Mr. and Mrs. Roger Sullivan, the candidate's brother, Charles Bryan, his son, William Jennings Bryan, Jr., state chair Charles Boeschenstein, Cook County chair William O'Connell, and a host of other party dignitaries waited expectantly at the railroad station even as massive crowds were shivering at Dexter Park, Chutes Park, in a tent at the corner of Division and Leavitt streets, at Logan Square Baseball Park (where it was reported 25,000 milled impatiently), as well as along the streets. The banners were hung, the signs were in hand, the bands were ready, and the speeches prepared, but the appointed hour came and went—no Bryan.

A telegram arrived explaining that he would be delayed until 10:00 p.m. When he failed to appear then, more desperate telegrams were exchanged; the parade went ahead, while J. Hamilton Lewis moved around the city attempting to salvage the rallies. But the crowds had already thinned considerably and soon began to disperse. It was not until after midnight that the tired and pale Peerless Leader finally arrived, profusely apologizing as he extended his hand to Sullivan. The boss, smiling, suggested that his candidate belonged in jail for making them wait so long. Bryan responded that he was probably right, but that he had been delayed by too many speeches in Indiana, followed by a breakdown of his train engine. Thoroughly exhausted, he went directly to the Auditorium Annex (where the national headquarters was located) and an apartment reserved for his use. He was soon snoring in bed. Sleeping late into the next day, he only briefly consulted with the local leadership before departing for Nebraska. Sullivan, jokingly, blamed the delay on a Republican plot, but it was undeniably a poor ending to an already faltering campaign.[49]

The election was yet another debacle. Bryan lost nationally by numbers that, while improving upon Parker's four years earlier, were less than in his first two bids. In the Electoral College, Taft received 321 votes to Bryan's 162; outside of the South (including Oklahoma), the Democrat only just managed to carry his home state of Nebraska. In Illinois, the totals were equally lopsided, and The Commoner won only thirty-nine percent of the vote. Cook County also went for Taft by the substantial margin of about 80,000 votes. The only vaguely bright spot was in the gubernatorial race. Stevenson lost, it was true, but by the relatively close margin of 526,912 to Deneen's 550,076, and he actually managed to carry the city of Chicago (though not Cook County). But he had no coattails;

the entire state Democratic ticket, as well as that of Cook County, went down to defeat by totals that more closely resembled Bryan's poor performance. Moreover, the Republicans easily retained their control of the state legislature.[50]

Although the rejection of Bryan nationally and in the state was widely expected, there also had been a reasonable hope that Stevenson might win, and Sullivan had expressed his belief that at least Cook County could be carried. It was a thoughtful Roger Sullivan, therefore, that reporters hounded with questions that somber election night. Where others blamed Bryan or reiterated the usual charges of Republican misdeeds, Roger pointed no fingers and offered no analysis, contenting himself with the simple statement that "the wisest thing to do is to keep silent."[51]

3

"I am not a boss"
(1909–1910)

"He flies the flag of Democracy for the purpose of enslaving the people of this state!"—Raymond Robins, social activist

At the heart of the Democratic defeats in the elections of 1908 was the overarching shadow of one man and what he represented. He, and what he did, would impact a changing political landscape in Chicago in ways that would challenge Roger Sullivan and his ability to adapt and lead. In an age of giants and geniuses like William Jennings Bryan, Woodrow Wilson, William Howard Taft, Mark Twain, Thomas Edison, Henry Ford, Oliver Wendell Holmes, Sigmund Freud, and Albert Einstein, President Theodore Roosevelt would stand above them all in defining the era. For many, his energetic style as chief executive was an apt representation of a young nation that just recently witnessed the close of its frontier and its own emergence as the world's leading industrial power. He was the first chief executive to implement the influence of a growing consensus for reform. After Roosevelt, the issue was no longer whether government should concern itself in detail with addressing the challenges of the new industrial age and society, but merely the extent and direction of its intervention. Taft may have been the victorious candidate, but the election in 1908 was a referendum on Roosevelt and his policies, and the country responded with enthusiasm.

Becoming president at the age of 42, following William McKinley's assassination on September 14, 1901, Theodore Roosevelt was the first to occupy the office during the industrial age to see government as something other than as the protector of the status quo. Instead, he conceived of it as a kind of referee in American society, representing neither labor nor capital, but only the best interests of the American people. Above all, he believed in fairness, what he eventually would labeled as a "Square Deal."

This first became apparent during a coal strike in 1902. Usually in the past once a labor conflict became either violent or a perceived obstacle to the economic well-being of the nation, the federal government would respond with injunctions and troops on the side of management. Roosevelt changed the rules by insisting upon arbitration and an eventual compromise—a major step forward for the cause of unionism. Similarly, he reactivated the largely moribund Sherman Anti-Trust Act of 1890, which made restraint of trade and competition illegal. The courts, in contradiction to the intent of its passage, often utilized this law against labor unions on strike or engaged in a boycott. The Roosevelt administration used the law to focus upon many of the monopolistic industrial combinations generally known as "trusts" (after trust companies set up to exchange stock with and to manage any number of other companies) that had been its supposed target in the first place. He directed his justice department to initiate suits against Trusts in egregious violation of the act against the interests of the American people (towards others not so judged, he remained tolerant). The most famous case concerned the Northern Securities Corporation, which was designed to coordinate the Great Northern and Northern Pacific Railroads, and thus create a monopoly on rail transportation in the northwest. In 1904, the United Sates Supreme Court ordered its dissolution. Other actions were brought against the American Tobacco Company, the General Paper Company, the DuPont Chemical Company, the New Haven Railroad, and the most hated trust of them all, the Standard Oil Company (broken up in 1911).

He kept going. At his urging, Congress passed the Elkins Act (1903) and the Hepburn Act (1906), both designed to more greatly empower the Interstate Commerce Commission, created in 1887, as an agency to oversee transportation companies, and railroads in particular. As a signal of the permanency of this broader federal regulatory role, the Department of Commerce and Labor in 1903 was established. Consumer protection was also expanded with the Pure, Food, and Drug Act (1906), and the Meat Inspection Act (1906), both inspired by Upton Sinclair's famous muckraking book, *The Jungle,* which detailed the often nauseating abuses of the Chicago packing industry. Moreover, as a sportsman and a naturalist, Roosevelt was strongly interested in preserving the country's natural resources, which many felt were being pillaged by business interests. In all, twenty-one new national forests were designated during his administration, and in 1902, a Bureau of Reclamation was created to restore despoiled land. Later, he presided over a conference of governors that set into motion events leading to a National Conservation Commission. By 1904, his renown was such that he was reelected over Alton B. Parker by the largest popular margin yet in American history, and in 1908, he was, if anything, more beloved. Even at the Democratic convention in Denver that year his name, when mentioned, evoked noisy applause and cheers.[1]

William Jennings Bryan, though two years younger than Roosevelt, seemed in contrast to be an anachronism. His great cause of free silver was now irrelevant, and his anti-imperialism unappealing to a nation generally pleased with Roosevelt's assertions of American power overseas, including the seizure from Colombia of the land needed for an inter-ocean canal in Central America. The Commoner's efforts to modernize his message with calls for greater control of the corporations and for broadening governmental regulatory powers seemed merely pallid and opportunistic echoes of the president. Moreover, Bryan suffered from the fact that he was still perceived by many Americans as associated with a Western based agrarian "radicalism." In contrast, Roosevelt, although his policies represented real departures, was accepted—at this point anyway—as a comparatively reliable member of America's Eastern establishment.

With the election results underscoring the change in American politics as represented by Roosevelt, Roger Sullivan began a process of accommodation that, while not always consistent, would reappear as events demanded. With increasing frequency in the years ahead, he turned to the use of reform as a political tool. Ultimately, he would even try on the toga of reformer for himself and once again seek political office.

Just weeks following the elections of November 1908, a joint meeting of the state Democratic committee and key legislators was called to gather at the Sherman House in Chicago. Roger gave a talk outlining his conception of the Democratic agenda for the upcoming Forty-Seventh General Assembly. It was remarkably progressive and included demands: (1) that the Republican-dominated legislature outlaw paying off political debts through enforced contributions from state appointees, (2) that a system of accountability be introduced for all expenditures including the publication of the state payroll, (3) that an extension of civil service to all Cook County offices be implemented, (4) that a general reduction of Cook County offices including a consolidation of all the clerks of the various courts be accomplished, and (5) that the jurisdiction of the county election commission be extended to all elective offices. To facilitate this program a legislative committee with a reliable downstate ally, Arthur W. Charles, as chair was appointed. To assist him were Ernest Hoover, Thomas Scully, and Gene Sullivan (none of whom were currently legislators).[2]

Not surprisingly, the opposition was skeptical about this commitment to progressive reform. The *Chicago Tribune*, for instance, in the most sarcastic tones possible, attributed most of the new Democratic goals to recognition of the permanence of Republican control of the Cook County government, and a desire to cut down on county patronage. In fact, when the Democrats returned to power in the county in 1910, these demands for change were nowhere to be found. Also not surprising was that the legislature declined to respond to any of the proposals. With heavy Republican majorities (28 to 13 in the Senate, and 89 to 64 in the House), not even the deal-making skills of Sullivan, who worked especially hard to expand the Cook County civil service, had much impact. In fact, the 47th General Assembly proved remarkably resistant to anything resembling reform.[3]

Instead, the question that became the Assembly's primary focus in the spring of 1909 was the purely political issue of the election of one of Illinois' United States senators. This would ultimately evolve into one of the scandals of the age, and would stimulate the clamor for change. Although Roger Sullivan was not implicated in anything untoward, the controversy called into question the state's political culture, and therefore his position and that of his organization.

Before the ratification of the Thirteenth Amendment in 1913, United States senators were chosen by legislatures in conformity with the Constitutional Convention's original intent that the Upper House represent state governments. As a consequence, senators had been almost exclusively senior state politicians able to secure the support of the organizations of their parties, and often much of that of the opposition as well (both frequently being necessary for election). A senatorship was prized as the highest honor a state could bestow.

Although in preponderance in the legislature in 1909, the Republicans were badly divided. The incumbent, Senator Albert J. Hopkins from Aurora, had, it was true, won the G.O.P.'s advisory primary. But his plurality of just 43.3 percent of the vote was small, and his chief opponents, Congressman George E. Foss, and former Congressman, William "Billy" Mason, promised to take the fight to Springfield. There the divisions of the legislative groupings were split among the followers of Governor Deneen, who were considered "progressive," assemblymen loyal to Albert Hopkins, who included a number of those associated with the federal faction of Mayor Fred Busse and the city's postmaster, Dan Campbell, and a coterie loosely bound to Congressman William Lorimer. Hopkins' backers mostly came from Chicago, and were judged to include the more conservative legislators, or at least those with the least commitment to the rhetoric of reform. None of the alliances were particularly stable, and, as Roger Sullivan explained, "the men [among the Republican legislators] who are strong enemies to-day [sic] may be friendly six months from now."[4]

If anything, the Democrats were even less unified. They, too, had their legislative factions, especially in the House. The most powerful of these was led by Lee O'Neil Browne of Ottawa, the minority leader, whose circle of about thirty received eight of the prized chairmanships. He also enjoyed the backing of Anton Cermak's United Societies for Local Self-Government, Chicago's pro-liquor or "wet" lobbying group. This placed him ideologically in opposition to those led by Thomas G. Tippet of Olney, whose approximately twenty-six downstate associates as a rule took an anti-liquor, or "dry" posture. Lastly, there were eight Sullivan loyalists, who generally would do his bidding without question. The Chicago leader could also usually count upon the Tippet men, though he did not countenance any "dry" legislation. His relationship to Browne's men was more complex, complicated by an intense personal antagonism between the two men, the origins of which are not clear but were apparently founded in past factional battles for control of the state party machinery.[5]

Roger Sullivan's position on the senatorial question was identical to the official line of the state committee: all Democrats in the legislature should support their primary victor, former-gubernatorial candidate, Lawrence B. Stringer. Beyond this, his primary participation, by his own substantiated account, was to hurry to Springfield at one point to "busy himself a bit" (a classic example of Sullivan understatement) to prevent Democrats from switching over to Hopkins. According to later reports, he was more than "busy," and actually threatened "to break every bone in the political body of each and every one of you if you sell out to Hopkins," and/or take "any dirty money." All of this was in collusion with Stringer, as the Democratic candidate would later affirm. Though it would be speculated that he took a larger role in the senatorial balloting, this was not substantiated despite intensive scrutiny by two special committees of the United States Senate.[6]

Predictably, when the General Assembly took up the issue in late January 1909, a deadlock immediately ensued. While the incumbent Hopkins could count upon a clear plurality of Republicans in both houses, his totals were insufficient for election and declined with each ballot. It soon became apparent that the man with the greatest influence was the eventual victor, Republican William Lorimer.[7]

Lorimer had known Roger C. Sullivan since the Democratic leader "came to Chicago" in the 1880s, and considered him a "close friend." Their families were neighbors and had "been very, very, intimate for a long time." Both men were passionate about yachting, and Roger's boy, Boetius, attended school with Lorimer's sons. Sullivan admitted their personal relationship, but politically, the two men remained on opposite sides. When mutual interest dictated, however, they would consult and cooperate. Going outside party lines to seek support even in an internal factional dispute was not common, but not rare either.[8]

Between January and late May 1909, Lorimer schemed with his allies in Springfield. One of his early plans was to convince Governor Deneen to make a run. Over the course of a few weeks the two formed a brief alliance. However, Deneen was unwilling to alienate legislators based upon his remote chances. Instead, he was duly inaugurated for his second term as the state's chief executive.[9]

Meanwhile, the Democratic support for Stringer was steadily eroding. On January 19, Democrats in the House gave him seventy-six votes and those in the Senate, fifty-seven. By the vote on March 24, his totals had fallen to just twenty-three in the House and twenty-seven in the Senate. And thereafter his numbers diminished still further. Sullivan and the state and Cook County leadership now moved in to do their best for their candidate. On May 15, John McGillen, secretary of the Cook County Central Committee, and one of Sullivan's lieutenants, telegraphed a stern admonishment promising that "ignominious oblivion" awaited the "perfidy" of those who failed to back their party's candidate. This evoked only anger and defiance. Representative Anton Cermak, for one, tersely responded that: "I have your wire. I need no advice." Others responded similarly, and the number of those standing pat declined still further. On May 25, Stringer received just one Democratic vote in the House.[10]

The following day, it all came ended when William Lorimer, who had received no votes to this point, was suddenly elected. His total was fifty-five in the state senate, of which thirteen came from the Democrats. However, in the lower chamber, forty-seven Democrats joined with forty-two Republican representatives to give him the victory. This was not totally unexpected. For weeks the press had been reporting that deals were being negotiated to secure his election.[11]

The key to the Democratic vote was Representative Lee O'Neil Browne, who actively worked for the Republican. Sullivan, for his part, made his feelings clear that any such agreements would be "bad politics." However, in the end most of his immediate followers in the legislature supported Lorimer and were involved in bringing over members of the Tippet faction. While Sullivan had been in contact with Lorimer and was in Springfield as recently as the second week of May, purportedly because of a Chicago waterway bill that failed, the word among the Browne men in the capital city was that the Chicago leader, in face of Stringer's failing campaign, was no longer "concerning himself with the senatorial ambitions of any known person." Lorimer would confirm this years later, testifying that: "I do not know, either directly, or indirectly, of one Democrat that Mr. Sullivan tried to influence on my behalf," but also that "Mr. Sullivan knew I was a candidate, and that I expected to get Democratic votes, and I just reasoned that I would get the votes of his friends." Sullivan was always consistent in claims of noninvolvement. He explained that the McGillen warning had been directed against a Lorimer candidacy, which, he had not, in any case, taken seriously. Instead, he had hoped that the deadlock could be brokered in Stringer's favor. No serious evidence ever emerged to contradict this statement, although it is difficult to believe that Sullivan's political judgment was not more astute.[12]

With all of this at last out of the way, Roger, with John Hopkins, was able to embark upon a highly anticipated tour of Europe. Accompanying them as a last minute addition was the secretary of the Democratic National Committee, Urey Woodson of Kentucky. Also along were Mrs. Helen Sullivan and the couple's four daughters, Mary, Helen, Frances, and Virginia. They focused upon eastern and southern Europe, traveling through Germany, down the Danube River and into the Austrian-Hungarian Empire. They then shifted north and eventually arrived at the Spitsbergen Islands in the upper reaches of recently independent Norway. Palaces were visited, but poverty "a hundred times over that in the worse spots of Chicago and New York" was also observed. Nor was Roger impressed with the European style of government-owned transportation: "as for service, comfort, and convenience the American railways are infinitely finer." Concerning the municipally owned public transportation pervasive throughout the continent, all he could say "is that if the company in any city in this country gave the same kind of service, the people would tear up the tracks." Such was Roger Sullivan's first public pronouncement upon the issue that had been for years an important focus of his city's political conversation.

All in all, however, he and his companions had a wonderful time on this tour of "good cheer." Still, it was a relief to get back home. As they arrived in New York harbor on the liner *Kaiserin Auguste Victoria,* and passed the Statue of Liberty, he later recounted to reporters, "we took off our hats, and bowed in reverence and joy to the symbol of our country's freedom and greatness." Exhausted, but exhilarated, Roger, for once, did not want to talk politics.[13]

But politics would not wait. Lorimer's election opened up a congressional seat. Special conventions in the Sixth District were held in October, but it fell to Roger Sullivan and William Lorimer to do the actual selection of their parties' candidates. There was some speculation that Roger's brother, Frank, might be given the nod, but in the end Frank S. Ryan was tapped to run against the Republican, William J. Moxley. This oversight of candidate selection by Sullivan and Lorimer caused some resentment, and provided an excuse for an independent "reform" bid, backed by the *Chicago Tribune,* of Republican Dr. Carl L. Barnes. In public anyway, he was motivated by an unalterable opposition to the "political union of William Lorimer and Roger Sullivan." Since Lorimer's election by the legislature, these charges of collusion became increasingly frequent, while the press would write, in moments of hyperbolic fury, of a Lorimer-Sullivan machine. Given the history of private cooperation that did on occasion exist among many of the leaders of the two parties, given both men's dedication towards the kind of political efficiency that some degree of coordination could bring, and given their personal relationship, the charges had some appearance of credibility. However, as the upcoming special election and later events would prove, they were greatly overstated.[14]

In fact, the chief characteristic of the campaign would not be collusion, but treason. Sullivan and John McGillen, secretary of the county committee, felt the need to appear at a meeting of the precinct captains of the Sixth District to attack scathingly those who were defecting for personal gain, as well as to confront and confound Republican-initiated rumors that the boss was actually backing Moxley. The words were harsh. However, in the end, the tirades had little effect; Ryan was trounced. Roger was furious and raged about the "cheap Democrats, who had been bought up in bunches" and who had "deliberately sold out" their candidate and their party. Soon afterward, his sometime friend, Alderman Johnny Powers, was thrown off the Cook County Democratic Committee for supporting the Republican Moxley, something he admitted but which he justified with the excuse that Ryan (somehow) was not actually a Democrat.[15]

Well might Roger Sullivan have been irritated and concerned about the defiance of so many Democrats. Making it worse, this was another in a lengthening string of defeats on his watch since 1907, including the recent Democratic loss of a majority on the city council in the April 1908, elections. He could, it was true, hardly be blamed for Mayor Edward F. Dunne's eccentric political behavior that had killed his reelection bid, or for the drag upon the party of the renomination of Bryan. Still, this lack of electoral success provided ammunition for potential rivals. And already the most dangerous competition possible was beginning to reemerge.

Carter H. Harrison II, had been insinuating himself back into the Chicago party since 1907, when he eagerly volunteered his services as a possible substitute for Dunne as the mayoral nominee. However, his selfless offer was ignored. In the 1908 fall elections, he made himself available to speak for Democratic candidates, only to be brusquely refused by the Cook County Democratic Committee. Instead, he spent his time campaigning for Bryan around the country. Throughout the following year, he quietly strengthened his relations with many of his old supporters, and it was becoming increasingly clear that he was intent upon staging a comeback.[16]

The former mayor would build not just upon his body of friends among Chicago Democrats, and his record as a winner, able to boast of four victorious mayoral races, but also upon the rising tide of reformism throughout the nation, a tide that threaten to become a tsunami in Chicago and Illinois because of two major scandals. The first of these involved the administration of Republican Mayor Fred Busse. Responding to numerous allegations, the city council had appointed a special commission under the chairmanship of Alderman Charles E. Merriam. A professor at the University of Chicago in the young field of political science, he epitomized the progressive "expert," and was unrelenting in his probe.[17]

In late 1909, his commission began reporting its findings, and revelations continued into the summer of the following year. They were not pleasant. Chicago's government, it was found, was rampant with inefficiency, favoritism, and outright corruption. The city was paying too much for inferior oil; it was also overpaying, perhaps even twice, for the same deliveries of coal, and there were suggestions of kickbacks; in the city clerk's office a notary public had set up a "private business"; the sewer commission was replete with failings; the interest on police pensions had gone missing; phone expenses were out of control; supplies for the fire department were overly expensive and of poor quality; worse of all, from Merriam's point of view, the entire system of accountancy was incoherent—and so it went.

Adding to the public controversy were revelations of personal corruption among the men around the mayor: one old friend managed to secure an untoward $45,000 profit for sewer construction, another made a killing selling the city overpriced manhole covers, and still another, Busse's secretary, Harry A. Smith, organized the Chicago Fire Appliance Company to obtain a monopoly on providing city office equipment, which turned out to be unduly expensive and inferior in quality. Estimates of the city's losses ran from thirty to fifty-five million dollars.

Fiery commission meetings attracted press attention as Comptroller Walter H. Wilson fought a rear-guard action against aspects of the investigation. Others outside attempted to secure an injunction to halt the commission's funding, only to be thwarted in court and by a Citizen's Association's pledge to raise private subscriptions to keep it going. However, the mayor promised change, Public Works Commissioner John J. Hanberg resigned, and grand jury investigations were begun. Even more dramatically, Busse summarily removed three members of the municipal Civil Service Commission accused of neglect of duty. After the Merriam group ended its investigation in the summer of 1910, a new private organization, to be eventually called the Bureau of Public Efficiency, was created to maintain oversight. The President of Sears, Roebuck & Company, noted business philanthropist, and a leader of the Jewish community, Julius Rosenwald, became its chair. Walter L. Fisher, soon to be Taft's Secretary of the Interior, sat on its board.[18]

Although Sullivan was not involved, the foibles of the Busse administration facilitated growing concerns about Chicago's political culture, and this presented obvious dangers to his Democracy. Far more impactful, however, would be the Lorimer Scandal involving allegations of vote buying during the 1909 senatorial race in the legislature. Again, Roger Sullivan was not implicated; indeed, it would be proved that he had done his best to prevent the events that would come to scandalize the state and the nation.

Yet, as Illinois' leading organizational Democrat, the seemingly endless succession of sordid revelations was hurtful.

On April 30, 1910, State Representative Charles A. White, a Democrat, confessed to Clifford S. Raymond, the chief editorial writer of the *Chicago Tribune*, that he and others had been paid to help elect William Lorimer United States senator. Moreover, he alleged that Lee O'Neil Browne, the Democratic minority leader in the Illinois House, had been a ringleader in this illegal conspiracy, and arranged a payment of $850 for his vote. White also claimed that he had only participated because he wanted later to reveal the details of the nefarious plot. In fact, Raymond was already well-aware of events because Roger Sullivan, back in 1909, had purposely acquainted him with his own understanding of the details. The writer counted the Democratic leader as one of his "warm personal friends," and not long following Lorimer's election, he dropped into the Democratic leader's office in the People's Gas Building to learn the latest political gossip. Brennan and other lieutenants were present, and when the discussion turned to Illinois' junior senator, all was revealed in confidence. As there was no corroborating evidence, Raymond kept the knowledge to himself until White appeared, and his conversations with Sullivan were only made public forty-one years later. Sullivan's motives, at least in part, were founded in his disgust at Browne and the other Democrats for abandoning their own party's candidate.[19]

The *Chicago Tribune* published White's revelations with screaming headlines, and thereafter pursued the story relentlessly. The rest of the press, sensing blood in the water, soon joined in a journalistic feeding frenzy. A grand jury probe was convened, and on May 6, 1910, Browne was indicted for bribery. Meanwhile, two other Democratic representatives were charged with perjury for their testimony before the jury. One of these, Michael S. Link of Mitchell turned state's evidence and supported White's allegations. The legislature began its own investigation. This led to more indictments with a Sangamon County grand jury accusing five state senators of either bribery or perjury before the legislative committee or both. Browne went on trial on 7 June 1910 and seventeen days later the case went to the jury. After deliberating 115 hours and 20 minutes, it came back hung by a margin of eight to four. A retrial began in August, and on September 9, Browne was acquitted.[20]

As the controversy unfolded, Lorimer, who denied all knowledge of any vote-buying, asked the United States Senate to conduct its own inquiry. Beginning in June 1910 and continuing throughout the remainder of the year, a subcommittee of the Committee on Privileges and Elections, held hearings in Washington, D.C., and Chicago. On December 12, it concluded that Senator Lorimer was blameless and as only four votes were purchased in the legislature, and as he would have been elected without them, he, therefore, should not face disciplinary action or expulsion from his office. These conclusions and recommendations were immediately challenged on the Senate floor and in 1911, new hearings before a new subcommittee were begun.[21]

Protest meetings erupted around Illinois and the scandal became an epicenter of public outrage over the next two years. Though Democrats were implicated in the bribery, the Lorimer scandal, together with the revelations of tawdry mismanagement in Chicago as revealed by the Merriam Committee, rebounded—temporarily at least—in the Democrats favor as the "out" party. They, naturally, were profuse in their own indignation and self-righteousness, doing their best to appear as a party of reform.

Roger Sullivan, too, did his part. Even as the Merriam Commission was confronting the city with the foibles of the Busse administration, but before the Lorimer story broke, he and his supporters in the legislature diligently applied themselves to the passage of yet another primary bill (to replace the one most recently overturned the Illinois Supreme court), which by its breadth attracted the approval of even the most dedicated progressives. It was a tough fight as a bipartisan group, led by Lee O'Neil Browne and others, fought hard to limit its range. But in the end, a coalition of Sullivan Democrats and Republican followers of Governor Charles Deneen were able to put it through.[22]

The voters 'exasperation began to pay off in the aldermanic elections in April 1910. Of the twenty four incumbents running for reelection (for thirty-five seats, half of the seventy-member council was elected each year), ten were thrown out (eight Republicans and two Democrats). This returned the Democrats to a majority.[23]

With something at last to celebrate, Roger Sullivan took the occasion of the annual Jackson Day Banquet held, as usual, at the Iroquois Club, to present a kind of political manifesto. Introduced as "a practical man," his words were plain and direct. The party "has had too much theory," he argued, and this must stop; "we've taken up the theory of this man or that, and one after another these theories have driven the rank and file out of the party." Instead, what was required was a return to "our old fundamental principles," to rebuild the base. Another problem was that there had been too much "individualism" lately. This was all very fine, he conceded, but it should be confined to "within the party organization." What was needed, he argued, was "more organization," and "more rank and file" made up of "businessmen and laboring men," sustained in the party "by more social life." "A party cannot live on office seekers and office holders." Lastly, in a clear reference to rival Carter Harrison, he called for a "new class of candidates," and "to cut loose from those who have run so often, run to defeat!" Do these things and "the time is ripe for us to win."[24]

However, there was a sizable number who did not share Sullivan's vision of a party marching in lockstep behind his leadership. By mid-summer a loose coalition of opponents was coalescing. Leading the dissent was Bobby Burke, who began mending fences with Harrison, and a brief-lived organization was created called the New Democracy, led by Maclay Hoyne and Oscar F. Meyer, which blamed Roger for "successive and crushing defeats." In late July 1910, they joined with Carter Harrison, Edward F. Dunne, William Dever, and Andrew Lawrence, leader of the Hearst faction (and publisher of the Hearst papers in Chicago), to demand their share of the county candidates for the fall elections. As usual, Sullivan sought unity in face of division, and repeatedly attempted to hammer out an agreement acceptable to all.

To this end, the county committee appointed a "harmony committee" of Sullivan, William O'Connell (with strong ties to Dunne), Adolph Sabath (who was close to Harrison), George Brennan, and others to meet with the "insurgents," as they were being labeled in the press. Meetings were scheduled, and then cancelled, and then rescheduled again. Finally, on July 11, 1910, a reasonably harmonious gathering of representatives of all the major factions was held, and a slate selected. Sullivan's man, Henry Stuckart was to run for sheriff. William O'Connell, a friend of both Sullivan and Dunne, received the nod for County Treasurer. Frank Hoyne, Maclay's brother, was to run for the board of review, and it was agreed that Dever would stand for superior court judge. However, Carter Harrison, though represented at the meeting, balked and threatened to run his own candidates. He simply wanted more, and in particular he wanted his man Michael

Zimmer, to be the party's choice for the sheriff of Cook County nomination. Moreover, Dever declined the honor of the nomination for judge, citing other plans.[25]

With Roger's best efforts failing, the county committee as a whole, with his approval, weighed in, and convinced Harrison and the others personally to attend yet another meeting. Harrison, Dunne, Lawrence, Dever, John Traeger, and Roy D. Keene for the "insurgents" or "allies," as they were now styling themselves, all came. Representing the "regulars" were Sabath, O'Connell, Frank Burke, Alderman James M. Dailey, and Stanley Kunz. Sullivan did not attend, but remained nearby at the county headquarters with friends. Finally, after hours of haggling at 1:30 a.m. an agreement was reached. Zimmer would run for sheriff, and Harrison was to choose the candidate for president of the county board. He would later name John Owens, long an opponent of Sullivan. Dever agreed to run for judge, while other slots were distributed to general satisfaction.[26]

The man least sanguine about the outcome was Roger Sullivan. "There is nothing in this ticket for me," he lamented before the county committee. This was something of an overstatement as many of the nominees for the lesser posts were his friends, but still it was an accurate reflection of the compromises necessary for harmony. But the list, unquestionably included men who were his "bitterest foes." Nor could he be silent about the recent spate of attacks upon him, most coming from participants, or their representatives, at the meeting. Though he admitted that he was "an influential member of this committee," he hardly could be held responsible for recent electoral setbacks. Was it not true that elections had also been lost during both Harrison and Dunne's tenures as mayor? As to intimations that he was somehow corrupt, had he not served as probate clerk, and had not the books of that office been thoroughly reviewed by the Merriam Committee and others with nothing untoward found? "Talk about your spirit of fairness. There is none of it here." Despite all, he recommended that the Cook County Committee "support the motion to adopt the ticket as drafted." And so it was done.[27]

Sullivan's defensive tone was not feigned. Since 1908, he had done things largely his way, and now he was being challenged not just on the basis of power—that he could probably accept—but also upon hurtful charges of political incompetence and possible corruption. His attempt to reinvent himself as a modern political leader and businessman dedicated to party efficiency, one who also recognized the need social and governmental reform, had been ignored or ridiculed. Instead, he found himself caricaturized as just another big city "boss."

This was made explicit at a mass meeting on July 21, in the central Illinois berg of Lincoln. Two hundred downstate Democrats gathered in the hometown of defeated senatorial candidate, Lawrence B. Stringer, to denounce Lorimer and their own party leaders. Chaired by Sullivan's old enemy, Ben Caldwell, the featured speaker was social activist and one-time member of Mayor Dunne's school board, Raymond Robins. Robins excoriated Lorimer and his Democratic supporters, labeling Lee O'Neil Browne a "pirate." He also used the occasion to attack the established political system and Roger C. Sullivan. Sullivan was, he conceded, "in his personal way ... a very decent man." However, he stands "in the night time" with those politicians who are "faithful to the public service corporations that will plunder the people." Moreover, "he owns largely one of these himself." Therefore, "he can't be honest with the Democrats if he wants to be; that is impossible ... [because] he flies the flag of Democracy for the purpose of enslaving the people of this state!" Removing men like Lee O'Neil Browne, he argued (ignoring Sullivan's antagonism towards the Representative), could only be brought about if they dispensed with

Roger Sullivan and the system he represented. However, for all of the rally's
noise, its impact was undercut by the
deliberate absence of important downstate Democrats like Henry T. Rainey
and Stringer.[28]

But within days, these same
themes would be voiced much more
tellingly as Sullivan came under a barrage of criticism from the president of
the Municipal Voters' League (MVL),
Clifford Barnes. In a widely circulated
bulletin, Barnes, writing anony-
mously under the League's moniker,
accused Roger of numerous political
sins. Most importantly, Sullivan had
allegedly ordered the committees of
what were described as "his districts":
the Nineteenth, Twenty-First, and
Twenty-Third, to run only one candidate for the Illinois House. As each
district had two representatives, it was
asserted that this was an unfair tactic
to unify the Democratic vote to assure
at least the election of a single man.

Raymond Robins (Library of Congress, LC-DIG-
ggbain-21748).

Sullivan was accused of taking a particular interest in one of those who ran, John
McLaughlin, said to own a construction business in which the Chicago leader held an
interest.

A war of words in the press followed as Sullivan flayed Barnes as a "once indicted"
unnamed member of the MVL governing board, while also attacking his other reform
critics like Raymond Robins, George Schilling and Alderman William E. Dever. "I am
not a 'boss,' I have never been one," he angrily proclaimed "I am utterly disgusted," he
told another reporter," with the vicious, lying, and deceiving utterances of certain pseudo-
reformers, and noted squaw-men of the city, who never do anything but agitate!" To
restore his good name, he decided, after consulting with John Hopkins, George Brennan,
and others, to accept an invitation to meet with the executive council of the League to
discuss this and other allegations.[29]

The two hour meeting at the Mid-Day Club with the MVL's executive board was
beset by belligerence and anger, all of which was reported verbatim to an eager public
by the press. Intimations of dishonesty would be flung with increasing disregard for convention or courtesy. However, everything began convivially enough with an elaborate
lunch consumed as Clifford Barnes and Roger sat together exchanging pleasantries. Then
it began. Barnes announced officially that the purpose of the gathering was to investigate
their guest's role in the selection of House candidates in the three districts in question.
While maintaining his belief in Roger's pivotal role in the matter, he also admitted that
he could be mistaken.[30]

This was Sullivan's cue. He explained he had come to counter these false charges, which were being used to make him "a goat." "Men," he pleaded, "this story about Roger C. Sullivan is not true; it cannot be substantiated and verified!" He then polled each member of the committee about his belief concerning the allegations of his responsibility for the district committees' nomination of a single candidate. All claimed to be withholding judgment. He then asked whether they lent credence to the charge that he held an interest in Representative John J. McLaughlin's construction business. Again they collectively declared that they had not reached a conclusion. Now Sullivan directed his attention to a statement in their bulletin "that I secured a good position for a man, and then flooded him with letters asking him to appoint a lot of bum politicians to jobs." Who was that man, he now demanded of Barnes? The MVL's president, flustered, tacitly admitted his authorship but declined to reveal his source. However, he assured Sullivan the man in question would testify in court, if necessary. Despite Sullivan's repeated demands, and intimations that it might have been Raymond Robins, which was denied, Barnes refused to say more.[31]

Now the Democratic leader, feeling his point had been made, began insisting that as there was no evidence, the committee should issue a statement exonerating him. This prompted the angry entry into the discussion of former league president and Barnes' co-conspirator, George Cole, who warned Roger that he was "not going to run things here!" This inspired a retort from Sullivan that he had a right to defend himself.[32]

Cole, now taking charge of the prosecution, turned to events in the districts, making a point of emphasizing Sullivan's power in his party. Had he not dominated the 1908 Democratic selection of candidates? Yes, Roger admitted, but "modesty" forbade him from saying more. Moreover, he argued, it should be remembered that there had been an open primary to elect the delegates. Only fifteen percent of registered Democrats actually had voted, sneered Cole. "Well, with all of your purity, George," responded Sullivan, inspiring some smiles, "you can't make all the people vote." What about the gas regulatory bill of 1905, Cole with increasing heat now demanded? Had Roger not lied when the two of them had agreed at the time that there was to be no interference? Sullivan allowed that his business interests were concerned, but he argued that he actually used his influence to convince the executives of the other gas companies to accept regulation as the alternative to municipal ownership. Moreover, had not George and he collaborated on parts of the bill?

Nor, for that matter, was Roger ashamed of his interest in gas. What was the issue with the Ogden Company, anyway? Had they not offered to the people cheaper gas than the monopoly? Cole allowed for the truth of this statement,

George Cole (*Illinois Political Directory, 1899*).

but attempted to regain ascendency in this increasingly polemical dialectic by spewing forth more questions in rapid succession. Sullivan began to speak over him in an attempt to reply, and confusion ensued. Out of the disorder and mutual recriminations that now followed, the Democratic national committeeman reiterated his insistence that not only was he "not a boss," but that the source of his influence was nothing more than "on the lines of moral suasion."[33]

During his discourse on his company, Sullivan cited the involvement of board member Adolf Kraus, who was an Ogden investor. Kraus admitted this, and also expressed his wish that he had put more money into the firm because of Sullivan's skill as a businessman. Changing the subject somewhat, he paid Roger the compliment that "it takes brains and ability to be a leader of men, to be a political 'boss,'" and in this light, the title carried no stigma. Flattered, Roger murmured that respect "was all I want."[34]

Cole now returned to his attack with a quick-fire interrogation. Had Sullivan not opposed the primary law of 1906? Yes, but he had supported that of 1897, and "helped make the present law" in partnership with Governor Deneen and his legislative supporters. Had he surreptitiously colluded with Lorimer in the election of Ryan over Moxley in the Sixth Congressional District? No, and Cole admitted that about this, at least, he believed Roger. Had he been a part of any deal to elect Lorimer senator? Absolutely not, and while, of course, he had met with the Senator before and during the session, it was about other matters. Moreover, if the League were going to be so self-righteous on this point, where were they, by the way, when he was in Springfield thwarting the conspiracy to reelect Hopkins to the senate with Democratic votes? What about Ben Mitchell, one of the district candidates at issue, was he not one of his men? Sullivan responded in the positive, but pointed out that previously the legislator had been someone Cole had endorsed. This brought no contradiction. Had he not agreed over a year before to endorse the selection of two candidates in all three districts? This was true, the Democratic chief explained, but things had changed. Then the selection of candidates was the responsibility of conventions, where he might have influence, but then they became chosen by committees elected through direct primary over which he could exercise relatively little control.[35]

This prompted a heated exchange. Cole angrily reiterated his belief that Sullivan could direct the district committees at will. Sullivan, who had been earlier denied the right to introduce the letters he had written to the committees to prove his point, now asked in exasperation whether he was expected to "buy them?" "It is something you have done before!" was the shouted reply. "You mean I used money?" growled a red-faced Sullivan. "Well I brand any such statement as a plain, bold lie!" Cole, still heated, confessed that he did not mean with money, "but that there are other ways." When the noise died down, Roger was allowed at last to clarify his position: "I am just as much in favor of two candidates as Mr. Cole is," he summarized, but "the statements [in the bulletin] by Mr. Barnes have been unfair and dishonest." With this, the meeting the atmosphere cooled, the committee agreed to defer all conclusions until a later session, and then it adjourned. Roger and Cole shook hands, but "without that old time friendliness, which had been noticeable between them."[36]

By any objective reading, it was Roger Sullivan who came off best at his "trial." His accusers were simply unwilling, or unable, to present proof of their charges. In the end, they did little more than engage in name-calling, and it was they who allowed their emotions to cloud the session. In contrast, Roger Sullivan arrived armed with documentation and references to support his case, and won a moral victory in not being permitted to enter them as evidence. Moreover, he compelled the committee to admit its uncertainty about the charges, thus underscoring the truth of his contention that the offensive pamphlet was the creation of just Barnes and Cole. He then extracted an admission from Cole that he did not believe that Sullivan had secretly supported Moxley, which was followed shortly by a statement of admiration (of sorts) from one of the committee's leading members. Nonetheless, the press chose to spin the story against him, and within days the executive board of the Municipal Voters' League, by an unrecorded vote, judged him "guilty" of having the power to dictate the number of candidates in the three districts in question, and haven chosen to run just one as an act of political corruption. This decision was effectively a declaration that Roger C. Sullivan was a "boss." and therefore, by implication, the enemy of reform.[37]

Sullivan attempted damage control. At a meeting of the state committee, where Roger was "influential," a statement was issued demanding that district committees select the usual two candidates for the state House. However, a month later, the Cook County Committee, of which Roger was secretary, also made clear to the same committees locally that they "are free to act as they see fit on these candidates," and the single nominations in the Nineteenth, Twenty-First, and Twenty-Third districts stood. Ironically, in late August, George Cole announced his intentions to vote in the Democratic primaries, a statement that brought a cheerful response from a Sullivan who offered the "glad hand of welcome." In good humor, but with subtle sarcasm, he continued: "He called me a boss. Well, I don't say that I am. But I will gladly resign whatever position I have to Brother George and I haven't the slightest doubt that he'll be able to run the job better than I could."[38]

Perhaps coincidentally, perhaps not, within a few weeks of the MVL "debate," an article appeared in *Good Government*, the official journal of the National Civil Service Reform League, which reviewed the progress of civil service in each state. Concerning Illinois, it singled out Roger C. Sullivan for praise for "coming out openly" for dispensing with the spoils system. In an accompanying interview, he stated his intention to obey the popular call for restrictions on patronage. After all, as he had already demonstrated that it was possible to be politically successful without direct access to city hall patronage, "the civil service movement has no terrors for me." Though his enemies might conveniently overlook his stance on civil service, he was never meaningfully accused again of being its opponent.[39]

Any hope that Sullivan's overarching paramountcy might be diminished by this latest set of controversies were soon dispelled. The primary elections in September 1910, gave him an absolute majority at the Cook County convention. They, in turn, selected a friendly county committee with John McCarthy, formerly chair of the Department of Public Works, replacing O'Connell (now officially candidate for county treasurer) as chair. This was not accomplished without the opposition making noises about a fight, but the Sullivan Democracy led by George Brennan, John J. McLaughlin and others at the convention (it was not thought necessary for Roger to be present), was so obviously in control that Harrison, Dunne, and Andrew Lawrence did not even bother to attend.[40]

The primaries also returned a Sullivan majority to the state committee (in Cook County his loyalists won six of ten seats), which to his satisfaction reorganized itself with the incumbent Charles Boeschenstein again as its head. The state convention held in East St. Louis on September 23, 1910, operated, as was becoming usual, under his thrall.

There was speculation that there might be a bolt or some other kind of demonstration against him, but nothing happened. Instead, in keeping with the general anticipation of impending victory, it was a largely joyous affair—for everyone except Lee O'Neil Browne.[41]

Though recently acquitted of charges of bribery, he became the target of convenience for the general antipathy against all those Democrats in the legislature who voted for Lorimer. Nor was his position helped by his longstanding feud with Sullivan. Browne still retained sufficient status to be named to the committee on resolutions, but, when his name was announced to the convention, it was hissed so loudly that the former House minority leader, now "white faced," rose and demanded recognition to respond. This inspired more jeers and catcalls, and he was pointedly ignored by the chair, Congressman Henry T. Rainey. Later, when the committee met, he attempted to block a resolution condemning bribery, bribe-takers, and Democrats who helped elect Lorimer, which, understandably, he took personally. Sullivan, in person, intervened under the proxy of committee member and ally, former alderman Thomas Little, and insisted the plank be inserted into the platform. He did, however, agree for it to be redrafted to remove offensive phrases like "jackpot legislation," and "bathroom tactics." Later, when the revised version was read before the convention, Browne again tried to speak, vainly screaming but barely heard amidst the derisive chorus around him.[42]

In keeping with Sullivan's overarching strategy of embracing reform, the remainder of the platform was equally progressive. Included among its planks were condemnations of business trusts that restrained trade and created monopolies, and railroads that charged unfair rates, and high tariffs. The Democrats also favored governmental economy, an amendment to the Sherman Anti-Trust Act to exclude labor as a commodity and, therefore, from injunctions during strikes, and the removal of partisan influence in state educational and charitable institutions (where "Boss Rule" was as "intolerable ... as it is elsewhere"), direct democracy through initiative elections by the people, conservation of natural resources, the Lake-to-Gulf waterway, better roads, and "clean and upright politics" to be augmented by campaign finance reform. In addition, it included a demand to end:

> the spoils system by which is meant the appointment of the servitors of political bosses to offices of trust and responsibility as a reward for political services regardless of character or fitness to serve, as a fruitful source of graft and corruption in our state.

Although his political enemies might view the platform, and this section in particular, with cynicism, Sullivan wanted it to be made clear that he feared neither the direct voice of the people through primaries, nor the limitation of patronage through civil service. Doubtlessly he also perceived no irony in the condemnation of "bosses," being still insistent that he was not one. The convention moved on to the nominations for the minor offices of state treasurer, superintendent of public instruction, and trustees of the University of Illinois. All were hand-picked by Sullivan or his lieutenants and accepted without much discussion.[43]

Though the progressive pretensions of the Democrats were belied by the renomination by the district committees of most of those who had voted for Lorimer (as was also true among the Republicans), in Cook County, they remained confident that the current wave of public dissatisfaction would carry them to victory. Locally the impact of the anger associated with the scandals of the Busse administration had been evident in the spring aldermanic elections, and this, together with the effects of the unfolding Lorimer controversy, was expected to be decisive in the outcomes.

For once, the local Democrats were able to pull together in a temporary truce between Sullivan and the "regulars" on one side, and Carter Harrison, Edward F. Dunne, Andrew Lawrence, William Dever, and the "insurgents" on the other. This armistice would not always be placid; unkind sentiments were still occasionally expressed, as was resentment of Sullivan's oversight of the party's campaign, but the overt political warfare that characterized the previous summer was suspended. Roger vigorously threw himself into the fray, motivated in part, no doubt, by a desire to prove that he was not the source of recent electoral disappointments. Meetings were held, and party discipline restored and enforced, while even the Republican press purported to be impressed by Sullivan's efficiency and dedication. Still, as was customary, both sides maintained at least the facade of optimism right up to Election Day; state Republican chair, Roy O. West, had no doubts, in public at least, that the elections held on November 9, would bring a G.O.P. "plurality."[44]

For all the interest generated in the world of Chicago and Illinois politics by the 1910 elections, it paled to relative insignificance compared to the greatly anticipated and spectacular return of Halley's Comet—first visible in March and the center of much public attention. In ancient times such awe-inspiring displays skyward were said to be portents of impending doom. Well might the local Republican Party have taken heed. In massive landslides, they lost just about everything by substantial margins in Cook County. From the office of sheriff to the Superior Court judges, from Probate Clerk to the county commissioners and their president, Democrats were swept back into office reversing the growing GOP ascendency of recent years. The only Republicans left standing were some incumbent municipal court judges. Sullivan might be displeased with many of his party's candidates, but these successes were impressive affirmations of his leadership—and power.[45]

William Lorimer (*Illinois Political Directory, 1899*).

Still the elections brought no peace. In just over three months, mayoral primaries were scheduled. In the context of growing expectations of a Democratic victory, the nomination was becoming an ever more effulgent prize. The party wars were now to resume, and with unprecedented ferocity.

4

The Battle of the Seventh Regiment Armory (1911–1912)

"To hell with Roger Sullivan!"—Anonymous delegate, September 1911 convention

On December 2, 1910, Carter H. Harrison II formally announced his entry into the mayoral race. He brought impressive advantages. As the son and namesake of a political legend and a former mayor, he was broadly recognizable. Moreover, his relatively successful tenures as the city's chief executive officer contrasted well to both Edward F. Dunne's overly idealistic but controversial administration and that of Republican Mayor Fred Busse, now tainted by corruption. With considerable credibility, Harrison could claim to embody a return to stable, even reasonably "clean" government.

His platform was accordingly pragmatic and devoid of grandstanding. At its heart was a promise for a reduction of gas from ninety to seventy-five cents (per thousand cubic feet), as well as the lowering of telephone rates, the replacement of aging bridges, universal transfers on the street railways, the construction of subways, and positive changes in city procedures for purchasing coal. Although plainly composed, it also included incidental nods to such reformist icons as eventual municipal ownership of the public utilities, the introduction of direct democracy through the initiative, referendum, and recall, and a call for the elimination of graft. For many, this kind of reformist posturing was difficult to take seriously, especially as the emerging Harrison coalition included such Municipal Voters' League bêtes noire as Johnny Powers, who came over (for a while) from the Sullivan Democracy, as well as the notorious First Ward Aldermen Michael "Hinky Dink" Kenna and "Bathhouse" John Coughlin. In fact, the candidate would make little pretense of running a reform campaign. Instead, his more important political tactic and asset was a newly negotiated alliance with New York publisher William Randolph Hearst. Their "H-H" faction and its rivalry with the Sullivan Democracy were to define party politics for the next four years.

In the early decades of the twentieth century, William Randolph Hearst was a fixture of American life. Born rich and idle, he revealed, upon taking over his late father's *San Francisco Examiner*, a heretofore unsuspected talent for anticipating popular tastes. Success inspired him to move east and purchase the nearly defunct New York *Journal*. He became, with Joseph Pulitzer of the New York *World*, a leading purveyor of yellow journalism, which thrived on the controversial, the sensational, and the titillating. His press empire soon grew to include a chain of newspapers across the nation as well as numerous popular magazines.

With a self-image weaned on the pride of massive wealth and easy success, his thoughts turned to politics. In 1902, he was elected to the first of two undistinguished terms in the United States House of Representatives. He then set his eyes upon the Democratic presidential nomination, an ambition that, with his money, and in the temporary absence in 1904 of Bryan as a viable candidate, appeared feasible. He used his newspapers and operatives in several states to build political operations. In most places this yielded a small return, but in Illinois, Hearst became for a time a real power within the party.

He owned the *Chicago American* and the *Chicago Examiner*, the latter run by the local manager of his forces, Andrew Lawrence, and these (most particularly the *Examiner*, the *American* being little more than a tabloid) provided effective tools for self-promotion. He also authorized prodigious spending, which, especially in downstate Illinois and among Bryan men, proved effective towards creating immediate, if superficial, allegiances. Neither Roger Sullivan nor Mayor Harrison was comfortable with this kind of carpetbagging, but both went along as Hearst was not concerned at this point with issues of party governance. The 1904 state Democratic convention formally endorsed Hearst for president, but at the national conclave, Sullivan and Hopkins, who controlled the delegation, worked for Alton Parker.[1]

Thoroughly disappointed, Hearst become an unpredictable and frequently disruptive force in the state, one always on the side of any reform currently being promoted, despite which many progressives found him untrustworthy. In 1904, his newspapers began imprecating Carter Harrison for the benefit of Edward Dunne, which contributed to the mayor's decision not to seek reelection. With the elevation of Dunne, the publisher shifted the focus of his opprobrium to Sullivan and Hopkins. In August 1906, the Hearst forces organized formally in Chicago as the Independence League, one of several around the United States created to promote the publisher's office-seeking (at this point he was vainly reaching for the governorship of New York). In the 1907 municipal elections, the League vigorously backed Dunne for reelection, and was one source of his refusal to compromise on the issue of immediate municipal ownership that led to his defeat.[2]

In 1908, Hearst presidential pretensions became suddenly irrelevant with the resurgence of William Jennings Bryan. Using the excuse of the Commoner's deal-making with Sullivan, Tom Taggart of Indiana, and other Eastern urban leaders during the national convention, he directed the Independence League to become the Independence Party. This group held a national "convention" in Chicago on July 27 and 28, and, contrary to expectations, did not nominate Hearst, but, instead, the completely unknown Thomas L. Hisgen of Massachusetts, an independent oil producer who had fought the Standard Oil Company, and who had been an unsuccessful gubernatorial contender in his state. Bryan's name, when mentioned at the gathering of the publisher's men, was greeted by hisses and boos. The "party" just managed to secure a place on the ballot in 33 states, and its advocates showed no restraint in their disdain for the Commoner. However, Hisgen's vote was negligible, which ended the Independence Party—but not the publisher's political hobby.[3]

Now in late 1910, Hearst and Harrison proved to be a perfect marriage of convenience. Harrison brought political credibility and a ready-made political network, while Hearst provided money, publicity, and a paid staff willing to do or say whatever they were told. Together they aspired to replace Sullivan and his organization. The first step was to secure the mayoral nomination for Carter Harrison. Opposing was Sullivan's hand-picked candidate, Andrew J. Graham, an old friend and associate who had made his fortune as a prominent West Side banker.

Born and educated in Chicago, Graham went to work in business at the age of fourteen. In 1871, following the Great Fire, his father, John, opened a bookstore that his son helped manage. Upon the elder Graham's retirement, Andrew opened a bank specializing in real estate and loans. As a banker, he developed a reputation for making financing available to small borrowers; "he was of the common people himself, and he had faith in the common people." He also became known for his quiet charitable activities, maintaining, for example, a standing account at a local restaurant for the hungry and homeless men who approached him on the street. Consequently, he enjoyed a quiet, but broad, popularity in his section of the city, and having no a political record, he was personally unassailable. On the December 9, 1910, he formally made his announcement in response to the entreaty of something called the Andrew J. Graham Businessmen's Association.[4]

His platform was straightforward with a major focus upon the elimination of the kind of graft associated with the disgraced Busse administration. More unusually, he also advocated the unification of the governments of Chicago and Cook County, which, if it had been realized, would have undoubtedly served the interests of Roger Sullivan. Like Harrison, Graham wanted subways and universal transfers. Unlike Harrison, he specifically endorsed "personal liberty," a euphemism for the protection of access to alcoholic beverages, and a clear bid for the support of the powerful United Societies for Local Self-Government (as all the candidates would eventually affect a pro-wet stance, the organization declined to make an endorsement during the primary). Less than a week later, the managing committee of the Democratic Cook County Committee voted to back Graham. Of the 84 members present, he received the votes of 63, while former Sheriff John E. Traeger took two, and Harrison none. The remaining fourteen (five members were absent) abstained. Among their number were William Dever and County Treasurer-elect, William O'Connell, who were acting on behalf of their old friend and ally, former mayor Edward F. Dunne.[5]

Following his defeat for reelection in 1907, Dunne maintained a relatively low political profile. Nonetheless in 1908, he campaigned for Bryan throughout the North and East. Thereafter he became more active as a speaker on various topics both within and without Chicago, most frequently upon some aspect of municipal ownership. With time and the revelations of the mismanagement of the Busse administration, his reputation for incorruptibility began to outweigh the failure of his program as mayor. The *Inter-Ocean*, a Republican newspaper, once owned by Charles Yerkes, years before the symbol of the evils of local public transportation, noted this fact in 1908, when it wrote of him that "With his entire rainbow chasing as mayor, [he] left his office with public respect undiminished … his personal sincerity was so transparent, and in his hands government power was so visibly impartial, that it could not be otherwise."[6]

For all of that, there was little expectation that he would again seek the mayor's office, at least not in 1911; against the resources of the Sullivan and "H-H" organizations, his chances appeared quixotic. However, as the only mainstream Democratic politician who could reasonably present himself as a reformer in a year when that seemed to matter once again, and with an impressive following among the city's Irish middle class, he was not without political advantages. This became clear when, just after he announced his candidacy on November 19, 1910, such well-known political and reformist figures as Alderman John J. Bradley (who would serve as his campaign manager), County Treasurer William O'Connell, William Dever, Margaret Haley of the Chicago Federation of Teachers, Clarence Darrow, and Raymond Robins lined up in support.

His platform was similar to those of his primary opponents in its focus upon practical issues. There were the obligatory calls for lowering the price of gas and electricity, in addition to demands for better water service, pickups of garbage at night, the construction of subways (to be eventually owned by the city), and the consolidation of the Chicago, Cook County, and parks administrations. Things that had to go included graft, bomb throwing—something nobody, outside of a few anarchists who generally did not vote, appeared particularly to support—and fake reform, all which was to be replaced by a spirit of government emphasizing "decency towards and fair treatment of the citizen from public officials." Though Dunne began energetically, he was not at first recognized by the press and most professionals as a serious contender.[7]

Without much difference in the platforms, the primary race soon devolved into a round of personal attacks. In this, Hearst's *Examiner* excelled by identifying Graham with Sullivan, ubiquitously (and falsely) acclaimed as the "defacto president of the People's Gas Light & Coke Company," the local utility trust. Graham's candidacy, readers were assured, was just a scheme to keep gas prices high. Near the end, the paper also began cleverly caricaturing Sullivan as "Jolly Roger," a calorie-challenged jovial pirate cheerfully bent upon exploitation and corruption.[8]

On the stump "Our Carter" used similar tactics, bragging about frustrating "the "gas dictator" and his scheme for self-enrichment in refusing "to lend a hand in a game of blackmail and holdup" by vetoing a measure back in 1903 to allow the consolidation of the Ogden Company with the People's Gas and Electric. As the race progressed, he became ever more vitriolic, presenting himself as "the Anti–Roger C. Sullivan and Anti-Gas candidate," even as he proclaimed that "Roger Sullivan is not a Democrat," and neither, therefore, was Graham. Meanwhile, Harrison's backers competed to find the most colorful simile to express the seemingly infinite dimensions of Roger's evil. One speaker likened him to "a modern Roman emperor [who has] converted his coat-tails into the chariot to which he ties his meek and humble captives for parade and exhibition before the Democrats of this great town!"[9]

In response, Sullivan took to the stump, something the city had not witnessed for nearly two decades. In his first major appearance, held before a crowd of about a thousand in the Fifth Ward, he admitted his presence on the platform represented something new: "In talking here tonight I break my policy of years not to make public speeches." He was now speaking out, he explained, because of the Harrison campaign's attacks his connection to the Ogden Gas Company. As he had before the Municipal Voters League the previous summer, he admitted to his interest in the enterprise, but argued that, even as he was lowering prices, Harrison was acting like a "chum" of the gas monopoly. It was a theme he developed further around the city in the days ahead, always admitting unabashedly that he had profited, but also insisting that he and his partners had saved the consumers money. In other speeches, he proclaimed his purity of purpose as a party leader, somberly telling his listeners that his "sole ambition in life" was "to build up the Democratic party into a pure, clean, and efficient organization that will win and hold the confidence of all men, and be a haven for the common people!" Hearst's men were special targets, castigated for hypocrisy in their scurrilous depictions of him as corrupt even as

"Jolly Roger," *Chicago Examiner*, February 2, 1911.

they were courting the support of the likes of such as "Hinky Dink," "Bathhouse," and "Bobby" (Burke). Roger spoke passionately, and while he was not as grandiloquent as Harrison or Dunne, his plain speech and direct style were well-received.[10]

Sometimes the growing rancor spilled over into the streets, at times to almost amusing levels. Heckling was common at all of the candidates' meetings, but the Graham campaign also created controversy with the introduction of messages plastered on as many as three thousand billboards, some that were changed each week. At first most featured rather pedestrian slogans like "No Graft at the City Hall" and "A Seat for Every Pupil in the Public Schools." Then someone hit upon the tactic of using Hearst quotes and cartoons from 1904 that vilified Carter Harrison. Not surprisingly, many of these were torn down almost as soon as they appeared, provoking the random brawl.[11]

Of some historical interest was the Graham endorsement by the boxing heavyweight champion of the world, Jack Johnson. The first African American to hold the title (won just months before in his famous bout with Jim Jefferies in Las Vegas), he was highly charismatic and uninhibited. He appeared, with other pugilists, at a First Ward meeting for Sullivan's aldermanic candidate, "Colonel" Leopold Moss, who was running a doomed campaign against "Hinky Dink" Kenna. His speech went over well as he verbally pummeled Harrison and Kenna: "What has Hearst or Harrison done for the laborer?" he demanded, "What has Hinky-Dink done for the poor man? Nothing!" he insisted. "Instead of making the landlords build good lodging houses, they put everything into saloons, and the saloons are in the syndicate!" He also questioned Aldermen Kenna's apparent claims to have a right to the ward's votes: "I have a right to do anything I want with [my vote]. We are all free, ain't we?" Nor should they be impressed by anything that Carter Harrison's martyred father might have done: "Don't let 'em tell you what [his] father did. Gee, my old man did a lot of things, but that never got me anything. I had to bring home the bacon myself. What my father did didn't do me no good in that ring in Reno. Believe me, Carter Harrison can't comeback!" Perhaps almost needless to write, even at a gathering apparently unadorned by representation of the distaff side of humanity and held in the very tough First Ward, no one thought to challenge or heckle the Champion as he spoke.[12]

Meanwhile, Edward F. Dunne's campaign was gaining ground. For weeks both of his opponents and the press, tried to ignore him. However, this changed as Dunne's broadsides against both of his rivals began to take their toll, and when he unexpectedly secured the endorsement of the Chicago Federation of Labor. Harrison was blamed for Dunne's defeat for reelection in 1907, a serious charge in a party primary, while Graham was dismissed as the mere tool of Sullivan: "If Mr. Graham would be elected mayor, and the gas question were up," Dunne asked at one crowd, "wouldn't he advise [sic] with his old friend, 'Boss' Sullivan?" He blamed the "Boss," too, for his defeat in 1907. Graft and corruption were also addressed, and Harrison's (re)association with "Bobby" Burke was a regular talking point.[13]

The dynamics of the race began to shift in Dunne's favor. The odds at Jim O'Leary's "temple of chance, sport, and sad libation" at 4183 South Halsted Street, where sportsmen met to drink and bet (the closest thing to a poll in those simpler times), initially stood at 4 to 5 for Graham, 8 to 5 for Harrison and 5 to 2 for Dunne; within weeks, these shifted to 3 to 5 for Graham, Harrison 9 to 5, and 7 to 7 for Dunne. Only now did Carter Harrison respond to charges of party disloyalty. Rather weakly, he explained his refusal to back Dunne in 1907 as a fair return for his opponent undercutting him in 1904. Dunne cleverly just cited this statement as proving his point.[14]

By the closing weeks of the primary contest, Dunne had dropped most references to Graham and Sullivan, even as he laid claim to the reformist sentiments that had become so potent with the Busse and Lorimer scandals. However, Carter Harrison also was doing well in convincing many regular Democrats of his electability and willingness to dole out patronage. Graham's chances dwindled. Reports appeared that the Sullivan Democracy, or at least some of its significant segments, was quietly shifting over to Dunne. Late in the campaign, Harrison began making these allegations a central theme based upon the fact that some of the Graham billboards were replaced by those proclaiming the virtues of Dunne. Significantly, too, Sullivan disappeared during the campaign's final phases.[15]

If in fact there was a shift (and that remains unclear), it almost worked. The final totals were 55,116 for Harrison, 53,696 for Dunne, and only 38,578 for Graham. The victor's plurality of 1,420 votes was so thin that Dunne and his supporters demanded a recount, which was granted, but did not change the outcome.

The primary was a serious setback for Roger Sullivan. It underscored the toll taken by the growing series of electoral defeats. However, as portentous as the return of Harrison may have been, Sullivan remained the most powerful Democrat. Of the thirty-five aldermanic nominees, twenty were counted as his men, as were most of those nominated for the city's other offices.[16]

Hungry for victory and the plums it promised, the local party for the most part rallied around Harrison for the election. Roger Sullivan remained silent, but within weeks, allies like John McCarthy, chair of the County Committee, and others like Anton Cermak, who had backed Graham, in addition to most of those who had been for Dunne, including William O'Connell and John J. Bradley, gave public notice of their support. Having no patronage ambitions and believing that he had been denied the nomination by the possibly illegal manipulations of some of Harrison's less reputable "friends" (conspiracy theories abounded in all directions), Dunne was less quiescent. Upon halting the recount, he did ask his supporters to back his rival. However, he then pointedly left town. Harrison did his best to appease his opposition, and this went far towards assuaging any lingering anger.[17]

The election promised to be a hard fight. The Republicans, in an effort to repudiate Busse and what he had come to represent, chose Alderman Charles Merriam, the man most responsible for the revelations of municipal corruption. The Merriam campaign quickly took on the aspect of a progressive jihad. The election of 1911, amidst a swelling of reformist sentiment, had become transformed into a referendum on the Windy City's political culture.

Merriam swamped his principal primary opponents, John F. Smulski, a successful banker and leader of the Polish community, who was also backed by Governor Charles Deneen, and John R. Thompson, a successful businessman and the heir to Busse's following. "The Professor" (he was, of course, a professor of political science at the young University of Chicago) as his friends and foes alike styled him, composed a platform calling for efficient and clean government. This was meant to define his conception of "Progressive Republicanism" as something that was rooted in the "the value of conservation as applied to municipal affairs as in relation to state and national interests." It would be "a straight challenge to the graft system, spoils system, and the special privilege system." His words were a siren song to many of Edward F. Dunne's reformist friends, who, without a word of condemnation from the man who had been lately their candidate, defected to the Republican nominee. Leading the pack was social activist Raymond Robins, who spoke extensively for his newest hero. Others of the claimed 1,000 associated with the Progressive Democratic Club for Merriam included Margaret Haley of the Chicago Teachers Federation, John J. Fitzpatrick of the Chicago Federation of Labor, which openly endorsed the Republican, Edwin F. Wright of the Illinois Federation of Labor, which did not, and, late in the campaign, a thoughtful Clarence Darrow. A number of Dunne ward clubs came over en masse as well. However, most of the Republican regulars, unfortunately for the Professor, were less impressed with his high purpose than they were with the implied threat to themselves of his platform.[18]

But Merriam proved not entirely inured to political reality. Connected as an alderman to the "dry" side of the simmering liquor issue, he now carefully framed his position on the subject in terms of home rule and democracy. Accordingly, he proclaimed opposition to "blue laws," i.e., Sunday closings of saloons, and his belief in obeying the will of the people of Chicago, which, as he conceded, overwhelmingly opposed any interference with this particular expression of "personal liberty." Harrison, whose use of the issue in the primary met with limited success, had his followers initiate a massive drive to solicit the endorsement of the United Societies for Local Self-Government, the powerful dry lobbying group with its vast influence (and money). Many promises were apparently made with remunerations of one kind or another possibly remitted, and the organization at last came out for "Our Carter" as someone who had always "championed the liberal cause." Apparently one factor in their decision was Merriam's reported directorship of the Hyde Park Protective Association, a group that, among other things, supported Sunday closings and other "dry" measures. In vain, the Merriam camp issued a flyer, written by campaign operative Harold Ickes, explaining that the association was not anti-saloon, just anti-blind pigs, or unlicensed operations. It was even felt necessary for Merriam to deny having ever voted for the Prohibition Party.[19]

The campaign rapidly became ugly. At one point, Harrison sued the *Chicago Tribune*, which was booming Merriam with evangelical fervor. The newspaper had featured a series of articles written by Charles J. Powers, depicted later by the former mayor as "none too clean physically or morally, but brilliant." These focused upon the Democratic candidate's previous tenure in the mayor's office. Skillfully composed, they were long on innuendo but short on substance about supposed shady dealings. However, in late March, an allegation was made concerning the restoration in 1901 of a saloon license, supposedly in return for a campaign contribution. Harrison, very publicly asked the prominent local attorney and Democratic operative, A.S. Trude, to file suit, prompting the publication to pull the articles, and thus allowing the former mayor an opportunity to portray himself as a victim of the "interests." Having served its purpose, the suit was dropped after the election.[20]

Meanwhile, the rhetoric of Merriam's supporters, particularly those who came over from Dunne, became ever more petulant and abusive. Raymond Robins especially specialized in vituperation and attack. At one point, he sickened his audience with graphic accounts of "children [dying] like flies in the typhoid alleys of the west side" because of "Harrison's misrule."[21]

In contrast, Clarence Darrow, speaking before a massive rally of laboring men, provided measured explication of the meaning of Merriam's campaign. Framing the contest in the context of the political assumptions and practices that had spawned Carter Harrison and Roger Sullivan, the man destined to be an American legal legend argued that the real challenge was the unfortunate fact that "the city of Chicago is little more than a great business cooperative." However, where Sullivan and other regulars might see this as a mere truism—a natural outcome of a marriage of human nature and politics as interpreted through the commercial prism of the city, Darrow, reflecting much contemporary progressive thought, questioned its premise on the basis that business activities of a city have no more relation to politics than to religion—possibly not as much, for some of the Ten Commandments at least are applicable to business, but none of them have much place in politics. [Thou shall not lie?]

Municipal government's only legitimate function was to provide services, and it made no more sense to expect professional politicians to demonstrate practical skills in this regard than it did to turn to someone who "could carry a ward" to design a sewer. It followed, therefore, that the search for the next mayor should have nothing to do with his politics—those were meaningless—but should be based instead upon an ability to do the job of building bridges, sewers, and public buildings, as well as generally manage the city efficiently. And that man was Charles E. Merriam, an apolitical expert trained in political theory and urban management.[22]

Of course, to others, like Roger Sullivan, what was missing from Darrow's otherwise impeccable logic was a recognition of the need for leadership that would not only be efficient in its pursuit of these practical matters, but which could also achieve successful outcomes through the creation of a working consensus among the competing interests within the city. Leadership, in other words, by those versed in the very political skills Darrow found irrelevant. Less melodramatic, but possibly more effective than either Robins' tirades or Darrow's dialectics, were endorsements of Merriam by several important Republicans including the new Secretary of the Interior, Walter L. Fisher, who most assumed was representing President William Howard Taft, and Governor Charles Deneen, who came to Chicago and spoke.[23]

As the contest entered its final phase, both candidates worked themselves into exhaustion. Merriam, who unlike his supporters generally avoided personal attacks, spoke at as many as fifteen meetings in a single day. Harrison also trying to keep his message positive (at his most negative, he merely insinuated that his experience was more meaningful than any set of theories advocated by a school teacher) in contrast delivered a mere nine speeches in one twenty-four-hour period. Both camps were, as usual, publicly optimistic, but the consensus among observers was that Harrison was ahead. On Election Day, this was affirmed when the Chicago electorate narrowly voted to keep municipal politics as they were. Carter H. Harrison won with 177,997 votes to Merriam's 160,672, a plurality of just 17,325.[24]

Merriam's defeat, beyond demonstrating the strength (temporary as it proved) of the theme of reform, had many fathers. Harrison's campaign was energized and well-run, and not above the use of traditional, if shady, political methods to achieve victory—a fact that even the new mayor-elect would eventually admit. Also important was the crusading alderman's simple lack of political skill in appeasing the regulars of his party, who could hardly be expected to be enthralled with the possibility of a chief executive whose entire stated purpose was to undercut their vocation. Some reassurance might have gone far, but none was forthcoming. Still another source of his defeat might well have been an additional, but largely unrecognized, implication of Merriam's alleged membership in the Hyde Park Protective Association.[25]

The Association was not unlike many found throughout urban America in this period of rapid change. It was mostly known for its opposition to saloons and the sale of liquor within its community, and Merriam was believed to be its supporter. This, as noted, unquestionably hurt him among the members of the United Societies, ethnic groups like the Germans, who were ardent in their support of "personal liberty," and Chicago's working men in general.

But the Association had also earned a more sinister reputation as anti–African American. In 1909, it publicly devoted itself "to rid the district of colored residents." This was in response to the early phases of the "Great Migration" of Southern African Americans into Northern urban centers. This brought a steady increase of Chicago's black population from just over 14,000 in 1890 to more than 44,000 in 1910, a figure that itself would more than double by 1920. Even as the election campaign of 1911 was underway, an African-American family was being stoned for having the temerity to move into the community. Just seven months hence, in early 1912, the Hyde Park organization would strive in vain for the introduction of Jim Crow style segregation into local schools. The extent of the Republican candidate's affiliation was, by the account of his defenders, limited to his name appearing on its letterhead as a member of its board of directors. This was, it was claimed, merely an honorific appointment, one shared by all aldermen in that part of the city.

In an open letter published on March 18, 1911, in the *Chicago Defender*, the leading African American publication in Chicago and the nation, Merriam denied all membership in this or "any other organization having for its purpose discrimination." These stories were based upon nothing but a "scurrilous report," he assured the readers, by "despicable men using despicable methods" to "alienate the large colored vote from its natural alliance" with the Republican Party, the party of Abraham Lincoln. However, it could not be denied that his name was on the stationary, or that he had not previously sought to have it removed. The very fact that he felt it necessary to publish his denial in the *Defender*, spoke to the damage the rumors were believed to be causing, and the Second and Thirtieth Wards, where the black population was most concentrated, did in fact return strongly for Harrison. Further substantiation of the impact of the issue appeared in an article in the *Defender* published just days following the election in which a reduction of the black vote for Republicans was admitted (though for more general reasons of G.O.P. neglect and without any reference to the Hyde Park group). While more study is required to determine the exact correlation between the rumors of Merriam's participation in this racist organization and the outcome, 1911 may well have been the first election in Chicago in which the African-American vote was decisive—a historical moment.[26]

Riding a wave of euphoria, Carter Harrison and his allies now turned to "fight to wrest the Democratic Party from Roger Sullivan." Within weeks of the inauguration in April, a formal meeting of a "committee of 25" was called for the purpose of creating something called the "Progressive Democracy." On May 4, Andrew Lawrence, editor of the *Chicago Examiner* and Hearst's point man in the city, arranged for a massive banquet to launch the new group. Present were most of the familiar local names. But also present were downstate Bryan leaders Millard Fillmore Dunlap, and Judge Owen Thompson. Although, in large part, the new faction was little more than the reconstituted "city hall crowd" from days of yore as conjoined to the Hearst aggregation and its imported money, the presence of Dunlap and Thompson also made this something new. For the first time Sullivan's factional rivals in Cook County were linked up with his downstate enemies.

Their common purpose was simple and direct: to create their own shadow Democratic organization from the state committee down to the districts, and then to use it to overthrow the existing party leadership in the primaries scheduled for the coming spring.[27]

However, cracks began to appear almost immediately in the Progressive Democracy's impressive facade. Despite their opposition to their national committeeman's dominance of the party, the downstate Democrats in the new alliance were not about to defer to the dictates of Harrison or Andrew Lawrence. Neither Thompson, nor the others, had any desire simply to replace one urban "dictator" with another in person of the mayor, or to surrender their freedom of action to the ambitions of a distant New York publisher. Thus, when a second meeting was held in September 1911 at the LaSalle Hotel in Chicago, the downstaters, led by H.N. Wheeler, state committeeman and editor of the *Quincy Journal*, refused to endorse Lawrence as their candidate to replace Sullivan on the national committee. They also balked at any kind of formal statement of praise for Hearst, all the while demanding their share of the appointments to the proposed congressional district committees as the price for their further participation.

Once these matters were settled to their satisfaction, and the focus upon the common purpose restored, what followed were heated even festive denouncements of "Lorimerism, Sullivanism, and Browneism" (for Lee O'Neil Browne, accused head conspirator in the vote buying scandal associated with the election of William Lorimer to the Senate in 1911), which had "disgraced, dishonored and debauched," the party. It was Sullivan's fault that Lorimer was elected: "If Roger Sullivan could let fifty-two Democrats vote for Lorimer, he forsook all the rights he had as national committeeman, and surrendered himself and us to degradation!" Others were similarly sweeping in their condemnation, inspiring one delegate in the full throes of vitriolic passion to cry out spontaneously, "To hell with Roger Sullivan," to general cheers. With their spleens amply vented, the delegates agreed to support Carter H. Harrison for the presidency of the United States (something the Hearst men definitely did not want, but did not dare to oppose openly). After adjournment, the committee of 25, or most of it, met and agreed to hold their own state convention on 4 October 1911 during the upcoming State Fair, a time when political leaders usually gathered in Springfield to do a little politicking.[28]

This, proved to be a strictly stage-managed, if riotous, affair. Something of its tenor became apparent when the aforementioned H.N. Wheeler attempted to defend some of the party's regular leaders against some of the more bitter attacks. The chair, Carter H. Harrison, refused him recognition, and then the hapless Democrat was physically assaulted to the sound of cries to "throw him out!" He was only saved from personal injury by the intervention of Congressman Adolph Sabath and Thomas Rees, publisher of the *Illinois State Register* (Springfield). All of this was within minutes of the adoption of a platform calling for the protection of "human rights." Predictably, the rhetorical scourging of Sullivan was once again the centerpiece of every address as old enemies like Dunlap, Thompson, Andrew Lawrence, and Sheriff Michael Zimmer proclaimed the need for a "leadership that will fight for Democratic principles and not for partisan spoils," and for the end of "Lorimerism and Sullivanism." According to plan, Congressman Henry T. Rainey, who had been very tentative in his acceptance, was selected as the compromise candidate to replace Sullivan on the national committee.[29]

Roger Sullivan was not slow to respond. At his direction, and even as his enemies gathered, the state committee was also meeting to prepare and plan a counteroffensive. On the eve of the "H-H" conclave, he issued a statement dismissive of the entire movement as nothing more—when one brushed "aside all befogging and befuddling claptrap"— than an attempt to secure the presidential nomination for Hearst. Moreover, it was only because he had refused Lawrence's direct appeals to back the publisher that he was now being scorned Harrison, he wrote, was simply repaying the Hearst forces for their support of his vain demands in 1910 to name some of the Cook county candidates. While all true, Sullivan's assessment was incomplete, excluding as it did all reference to his knowledge of Harrison's own presidential ambitions as well as to his now organized opposition's immediate purpose in capturing the party machinery in Cook County and the state. Nor did he address the many references to "Lorimerism," a theme that Hearst's *Chicago Examiner* had been using for months in an attempt to link Sullivan to the now re-emerging scandal.[30]

Wisconsin's Senator Robert LaFollette revived the issue in the spring of 1911, by introducing a resolution calling for a new investigation based in part upon evidence revealed in the various trials of the compromised state legislators. LaFollette's motion was approved, and a new subcommittee of the Committee on Privileges and Elections (to be known as the Dillingham Committee after its chair, Senator William P. Dillingham of Vermont), began hearings in Washington, D.C.

All that summer, the newspapers were filled with the testimony of such luminaries as Cyrus McCormick, president of the International Harvester Company, Henry Kohlsaat, editor of the *Chicago Record-Herald*, Governor Charles Deneen, and Lawrence B. Stringer. Much of the impetus in the subcommittee came from a relentless Senator John W. Kern of Indiana, who had been Bryan's running mate in 1908. After a recess in August, they reconvened in Chicago that October. Roger Sullivan was called to the stand. He chiefly reaffirmed his previous public statements that he had not heard beforehand of any deal concerning Lorimer's election, and that he was never a party to any such conspiracy. He did admit, however, that Lorimer enjoyed strong contacts in the Democratic Party, probably more than any other Republican in the state. Sullivan's success in torpedoing an earlier scheme to sell Democratic votes to reelect Albert Hopkins was also discussed. No attempt was made by Kern, or any other member of the committee, to tie him directly to Lorimer's selection, and no witness ever came forward to contradict his testimony. Further substantiation was provided when Lee O'Neil Browne (protected by his acquittal from any legal sanctions) admitted his role as Lorimer's sole agent.[31]

The hearings in the Windy City ended in November, but were resumed in the nation's capital in February. In March 1912, the subcommittee voted by a margin of five to three to absolve Lorimer of any wrong doing; however, the three dissenting members took their case to the Senate floor where, by a vote of 55 to 28, he was judged as equally guilty as those state legislators who took bribes to vote for his candidacy. He was then formally expelled. The disgraced former-senator returned to Illinois to a hero's welcome from his friends and supporters, but he would thereafter be a fading force in state politics.[32]

The specter of Lorimerism generally played in favor of the Democrats, and was frequently referenced in their speeches and campaign literature. However, there were indications that the issue was losing its potency, at least in Cook County, Illinois. It certainly had no discernible effect upon Harrison's failed attempts to challenge Sullivan's control of the judicial nominating process in the fall of 1911, or in the subsequent elections. The Democrats once again negotiated a temporary internal truce and campaigned diligently, but the results were disappointing. Of eleven seats on the bench, the Republicans took seven, a clear contrast to the previous year, when there was a Democratic sweep. The

Sullivan testifies (Sullivan family collection).

Sullivan-dominated County Committee tried to make the best of the situation, pointing out that even these results represented a relative success compared to the Democratic averages over the last decades. Still, there was some inevitable grumbling about the "H-H" faction not doing its part, which was probably true.[33]

However, even as the acrimony heated up between the two factions, and even as he was being questioned about Lorimer's selection, Roger Sullivan also found himself distracted by growing demands from his family. His role as pater familias over his vast clan of relatives was always central in his life. Sullivan unquestionably loved and cherished his wife, his daughters, his brothers, his sisters, his uncles, his aunts, and his many cousins (whether in America or back in Ireland), but it was his only son, first-born, Boetius (an old clan name, and also that of Roger's elder brother, spelled as Boetious), who was the clay in which his hopes and aspirations were most clearly molded. As the son of an Irish immigrant father who worked as a notions' store owner and a traveling peddler, Roger made his way up in the unforgiving and sometimes seamy worlds of business and politics through talent, hustle, and hard work to become a multimillionaire entrepreneur and a major political leader. But he wanted something more for his son, and Bo was provided every advantage possible to secure his place among the nation's elite.

The Sullivan family (Sullivan family collection).

Following early years at a local parish school, young Sullivan's education continued at the exclusive Phillips Academy in Andover, Massachusetts (founded in 1778; Paul Revere designed its seal; John Hancock signed its incorporation, and George Washington's nephews were among its alumni). Following graduation in 1905, he attended Yale, where he received his bachelor's degree in 1909.

In 1912, he completed his law degree at Harvard, and returned to Chicago to begin his legal career as a clerk with the firm of Sears, Meagher & Whitney, which, by the time of his retirement as senior partner thirty-two years later, had become Cooke, Sullivan & Ricks. Boetius was popular among his many friends, known as the "Million Dollar Kid," (a nickname at Harvard because of his generosity in his willingness to share his lavish allowance) and the "Boy with the Golden Smile." He became every inch the American aristocrat graced with education, manners, gentility, and a strong social consciousness conjoined with a sense of noblesse oblige. He was everything for which his father could have desired, and he became a valued friend and confidante in the years ahead. The Sullivan daughters were also afforded every opportunity for education and travel in the contemporary context of their gender.[34]

Bo's wedding was held on Wednesday morning, December 27, 1911, at St. Matthew's Church. His bride was Miss Mary Loretta Connery, the daughter of James P. Connery, a wealthy coal executive, and Washington Boulevard neighbor. It was an elegant event reflecting Roger's stature that attracted considerable press coverage. The bride wore white satin with a full court train, complemented by a veil of Brussels lace held in place by a strand of pearls and orange blossoms. Her maid of honor was her sister, Helen, who was graced by a gown of "delicate pink charmeuse satin with an overdress of white lace robes over white satin with a Watteau train of pink satin" topped off with a large pink, plumed hat. There were four bridesmaids, including the bridegroom's sister, Mary. They were dressed tastefully in white lace robes over white satin also with Watteau trains of pink satin. Former mayor John P. Hopkins, who looked upon Boetius as a surrogate son, served as best man with all of his own many sisters also in attendance, but almost no other political figures were present. After the ceremony, a breakfast for was held for family and intimate friends at the home of the bride. The young couple returned east to reside temporarily at the plush Hotel Somerset in beautiful downtown Boston, while Bo completed his studies.[35]

Over the next several months, Roger would also endure the bittersweet experience— and considerable expense—of giving away three of his four daughters in marriage. All would marry well, but for reasons perhaps of economy or maybe because of simple exhaustion, these ceremonies of love became progressively less ostentatious. The first, however, held for eldest daughter Mary, was, like that of her brother, also clearly meant as a public declaration of Sullivan's social position. Presided over by Bishop Peter Muldoon of Rockford as assisted by six priests, the music was specially composed by the director of the Sistine Chapel at Rome—a singular honor. She was followed to the altar by Helen on November 26, 1912, and Frances on April 30, 1913. Virginia Hopkins would wait until April 17, 1918, to be wed in a relatively Spartan ceremony in keeping with wartime austerity.[36]

On the eve of the proud Papa escorting his daughter Mary down the aisle, a desperate fight between the Sullivan Democracy and the Hearst-Harrison group for control of Cook County Democracy broke out on the streets of Chicago, one which briefly threatened to escalate into a real civil war. Despite its disperse nature, the "H-H's" control of city hall patronage made it a formidable force, a fact recognized by numerous politicos heretofore within the Sullivan ambit who now chose to defect. Some of these, like Thomas Little, who came from Roger Sullivan's home ward, were formerly close associates of the "boss" and high in his counsel. Others were semi-independent operatives boasting their own political base who now seized an opportunity to advance their political fortunes. Among

Boetius' wedding party in the Sullivan home. Note John P. Hopkins sitting in profile on the left and the photo of Roger Sullivan on the wall (Sullivan family collection).

these was Maclay Hoyne, a rising star in the party, but even more important was Anton Cermak, the man who in 1927 became the third "boss" of the Chicago Democratic Machine. Cermak was the leader of the Bohemian community, and secretary of the United Societies for Self-Government, the city's leading "dry" organization. He was an especially prominent and influential leader. His defection added considerable strength to the "H-H" crew.[37]

Almost immediately after Harrison's election, his faction began confidently making plans for the April 1912 primaries. These would determine not only local and state candidates, but, even more importantly, the delegates for the Cook County convention, which elected the county committee. It would also send representatives to the state convention where the state committee would be selected. Control of the local party machinery depended upon these outcomes, and if some of the downstate members of the faction were successful as well, a state-wide paramountcy might be possible.

But the stakes were even higher than this, at least for Mayor Carter H. Harrison. He had inherited his father's White House dreams, and his triumphant return to the mayor's office in 1911 reignited his dormant ambition. However, although recognized nationally as a viable contender, his candidacy failed to inspire much local enthusiasm. Symbolically, the Iroquois Club, the social club of the Chicago Democratic Party, turned down his appeals for support. Worse, his allies in the Hearst press, reflecting the still viable political hopes of their master in New York, ignored his ambitions. According to the mayor's own recollection years later, Roger Sullivan offered in person to back Harrison for the nomination in return for uncontested control of the Illinois delegation. Fearing that the national committeeman could not be trusted (or hoping to build his campaign upon his success in overthrowing the "boss"), the mayor "declined with thanks."[38]

As events ultimately unfolded, Carter Harrison would have been better served had he accepted Sullivan's offer (if in fact such an offer occurred, the mayor's memory was sometimes defective in his autobiography from which this account is derived). However, the initial test of strength between the two factions seemed at first to justify his decision. The February aldermanic primaries went well for the Hearst-Harrison forces, which won 22 of the 36 nominations. The subsequent sweep of the elections on April 2, put twenty-five Democrats in the thirty-six-member city council, providing the mayor with a working majority and strengthening his political hand.[39]

However, Harrison's growing power in alliance with Hearst was also beginning to create considerable unease among the city's Democratic professionals. While the backing of the publisher's newspapers was unquestionably a contributing factor to the mayor's reelection the previous year, Hearst was also someone who evoked an instinctive mistrust and even loathing. Many Democrats around the state remained concerned about the linkage of their party to the agenda of the rich New Yorker. Even as the all-important major primary (scheduled for April 9, 1912) was approaching, the Sullivan Democracy exploited this connection to great effect, especially in the downstate contests for national convention delegates.[40]

Something of the intensity of the factional battle that now ensued can be ascertained by the fact that Sullivan personally spent the huge sum of "between $40,000 and $50,000" on the campaign (something more than a half a million dollars in the second decade of the twenty-first century). Both sides held back nothing in what was shaping up to be a decisive battle. Although much energy was expended in the public campaign, much of the most important politicking took place privately, as both factions used every tactic possible, including some that likely skirted or passed over the edge of legality, to convince, cajole, or compel political operatives across the county and the state to fall into line.[41]

Using its usual poison, the Hearst Press again framed things in terms of Sullivan and his supposed corruption. Attempting as always to present itself (and Harrison) as an advocate of reform, the *Examiner* editorialized that the real issue was the elimination of "the political boss," which would mean "that there would be no more professional go-betweens of the Roger Sullivan type to milk corporate treasuries with one hand and pilfer the people's treasury with the other." Of course, what the editorial writers neglected to mention was that the "H-H" group was held together by precisely the same means as the Sullivan Democracy. As before, there were brilliant cartoons portraying Sullivan as a stereotypical fat political boss, or alternately as, yet again, Jolly Roger, who appeared mostly in the guise of a pirate, but at least once as a side-show freak.[42]

From the beginning, based upon discrepancies between the apparent recordings of the election judges and clerks, which appeared to substantiate a Sullivan win, and those of the Harrison-dominated Election Commission, which claimed H-H majorities, the outcomes of the crucial country convention delegate races were unclear. State-wide, however, the Sullivan Democracy emerged triumphant; the vote in the Congressional Districts guaranteed the support of twenty of the twenty-five members of the new state committee. In Cook County, a majority of the Sullivan slate of candidates for public office was nominated with undisputed majorities in the towns of Cook County outside of Chicago. The

"H-H" faction's main victories came in the renomination of incumbent County President, Peter Bratzen, the selection of Anton Cermak to run for Bailiff of the Country Court, and Maclay Hoyne's win over Sullivan's man, James J. Kelly for State's Attorney. But their loud claim of having elected a majority of delegates was undercut with the revelations of the Harrison camp's short-lived scheme to gain control of the county party convention premised upon a minority return.

According to the state primary law, every delegate in each precinct was entitled to a single vote at the convention plus one additional vote "for every fifty votes or major fraction thereof of his party" as cast in the last election. Insisting that they had carried the "lodging house" wards that historically returned large Democratic majorities, the "H-H" men crowed they would have the votes in the convention even if they did not have the delegates. The idea had all of the hallmarks of improvisation, and it quickly disappeared when greeted with derision by the Sullivan Democracy and the press. Harrison men did not dare to have this scheme adjudicated in court, as certainly they would have done had they felt they had a case.[43]

The Sullivan faction, on the other hand, gave every appearance of confidence. Within days after the primary, they were claiming "at least" 900 of the 1,492 county delegates. The "H-H" leadership became desperate. Although ninety-two contests had been filed by the mayor's faction—a certain sign that the returns had not turned out as they hoped— as things stood, county chair and Sullivan ally, John McGillen, would be temporary chairman of the convention with the power to disqualify any of their men. Two conferences were hurriedly arranged for Saturday, April 13. The first was held at the offices of Andrew Lawrence, editor of the local Hearst papers, who met with County Judge John Owens, Anthony Czarnecki, secretary and William H. Stuart, chief clerk of the Chicago Election Commission (the body's sitting chair, Charles Kellermann, who was an ally of Sullivan, was not invited). The other met at the Briggs House hotel, where Mayor Harrison huddled with his chief of police, John McWeeny and Cook County Sheriff Michael Zimmer.

A plot was hatched to save the "county $150,000 electing precinct committeemen" and to prevent the likelihood of having "two men over at the LaSalle Hotel run the convention." As county judge, Owens had a legal claim to the "entire management and control of all elections in Chicago." It was decided to use this authority to seize the convention. Owens would appoint Czarnecki as McGillen's replacement as temporary chair. The justification for this would be a petition supposedly (and very questionably) signed by a "majority" of the "precinct committeemen/county convention delegates." The list included many of those who lost the primary but who the "H-H" faction insisted would have been selected but for the flagitious machinations of the Sullivan organization. Harrison and Zimmer were to provide "the muscle" in the form of large contingents of police and "special deputy sheriffs" to be mobilized "to prevent gavel rule." To give an appearance of fairness, both factions were to be invited to provide "checkers" of each delegate's credentials, and the same measures were to be applied in their entirety to the Republican county convention.[44]

The news of this conspiracy was greeted with outrage. McGillen called it a "farce"; Sullivan saw it as "martial law used to circumvent the will of the people," and promised that "if the Harrison-Hearst-Owens crowd thinks we are going to be robbed of our just rights they are badly mistaken!" The Republicans, too, were unhappy with having the governance of their convention taken over by Owens, and, in fact, their convention was organized as usual and without the extraordinary altercation of that of the Democrats.

Following a hurried meeting, the Sullivan forces obtained an injunction from one of their own, Superior Court Judge Michael L. McKinley. It did not address the question of the primary returns. However, based upon the fact that Chairman John McGillen was the lessee of record of the convention site at the Seventh Regimental Armory, it upheld his property rights by setting aside Owens' order and directing that there be no interference. The court order was served upon Czarnecki, Zimmer, and McWeeny, as well as Charles H. Kellermann and Howard S. Taylor, both Sullivan-friendly Democratic members of the election commission who were uninvolved in the Harrison plan. As the Superior Court judicially outranked the County Court, in strictly legal terms this should have ended the matter. Nonetheless, there was no absolute confidence that the "H-H" forces would abandon their desperate gamble. As further insurance, Daniel Moriarty, Sullivan's defeated candidate for the presidency of the County Board, and the colonel of the "Fighting Seventh," a predominately Irish regiment of the Illinois National Guard whose armory was the subject of the dispute, was reported as ordering a small contingent of his men to occupy immediately the building on Wentworth between Thirty-third and Thirty-fourth Streets. Now the press began to speculate eagerly about the prospect of "bloodshed."[45]

At about 2:00 p.m. Sunday, April 14, 1912, eight city policemen led by Chief McWeeny reported to the armory and took positions at its four corners. Captain Thomas P. Octigan, in charge of the troops that were allegedly inside (the press claims were never substantiated), called to the Chief from a window above the main door to remove his force immediately, noting that their presence was in violation of McKinley's injunction, and warning that "there will be trouble" if any attempt were made to force an entrance. McWeeny refused to withdraw, but agreed not to interfere with the soldiers, over a hundred more of whom were reported as entering the building.[46]

So things stood until shortly after daybreak, Monday, April 15, 1912. By 7:00 a.m., there were supposed to be 120 guardsmen inside surrounded by 300 policemen aided by 200 recently arrived special sheriff's deputies. Soon the sergeant-at-arms of the convention, William "Billy" Skidmore appeared. He slipped past most of the police, and was almost to the entrance when he was intercepted by a police captain and "sent on his way." The Sullivan precinct committeemen now began to gather by the hundreds across the street, even as large numbers of "H-H" delegates began passing by on their way to their rendezvous at nearby Walla Walla hall at West 37th street and Wentworth. Also on hand was a growing crowd of onlookers, who eagerly hoping to witness a brawl. Just after 9:00 a.m., State Adjutant General Frank S. Dickson hurried up, having been sent by Governor Deneen who had been notified of the situation by Mayor Harrison. Over the protests of some of the police, he sought admittance. Captain Octigan called to him that it was impossible to let him in, as they had lost "the big key." Not long afterwards the "big key" was apparently found, and he entered to discuss the situation. Upon being assured that the agreement of mutual noninterference between the police and soldiers still stood (and perhaps finding that there was no body of troops within), he left satisfied that an actual civil war was probably not going to break out this day in Chicago.[47]

At 9:20 a.m., Czarnecki arrived followed by Zimmer, and they in their turn demanded entry into the hall. They were rebuffed by Octigan, who first insisted that he could not hear them, and then informed the esteemed gentlemen that as the building was "the property of the state of Illinois," and contained items worth $25,000, he would not be responsible for their presence inside. Czarnecki and Zimmer retreated to confer.

At this point, the generals of the Sullivan faction, George E. Brennan, John McGillen, and George L. McConnell, secretary of the Cook County Democratic Committee, came upon the scene. Roger, himself, never was present, being otherwise occupied with the impending wedding of his daughter Mary scheduled for just one day hence (although it is difficult to believe that he was not kept informed of every development). McGillen attempted to assert his right as the lessee of record to enter. When rebuffed, he responded by loudly reading McKinley's injunction. In reply, Sheriff Zimmer just cited his authority from Owens. Frustrated, the Democratic county chair withdrew with his comrades to the waiting taxi across the street that would serve as their battlefield headquarters (allowing the one-legged Brennan the ease of sitting down). Behind and to their sides were four long and orderly lines of Sullivan delegates. This was all an immense disappointment for spectators, who anticipated a brawl.[48]

Some of the crowd's frustration was soon assuaged when, at about 11:00 a.m., Judge John Owens "dashed up" in an automobile and took "personal charge." Now events began to unfold rapidly. Accompanied by Zimmer, McWeeny, and a number of deputy sheriffs and policemen, Owens pounded on the four-inch-thick door, upon which was pinned a copy of McKinley's injunction, demanding loudly for the doors be opened "or they would be "chopped down." He did not actually threaten to blow the building down, but the effect was much the same. From a window above, the gallant Captain Octigan first denied again that he had the key. Then, while not actually saying: "not by the hair of my chinny chin chin," he did insist that the door could only be opened on the orders of John McGillen. Angrily, Owens, promising to arrest Octigan "at once," directed the Assistant Chief of Police, Herman F. Schusettler, to force an entry. He began swinging a handy axe, until, quickly tiring, he turned the job over to an ordinary policeman, reserving for himself the honor of the last few blows. The oaken structure was reduced to shards in minutes; then a second interior door was subjected to the same brusque treatment. An improvised barricade beyond was pushed aside, and they rushed in. Except for Captain Octigan, who was held, but released later on a writ of *habeas corpus*, and another officer briefly detained for being "impertinent," the armory was found to be empty as the troops supposed to be present had apparently absconded earlier (somehow escaping the notice of the myriad reporters on the scene) by another egress.[49]

The "H-H" delegates had returned and taken up a position on the armory side of the street where they had been standing for a number of hours, all the while engaging in an ongoing exchange of "uncomplimentary comments" and "minor fights" with their erstwhile Democratic brethren on the opposite sidewalk. They briefly adjourned at about 10:30 a.m. to Walla Walla Hall to caucus and elect temporary officers. Following this, they gathered again outside the Armory to begin their entry. Only forty minutes had passed since the first blows were struck at the armory entrance.

The march inside took some time. As it was proceeding, John McGillen ordered a small party of his own men to infiltrate and to reconnoiter. Based upon their intelligence, it was decided that the Sullivan delegates should continue waiting outside. The "H-H" version of the Cook County Democratic Convention proceeded. As per Owens' order, Czarnecki took charge as temporary chair. Facing him on the front row were such factional sachems as the First Ward Aldermen, Michael "Hinky-Dink" Kenna, John "Bathhouse" Coughlin, Congressman Adolph Sabath, and Johnny Powers. Hoarse laughter rang out when Czarnecki asked if either McGillen or any of the Sullivan checkers were present. The convention organized, endorsed the candidates as chosen in the recent

Assistant Chief Schuettler Battering
Down Doors of Armory

Battering down the door, *Chicago Examiner*, April 4, 1912.

primary, ratified a county platform, elected delegates to the state convention, selected a
new county committee headed by Robert Redfield, and then adjoined.[50]

As their factional rivals were still convening, the Sullivan leaders at last announced
a plan for their foot-weary troops. They would meet at Liberty Hall at 3000 Union, a
small facility located over a saloon five blocks away. A large contingent began to march
in that direction singing a spontaneously composed ditty based upon "John Brown's
Body," with the two recorded verses proclaiming: "We'll hang Mike Zimmer to a sour
apple tree" and "John E. Owens is a very large piece of cheese." Upon arrival, they settled
upon their own delegates and platform, and elected John McGillen as chair of their version of the Cook County Managing Committee. However, it was decided for the sake of
legitimacy to reserve for the "H-H" faction a number of delegate seats for the state convention based upon the Sullivan interpretation of the primary results. And so a most
remarkable day in the political history of Chicago politics at last drew to a close. It was
one that saw two Democratic county conventions sending two delegations to Peoria and
electing two county committees. While violence was avoided, thanks in large part to the
restraint of the Sullivan men, a kind of civil war had in fact broken out in Chicago.[51]

Public attention was almost immediately diverted by the stunning reports of the sinking of the *Titanic*, and this helped reduce tensions. However, it all became news again when Judge McKinley ordered a hearing to allow Owens, Czarnecki, Zimmer, McWeeny, and Schusettler to explain why they should not be held in contempt of his court. Owens' immediate response was to threaten to issue his own contempt citation against McKinley. This proved, however, to be mere posturing. The hearings began on April 28, 1912, and the matter was not fully adjudicated until several weeks later. Appearing for McGillen, the officially aggrieved party in Owens and company's disregard of the injunction, was attorney Alfred Austrian, who insisted heatedly upon jail time for the miscreants. Owens was alternately humble and defiant, and generally argued that not only was he within his rights as county judge to ignore the order and take control of the convention, but that, regardless, he was only accountable to the state supreme court. How he arrived at this conclusion when the most recent version of the Illinois primary law specifically stated: "the county central committee shall meet at the county seat and organize such meeting to be called the county convention," was not immediately apparent.

One amusing incident occurred when the attorney for Owens, E. B. Tolman, felt the need to read a letter into the record in which Mayor Harrison, who just managed to avoid a contempt citation himself, denied newspaper reports of having described Judge McKinley as a "whippersnapper." Eventually all were found guilty of contempt, fined $500, and sentenced to six months' imprisonment. Notices of appeal were immediately filed, a stay in the sentence granted, and more than a year later, on June 18, 1913, the state supreme court vacated the contempt conviction on the grounds that the injunction upholding McGillen's property rights was valid but only in the sense that he was an agent of the Cook County Democratic Party, the political rights of which took precedence, and which were beyond McKinley's jurisdiction. However, the court also took Owen to task for "an inexcusable disregard of the law" in attempting to seize control of the convention; he was in no way authorized by statute for his deed. In sum, Owens and his co-conspirators were held to be legally in error, but escaped all penalties. The court made no ruling on the relative merits of the "H-H" and Sullivan factions' claims to control a majority of the delegates, or the legitimacy of either county convention.[52]

Though dramatic, the storming of the Seventh Regiment Armory proved to have little impact upon the immediate future of party governance. The "H-H" version of the county committee went on claiming an unrecognized sovereignty for the next two years, but it was the Sullivan Democracy that was officially sanctioned nationally and controlled all party assets. The new state committee met on April, 18 1912, the eve of the state convention, and voted to recognize only 67 of the 404 "H-H" delegates. Many downstate members expressed their "disgust" at the events at the armory, and the Sullivan men claimed, in any case, to have more than enough delegates from outside of Cook County to be in control of the impending Peoria assemblage. Secure in his ascendancy, Roger in his crowded hotel suite that night, for once threw "off the reserve that usually mark[ed] his utterances" and let loose with a barrage against his antagonists: "The issue here is not Sullivanism!" he insisted:

> The issue is whether William Randolph Hearst, his agents, and hired assassins can control the Democratic Party of Illinois! I don't count in this thing. It is nothing I want personally ... [but] if Harrison and "Andy" Lawrence face me [in the state convention], I will call things by their proper names, and I won't mince words doing it![53]

Whether out of fear of the wrath of Sullivan, or, as is far more likely, because they rec-ognized that their strength was insufficient to make a stand, the "H-H" leaders decided to hold their own rump convention at a Peoria skating rink. Joining their delegates from Cook County was a scattering of downstaters, including the usual crowd of M.F. Dunlap, Owen Thompson, and Congressman Henry T. Rainey. There were overtures made in the course of the day to lure them back into the fold, but these were unsuccessful. Both con-ventions chose delegates for Baltimore, and as in 1908, a fight over recognition became inevitable.[54]

Sullivan also used the occasion to announce his intention to resign as national com-mitteeman. For the last four years he had manfully done his duty despite his original wish to forego the honor. This time he took no chances of being drafted again, and made his disinclination known early (he would actually continue to serve until the national convention) as part of a carefully laid scheme to have Charles Boeschenstein smoothly take his place. Arthur Charles from Carmi, an ally of long standing, would replace Boeschenstein as state chair.[55]

In contrast to their heated fight for control of the various delegations, Roger Sullivan and his organization did not take sides in the primaries for the state offices. This was their usual practice (with exceptions), one that helped alleviate any fears on the part of downstate Democrats of domination by Chicago. Moreover, in an unpredictable and unusually volatile election year in which the winds of reform were blowing with hurricane force, this was an especially prudent strategy; although Sullivan was exonerated of involvement in the Lorimer scandal, the widely held perception of him as a political boss could rebound unpredictably should he front a state slate or gubernatorial candidate.

Despite this, he was approached by a representative of one of the leading contenders for the nomination for governor, former Congressman Ben Franklin Caldwell, a banker and farmer from Sangamon County. This was Walter Townsend, the editor of the *Illinois State Register*, the Democratic newspaper of record in the state capital of Springfield. According to Townsend, Sullivan agreed that Caldwell was "a fine man and a fine Demo-crat," but admitted that should he make a choice, his man would be Samuel Alschuler, to whom he was "a little closer personally." Alschuler, a prominent attorney in Aurora, ran as the Democratic gubernatorial nominee in 1900 and served in the state legislature from 1897 to 1901 (in 1915, he would be appointed to the federal bench), but he was also backed this time by Carter H. Harrison. However, Sullivan believed that the likely victor would be the third major candidate, Edward F. Dunne, who, it was Townsend's impression, was probably the man that the Chicago leader found least desirable.[56]

Sullivan's political judgment was, as usual, astute. Dunne had made a smooth tran-sition from his near-victory in the mayoral primary of 1911 to becoming the leading con-tender for his party's nomination to become the state's chief executive. Besides being by far the most charismatic of the three, and a very effective public speaker, Dunne was the only member of the Chicago and Illinois Party's leadership who could with any credibility claim both party regularity and a meaningful record as a progressive. His candidacy brought forth his usual backers among the Windy City's reformers, but he also had taken the time build a professional organization led by the Cook County Treasurer, William O'Connell. He concentrated his efforts in the downstate to counter any apprehension that Democrats might have felt about a former mayor of Chicago becoming governor. He need not have worried unduly; although Caldwell was especially popular outside of Cook County, Dunne was a strong second choice, if only because he was perceived as a vote-getter in a year when it seemed that the Democrats had the best prospects since 1892 for victory in the state elections. Portraying himself throughout the state as the opponent of "Jackpotism" and "Lorimerism," Dunne won the primary with the substantial margin of 131,212 votes (of which 106,253 came from Cook County) to Alschuler's 87,127, and Caldwell's 71,972.[57]

Both factions endorsed Dunne and the other primary victors, as well as the state platform that—by the grace of Sullivan—he composed. It was, predictably progressive, advocating the initiative, referendum and recall, the direct election of United States Senators, consolidation of Chicago's park boards, reduction of the number of state offices, and better roads. However, missing was a plank favoring woman's suffrage, so ardently desired by the representatives of that rising movement, and one Sullivan would have preferred to be included.[58]

With the challenges of the primaries and the conventions now resolved, if not overcome, all attention turned to the upcoming national convention. Unexpectedly, it would be Roger Sullivan who would be decisive in determining the nominee. Having repeatedly frustrated the aspirations of William Jennings Bryan and his associates in Illinois, Sullivan in Baltimore would find himself embroiled yet again with his old nemesis in an epic power struggle. This time the stakes were the highest possible: Bryan's status as leader of the Democratic Party, and the making of a president of the United States.

5

Roger C. Sullivan and the Democratic Convention (1912)

"It was Bryan and Sullivan who did the Trick."—James Kerney, *Political Education of Woodrow Wilson* (New York: Century, 1926), p. 234.

The drama in the Illinois Democratic Party during the spring of 1912 was only a sideshow compared to the political theater that would be that year's presidential race. This framed Roger C. Sullivan's emergence as an important actor on the national stage and represented a climax of his political career. Ironically, Sullivan was initially reluctant to become engaged, taking a "hands off" policy towards his state's presidential primary. Instead, it was his rival, Carter Harrison, who threw his resources behind the frontrunner, Speaker Champ Clark, who won Illinois with a plurality of over 140,000 votes. However, instead of becoming president, Clark, thanks in part to Sullivan, was to become one of the more tragic figures in American political history.[1]

James Beauchamp Clark was an Appalachian of genuine mountaineer stock, hailing from eastern Kentucky and West Virginia before moving to the Show Me State as a young lawyer. First elected in 1892 to Congress, in 1910 he became speaker of the House of Representatives. He enjoyed a reasonably close friendship with Bryan, whom he had known since 1892, and had consistently backed for the presidency. Having won most of the presidential primaries (first used during this campaign cycle), as well as the endorsement of more state committees and caucuses then all of his rivals put together, Clark was now clearly the leading candidate. His record was reasonably progressive. However, among the younger and more "sophisticated" members of the party, he was viewed with doubt. Some of this appeared to be sheer snobbery, as many intellectual commentators seemed to view the speaker with bemused contempt; what could they make of a candidate whose campaign song celebrated a "houn' dawg" (this being forty-four years before the advent of Elvis Presley)? Moreover, though he had managed to be on the "right" side of most policy fights, if he had:

> any conception of the vital, burning questions, the American people are asking, any grasp of the issues and problems on which the voters are sharply divided as never before since the dark days before the Civil War, any comprehension of the great readjustments that are going on across party lines as the Progressives [sic] and Conservatives [sic] are reclassifying themselves, one finds no evidence of it in his conversation or recorded speech.[2]

It was the governor of New Jersey, Thomas Woodrow Wilson, who inspired the enthusiasm of the more youthful and better educated in the party. His background as head of Princeton University came at a time when there was broad respect in American society for academia and this helped transform him into a national celebrity and presidential candidate. In addition, he was well-known as a political scientist, a role that fit neatly into the progressive celebration of the expert. As his state's chief executive, he was aggressively reformist. Moreover, he made a remarkable appearance, and was a skilled speaker able to evoke with a few well-crafted phrases the highest idealisms. For all of his brilliance, however, many remained unimpressed—including most of the voters in the primaries. He won in only five of twelve states, with the results in the various caucuses being equally disappointing. By May 1912, even the candidate was prepared to admit that he no longer had "the least idea of being nominated," and believed that he could count on only 327 of the 1,099 delegates that were to gather in Baltimore for the national convention.[3]

Two other men of some importance were also in the running. Judson Harmon was the moderately progressive governor of Ohio, but was felt by Bryan and others to be too closely tied to the corporate interests. Nor was his "safe and prudent mentality" likely to attract much enthusiasm in an election year centering upon reform and change. Harmon did manage to win the Ohio presidential primary, and ran an active campaign. Oscar Wilde Underwood, United States Congressman from Alabama, was the favorite of most Southern Democrats. He could point to a distinguished record as a legislator and party leader, but suffered from the fact that he was a Southeron who was "part of the generation that has grown up since the late unpleasantness."[4]

But the race was not as clear as it seemed; Clark's position as the front-runner was much belied by the shallowness of his support, and there was private agendum in every direction.

Although committed to Clark by the speaker's plurality in the Illinois primary, Roger C. Sullivan had no great affinity for the man from Missouri. Indeed, before the voting, it was the general assessment that he would not "shed many tears if the candidate of Harrison and Hearst [Clark] were beaten." In fact, the Illinois boss, who was known for respecting education and educators, held Governor Wilson in high regard. In 1910, at the request of a mutual friend (Edward Nash Hurley), he helped lobby James Smith, the New Jersey Democratic boss, for the gubernatorial nomination of then president of Princeton University. Moreover, Wilson, the Eastern conservative and former "gold" Democrat with a long record of opposing Bryan and Bryanism (although the governor was currently doing

Champ Clark of Missouri (Library of Congress, LC-USZ62139527).

his best to placate the Commoner), was much closer ideologically to Sullivan than Clark, the Western Bryan Democrat. Even Wilson's relatively recent adoption of a progressive agenda, having only converted to the cause of reform in 1906, was of little consequence. Sullivan was on the record as supportive of the direct primary, civil service, governmental oversight of public utilities, and—unlike the governor—of women's suffrage. Moreover, he had overseen and approved a series of very progressive state platforms. But regardless of his feelings towards either Clark or Wilson, of overarching importance for a practical politician like Roger C. Sullivan was the nomination of a candidate who could win, and who most decidedly was not William Jennings Bryan.[5]

For his part, the Commoner had counted Clark as among his consistent and reliable allies; the speaker was active in each of his leader's campaigns, and was among those blessed with an invitation to spend a weekend at Bryan's mansion outside Lincoln, Nebraska. However, the Peerless Leader's feelings of friendship did not run very deeply. As a delegate from the Cornhusker State where Clark easily won the primary, he, it was true, went to Baltimore as a delegate for the man from Missouri. But tellingly, he did not exercise any of his massive influence on behalf of his friend.

And it would be Bryan who dominated the 1912 Democratic National Convention. He was the party's leading figure, the reigning champion of intraparty paramountcy. As a party icon, he was equaled in the past only by Andrew Jackson, and would be superseded in the future only by the greatest American politician of all time, Franklin Delano Roosevelt. Despite any compromise he may have made in 1908 with Roger C. Sullivan and the "interests," he remained the darling of the populist wing and the Democrat's greatest celebrity. The possibility of his third renomination remained a subtext of every political conversation.

But Bryan had repeatedly made clear his disinterest in another run. In January 1912, he insisted: "I am not a candidate for any office, and what I say ought to be accepted.... I believe now that there are others who can poll more votes than I can." Thereafter, he became "highly indignant" by an effort to enter his name into the Nebraska primary and he moved quickly to block an attempt to run him in California. At the convention, he adopted the contrary tactics of moving about the floor discouraging any thought of his nomination, while leaving the hall when rumblings of a stampede began to be heard. It was a testament to his power—not to his weakness—that he never received more than seven votes.[6]

Some of the most faithful sadly accepted him at his word. One James G. Waite, a Bakersfield, California farmer, for example, at last broke his vow, dating back to 1896, to remain unshaved until the Great Man was in the White House. Just weeks before the Baltimore conclave, and witnessed by "half the town," he sadly unwound his whiskers from the spool where they were stored, and surrendered them to a local barber. "I guess Bryan has no chance anymore," he lamented, "I've forgotten why I was such a durned [sic] fool."[7]

Many others remained certain that Bryan was "looming large as a candidate." Pittsburgh Democratic leaders created a betting pool with the smart money on a third renomination. Even a politician as astute as Chicago's mayor, Carter H. Harrison, was firm that in the end the Nebraskan would be the standard bearer. Bryan added fuel to the ruminations by not issuing an unequivocal statement removing himself entirely from consideration. Meeting with Democratic senators in Washington, D.C., in late April, he left the impression that "under certain conditions," he "would not decline the nomination." Years later this same ambiguity appears in his memoirs: "I told all who inquired [at the convention and before] that nothing but a situation which [sic] made the whole convention regard my nomination as necessary justified my considering the nomination."[8] However, there was no doubt of his appeal among the delegates. One contemporary account judged they were divided roughly in thirds, with one part "positively opposed," another part ready to embrace his nomination enthusiastically, and the remainder open to his selection under the right conditions. As impressive as these numbers were—given that he had trice led the party to defeat—they also revealed the problematic nature of his possible candidacy. Two-thirds of the votes were required, and there was no doubt that any hint of Bryan entering the lists would instantly unify Roger C. Sullivan and the other Eastern conservatives into a prohibitive opposition.[9]

And already some conservative speculations were bordering upon the paranoiac. Had Bryan not already undermined the hopes of Harmon by labeling him unfairly as a "reactionary," as well as those of Underwood, accused of kowtowing to the "Wall Street Crowd?" Had he not done so without any compensating indication of real support for either Wilson or Clark? Was he not appearing to be playing off the two front-runners by boosting ever so slightly with a few friendly statements the cause of the governor of New Jersey, while reiterating his intention to vote for the speaker, his supposed first choice? Was there not the danger that the "Peerless Loser" would "call into play all his genius for stampedes, all his adroitness, all of his magnetism, in an effort to nominate himself in Baltimore"? The press could not leave the question alone. Even a newspaper as relatively obscure as the African-American *Broad Ax* (Chicago) was convinced of Bryan's "itching desire" to try again, and as late as May 1912, the vehemently anti–Bryan *New York Tribune* was predicting that: "It looks more and more like a deadlock in Baltimore, out of which Mr. Bryan will emerge again as he did in 1896.… Preparations are well along to install the apparatus from which he will appear as the deus ex machina at the psychological moment for brushing aside the other aspirants."[10] Where his contemporaries were inclined to interpret Bryan's actions before and during the convention of 1912 in terms of his ambitions, the historians, as a rule, have accepted the Commoner's own explanations of high purpose. Most have described his role as heroic, as the leader in a fight against the forces of "reaction." This facile interpretation also has been one source of the neglect of Sullivan's key role in the outcome.

Bryan's earliest biographers are unabashed in their assertion that his motives were self-evident in his having "turned the tide in the bitter, long-drawn out fight," in standing fast against a vast right-wing conspiracy of Eastern conservatives led by Charles Murphy of Tammany Hall bent upon foisting a reactionary upon the party. One of these, Wayne C. Williams, writing in 1936, does admit that "Bryan, however, continued to feel and without doubt to hope that a situation … would justify submitting his name," but also credits him for working all along for the nomination of the progressive governor of New Jersey.[11]

More recent works have repeated this theme in less absolute terms. David D. Anderson in *William Jennings Bryan* (1981), for instance, argues that the Commoner's role "in defining the progressive limits of the convention has been misinterpreted almost constantly" as either an attempt to destroy old enemies or to stampede the convention towards his own nomination. Instead, he contends it "was a courageous and skillful movement by which the reactionary power in the party was virtually neutralized." Presumably meaning Charles Murphy, who undeniably disliked Wilson and Bryan did consider "reactionary," Anderson makes no reference at all to Roger Sullivan or the other Eastern conservative leaders who were decisive in determining the nominee. Louis W. Koenig, *Bryan* (1971), does recognize that Wilson was "put across the goal line" not through Bryan's quarterbacking but in an offensive drive led by Sullivan and the other regulars. However, he is certain that they did this "only after they tried by might and main and ruse" to "nominate some other candidate who was unprogressive or whose progressive ties were thin." Regrettably, Koenig provides neither evidence nor a coherent account of these supposedly strenuous efforts to keep the nomination from Wilson. Nor for that matter does he identify anyone in particular as their likely champion. Michael Kazin, the author of the most recent Bryan biography, *A Godly Hero* (2006), appears to uphold the thesis that the Peerless Leader was focused upon clarifying and defining the party's commitment to progressive principles, but he sees a personal motive in the Commoner's success in reasserting himself as "the star of his party." The nomination of Wilson, though achieved without direct assistance from the Nebraskan, was in the end therefore "all he could desire." Kazin also does not include a meaningful discussion of the impact and importance of the widely held contemporary belief that Bryan was working for himself.[12]

Where other historians assume Bryan's central role, his most meticulous biographer, Paolo Colletta, in his *William Jennings Bryan: Progressive Politician and Moral Statesman, 1909–1915* (1969) is less certain about his importance at convention, maintaining that other factors exceeded the impact of anything the he might have done. At the same time, Colletta recognizes Sullivan and the other Eastern conservatives' concerns about Bryan's manipulations. However, he does not address the fact that in the normal course of events—because of the implacable opposition of these Eastern conservatives—Bryan stood no chance for the nomination in 1912. Without the understanding that his selection was achievable only through the extraordinary circumstance of an otherwise unbreakable deadlock, his interpretation of Bryan's deliberate alienation of Charles Murphy of New York, and others, as evidence of a disinterest in the nomination becomes less convincing. Bryan had nothing to lose in confronting Murphy (who would oppose him regardless), but much to gain in establishing himself as the party's progressive arbitrator and leading symbol of reform should all of the declared candidacies cease to be viable because of gridlock. In the end, Colletta offers no clear opinion about Bryan's actual intensions.[13]

Whether he intended to seek the prize for himself or was "at his heroic best" stoking simultaneously angst and hope to achieve some noble set of ends remains unclear. William Jennings Bryan was not a man given to verbal inexactitudes. Moreover, he was consistent in his statements of disinterest, and took no direct affirmative action. Still, he would have been more than human if the embers of his great ambition had not continued to glow somewhat. In the end, there are but three certainties. First, William Jennings Bryan would kill the momentum of Champ Clark thus creating a deadlock. Second, it was the apprehension that the Nebraskan was attempting to maneuver his way to the nomination that would shape the actions of Roger C. Sullivan and the conservatives. Third, Sullivan, as their leader, thwarted the possibility of Bryan's selection by moving decisively to break the impasse to the benefit of Woodrow Wilson[14]

With the breakup of the Republicans just days before, and Theodore Roosevelt's announced intention to create his own third party, the delegates gathering in Baltimore on June 25, 1912, might have been expected to have been imbued with unalloyed joy and optimism. Instead, in part because of Bryan, in part because Clark was found by so many to be uninspirational, an element of tension and uncertainty already affected the Democrats beneath the surface jocularity. Also unquestionably contributing to the tempers and passions of this remarkable convention, were the miserable conditions the delegates and visitors endured for their extended stay in Maryland's first city.

Baltimore was proud to be the site; it had paid $100,000 for the privilege. It had not hosted the Democrats since 1872 (and the Republicans after 1864), and plans and preparations were carefully discussed and implemented. From the mayor on down, everyone purported to believe that all was ready. They were wrong.

Initial predictions of the crowds were put at 25,000. Later the national press would estimate, with pardonable exaggeration given crowded conditions, that the city's population of just over 550,000 souls was doubled. Whatever the exact size of the crowd, everything broke down. For hours on end, the streets were blocked by the multitudes that were so thick that they halted the trolley cars in which people were "packed like figs." The hotels were filled to bursting, with four and five strangers sometimes sharing a single room. The Illinois delegation, which reserved rooms on the fourteenth floor of the *Belvedere* endured exhausting trips up and down seemingly endless flights of steps because the few elevators were slow and in such demand. Restaurants were impossible, and it could take two hours to have a simple lunch served. The telephone systems were almost dysfunctional, with many of the hotel switchboards so overwhelmed by internal calls as to forego answering outside lines entirely. Taxis were at a premium and almost nonexistent at the rail stations, where a milling herd of delegates, press, and visitors seemed to be always waiting for transportation. Adding to the constant din in the streets and public areas—not excepting even the hotel lobbies—was the sound of band music playing incessantly. Favorite tunes included: "Everybody's Doin' It," and, "There'll Be a Hot Time in the Old Town Night," which was an appropriate metaphor for the heat of that Maryland summer—according to one delegate, a "fireless cooker"—that added considerably to the collective discomfort. The main hotels themselves, the Belvedere, the Emerson, and the Rennert, were a half-mile to a mile from the convention site, requiring long walks by the delegates through the already crowded streets. However, just about everyone tried to make the best of things, and there was reportedly a pervasive mood of bemused tolerance and endurance—at least for a while.[15]

Conditions were not much better at the Armory where the convention convened; the two hundred ushers were not properly trained and did not actually usher much, with the result that the throngs were free to wander about looking for their assigned seats on the floor and in the stands. That is, when they could get in; the authorities in their wisdom initially placed a single ticket-taker at the main entrance. There was also some confusion as to what door to use. Tickets might be marked "front entrance," but sometimes the only ingress available was at the side. Even the delegates had trouble collecting their credentials. All of this stood in stark contrast to the efficient way things had been run at Denver four years earlier, when Roger Sullivan had been in charge of arrangements. And, of course, the discomfort brought by the hot weather and the even hotter auditorium—the common comparison being an "oven"—was compounded inside by the close proximity of over 14,000 sweating and smelly bodies (deodorant had been invented, but was not widely used, especially by men who would not embrace what most considered a feminine affectation until after World War II), made all the more odiferous by the "intense but prevailing excitement" of the occasion. Nor did the heat merely bring sweat and odor; it also added the sound "of thousands of fans beating the stifling air" to the usual dull murmur punctuated periodically by deafening cheers. Not coincidentally, perhaps, no major party national convention has been held since in Baltimore.[16]

It was amidst these lamentable conditions that Bryan began his quest for the domination of events. On the first day he challenged the national committee's choice for temporary chair, Alton B. Parker, an Eastern conservative and the party's 1904 presidential candidate. Failing to convince Senator John Kern of Indiana (Bryan's running mate in 1908), or anyone else that was ideologically correct, to be his stalking horse, the Commoner ran himself. Though he lost, the vote of 579 to 510 (Illinois voted for Parker) revealed his still impressive following among the delegates, and set the scene for further machinations. Subsequently, Bryan's friend, who was liked by the regulars as well, Ollie James of Kentucky was selected as permanent chair. The next day, the Nebraskan parlayed his political capital into a suspension of the unit rule for all delegations, except for those, like Illinois, elected through congressional district caucuses or conventions. Again the vote, 565½ to 491½ (Illinois voting "nay"), underscored Bryan's power to impose his own definition of the progressive agenda upon the convention. However, his victory was more symbolic than real as many of the states affected, like New York and Ohio, were so politically organized as to vote generally as a unit in any case. Soon afterwards, Bryan was offered the chairmanship of the Committee on Resolutions, but declined in favor of Senator John Kern, his running mate four years earlier. He did consent, however, to serve on the subcommittee responsible for the platform, which, in an unprecedented move, would not be presented to the convention until after the presidential nominee was chosen. This was justified as an attempt to avoid repeating the experience of 1904, when Parker had made his candidacy conditional upon a stronger statement of support for the gold standard than the platform's vague phrasing.[17]

Meanwhile, Roger Sullivan was brushing aside Carter Harrison's quadrennial challenge to Illinois' representation. Having lost in 1904 and 1908, the mayor promised this time to make "the fight of his life." Following a pilgrimage to New York City to consult with William Randolph Hearst, Harrison arrived confident with 300 of his "delegates" and the Cook County Democracy marching club in tow. However, the mayor badly misjudged the situation. Champ Clark, had been endorsed by both Peoria conventions, and though he was backed by Hearst, he had nothing to gain in alienating the powerful Sullivan. Moreover, Harrison was on the record professing an "instinctive repugnance" towards the second contender, Governor Woodrow Wilson of New Jersey. Both Clark and Wilson's forces backed Sullivan, but given the one-sided nature of the conflict, this certainly did not create any obligation—especially in the all-important matter of the nomination. When the national committee voted unanimously to seat the Sullivan men, the case went to the Credentials Committee. Harrison was on the defensive throughout his appearance because of the extraordinary events associated with the Cook County convention(s). These were an embarrassment to the party. Even as the mayor admitted being responsible for the presence of the police at the Seventh Regiment Armory on that April day, he claimed his involvement as being no more untoward than his provision of special protection for some of the Roosevelt delegates during the Republican convention, held in his city. Roger Sullivan, during his testimony, characterized Harrison's words as "beautiful" but "incorrect." "We whipped them to a standstill by a direct vote of the people," he insisted, "and left them with nothing but the police force and the deputy sheriffs." In fact, there was little real doubt that it was he, and not the mayor of Chicago, who was the actual leader of most Illinois' Democrats, especially of those outside of Cook County. When the vote was called, his delegation was upheld by 40 to 10 with two abstaining.[18]

A Clark demonstration at 3 a.m. (Library of Congress, LC-DIG-ggbain-10552).

As Harrison now gave up the fight, the full convention accepted the majority report of the committee without much comment. The mayor—once considered a serious presidential possibility—was unable initially to obtain tickets to the hall despite requests, and then pleas to William Skidmore, a Sullivan man and Illinois' ticket dispenser (and the sergeant-arms of the Sullivan version of the Cook County Democratic Convention). These evoked only the brusque response of "nothing doing for that Harrison bunch!" Upon learning of the situation, Sullivan arranged for two passes for seats on the platform to be sent over. Harrison (who was a good hater) chose to interpret the gracious gesture as a "deliberate insult" and angrily refused to be obliged to "Mr. Sullivan for my presence there!" Instead, he left fuming to "pick out the best seat I can find."[19]

William Jennings Bryan stayed out of the Illinois seating fight. He had much more important issues to consider. He was now preparing his first major step toward complicating the presidential nomination. On Thursday evening, June 27 (the third day), he introduced a resolution declaring the convention "opposed to the nomination for any candidate for President [sic], who is the representative of or under obligation to J. Pierpont Morgan, Thomas F. Ryan, August Belmont, or any other member of the privilege-hunting and favor-seeking class." As originally written, it included a paragraph asserting the convention's right and duty to remove from the national committee any member "who represented predatory wealth." This was clearly directed at Sullivan, among others. However, Charles Bryan convinced his brother that this would inspire considerable opposition as an intrusion upon the rights of the state parties, and it was removed. Retained, however, was a demand for the "withdrawal from this convention of any delegate or delegates ... representing the above-named interests." Morgan was the nation's leading financier, and long an object of scorn and hatred as the chief symbol of the "interests" August Belmont was (like his father after whom he was named) the American representative of the Roth-schild interests, and was noted for among other things, his capitalization of the New York Subway; Thomas F. Ryan was another financier who had first invested in New York's streetcar lines and then in insurance. In 1908, he was indicted for corruption, but the charges were later dropped.

By his own account, Bryan originally included a reference in the resolution to the success of "Wall Street" in controlling the recent Republican convention and renominating President William Howard Taft. While moving towards the platform to speak, however, he was introduced to Mrs. Taft, who was present as an observer (as Bryan was at the earlier G.O.P. gathering). Always the gentleman, he pulled the reference in deference to the sensibilities of the dear lady. Just before the roll call on the resolution, he also withdrew the paragraph calling for the removal of interest-obliged delegates, something he may have intended all along to assure passage. Pandemonium ensued—Belmont and Ryan were actually present as delegates from New York and Virginia respectively—and death threats were hurled from the floor (though Bryan did not learn of them until afterwards), but the resolution passed overwhelmingly by a margin of 883 to 201½.

The vote was an undoubted reflection of the desire of most present to appear pro-gressive. Without its second paragraph, it was in any case symbolic, so even Illinois and New York (the latter in part on the advice of Sullivan) voted in the affirmative. However, what Bryan accomplished was to prove to be more important than was immediately apparent; he had emphasized and reinforced the divide within the convention between the Eastern conservatives or "regulars," and those of the Western wing and others more vociferously dedicated to progressivism. This would prove be an important factor in enabling the subsequent stalemate in the balloting for the presidential nomination.[20]

When the noise and confusion brought by Bryan's resolution against the influence of Morgan, Belmont, and Ryan at last abated, the Thursday evening session moved on to the nominations. The names of the prospective nominees were presented in turn accompanied by florid rhetoric and vociferous demonstrations. Each was lauded as the potential savior of the nation to the sounds of hosannas meant to inspire blind passion and a suspension of every contrary sentiment. This went on and on; it was not until 6:43 a.m. Friday that the speeches and the histrionics were concluded. There was just time for one ballot, and this confirmed expectations: Clark 440½, Wilson 324, Harmon 148, and Underwood 117½. In addition, Governor Thomas Marshall of Indiana, a protégé of Thomas Taggart, received 31 votes, while Governor Simeon E. Baldwin of Connecticut was given 12, and William Jennings Bryan one. The exhausted delegates, adjourned at 7:30 a.m., having sat for nearly twelve hours.[21]

Balloting resumed after the convention reconvened at 4:00 p.m. for another session that was destined to last well past midnight. The atmosphere was to become even hotter, both literally and figuratively. Between the second and ninth ballots there was little change (a short recess was called after the fifth ballot from about 7:00 p.m. to 9:42 p.m.). Clark's total rose to 452, while Wilson's stood at 351½. Both men benefited from a steady decline of Harmon's support.

What many initially assumed would be the defining moment came on the tenth ballot, when the New York delegation led by Charles Murphy, switched from Harmon to Clark. This provoked an exodus from the Ohio governor to the Missouri congressman. Permanent chair, Ollie James announced Clark's majority, which was still considerably short of the two-thirds necessary for nomination. This prompted an immediate protest for being prejudicial from A. Mitchell Palmer of Pennsylvania, one of Wilson's floor managers. Meanwhile, a spontaneous demonstration briefly broke out for Bryan when he was observed going over to the Oregon delegation; perhaps the Beaver State was about to introduce his name? The chant of "Bryan, Bryan" echoing through the crowded hall could not have given much comfort to the declared candidates or to Roger Sullivan and the Eastern conservatives. Two more ballots were held before adjournment was moved by Sullivan at about 3:30 a.m. Saturday. The totals at this point were: Clark 547½, Wilson 354, Harmon 29, Underwood 123, Marshall 30, with one each for Senator Kern of Indiana and his mentor, William Jennings Bryan.[22]

Only Martin Van Buren on the first ballot in 1844 ever secured a majority in a Democratic national convention and failed to be nominated. Wilson campaign manager William McCombs despaired, and advised his candidate to withdraw. A telegram of congratulations to Clark was composed. According to two separate accounts, one from Joseph P. Tumulty, Wilson's private secretary, and the other from Frank Parker Stockbridge, who oversaw the governor's publicity, it was Roger Sullivan who stiffened the backbone of their campaign and their candidate. Upon learning of the message of doom sent to Wilson, so Tumulty relates, the Illinois leader, "who had been in conference with Bryan," rushed over and told McCombs: "Damn you, don't do that! Sit steady in the boat," or words to that effect (Stockbridge presents a similar account but without the mild profanity). Wilson did not withdraw.[23]

Sullivan, as well as the rest of the Illinois delegation, remained committed to Clark by the state's primary. His action to keep the governor in the race makes best sense in terms of his apprehensions about Bryan. Woodrow Wilson was the most credible progressive candidate, or at least the only one generally accepted as such (in this election cycle everyone was a "progressive"). Alone among those seeking the nomination, he backed Bryan's bid for the temporary chairmanship. If Wilson withdrew, his men, who were as a body the most reform-minded present, could collectively turn to the Nebraskan, accepting his earnest presentation of himself as the paramount champion of progressive principle at the convention. A general stampede could ensue for Bryan. This was far from a fantastic scenario. After all, the Commoner had achieved just this effect in 1896 with a single speech. Even failing this, Wilson's delegates could well forgo Clark, who for many was neither sufficiently dynamic nor progressive, in favor of scattering their votes among the other candidates or perhaps uniting behind some dark horse. This, too, could create a deadlock resulting in Bryan's nomination. In short, Wilson's continued candidacy was the best safeguard against a spontaneous movement towards Bryan, and therefore had to be maintained.[24]

Moreover, Sullivan, the astute politician, by this point recognized that Clark's nomination was by no means assured; New York's shift and his majority failed to create the overwhelming bandwagon effect that might have been expected. It was also becoming clear that Clark could not achieve the two-thirds necessary for his nomination without converting a substantial percentage of those presently voting for Wilson, and the ideological dynamic as being reinforced serially by Bryan was making that increasingly unlikely. There was a real possibility, therefore, that it might in the end come down to Wilson or Bryan, and there could be no alternative at all to Bryan if Wilson withdrew.

And subsequent events would only substantiate further Roger Sullivan's trepidations. The convention reconvened at 1:00 p.m., Saturday, 29 June 1912, and following the preliminary prayer, the thirteenth ballot began. When the roll came to Nebraska, Bryan asked leave to speak to explain his state's vote. He was, with one stroke, about to damage the candidacy of Champ Clark irrevocably and deadlock the convention. He explained that he was changing from the speaker to the governor of New Jersey in response to the shift of the New York delegation to Clark. Because the convention had voted by a margin of four to one not to nominate anyone under the influence of Morgan, Belmont, Ryan, and the "privilege-seeking, favor-hunting class," and because the New York delegates were dominated by Charles F. Murphy, the head of Tammany, who represented "the influences that nominated a republican [sic] candidate" (Taft), therefore, Bryan concluded, the selection of someone backed by New York would mean someone compromised by these interests. For this reason, he was going to "withhold [his] vote from Mr. Clark as long as New York's vote is recorded for him" and would "not be a party to the nomination of any man" who could not carry out as president the substance of his resolution. He was both applauded and jeered. He then demanded a roll call of his state delegation, which was pledged to Clark, but now recorded twelve for Wilson and but four for the speaker. Not unexpectedly, this provoked a storm of noise and angry rebuttal. One Clark delegate from Oklahoma, referencing the "Cross of Gold" speech from 1896, proposed that Bryan was now crucifying the party on the "cross of selfishness," a clear reflection of the growing belief that the man from Nebraska was seeking a path towards the nomination.[25]

Maurice Lyons, the secretary of William McCombs, Wilson's campaign manager, would later write that it was Wilson who was responsible for Bryan's coup. The governor, so Lyon's account runs, called McCombs on the telephone during the thirteenth ballot, to dictate a message from the governor to Bryan. Wilson professed to believe that the "present deadlock" was due to the manipulations of the New York delegation to "bind the candidate to them." It was both his "duty, he now believed," and the other candidates' as well, to refuse to accept the nomination "if it cannot be secured without the aid of that delegation," the "supreme consideration" being to keep the party free of "private control." It was this missive, Lyons asserts, that inspired Bryan's act. To prove his contention, he reproduces in his book a photograph of part of his notes of the dictation taken from Wilson, though not the critical section. Bryan made no mention of such a message, either at the time or in his memoirs, nor does Lyons appear to be corroborated elsewhere. Moreover, Wilson was probably enough of an astute politician to know that it was not productive to alienate those upon whom might depend one's future (until one does not need them), as surely this would have done had word leaked out that he was the source of this provocation. It is also to be wondered that William Jennings Bryan, the only Democrat at his point to win his party's presidential nomination thrice, would need or heed anything strategic from the governor of New Jersey, whose direct political experience did not as yet extend to fully two years. Still, such a message would have been consistent with Wilson and his campaign team's focus upon staying close and in favor with Bryan, and it would have been a brilliant tactic to use the Commoner's purported pursuit of ideological purity to checkmate Clark.[26]

Although it was the general consensus during the convention that Bryan's speech effectively crippled Clark's chances, one of Wilson's best biographers, Arthur Link (echoed

Sullivan with allies at the 1912 convention (Library of Congress, LC-DOGG-ggbain-11260).

by Paolo Colletta as noted above) in *Wilson, The Road to the White House* (1947) contends that the speaker's campaign was already fatally weakened by a coalition of Wilson and Underwood delegates. These, he writes, by holding "their ground" in the tenth and eleventh ballots had thwarted the threat of a Clark "landslide." Bryan's speech and its impact were therefore not the decisive element in the demise of the speaker's hopes.[27]

This view, however, greatly underrates the Nebraskan's power. This was the party's greatest living figure, "no other individual matched his influence at Baltimore." He was able to dictate the ideological context of the convention and its platform, while also inspiring both hope and fear that he might yet win the nomination despite his explicit denials of any such intention. It was he, more than any other, who shaped events. Moreover, in just a few days the Wilson campaign, with considerably less momentum, was able to overcome an opposition from the Clark delegates that was much more determined than any earlier marriage of convenience between those of Underwood and the governor. It is not unreasonable to believe that the speaker would have—but for the intervention of Bryan—achieved a similar success. Perhaps most importantly, this interpretation flies in the face of a cardinal rule of politics: everyone loves a winner, which, until Bryan spoke, Champ Clark had been.[28]

Some, including the Hearst press, which was vigorously backing Clark, assumed at first that Bryan was attempting to create a stampede for Wilson. Significantly, however, the Nebraskan did nothing further to promote the governor. Logically, if he wished to nominate Wilson, he would have openly called for his selection, or at least begun working quietly on his behalf among his men in the delegations. In short, he would have acted in a manner anticipating the role that President Harry S. Truman initially played for Adlai Stevenson in the 1952 Democratic convention. But the Commoner did neither.

Over the next ballots Wilson's vote rose by only small accretions, while Clark's fell in equal proportion. On the fourteenth the totals read: Clark 553, Wilson 361, Underwood 111, Harmon 29, Thomas Marshall 30, and John Kern of Indiana two, and on the twenty-fifth: Clark 469, Wilson 405, Underwood 108, Marshall 30, Harmon 29, scatterings four. On the twenty-second ballot, Governor Eugene N. Foss of Massachusetts began to gain some votes, taking 43 in the twenty-fifth, but his momentum stalled and he never became a real contender.[29]

For those who feared a Bryan nomination, his actions assumed a sinister aspect; the renunciation of Clark had resulted in effectively equalizing the speaker's strength with that of the governor of New Jersey, creating exactly the kind of dreaded impasse that could result in the convention turning to the Nebraskan. For Roger Sullivan, this was of special concern as the leadership of the Eastern Democrats had largely fallen to him because Charles Murphy was effectively disqualified from any larger role by Bryan's denunciations. When the Commoner completed his speech, Sullivan sent over his chief lieutenant, George Brennan with others to ascertain the true nature of his motives. Apparently the explanations were not reassuring. Reportedly, Sullivan now allowed himself to be persuaded by the Wilson men to call a caucus during the twenty-sixth roll call, and based upon that, to offer a tentative promise to switch Illinois to Wilson, "on the first ballot after midnight," or on the next ballot—accounts differ. Unfortunately for the cause of the governor, one of his own floor managers, Congressman A. Mitchell Palmer of Pennsylvania, who was apparently uninformed of the purported deal, moved for adjournment before its terms could be fulfilled.[30]

Champ Clark was angry and hurt witnessing his seemingly inevitable victory being snatched away. It was such a ruthless and unfair twist of fate, especially as Bryan knew full well that Clark was in no way an operative of Tammany or of the "interests." It seemed to be hollow reasoning to repudiate the speaker simply for accepting the votes of the largest delegation at the convention, and for not supporting the effort to overthrow Parker as temporary chair. Nor could Clark and his backers forget that Bryan had not demonstrated the same ideological scruples in soliciting the backing of Murphy, Taggart, and Sullivan in 1908 during his last pursuit of the presidency. Moreover, it was infuriating that Bryan was not man enough to make his charges and position plain but relied instead upon innuendo. Like many others, Clark could only conclude that his erstwhile "friend" was after the nomination.

Upon learning of Bryan's switch, the speaker rushed from Washington to Baltimore to take the unprecedented step of directly addressing the convention to refute the insinuations that he had been compromised. He arrived after adjournment, and became convinced that the Wilson men had sent the convention into recess to keep him from speaking. His managers persuaded him to return to the capital, but he remained determined to hold on. His followers were no less stunned, incredulous, and furious. After Bryan's explication during the fourteenth ballot, a physical altercation nearly broke out between the Missouri and the New Jersey delegations that happened to be seated near each other, and the acrimony and frustration would burst forth repeatedly in the days ahead.[31]

The next day, Sunday, June 30, 1912, was supposed to be a time of greatly needed rest, but, of course, the politicking only increased. There was wide speculation that the convention might be compelled to turn to a dark horse to end the stalemate that was threatening what had appeared to be certain victory in the fall. Chicago Mayor Carter Harrison reflected one tenet of conventional wisdom in his belief that it would come down to either Bryan or his protégé, John Kern. Others were less certain. Conferences were held all that day among leaders and by delegations, but the most important involved Sullivan, Tom Taggart, James Smith, and Charles Murphy. They came together on very short notice in the early morning with most of the participants reportedly clad in pajamas and dressing gowns. Any kind of commitment that the Illinois leader might or might not have made the previous evening was now seemingly disregarded, as accounts emerged of "vague" discussions of various other possibilities including Pennsylvania's A. Mitchell Palmer (it is not certain if he were actually approached, the sources differ), and Senator Charles A. Culberson of Texas. Other reports suggested a possible return to Clark or a move to Underwood.[32]

One obstacle was Charles Murphy, who stood firm in his opposition to Wilson. What was clear was that Roger Sullivan and the others were exploring all contingencies and keeping all of their options open, but for the moment no change was forthcoming. The Chicago leader explained later that day: "our 58 delegates are instructed for Clark and our vote will not be changed unless we find it impossible to nominate Clark." Moreover, in public at least, he dismissed any thought that he might shift to Wilson: "We have no second choice."[33]

Some have interpreted these discussions as part of a larger conspiracy to stop Woodrow Wilson. Supposedly, this was motivated by the threat of Wilson's progressivism. This does not accord with the realities of the situation. There is no good evidence that that Sullivan, or for that matter any of the other organizational leaders (with the notable exception of Murphy, whose antipathy toward the governor was well known), were implicitly opposed to the governor of New Jersey or to his platform. Their goal was to win in November. In an election year in which reform was in the air, in which Theodore Roosevelt, perhaps the most personally popular man in the nation, had called forth the faithful in a progressive crusade so powerful that it had fractured the Grand Old Party, it made no practical sense to attempt to force another Alton Parker upon the Democratic Party. Nor, given the ideological configuration of the delegates, would it have been even possible.[34]

Instead, their problem was a convention stalemated because William Jennings Bryan had undermined the front runner. The obvious second choice was Wilson. However, Clark's "fighting blood was aroused" as was that of his followers, and their "chief object now was to prevent Wilson's nomination." This was a formidable impediment, as was Murphy. Accordingly, others were discussed and their merits weighed. None of them, not Clark, Underwood, or Harmon, however, could be remotely considered money-kings or creatures of Wall Street.[35]

Although the reputation of A. Mitchell Palmer has been tainted by his later role as Wilson's attorney general in the abuse of the civil rights of opponents of American involvement in World War I and afterwards those of Marxists, he was certainly no reactionary. In 1912, he was a liberal congressman from Pennsylvania, who recently deposed and replaced Boss James Guffey as the state's national committeeman. He, like Bryan and Wilson, advocated lowering the tariff, and he was on record as supportive of most other progressive causes. Not least, he was one of the New Jersey governor's chief floor leaders. Doubtlessly, he was looked upon as a potential dark horse, around whom the party might rally, much as had happened with James Garfield at the deadlocked 1880 Republican Convention. Culberson, whose name was discussed only in passing, was a progressive on record as favoring "the destruction of favoritism and privilege and private graft in public affairs." He, too, was no myrmidon of the "interests." In the end, no decisions were reached, and a wait-and-see attitude prevailed.[36]

But there was also clearly an emerging consensus that it might have to be Wilson after all as the only feasible alternative to the deadlock and the possibility of Bryan; fears were growing that the Peerless Leader might yet finesse his way to the nomination: "The proportion of Democrats in Baltimore who think Bryan wants and will to try to get the nomination," one observer wrote," is about nine out of every possible ten." If events continued to unfold as they were, who knew what the Nebraskan's next trick would be to disrupt the convention and perpetuate the stalemate, the end of which was "not in sight"? This was a perception the New Jersey governor's campaign team did their best to encourage, and on Sunday night, Sullivan reportedly conducted an informal canvass of the Illinois delegation and agreed in principle, though without a specific commitment, to shift to Wilson, but "at the proper time." However, all such reports should be treated with caution as there were also stories that Sullivan made a similar agreement with the Underwood forces. Taggart, on the other hand, unquestionably negotiated a more concrete arrangement, but only in return for Wilson's support for the vice presidential nomination of Indiana Governor Thomas Marshall.[37]

The Eastern Conservatives, the press, and the other delegates were not alone in recognizing the increasing possibility of a Bryan candidacy emerging from the ongoing stalemate. His wife, Mary Baird Bryan, records that as the convention deadlocked, she began urging her husband to begin an active effort. His reply was to the effect that he would only consent if no one else were able to be nominated (something that in the opinion of many, he was giving every appearance of facilitating). Hoping to help prolong the impasse, Mary, thereafter, made a point of urging those around her in the hall to join in the applause for Wilson.[38]

However, for all the intrigue, and deal-making, the initial votes continued to disappoint the Wilson camp when the convention reconvened on Monday. The twenty-seventh ballot brought little change. The Missourian still led with 469 votes, followed by Wilson at 406½, Underwood at 112, Marshall at 30, Harmon at 29, and one for Bryan. However, the fortunes of the governor of New Jersey began to improve on the next roll call as Taggart brought over Indiana's 30 votes. By the thirtieth-first ballot, almost all of Ohio had broken with Harmon for the governor, while half of the Iowa delegation and a scattering of others deserted Clark to give Wilson the lead for the first time with 475½ votes to 446½.[39]

Emotions became increasingly heated, especially among the speaker's supporters whose frustrations mounted as the nomination began slipping away. At the end of the thirty-third ballot, a near riot broke out when some of the Missouri delegates came to their seats carrying a banner upon which was inscribed a quote from Bryan, dating back to 1910, extolling their hero as "absolutely incorruptible," and "above reproach." "Take it over to Nebraska and show it to Bryan," was the cry. Standing in front of the Nebraska delegation, they began to taunt the Commoner and violence became a real possibility. The police quickly moved in, and escorted the object of the Missourians' scorn to the platform. There he confronted Clark's manager, Senator William J. Stone, inquiring force-fully if he were responsible for "this insult." Failing to receive a satisfactory answer, he descended and went to the Missouri delegation. Now standing in the midst of "the shriek-ing, excited mob" he demanded an explanation. "It was the only time in my life when I was in danger of physical harm," Bryan later recounted, but a half-dozen burly policemen surrounded him in time, and moved him back to the platform for his safety. Meanwhile fistfights broke out between the Missouri and New Jersey men, fights that spilled over into the press gallery. When Bryan tried to speak to quell things, he was told to "shut up" by an Ohio delegate, who was for Harmon, but who was then pummeled by a Wilson backer from his own delegation. Making things worse was the badly timed appearance of a Wilson banner, which was quickly ordered out. Calm at last having been restored, Bryan asked for the right to speak as a point of personal privilege. The Chair, Ollie James, "acting wisely" (Bryan's later words) denied his request. The Commoner instead returned to his seat with a police escort, and the convention resumed balloting. However, the ten-sion only increased as the session progressed, with "every shifting vote, every demand for a poll of a delegation, awaken[ing] bitterness," and the guards were repeatedly called to remove "offenders who got involved in quarrels." It began to look as though the Dem-ocratic Party might fall apart.[40]

There was some irony in the brawl between some of the Wilson and Clark men. On Sunday, the Commoner, it was true, at last let it be known vaguely that Wilson was his first choice. However, one source reports "that he suggested [on Saturday] to Governor Wilson that he withdraw his name [as] is testified by Wilson himself." He also had floated the idea that perhaps the convention could "adjourn for a month" to allow passions to cool (as had been unsuccessfully attempted in 1860). By Monday, some of the press was claiming that he was now behind the candidacy of his earlier stated second preference, Senator John Kern of Indiana. At the least "it is certain that Bryan favored.... Kern more than any other candidate except Bryan." Even as the convention now proceeded, further news stories were appearing that the Peerless Leader's son and brother were working the delegations on Kern's behalf (perhaps, it was suggested, as a means of reestablishing the deadlock). Meanwhile, his feelings for Wilson were being described as "lukewarm." The *New York Times* even wrote that former New Jersey Senator Jonathan H. Blackwell left the convention to warn Wilson that the Commoner was not his friend, and was looking for an excuse to withdraw his backing. The New Jersey governor, so the article stated, merely smiled with apparent understanding. Whether true or not, the story illustrated the growing belief that Bryan was following his own private agenda and was now seeking to subvert the Wilson candidacy that he had just so lately, if tentatively, embraced.[41]

As the day moved forward, however, even Bryan's quiet efforts (if they were in fact taking place) could not keep the governor from continuing to gain at the expense of his principal opponent in one weary ballot after another. In the thirty-ninth, Wilson passed the five hundred mark receiving 501½ to the speaker's 422. But he was still short a major-ity, and in the forty-second ballot, he slipped to 494, while Clark rose to 430. At about 12:30 a.m. the convention adjourned.[42]

Throughout, Sullivan and the Illinois delegation held for Clark as importuned with increasing desperation by the speaker's men and likely by the candidate himself. Repeat-edly the delegates caucused, and repeatedly they voted to stay with the speaker. The most recent of these votes came during the thirty-eighth ballot, when Roger sent the men out of the hall to confer (whispering to each as they left), while remaining on the floor himself. Only eight were for a switch to Wilson, seven were for Underwood, and most were content to stand pat until the governor of New Jersey at least received a majority. However, based upon this slender reed, the Wilson forces confidently predicted that Illinois would soon join them. To buttress their case with Sullivan, they redoubled their efforts to have a massive number of telegrams sent from Illinois to plead their cause—though it is doubtful that Sullivan, who knew a "snow job" when he saw one, paid much attention. By this point, Illinois was considered "pivotal," and was being closely watched by a number of other states. However, the Chicago leader continued to deny that any promises were being made despite the widely circulated reports of a general commitment to Wilson among the Eastern conservatives. Sullivan was still not convinced, despite Wilson's gains, that the right moment to act had come.[43]

But that time was almost at hand; the Clark campaign was on its last legs. Late in the day, the candidate was summoned by his team to Baltimore to discuss the situation. According to Clark's manager, Senator William J. Stone, as quoted in the *New York Times*, the speaker "was told that the intriguing of Mr. Bryan had made his nomination impossible, and that Mr. Bryan was engaged in an effort to kill off Mr. Wilson." He was urged to release his delegates for "some other progressive candidate" (Stone refused to affirm that he meant Wilson). Though not made explicit, apparently the antipathy towards a Bryan candidacy was now as much of a factor in the Clark camp as it was for Sullivan and the other leaders of the regulars. The dejected man from Missouri asked for time to return to Washington to consider his course.[44]

When the delegates gathered again that Tuesday morning, July 3, 1912, they were tired; this was already the lengthiest convention in living memory. Still, the commitment of those supporting the major candidates remained strong, and even on this fifth day of balloting, most clung grimly to their allegiances. Before the voting began, William McCombs, as he later recounted it, rushed to Sullivan and threatened to withdraw his man (evoking the specter of Bryan), if Illinois did not come over. According to Lawrence B. Stringer (one of the governor's point men in Illinois, and Sullivan's future primary opponent for the senatorial nomination), it was he who took the initiative to bring McCombs and Sullivan together at the "psychological moment when the die was cast." Roger's recorded response was: "Sit steady, boy!" In fact, Sullivan already knew that the states of Virginia, West Virginia, Alabama, Washington, and Maryland were waiting on Illinois to move and at last he resolved to act. By the time the forty-third roll call came around to Illinois, the delegation had canvassed and voted by a margin of 45 to 13 to back the governor of New Jersey. When called upon by the chair, Roger Sullivan rose: "Illinois casts eighteen votes for Clark, and forty for Wilson," he "roared." "Under the unit rule, adopted by the delegation, therefore, all fifty-eight Illinois votes are cast for Wilson!" Roger found himself "hugged and kissed" by Wilson supporters, and the object of jeers from those for Clark.[45]

However, though now undermined, the walls through sheer inertia remained standing even as fragments began to fall. On the forty-third ballot, Illinois was joined by West Virginia, taking Wilson's total to 602 votes. On the forty-fourth, Virginia and about half of Maryland came aboard, and the governor of New Jersey had 629. The forty-fifth saw little change and his count only inched up to 633. Finally, as the convention prepared for the forty-sixth the rumble of tumbling stones began to be heard. Before the vote, John Bankhead, Underwood's manager rose and freed his candidate's nearly 97 (as of the last ballot) delegates. He was followed by Senator William J. Stone who announced that Missouri would stay with Clark, but that the rest of the speaker's supporters were now released from their pledges. Then Edward H. Moore, political boss of Ohio, turned over most of the few remaining Harmon votes. Even New York joined the rush, which inspired no comment from Bryan, who had insisted he would vote for no man backed by Charles Murphy (Murphy's opposition to Sullivan's shift was reportedly "lulled" by a promise to shift back to Clark if necessary). It was soon all over; the final count stood at Wilson 990, Clark 84, Harmon 12, and two not voting. Sobs of joy and disappointment were mingled with cries of jubilation and frustration, Roger Sullivan had done it, the deadlock was broken and the possibility of another Bryan candidacy preempted. The Commoner, reportedly, stood silently overcome by "the emotions of hope lost and a life-time ambition again defeated."[46]

The convention recessed until 9:00 a.m. Wednesday, July 3, 1912, when the vice presidential nominee was to be selected. Before the names could be placed into consideration, a representative of Clark announced that the speaker declined to be considered. In the end, as arranged, Thomas Marshall, the protégé of Sullivan's friend and ally, Thomas Taggart, was given the nod.

The platform, for some unrecorded reason, was released by the Committee on Resolutions during vice presidential nominations. Though overseen by Bryan, a man not given to sparse expression, it was relatively straightforward, and included virtually every conceivable progressive demand including calls for tariff reform, a stronger anti-trust law, a federal income tax, the direct election of senators, the promotion of state presidential primaries, conservation, campaign finance reform prohibiting contributions by corporations, and closer regulation of railroads, telephone and telegraph services. However, missing was any reference to reform of the currency, once Bryan's primary political passion, and to woman's suffrage (something Wilson opposed, but Sullivan supported). It was a platform that matched Theodore Roosevelt's rhetoric, and it placed the Democrats squarely in the reformist vanguard. With the nominations at last completed, the platform ratified, and routine business concluded, the convention adjourned at 1:55 p.m. *sine die* (without a set date for reconvening).[47]

All the principal players claimed to be satisfied with the outcome. Roger Sullivan, basking in the acclaim of the Wilson men, professed himself to be "delighted" and "gratified that it came our way to nominate such a candidate of such a progressive character, who has such eminent qualifications for the high office that I believe he will attain." He explained that Illinois' move to Wilson was a response to the speaker's cause becoming futile, with Illinois's shift coming only after "Mr. Clark's friends admitted he could not win." Others in his state delegation were more specific in admitting that a key motive was the fear "that Bryan might come into the situation at any moment, and stampede the convention." In more measured and cooler tones, Bryan revealed his thoughts in a quickly composed article that spoke of his happiness with Wilson's nomination because he "is evidently very acceptable to the country." He considered the governor's "greatest asset" to be the fact that he joined in opposing Parker for the temporary chairmanship, but noted that probably his weakest point was "his former utterances" (i.e. when the governor had made disparaging remarks about Bryan in the past). However, he did concede that Wilson would "poll more of the progressive Republican vote than any other man we could have named." With considerably more sincerity, Bryan took the occasion to express his continued admiration for Champ Clark. The speaker was less magnanimous, grumbling that the nomination was lost "through the vile, malicious slanders of Bryan!" However, he, too, agreed to support Wilson.[48]

Much was made in the press (and in several subsequent accounts as well) of the supposed influence upon Roger Sullivan of his son, Boetius. Most of these stories originated with Joseph Tumulty, Wilson's private secretary. As he recounted it, it was his understanding that the younger Sullivan had become enamored with the governor years before in prep school when he heard him speak. Early in the campaign, so the account ran, he sought to convince his father to support Wilson, but was told that there was no reasonable alternative but to back Clark. In the end, Boetius, Tumulty recounted, won his mother, Helen Sullivan, to the cause, while wringing the concession from Roger "to use his influence for [Wilson], if there were a break from Clark." Though the Clark managers tried to hold him back when the time came, so Tumulty explains, Roger Sullivan insisted that he "had a private promise to fulfill, and kept his word" and thus Woodrow Wilson received the nomination. Tumulty would stick to this story over the years and would include it in his 1921 book, *Woodrow Wilson as I Know Him*.[49]

Helen and Roger Sullivan with their daughter, Virginia Hopkins Sullivan, at the convention (Library of Congress, LC-DIG-hec-01728).

While the basic facts were correct, the conclusion was not. Boetius was an early admirer of Wilson, having heard the governor speak at Yale, probably on March 18, 1908, at the Phi Beta Kappa Dinner (the topic that night was "The Training of the Intellect"), and he did convert his mother. There can be no doubt either, that the two communicated their devotion to Roger, and, according to Wilson's managers, Helen Sullivan did argue to her husband that helping to nominate the governor would "be remembered to his credit," especially as he was talking of a political retirement (which did not happen for eight years). However, she also cleared up any misconception about their influence during an interview shortly after the nomination. She admitted that she "had first heard of Mr. Wilson, through my son when he was at Yale" (not at Lawrenceville as Tumulty recounted it), and that she had "been an admirer ever since." Moreover, she was sure the nomination of "Mr. Wilson is a wonderful thing for the young men, because they brought it about," and "because it will bring all the young men into the Party, and we will be like one big family." However, she balked at the suggestion that she and her son had unduly influenced her husband: "Neither I nor Boetius wanted Mr. Sullivan to break his instructions to Mr. Clark until he had fulfilled them" by voting for the speaker until he could not win. On the other hand, Woodrow Wilson, as noted, possessed qualities that Sullivan found admirable. He also would have recognized the need of nominating someone with a progressive reputation to match that of Roosevelt. At the same time, there can be no question that he valued his wife and son's opinions. However, to suggest that he would allow either to be decisive in a political decision of such magnitude is to misjudge the man entirely. Still, it made a good human interest story, and there was never a useful purpose in denying it further.[50]

In the end, "it was Bryan and Sullivan who did the trick." Bryan prepared the way by destroying the Clark candidacy, and stirring the convention into a deadlock; Sullivan motivated by fears of Bryan's intentions moved in exactly the right way and at exactly the right moment to help herd the convention reluctantly along towards the governor of New Jersey, a fact broadly recognized at the time. Even Hearst's *Chicago Examiner* grudgingly admitted "it was Sullivan and his associates that gave Wilson the nomination." Events made clear that had Sullivan moved too quickly, it probably would not have had a decisive effect (it came close to failing in any case); on the other hand, had he tarried longer, the impasse may have endured indefinitely, such were the contrary and volatile dynamics at work in the convention. His primary concern, like that of the other regulars, was to thwart his old adversary, whose nomination under any circumstances, he doubtlessly felt, would be a disaster for the country, the party, and himself. In this sense, the results of the convention of 1912 can be understood most broadly as an extension of the ideological polarity present in the party since 1896, and most narrowly as another in a concatenation of conflicts dating back to 1904 between Sullivan and Bryan. It was not to be their last.[51]

6

"A Man of Belial"
(1913–1914)

"It is unthinkable that he should be chosen for a seat in the Senate."—*The Commoner*, February 1914

Shortly after the adjournment of the 1912 Democratic convention, Sullivan and his wife, Helen, attended a gathering of the most influential members of the party at Woodrow Wilson's home in Sea Girt, New Jersey. When the governor greeted the Chicago leader, he promised "Mr. Sullivan" to "never forget Illinois" for its decisive role in his selection. Sullivan became one of the campaign advisors, meeting with the new national chair and Wilson manager, William McCombs on at least one occasion in New York City, and, more importantly, with the national committee when it convened in Chicago to strategize. He sat in by proxy, and with John Hopkins and William Skidmore, he served as an official host for the meeting. His chief contribution appears to have been insights into fund raising. He also used his influence to bring the party's western command center once again to the Windy City. Offices were opened in early August at the Sherman Hotel, which by this point was effectively the home office of the Sullivan Democracy.[1]

While his new public prominence underscored his position "as the head of his party in his state," it was of little importance to the Hearst-Harrison faction, which still commanded considerable strength within the local political culture. They, it was true, suffered some loss of prestige because Hearst, ostensibly because the Democratic Platform did not include a provision for a stronger navy, withheld his endorsement of Wilson, while continuing to provide good press for the mayor. But having been humiliated in Baltimore, Mayor Harrison and company were in no mood for peace. Sullivan and his allies were at this point equally immersed in an ebullition of hostility; no one had forgotten or forgiven the events the events of the previous spring at the Seventh Street Armory.[2]

However, powerful voices were demanding a united front. Most directly concerned were the party's nominees for the Cook County offices, many of whom were Harrison men, to be sure, but none of whom were pleased by the prospect of an election campaign hobbled by a divided and distracted leadership. Added to this were the blandishments of the party's gubernatorial candidate, Edward F. Dunne. Because the state Republicans, like their national counterparts, had divided along progressive and regular lines with two complete slates of candidates, he was expected to win and, therefore, exercised an inordinate influence. Against all precedent, he, rather than the state committee, took over the management of the Illinois campaign, placing his own man, William O'Connell (who had always had a good working relationship with Sullivan) in charge. Even more important than Dunne's calls for peace was the Wilson administration's insistence upon unity in this important electoral state.[3]

In response, a "peace committee," with Sullivan represented by Alderman Dennis Egan, and Harrison by the three emerging powers of his faction, Congressman Adolf Sabath, Maclay Hoyne, candidate for state's attorney, and Anton Cermak, candidate for bailiff of the municipal court (a patronage-rich position), met with Dunne to hammer out an agreement. Despite walk-outs, in September it was at last announced that an agreement had been reached dividing power within the party as a step towards reuniting the two competing Cook County Committees. However, just as a unified meeting was scheduled for September 12, 1912, at the Hotel Sherman, Adolph

Edward F. Dunne (Library of Congress, LCUSZ62-123215).

Sabath issued a statement withdrawing the "H-H" faction from the settlement. His stated reason was that the Sullivan men allegedly arranged a deal on the side with a number of projected campaign committee members that would effectively place two of their own in charge. According to Sabath, the selected pair was "personally and politically objectionable to our organization and to Mayor Harrison," as "was clearly understood by Mr. Sullivan." Besides, the Congressman insisted, it was his associates who, in any case, were the actual legal organization of the Cook County Democratic Party, and they were already committed to the election of Wilson and Dunne. He hoped, but apparently doubted, that "the so-called Sullivan organization" would do the same. Of course, while the "H-H" men could count upon the recognition of Judge John Owens of the County Court as well as that of the Election Commission, it had been Sullivan whose men had been legally legitimized by the national convention.[4]

The Sullivan Democracy responded by electing James J. Townsend, president of the Chicago Stock Exchange and member of the state Democratic committee, as chairman of the Democratic campaign committee of Cook County. A highly respected figure, it was hoped that he would be universally acceptable. But exasperated by the obstreperousness of the Harrison men, Townsend subsequently was only just convinced not to resign. In the end, both groups would conduct separate campaigns with their own committees and treasuries. This lack of coordination left to the candidates responsibility for most of the leg work. For the first time in the running battle between Sullivan and Harrison, factional interest assumed a greater importance than electoral success.[5]

Even the august presence of Woodrow Wilson, who arrived in Chicago on September 19, failed to inspire the appearance of unity. Rather, his visit was characterized by school-boy jostling for place among the various leaders of both aggregations (but not by Roger Sullivan, who was not present at the reception or other events). The Iroquois Club delegation, performing the function of official greeters, was dominated by Sullivan men, but Sabath took upon himself to escort the candidate and to make the introductions. He pointedly, but unsuccessfully, attempted to ignore Sullivan's proxy, John McGillen.[6]

Three weeks later the presidential candidate was back in town, and this time both sides were better organized in their determination to bask in Wilson's glory. It began before his arrival in Chicago, when the governor of New Jersey was met at 9:30 a.m. in Joliet by national committeeman Boeschenstein and state chair Charles, who arranged for their private rail car to be attached to his train. When the candidate arrived at Union Station, Mayor Carter Harrison was there to extend an official welcome. However, in the subsequent parade it was Boeschenstein and Arthur Charles who rode with Wilson; Mayor Harrison had to content himself with riding in another vehicle with Edward F. Dunne. Adding color to the proceedings were the two County Democracy marching clubs, contingents of the Iroquois and Jefferson Clubs, and impressive numbers of prominent members of both factions. The advance work was done well, and large and noisy crowds turned out throughout the day. Wilson delivered his first speech at noon at McVicker's Theater, where the sizable audience applauded and cheered his attacks upon Roosevelt and Taft. This was the mayor's moment as it was his privilege to introduce the candidate. Next came a luncheon at the Iroquois Club, where the governor was the guest of the mayor, Governor Dunne, and former Vice President Adlai Stevenson. After lunch, the guest of honor was treated to a "women's reception," but there was such a "bargain counter rush" by his feminine admirers that Boeschenstein, Charles, and other Sullivan lieutenants only just managed to keep the governor from being mobbed.[7]

The main event was an evening address at the Sullivan bastion, the Seventh Regiment Armory, in which Wilson went on the offensive against his two opponents, the "system," and the special interests. A crowd of 6,000 produced the appropriate cacophony, but as the candidate was seated an untoward moment occurred. Either through design or by accident, the chair of the meeting, James Townsend, adjourned the proceedings at about 8:45 p.m. just as Mayor Harrison was rising in response to calls (probably by shills) for him to add a few words. The next day the mayor was livid, disowning all connection to the meeting: "Is this the brand of harmony these so-called Democrats are handing out?" he complained. "The mayor of Chicago … was ready to raise his voice on behalf of Gov. Wilson, Mr. Dunne, and the county and city candidates, but the blind jealousy of men like McGillen blocked the way to satisfy their hatred!"[8]

Townsend denied any intention of insulting the mayor, claiming that he had ended the meeting as soon as the scheduled speeches had concluded. The mayor had made no request to speak, but if he had, "he certainly would have been accorded instant recognition." Moreover, it was the general understanding that Governor Wilson wished to depart as quickly as possible for Canton, Ohio. Roger Sullivan, for once, was spared any direct criticism as he was not present at any of the proceedings in keeping with the lower profile he had been affecting since the national convention.[9]

However, for once, the Democrats of Cook County and Illinois could afford to be divisive. With the GOP divided nationally into Republican and Progressive Parties, both with separate tickets down to the local level, there was little chance that even fractious

Democrats could find a way to lose. In the event, November 5, 1912, proved to be a very good day to be a Democrat in Chicago and Illinois. For president, Illinois returned for Wilson 405,408, Roosevelt 386,478, and Taft 253,593, adding the state's twenty-nine electoral votes to the Democrat's national majority. Dunne also prevailed with 443,120 to Progressive Frank Funk's 303,401 and Deneen's 318,469. With him were elected Democrats as lieutenant-governor (the generally Sullivan-friendly Barratt O'Hara), secretary of state, auditor of public accounts, state treasurer, and attorney general (Sullivan's ally Patrick J. Lucey). Of the state's twenty-five congressmen, twenty were now Democrats (up eleven from the previous election), with just four Republican (down from fourteen), and one Progressive (from Chicago). In Cook County the Democrats won almost every office, including a very hard-fought contest for State's Attorney that saw the election of Maclay Hoyne. Anton J. Cermak was also victorious in his quest to become Municipal Bailiff. The Republicans did just manage to hold on to the presidency of the county board, the coroner's office, and the chief justiceship of the municipal court.[10]

However, victory also brought new complications to the already divided makeup of the Democratic Party in Illinois. At a stroke, a third major force was created in the person of the governor-elect, Edward F. Dunne. In his early career as a judge, Dunne never aligned himself with any of the party's factions; although when he was mayor and Carter Harrison was in California, he had cultivated an uneasy peace with Sullivan. Even his unsuccessful bid in the 1911 mayoral primary against Harrison was an entirely personal endeavor. He was, therefore, not obligated to either side. Now as governor-elect, he directed the distribution of state patronage based entirely upon his own interests. He was not exactly focused upon creating his own organization—he was not that kind of politician—but he understood the advantages of creating his own cadre of state appointees. In time, Dunne would move closer to Harrison to create what would be labeled the "reform wing" of the state party. Often it would function as little more than the agency of Wilson's appointee as Secretary of State and Sullivan's nemesis, William Jennings Bryan, but for the moment the governor-elect was aligned with neither the Sullivan Democracy nor the Hearst-Harrison faction.[11]

Dunne immediate concern was the organizing of the state legislature. In the House an impasse quickly developed over the selection of a speaker, which was necessary before the governor-elect could be inaugurated. With complex private agenda and real policy divisions like that over the restriction of alcoholic beverages in play, the fight went on for weeks. Finally, Roger C. Sullivan stepped in and provided a solution in the person of William Michael McKinley (1879–1964), a representative from Cook County (not to be confused with Champaign, Illinois Republican congressman, United States senator, traction operator and philanthropist, William Brown McKinley 1856–1926) who was elected on the seventy-seventh ballot.

"Although generally known as a Sullivan man," the new speaker also backed Dunne and was active on his behalf in the Twenty-Fifth ward club of Chicago during the primary; the governor would label him "a young man of good character, and a progressive democrat [sic]." McKinley pledged his full support of the governor-elect's legislative goals. But even with the full weight of Sullivan and Dunne behind him, it was a bitter battle, and in the end the new speaker received more votes from Republicans than Democrats. This prompted charges of some kind of bipartisan deal (bipartisanship being a pejorative epithet after the Lorimer scandal), which were probably true and likely involved committee assignments[12]

Thereafter, Sullivan, as had become his rule, largely stayed out of the legislature's affairs. Late in the session, however, he took the occasion to expound expansively upon the benefits of the "short ballot," a change advocated by many progressives, but which would not make it to the legislative floor in 1913. As he interpreted it, this would mean the reduction of the state executive branch to two elected positions, the governor and the lieutenant-governor. In Chicago, only the mayor would be chosen at the polls. All others should be appointed by these executives, he argued, as a sacrifice of democracy for efficiency. He even went so far as to disagree with his lieutenants, calling for the passage of a bill then pending in the legislature to eliminate partisan labels in elections. After Sullivan left for his much-anticipated vacation before the end of the session, John McGillen, a leading light of the Sullivan Democracy, lobbied successfully against the measure. For Roger C. Sullivan, boss of one of the strongest political machines in the country, to embrace progressive reforms that struck at the heart of organizational politics, and in doing so disagreeing openly with many of his associates was, at the least, unexpected (though he took no apparent action), while also speaking to his thoughts about the future.[13]

Sullivan departed Chicago for South America on May 14, accompanied by former mayor, John P. Hopkins, the Reverend Father Edward A. Kelly, chaplain of the Seventh Regiment of the Illinois National Guard, and the Reverend Father James F. Callahan of St. Malachy's church. They traveled by train to New York City, where they caught the Lambert & Holt liner, the *S.S. Vasari*. The *Chicago Tribune* reported as front page news that the ship's departure was delayed for fifteen minutes as cases of seasick "medicine," donated by concerned friends, were loaded from a tug. Just as this task was completed, another truck rolled up with still more "medicine," making for twenty-five cases in all. Though the abundance of liquid refreshment was more reflective of the devotion of others then it was of the traveler's appetites, nevertheless, Roger and company set out thus well fortified against any and all perils. The little party voyaged first to Uruguay, then on to Argentina and Brazil. Sullivan was reportedly aghast at the apparent widespread corruption present in the three countries[14]

They next caught a boat for Portugal, from where they journeyed by train through Spain to Paris. Here they met up with Roger's wife Helen, his daughter, Virginia, and Hopkins' sister, Adelia. In the French capital, George Ade, family friend, humorist, fabulist, playwright, and frequent columnist for the *Chicago Tribune*, (once called the "twentieth century Aesop") was invited to join the explorers. Spontaneously, it was decided to add the Russian empire to the itinerary. It was apparently a challenging experience; Ade later labeled the excursion as an "aftercurse." [sic]. Warsaw, Moscow, where Roger was presented by admirers with a silver-tipped walking stick, and St. Petersburg were among the cities visited. Afterwards the party traveled to England via Berlin. On August 23, 1913, they set sail from England for New York City aboard the luxury liner, the *R.M.S. Lusitania* (the sinking of which by German torpedoes in May 1915, nearly brought the United States into World War I). Among their fellow passengers in First Class were Senator Elihu Root and the Chief Justice of the United States Supreme Court, Edward White.[15]

The "boys" back home decided to arrange a royal welcome for their chief, and what was essentially the entire upper tier of the leadership of the Sullivan Democracy were all there with son, Boetius Sullivan, waiting at the Cunard Pier. Roger disembarked wearing "a rainbow shirt" ("one of those things one always gets in Paris"). He was duly grateful and flattered, and treated everyone to an informal dinner that night at the Waldorf, where he, his family, and companions had taken rooms. He tried to avoid political questions from the press, but conceded that, as a matter of principle, he disagreed with his men on the Cook County Board who recently blocked appropriations to fund a fraud inquiry into the local elections of the previous November (later he would break with the men entirely over this issue). He was more expansive a few days later upon his return to Chicago on the *Twentieth Century Limited*. Exhibiting his new affectation of smoking gold-tipped cigarettes, he expounded upon some of his current thinking. He did not mean to "knock" Chicago, he explained "because I think it is the finest and greatest city, bar none," but he felt that local government might benefit from Berlin's example by substituting a city manager, as an "efficiency expert," for a mayor. This office, he declared, doubtlessly with some thought of its current occupant, was "an obsolete ornament." He also endorsed the construction of a municipal subway, and he expressed his pleasure at the passage of statutory woman's suffrage by the state legislature stating: "The granting of women the vote was inevitable, and is welcomed so far as I am concerned."[16]

James J. Brady, left, Urey Woodson, Boetius Sullivan and Ben. F. Mitchell greet Roger at the dock (Library of Congress, LC-DIG-ggbain-14359).

Helen Quinlan Sullivan's views on woman's suffrage were also recorded by the press. She decried what she labeled as "militancy" among English feminists and their tendency towards tactical violence in their quest to secure the vote. She recounted her shock at the threatening tone of a suffragette meeting witnessed in London. On the other hand, she had nothing but praise for the "French woman," who not only eschewed "atrocious styles one sees on some women here," but who is "her husband's partner in everything." She felt pleased to believe that American women were most like the French, using "brains instead of coercion as witness the recent history in Illinois." Indeed, in her judgment, the ladies of America were "the world's brightest and most distinctive wherever you go."[17]

Roger and his party had an excellent time on their journey. Reporters were especially struck by his appearance of good health, looking as if he had shed twenty-five pounds and ten years. He was clearly refreshed and prepared to take on new challenges. Within days, reports began appearing that Roger Sullivan was planning a run for the United States Senate.[18]

First visual impressions aside, Roger Sullivan was far from the stereotypical crusty and seamy big city "boss" imbued with greed and a lust for power. As he had forcibly argued before the Municipal Voters League in August 1910, it was a characterization he felt deeply and vehemently rejected. As one political commentator explained years later: "While most politicians have the skin of a rhinoceros, Roger was as sensitive as a woman. The barbs hurled at him by his opponents, hurt him deeply. He would grieve for hours over an unfriendly reference to himself in the newspapers."[19]

As this quote implies, he was a man of genuine sensitivity, a dignified man, whose core values were rooted in his family and his religion. He was blessed with an intellect that, like most of his public utterances, was measured and logical, and this, with his natural gifts for human fellowship, served him well in business and in politics.

By 1913, he was a multimillionaire through legitimate venture capitalism, admittedly augmented by opportunities present in his political prominence, and he was the most powerful man in the most powerful political faction seen in Illinois. Moreover, as a national committeeman and kingmaker, he walked comfortably in the corridors of national power, influencing the policies and future of his party and country, even rising so far as to confront repeatedly on an equal basis William Jennings Bryan, one of the predominant figures of the age. It was, therefore, entirely reasonable, from his point of view, that he felt both prepared and worthy to seek the broader horizons promised by entry in the United States Senate. Who could question that Sullivan would fit neatly into that august body, where most members were either leaders, like Senator Robert LaFollette of Wisconsin, or representatives, like Senator John Kern of Indiana, of state party machines? He knew many of them, and would command immediate respect. Certainly, too, Roger Sullivan was as qualified as most already there, and easily as capable as J. Hamilton Lewis, or Illinois' other sitting senator, Republican Lawrence Y. Sherman. With his abilities and influence, he could emerge from the relative obscurity of intraparty celebrity into the public light as a recognized national leader. It would just be an added benefit that he also would be able to counter Lewis' often contrary voice in Washington, especially in matters of patronage.

However, it was not just a question of ambition. Sullivan, it was true, used the political and business systems as he found them to his advantage, but he was also a man of his times. Widely read and thoughtful, he had been making it clear, with increasing frequency in recent years, that he, too, understood the need for key reforms. Like many businessmen, he accepted that government regulation was necessary to preserve and protect competition from monopoly. Although an organizational politician, he had long backed primaries (which he usually won) to allow for the direct selection of party candidates. He supported women's suffrage, and revealed civic mindedness in being a sponsor of Daniel Burnham's famous 1909 City Plan for renovating Chicago's waterfront. He consistently stood with civil service reform (with one exception, in 1906, when he objected not to the principle but a specific part of a specific bill), for which, as early as 1910, he was recognized by the National Civil Service League. Sullivan also approved a series of very progressive planks in his party's state platforms. Nor was all of this simply the product of cynical manipulation. He had not, for instance, opportunistically embraced municipal ownership simply because of its popularity.[20]

In his own mind and those of a considerable body of politicos as well, he was a progressive businessman and political leader able and obligated to make a greater contribution. Now with the election of Woodrow Wilson, a man who many felt had the potential to be the greatest Democrat since Thomas Jefferson, a unique opportunity for service and advancement seemed to be presenting itself. Who could doubt that Roger Sullivan with his political gifts would be a major asset in the nation's capital for Wilson and the further implementation of his program, so grandly labeled the "New Freedom?" Moreover, as the Seventeenth Amendment to the United States Constitution, which provided for the direct election of senators by the people, was on the verge of ratification, he would achieve, if chosen by the voters, a complete legitimacy—and legitimacy, or at least respectability, was becoming important for Roger Sullivan.

Such must have been the direction of Sullivan's thoughts over the summer months of his travels through South America and Europe. The suddenness of the revelations of his interest in office suggests long conversations during the trip with his wife and John P. Hopkins in which every possible aspect was weighed and analyzed. Yes, he had long been a convenient whipping boy of the professional reformers, and yes, he had important enemies in Carter Harrison, William Jennings Bryan and others, but with his organization and a trust in the effectiveness of an honest appeal over their heads to the voters, a primary victory seemed more than possible. In addition, with the Progressive Party showing as yet no sign of fading away in the state, and the formerly Republican vote thus remaining divided, the prospects for electoral success were good.

Throughout the fall of 1913, the Sullivan campaign quietly moved forward. Initially, Roger neither affirmed nor denied his candidacy, which had the desired effect of maintaining interest. Only in stages did he allow his intentions to become clear. At a meeting of the Bobby Burke version of the County Democracy marching club (Burke having changed factional sides again), held on November 23, 1913, presided over by Cook County Clerk Robert M. Sweitzer, and graced by the presence of John McGillen, chair of the Sullivan version of the Cook County Committee, he was acclaimed as the ideal candidate for the senate, deserving and true. Had he not helped Woodrow Wilson win the nomination? Had he not for years led the party "without selfish motive?" The object of the fulsome praise was not present, but a week later, he led the ceremonies at a special New Year's party held at the Second Regimental Armory at Peoria Street and Washington Boulevard. Thirty-five hundred noisy and boisterous faithful friends (the Harrison party at 167 Randolph was not nearly so well attended) cheered their leaders, many of whom engaged in stirring perorations extolling Roger Sullivan's qualities as a potential United States senator. The program climaxed with a short speech by the man himself. He chose to avoid all direct reference to his possible candidacy, but he called upon everyone to follow Woodrow Wilson: "If we take up his theories and practices, there will be no apologies to make." The Seventh Regimental Armory band then struck up "Top o' the Morning," resolutions endorsing the national administration were passed, and all went home well-fortified to meet the challenges of the New Year.[21]

On January 17, 1914, Roger Sullivan at last issued a formal statement of intent. It was characteristically straightforward and businesslike without flourishes and frills. He made no claim that "insistent demands from all parts of the state" were compelling his candidacy. Yes, he had "many loyal and warm friends," who were urging him to run, but he was not going to "make a false start by pretending to be a coy or reluctant candidate." Why was he running? Because the honor of representing Illinois in the senate was "great enough for any man's ambition," and because he felt that in these times of change he had something to offer.[22]

What followed was a manifesto of his political beliefs, and they were remarkably Jeffersonian and progressive, not unlike those "of the large majority of thinking men in the country." He argued for new policies to meet the new challenges of the times under the banner of "democratic government for a democratic people." And what were the defining natures of these new challenges?

> The biggest problem of today is how to secure the greatest measure of comfort and happiness for our neighbor as well as for ourselves. This focuses attention at the problem at our doors—on the problems of the farm, the factory, and the mine; on how to have better homes, better working conditions, better business conditions, in other words, better conditions for everybody based upon the realization that the welfare of the individual everywhere is inseparably interwoven with that of the community. The rights of the individual are to be preserved, even if by so doing so the rights of the combined are curbed.[23]

In what was certainly a self-reference, he proclaimed that "the wise corporation manager of today is prepared to meet the new order of things," and to accept that "business organizations, especially public service corporations" have to accept either governmental regulation or governmental ownership. "The everyone-for-himself-and-devil-take-the-hindmost policy," of laissez-faire government recently so pervasive "has seen its best days." It was simple; fairness had to be reintroduced in society and the economy.[24]

Of course, the best way to bring this about was to back Woodrow Wilson, a president with the vision and leadership abilities of a Lincoln, now so necessary in these volatile times to lead the country to better things, and he, Roger Sullivan, was prepared to do his part. Moreover, he wanted it made clear that he stood unafraid to take his case directly to the Democrats in the primary and the voters in the election. He would abide with the people's will.[25]

To enhance his credibility, and to help shield himself from the inevitable "gas boodler" charges, he divested himself in the fall of 1913 of his last interests in the Ogden Gas Company and the Cosmopolitan Electric Company. They became the complete property of the People's Gas and Coke Company and the Commonwealth Edison Company, both now part of the massive utility system created regionally by Samuel Insull. After his arrival in Chicago in 1892 to become president of Chicago Edison, Insull cultivated a relationship with Sullivan that developed, through a growing mutual respect for the other's political and business acumen, into a personal friendship that ended only with Roger's death. They became friends with apparently some business ties. Some accounts, including that of Insull himself, have their relationship dating to their meeting on a ship bound from Europe in 1904, but in light of their shared interest in municipal utility matters, it is likely that they became aware of each other earlier. In truth, the Ogden Gas and Cosmopolitan Electric companies were after 1907 and 1909, respectively, with their facilities and products being leased out, little more than paper organizations in which Roger and his late brother, Gene, served as officers and drew salaries. Most of their value resided in their franchises not their facilities.

Consequently, Sullivan and the other shareholders were not giving up much, especially if the news reports were true and a handsome profit was realized from the deal. How much of a profit is difficult to ascertain as the structure of the transactions was complex involving leases, assumption of debt and installment payments, including shares of stock and cash, that stretched out over years, but at the time, one newspaper report placed the sale price of the assets of the Cosmopolitan Company alone at five million dollars. Under the terms of the Ogden deal, People's Gas, Light & Coke Company and Commonwealth Edison were to continue to lease all the company's facilities and assets, and simultaneously begin the process of purchase, agreeing to make payments to the remaining stockholders until December 31, 1945. By that time, the total amount to be paid was scheduled to exceed twenty-four million dollars. However, as early as 1920, it was recognized that the actual worth of the assets was closer to 1.7 million dollars, and in 1936 and 1941, the company wrote off the physical plant it acquired from the Ogden company as obsolete in an effort to reduce its property taxes.[26]

While the rewards from his investments in the Ogden and Cosmopolitan companies were certainly significant, it can be assumed that those involved on the other side of the transaction were equally astute businessmen in valuing the sale; it was worth a great deal just to eliminate a potential competitor. Most accounts regarding Sullivan's utility interests have been over-simplified and/or based upon questionable guesses and rumors perpetuated by political opponents (most especially Carter H. Harrison) to the point where they have become apocryphal and probably as reflective of the politically charged assumptions that surrounded Sullivan as of the truth. However, he must have been gratified by what were clearly the advantageous terms of the sale, and as he had long chaffed under the pressure of the periodic rituals of reformist outrage for his connection with the Ogden Company, this final disassociation would have been a relief.

Sullivan was not the only Democrat attracted by the opportunity for service in the senate. Soon others of disparate prominence were making similar announcements. Leading the lists were Lieutenant-Governor Barratt O'Hara (despite his general closeness to Sullivan), Secretary of State Harry Woods, Congressman Lawrence B. Stringer, and downstater, James Traynor, a minor candidate. None of these presented themselves as the anti–Sullivan candidate. But powerful forces involving the usual sources began to stir as soon as Sullivan's intention became known. Mayor Carter Harrison for a few weeks publicly threatened to become a candidate. When his bluff was called, he, knowing he had no chance in a state-wide primary, let the idea die. However, the mayor was to play the leading role behind the scenes in the months ahead in the effort to thwart his factional rival. Others were more immediately open in organizing their opposition.[27]

On December 23, 1913, a meeting was held in Springfield to create the "Wilson-Bryan League." Although it could boast the endorsement of neither the president nor the secretary of state, its name reflected the conceit of its organizers that it was they who embodied downstate Democratic progressivism, and who were, therefore, the legitimate representatives of the national administration. The League's driving force was Carl

Vrooman, a wealthy (he was educated at both Harvard and Oxford) farmer from Bloomington, who was flirting with the idea of entering the senate race. Vrooman and his family also provided much of the organization's funding. Two months later a formal banquet was held to discuss unifying the anti–Sullivan forces behind one candidate. Among the names considered were Vrooman, Kent E. Keller of Ava, Frank D. Comerford of Chicago, and state senator D. Duff Piercy, none of whom was deemed to be of sufficient stature to attract broad support. Consequently, no one was endorsed. Significantly, too, O'Hara, and Woods refused to become involved. In the months ahead, the League was to be an irritant to Sullivan's campaign, but "gained no actual power." Effective opposition would have to come from elsewhere.[28]

Governor Dunne was certainly not inclined to take on the Chicago leader. He was never a factional warrior, and Sullivan's strength was such that defeating him in the primaries was problematic in any case. Even success in turning back him back, however, would not eliminate his influence, which would be critical for the governor's renomination two years hence. Similarly, William O'Connell, the governor's primary political advisor, declined involvement. Nor was Senator J. Hamilton Lewis interested. He shortly issued a statement that he "was out of politics" as far as the senatorial nomination was concerned. Outside of the Wilson-Bryan League, only Mayor Carter H. Harrison continued to agitate for a united effort, allegedly to protect the progressive integrity of the party. Harrison's determination was strengthened by an April 1914 local primary victory over the Sullivan men, which returned control of the Cook County Committee to his faction, and the job as its chair to his main lieutenant, Adolph Sabath. However, for all of Harrison's bluster, as things stood, no challenge to Sullivan's candidacy would emerge from the more-or-less ephemeral "reform wing" of the Cook County and state parties unless something extraordinary and unexpected intervened.[29]

And of course something did. Perhaps inevitably, William Jennings Bryan, Sullivan's nemesis and the master of the extraordinary, moved in. Breaking with the Wilson administration, which consistently sought neutrality in the Illinois senatorial primary, the Secretary of State interceded dramatically with an editorial in the February edition of his newspaper, *The Commoner*. It was a clarion call for battle. Under the title of: *SULLIVAN, SENATOR? NO!*, he issued a *ukase* declaring that the "the democrats [sic] of Illinois should know it [is] … time to thwart his purpose, for it is unthinkable that he should be chosen for a seat in the United States Senate!" Why? Because Sullivan: " is to the democratic [sic] party, what Senator Lorimer was to the republican [sic] party," and would, he predicted, destroy all hopes for electoral success in the state in the fall elections.[30]

Bryan's initial instinct was to induce Governor Dunne to enter the race. The governor dutifully traveled to the nation's capital for a consultation, followed by a pilgrimage to New York City, to meet William Randolph Hearst. However, when he returned to Illinois, he announced that he was "not a candidate in any sense of the word." It was far from certain that he could win either the primary or the election, and he was unwilling to risk sacrificing the good-will of the Sullivan Democracy towards his own renomination and reelection in 1916. He did agree, however, to work with Bryan and Harrison to help identify a suitable candidate to oppose the Chicago leader.[31]

The problem was that none of the men running, or those who could be convinced to run, seemed a good choice. Bryan initially supported Vrooman, who had by now declared his candidacy. However, because he was relatively new and unknown throughout the state, and because he "had been so thoroughly stamped with the 'dry' idea [on the issue of the prohibition of liquor] that his candidacy would be a difficult one to make in Cook County," he was eliminated from consideration. More acceptable for Bryan, Dunne, and Harrison, was Congressman Henry T. Rainey of the Twentieth District. He was a dynamic politician with a solid progressive record, but he refused even Bryan's direct appeals. Failing here, the Secretary of State next suggested his old friend and ally, Judge Owen P. Thompson. He had long stood against Sullivan, and was Bryan's state campaign manager in 1908, but otherwise he had few factional enemies. Governor Dunne thought well enough of Thompson to have appointed him to the new Public Utility Commission. However, Chicago politician that he was, the governor was concerned about Thompson's dry proclivities. Nonetheless, Dunne arranged a meeting and offered his endorsement. Thompson, too, declined, judging it to be "a political mistake" to run against the powerful Sullivan, a tribute to both the leader's influence and to the astuteness of Thompson's instincts.[32]

It was now early summer, and many progressive Democrats were becoming impatient. Carl Vrooman, who was actively campaigning against Sullivan, went so far as to imply that Dunne, and by implication, Bryan and Harrison, were playing into Roger's hands. In fact, though it was not yet general knowledge, the trio had found their man, Congressman and former gubernatorial candidate Lawrence Beaumont Stringer. He was considered earlier, but because of past associations with Sullivan, he was placed near the end of the list. The refusals of Rainey and Thompson, the press of time, and the fact that Stringer so clearly wanted the job now all worked in his favor. In addition, he met a criteria suggested by Mayor Harrison that their candidate be a downstate man. This would facilitate, so it was felt, the chances for a strong vote outside of Cook County, while also allowing Dunne to couch his opposition to Sullivan in terms of fairer and more equal representation of the state (Senator Lewis being from Chicago).

Stringer was a native of New Jersey where he was born in 1866. At the age of ten, he moved with his family to Lincoln, Illinois. He graduated in 1887 from the local Lincoln University (later Lincoln College, originally founded in 1865 by the Cumberland Presbyterian Church), and in 1896 from the Chicago College of Law. He set up a practice back in Lincoln, and in 1900, he was elected to the first of two terms in the Illinois senate. In 1904, he was the sacrificial Democratic gubernatorial candidate in that Republican year. However, in 1905, he was appointed by his electoral opponent, Governor Charles Deneen, to the Illinois State Court of Claims. While on the bench, he ran unsuccessfully for the United States Senate, and in 1913 he resigned the bench to begin a term as a congressman. Almost immediately following his election, he began to work for his party's senatorial nomination.[33]

On June 1, 1914, Governor Dunne began to lay the groundwork by issuing a statement calling for a candidate who was both a downstater and a Wilson-supporter. Six weeks later, he and Mayor Harrison formally endorsed Stringer, and were soon followed by Bryan. With the exceptions of James Traynor, Barratt O'Hara, Harry Woods, and, of course, Sullivan, the other candidates dropped out. Kent E. Keller went to work for Stringer, as did Vrooman, who soon took up the job of Assistant Secretary of Agriculture. After six months of maneuvering and indecision, and just six weeks before the primary, the leaders of the self-styled progressive Democrats at last had acted.[34]

While his opposition was uncertainly working its way towards finding a candidate, Roger Sullivan was waging a highly effective campaign. In late April, he opened an office at the Hotel Sherman. His campaign manager was national committeeman Charles

Boeschenstein. Not coincidentally, the Democratic state committee was headquartered in the same building, and though not formally endorsing his bid, was unsurprisingly friendly to his aspirations.[35]

Most downstate regulars, including some who had opposed him in the past, were also moving into the Sullivan camp; by the end of the campaign, he was claiming the endorsement of 23 of the 30 downstate delegates to the 1912 national convention. Part of this support was rooted in the desire to back a winner, but they were also responding to the most recent round of federal patronage distribution. Lewis and Dunne, backed by Bryan, did their best to monopolize the control of all federal appointments within the state much to the despair and anger of many downstate politicians. In both September and December 1913, Sullivan, with George Brennan in tow, traveled to Washington to press President Wilson, his secretary, Joseph Tumulty, and Secretary of the Treasury, William McAdoo for a fairer share of the plums. The trips were reported as successes and Roger as being all smiles. However, many of the Wilson administration's subsequent choices did not please many powerful Democrats outside of Chicago, Democrats, who could hardly be quiescent at the prospect of Dunne and Harrison, a former mayor and current mayor of Chicago, electing a second senator and tightening up their grip on federal jobs.[36]

Sullivan began soliciting votes, logically enough, in the distant reaches of southern Illinois where he was least known. He began creatively with an extensive automobile tour in a "remarkable and unique campaign, perhaps without precedent." Starting out on May 11, he spent eleven days visiting literally dozens of towns and villages like Centralia, Waterloo, Nashville, Mount Vernon, Carbondale, and Cairo. Eschewing bands and hoopla, he concentrated upon extemporaneous talks with small crowds in the streets that he would roam sometimes for hours during the day. The nights were reserved for slightly more formal gatherings in halls. Throughout he engaged in good-natured banter with the crowds and often in friendly debate with those present who had opposed him in the past.[37]

Concerning his reputation as a boss, he pointed out that his very presence underscored his determination to achieve office based upon a popular mandate rather than upon the machinations of an organization. He also enjoyed contrasting his open campaigning to the furtive conspiring of his opponents. As he explained in Edwardsville: "I have gone to the people directly and I question the right or propriety of the use of tactics [by the opposition], the underground variety particularly, which were sent to the scrap heap when the direct election of senators became an actual legal reality." Who was it, then, that was being true to reformist principle of trusting the people? And who was it that could claim a special relationship with President Woodrow Wilson? As to the fact that he came from Cook County, he made a convincing argument that the mutual dependency between Chicago and the downstate made the issue meaningless. For the most part, he generally kept his themes positive, and even went so far as to publicly welcome the efforts of Carl Vrooman, who began following after him around the state to speak in opposition.[38]

The "populist" tactic worked, "the natives responded with joy," and Sullivan's tour was effective in countering his image as a "big fish." One downstate Republican newspaper (the confusingly named *Carlinville Democrat*) grudgingly admitted that he "has convinced Egyptians that he has neither horns nor cloven feet, and that he is a right good fellow." Echoing this sentiment, one local leader confessed, after attending Sullivan's address before the student body of the Southern Illinois Normal University, that: "We came expecting to see a ward boss, one of your Chicago roughnecks…. Instead, we found a man who knows what he is talking about and is our friend."[39]

Literally kissing babies, Sullivan frustrated his opposition by refusing to engage in invective. Even editorial blasts from Bryan in February and March evoked only mild rebukes for meddling in the affairs of Illinois, and the most he would ever say about his chief antagonist was that he was an "ingrate" for forgetting past favors. In fact, it made little sense for him to engage at this point in any kind of dialogue. He was the front runner, and it served no good purpose to risk further alienation of those whose support he would covet after securing the nomination. Also, of course, it would be unwise to allow others to redefine the issues of the campaign. Lastly, Roger Sullivan simply refused to be intimidated or otherwise affected by the self-proclaimed moral superiority and self-righteousness of his political enemies, especially as he was well-aware of their own imperfections. He preferred to let the voters judge his candidacy based upon "my character as a man," and this ap-

Roger Sullivan campaigning, *Belleville News-Democrat,* October 21, 1914 (Sullivan family collection).

proach went far towards undercutting his enemies' hope of reducing him in the public perception to being little more than (in the words of one editorial writer) "a Man of Belial."[40]

And his antagonists' limited and badly coordinated efforts only lightened Sullivan's task. To be sure, Lawrence Stringer had been campaigning for months. However, his efforts were completely overshadowed by the activities of the triumvirate of Bryan, Dunne, and Harrison. Ironically, the Commoner, who initiated the crusade against Sullivan, did not come to Illinois. He appears to have been checked by President Wilson, whose displeasure over Bryan's public intervention was purposely leaked to the press. William F. McCombs, who was now chair of the Democratic National Committee, arrived in Chicago in July to make clear the administration's neutrality. Federal appointees were forbidden from performing "managerial duties for any candidate," or participating in the campaign "to the point where the question could be raised as to the loyalty to the primary nominee." In an obvious reference to the Secretary of State, McCombs declared that "the Democratic primary in Illinois should be conducted without any outside influence." Consequently, Bryan first used the excuse of "Washington business," and then the outbreak of a World War in Europe in late August to remain out of the state. Deprived of his usual forum, the stump, he was compelled to confine himself to occasional editorial blasts in *The Commoner,* and to a final letter just before the primary election in which he predicted the doom of the Illinois Democratic Party should Sullivan be nominated.[41]

Lawrence Stringer was naturally disappointed by the administration's attitude. As an original Wilson-man in Illinois, he felt he had the right to be treated as something more than as a "stranger and outsider." Privately, he lamented that the president's fear of "displeas[ing] Mr. Sullivan" was so great it prevented "a pleasant look in my direction." In truth, Wilson found himself between two powerful camps, not just in Illinois, but in his own administration, where men like McCombs and Joseph Tumulty worked to dilute Bryan's poisonous antipathy towards Roger Sullivan.[42]

This left Carter Harrison. Beginning on August 26, the mayor spoke at a series of massive rallies in Chicago. Contrary to expectations, and perhaps in a grudging response to Sullivan's purposeful avoidance of vituperation, he promised not to engage in "personalities," or to be "acrimonious." Supposedly, this was at the request of Stringer, who usually stood by the mayor's side at meetings attracting little attention. Nonetheless, Harrison found no difficulty in lambasting Sullivan for, among other things, not being a Democrat in the traditions of Stephen A. Douglas and Woodrow Wilson, causing the defeat of William Jennings Bryan in 1896, and being "a man of gas," whose business associations disqualified him for high office.[43]

On August 28, Governor Dunne joined the mayor, and used similar themes. Sullivan, it seemed, had not just repeatedly betrayed his party in refusing to back Bryan in 1896, and himself in 1907, but also had sabotaged his attempts as mayor to bring fairer gas prices to the city. Moreover, according to the governor, Roger Sullivan was a "corporation" man whose first instincts were to protect the power of the wealthy, who represented the "reactionary element of the party," and who would be the "weakest candidate." For the next two weeks, the governor, the mayor, and Stringer stumped throughout the city.[44]

Meanwhile, Sullivan was concentrating upon northern Illinois, where he was greeted everywhere by large and enthusiastic crowds. In Peoria on July 15, he addressed the question of who was the "progressive democrat [sic]" in the race, claiming to be unsure "what those who are so free with the term mean when they employ it." However, he was certain that he was at least a "constructive Democrat," who believed "in making the Democratic Party a constructive party," and who believed "in the constructive work that President Wilson is doing." He used the same theme in Chicago, though at one point he did feel constrained to express his perplexity at the absurdity of a "group of Chicagoans, all officeholders … attempting to defeat me with the anti–Chicago cry!" He also managed to slip in some indirect references to Bryan, by commenting that the "great curse" of recent Democratic politics was the "political quack" distributing his "nostrums and fakes."[45]

Sullivan's statements of support for the president and the national administration frustrated and angered his opponents, especially those who were the most ideologically driven. It was they, or so they clearly believed, who were the real progressives and who, therefore, had the right to claim Wilson's mantle. Perhaps Sullivan had helped the president get the nomination, but as one furious backer of Stringer explained, it was only after he had "stood supinely by" wishing "at heart" for the nomination of Clark. He only went for Wilson because he had no choice, and because he was being "pelted and bombarded by telegrams from the democratic [sic] proletariat at home in Illinois." How can this boss, it was wondered, claim to be a loyal Wilson-man, while at the same time attacking

William Jennings Bryan, the secretary of state? Roger Sullivan never was and never would be a progressive, but was simply "a great reactionary conservative."[46]

Of course, missing from this analysis was the fact that most of those now opposing Sullivan had, like the Chicago leader, waited until very late in the Baltimore convention to support the then governor of New Jersey. Dunne and Lewis were originally Clark men in line with their leader Bryan, and Carter Harrison had been openly hostile, both politically and personally, towards Wilson. Only Stringer could reference any pre-convention relationship, but this carried little apparent weight with the perfidious president. Strictly in terms of political obligation, Sullivan could make the stronger claim on Wilson, and concerning the president's national policies, the Chicago leader was as supportive as any of those who were now criticizing him.

Despite being by every indication far in the lead, he continued to work indefatigably. In the last days, he focused upon Chicago, where his campaign reached a climax with the spectacle of five separate parades simultaneously marching through the streets proclaiming his virtues. Eventually they combined to create an impressive procession eight miles long. This was followed by a massive rally of 10,000 at the Coliseum that went on until 1:00 a.m. on election eve. Just days earlier, on September 4, Roger Sullivan released his final campaign statement. As always, he expressed pride in having taken his case directly to the people in all 102 of Illinois' counties. And as always, he explained his candidacy in terms of his devotion to President Wilson: "There is but one desire and ambition back of my candidacy," he explained, "to serve the people and the interests of my state and to help, to the extent of my ability, in carrying forward the policies which have already marked Woodrow Wilson as the greatest constructive president we have had in generations."[47]

Primary day, September 9, 1914, dawned with the usual universal predictions of victory, but it was Sullivan who proved—as was usually the case—to be the best political prophet. He won with 141,008 votes or forty-seven percent. Stringer was a distant second with 109,928, or thirty-seven percent, followed by Illinois Secretary of State Harry Woods at 24,947 or eight percent, Lieutenant-Governor Barratt O'Hara with 14,160 or five percent, and James Traynor with 7,294 or just barely three percent. Cook County returned heavily for Sullivan, where his total of over 35,000 votes was almost enough in itself to guarantee the victory. Elsewhere, he did surprisingly well, which was a tribute to both his campaigning and his organization. In all, he secured majorities or pluralities in nineteen downstate counties including White, Clay, and Jasper. Making the night even more joyful were massive victories in the Cook County primaries by Sullivan's men against a combined Harrison-Dunne slate. Sweetest of all was the defeat for renomination of the County Judge John Owens by Thomas F. Scully. The events at the Seventh Regiment Armory in 1912 were now at least partially avenged.[48]

The state convention in Springfield on December 14 was another predictable affirmation of Sullivan's ascendency. Congressman Henry T. Rainey presided over what was essentially a political spectacle; the only offices not predetermined by the primary were the trustees of the University of Illinois, and nobody much cared about them. Governor Dunne spoke in broad generalities about harmony and the foibles of the Republicans, but it was Roger Sullivan who was the center of attention as the senatorial nominee and keynote speaker. It was the most important address of his career. Heretofore, his speaking was confined to party gatherings or the stump. Now his task was to present himself as a statesman and a comrade-in-arms of Woodrow Wilson, worthy to enter the United States Senate.[49]

He began modestly, disparaging his words as "poor things," but assuring his listeners that it would not be with words with which he would "repay the faith" shown to him by the Democratic voters. Then, using his usual "crisp sentences," he launched a scathing attack on the G.O.P., arguing that despite the election of "Conservative Republicans, progressive Republicans, standpat Republicans, and reactionary Republicans," the country kept falling prey to predatory economic interests. To tremendous cheers, he decried the sixteen years of Republican rule before 1912 as "an era of economic reversion to the law of tooth and claw." This "cant and hypocrisy" facilitated the "wickedness of interlocking directorates" and economic monopoly. Only the election of Woodrow Wilson brought salvation, and it was his New Freedom with its downward revision of the tariff, its currency reform through the Federal Reserve Act, its strengthening of trust regulation in the Clayton Anti-Trust Act, and, not incidentally, its support of the Seventeenth Amendment bringing the direct election of United States Senators, that restored the nation to its people by freeing them from the influence of "big business." Moreover, it was not just domestic issues that mandated the need to reelect Woodrow Wilson, but also the world crisis brought by the onset of war in Europe. All could be confident that the wisdom of the president would keep the United States at peace. Sullivan received a tremendous ovation and demonstration. However, the success of his speech was belied by the underlying bitterness of much of his opposition.[50]

Lawrence B. Stringer, for instance, was privately furious, not so much at Sullivan, but at the Wilson administration, for being ignored. Still, he hoped the president would understand when passing out patronage that his "defeat was not a defeat" because he had had only six weeks before the primary after the belated endorsements of Dunne, Harrison, and Bryan, and because his campaign was conducted on a shoestring budget with a paltry volunteer staff. Against "the strongest organization known in the history of the state" and "inexhaustible resources," he felt that he did extremely well, and, most importantly, hoped that Wilson and Bryan would not forget his service to the progressive cause. Stringer, lately the great hope of the "reform wing," also makes clear his disinclination to help his party's senatorial nominee. As he no longer commanded much influence, this was of little consequence. Of far greater moment was an ongoing defection of a sizable body of liberal Democrats to the Progressive Party senatorial nominee, Raymond Robins.[51]

He had long been a political irritant. Although to many little more than a political gadfly and bohemian, Robins was to others an astute and dedicated reformer deserving of an influential voice. His was certainly an interesting life. Born in Staten Island, New York on September 17, 1873, Robins attended local schools in Ohio, Kentucky, and Florida, and graduated with a degree in law from Columbian University (now George Washington University) in Washington, D.C. He began a promising legal career in San Francisco, but then in 1897 went to the Alaskan Klondike to seek gold. Stories of the discovery of a vast fortune would follow him for the rest of his life, stories that at times he encouraged. However, while apparently self-sufficient, he never displayed great wealth. But it was about at this time that he found a greater personal treasure in Christianity, and became a Congregational minister. Thereafter, he devoted himself to his own vision of the social gospel by seeking to fulfill the mission of Christ through working to address societal problems, particularly as they affected the poor.

In 1901, he came to Chicago, which he believed to be the true financial center of the country and therefore of power, where he established himself as an advocate of the rights of working people. Mayor Harrison in 1903 appointed him as head of the Municipal

Lodging House. Around this time, he acquired a wife, Margaret Dreier, a remarkable woman who shared her husband's dedication to social activism. In the elections of 1905, Robins backed Republican John Maynard Harlan against Edward F. Dunne, but when the Democrat was elected, he offered his services. This began a cordial and enduring relationship. Dunne was sufficiently impressed to have appointed Robins in 1906 to the Board of Education. There he joined such other progressive luminaries as Jane Addams and Louis Freeland Post. The board pursued what many judged to be a "radical" agenda, especially in its accommodation of the desires of the Chicago Federation of Teachers and its leader Margaret Haley. The controversy this engendered led Mayor Busse upon taking office in 1907 to remove Robins and most of Dunne's other appointees. This resulted in a lengthy lawsuit that did eventually bring about their reinstatement but only just before their terms expired. After 1905, Robins presented himself as an anti–Sullivan Democrat, allying himself with the state forces associated with Bryan. In 1912, however, he moved into the Progressive Party, and subsequently served briefly as its state chair. Now in 1914, at the personal request of Theodore Roosevelt, he accepted his young party's senatorial nomination.[52]

Robins' candidacy was a source of real concern for Sullivan. Most importantly, it was a threat to his strategy of identifying himself with the progressivism of Woodrow Wilson in contrast to the more conservative Republican nominee, incumbent Lawrence Y. Sherman. At the same time, though he professed not to care, he could not have been pleased with the drain of party support and resources that came with the creation of the Democrats for Raymond Robins League. Many previously associated with the Wilson-Bryan League, including the new Assistant Secretary of Agriculture, Carl Vrooman, who actually came back to Illinois to campaign, jumped on the Robins bandwagon, as did many other liberal Democrats including Jane Addams and John J. Fitzpatrick, president of the Chicago Federation of Labor (which officially endorsed Robins) as well as national figures like Oklahoma's Senator Robert Owen, and Nebraska senator and Republican George Norris.[53]

Discouraging, too, was the fact that Democratic leaders like Governor Dunne, who was usually a guardian angel of party regularity, uttered not a word of reproach against those who were now abandoning their party. Although all formal opposition ended with the primary, and the governor and the mayor of Chicago reluctantly agreed to honor the outcome, their endorsements were often faint and even damning. In the closing weeks of the campaign, Dunne traveled to Chicago, and appeared with Sullivan, but confined most of his speeches to generalizations. On the other hand, Harrison, who also spoke extensively in the city, pointedly refused to mention his rival's name. Even when his party's senatorial candidate appeared unannounced at rallies at which he was speaking, Mayor Harrison declined to acknowledge his presence. Any thought that Sullivan's success in securing the senatorial nomination might dampen, even temporarily, the bitter factional divide proved to be unfounded. In early October, a unified Cook County Committee was organized based upon the wishes of Harrison, whose followers lost many of the nominations in the county primary, but won a majority of ward committeemen slots. Sullivan men were barely included.[54]

To counter the Progressive candidate and the defectors in his own party, as well as to lend credibility to his central theme of support for the national administration, Sullivan needed a direct endorsement from Woodrow Wilson. For months, Joseph Tumulty, the president's political secretary was importuned by various prominent Illinois Democrats for a letter of support. Among these was Congressman Henry T. Rainey. Although opposing Sullivan in the primary—he attended the founding banquet of the Wilson-Bryan League—he was now calling for unity behind his candidacy. He soon took upon himself the task of extracting a formal statement of support from Wilson. On October 23, he made his case to Tumulty that there was nothing "unreasonable when I ask that the choice of the Democrats in a fairly conducted Primary [sic] be endorsed by the President," especially as it "would mean many thousand votes for Mr. Sullivan." Moreover, something needed to be done to counterbalance Carl Vrooman, whose plan to ignore the administration's directive and speak for Robins in the state was now public knowledge. Three drafts of an endorsement were actually composed. Tumulty and William McCombs, chair of the Democratic National Committee both urged the president to act. But the much-coveted statement was not forthcoming. On October 25, Rainey wrote Tumulty again, this time to express his disappointment "that we have been unable to obtain for Mr. Sullivan and our Illinois ticket the endorsement of the president," and his concern that this failure would "cost us many thousands of votes in Illinois." However, he remained hopeful that the president might yet relent and repay his political debt.[55]

He never did. Loyally, Tumulty would later seek to explain that the idea "was countermanded by one of the advisors close to Sullivan" supposedly for fear of offending Theodore Roosevelt who was about to begin a tour of the state. It is unclear to whom Tumulty is referring, and the notion that anyone in the Illinois Democracy would be concerned about discomfiting the former president was a departure from reality. What is certain is that the candidate himself, Rainey, State Chair Arthur Charles, and virtually the entire Democratic establishment outside of Carter Harrison, Edward F. Dunne, and their allies, vainly sought the president's formal blessing.

Perhaps not least in Wilson's thinking was William Jennings Bryan, who was using his considerable influence to undercut anything that would assist Sullivan; indeed, one newspaper report had the Nebraskan threatening to resign if there were an endorsement. Wilson also may well have already begun to think of 1916 and keeping his progressive image unsullied by any association with men as vilified as Roger. Moreover, Woodrow Wilson had a life-long habit of ignoring political debts and personal obligations. The list of men who helped him in his career, many of whom counted him as a close personal friend, and who were then discarded is lengthy and includes George Harvey, Jim Smith, William McCombs, Robert Lansing, and Colonel Edward House. Woodrow Wilson declined to honor his obligations to Sullivan because he could, and because he felt it best served his own interests. To his credit, Roger never expressed disappointment nor held a grudge for a betrayal that allowed his opponents to make the case that he was not Wilson's man.[56]

Roger was probably more personally disturbed by the displays of prejudice against him as a Roman Catholic. Protestantism, as then broadly practiced, often still referenced the Reformation. Catholicism was by far the fastest growing affiliation in the United States concomitant with large-scale immigration from places like Italy and Poland. For these reasons, Catholic candidates excited a nativist response among some traditionally Protestant downstaters. Governor Dunne, when running in 1912, faced some anti-Catholic feeling, but his reputation for honesty and reform countered such fears. Roger Sullivan, on the other hand, was laboring under the weight of years of fabrications and exaggerations from his political opponents. He was easily cast into the sinister role of the big city boss sustained by Catholic immigrant hordes.[57]

Neither of his opponents raised the issue, of course, but placards did go up in southern Illinois proclaiming: "Roger Sullivan is a Catholic. Be A True American. Vote Against the Pope," and a sheet titled "The Menace" warning of a Catholic conspiracy to dominate the world, was circulated. Nor was all of this simply the provenance of the uneducated and ignorant. The Reverend J. R. Williams of the Presbyterian Church of Clayton, Illinois was probably representative of many when he explained candidly (in response to a Democratic letter requesting his support) that, despite being a fervent admirer of President Woodrow Wilson, he could not vote for Sullivan "because of his church affiliations." While he recognized that "every man has a right to his own religion," he could not in good conscience vote for a man who had sworn "allegiance to a FOREIGN [sic] power [the pope]," whose principles were: "'to hell with the government' ditto bible [sic], ditto public schools, ditto American flag, ditto song 'AMERICA' [sic], ditto Free Masonry [sic] and ditto every thing [sic] that is not ROMAN PAGANISM [sic]" He was also certain that neither "a single member" of his church," nor any other "liberty-loving patriotic American voter of my acquaintance" could either. Just to make sure his message was heard, the good reverend sent a copy of his letter to President Wilson, who passed it on to Joseph Tumulty. It was precisely to counter these predispositions that Sullivan began his campaign so informally downstate, but there was little else he could do against such bigotry.[58]

When confronted with something that he could fight, however, he moved with decisiveness and precision. During the primary contest, Carl Vrooman raised concerns about Sullivan's campaign finances, with the implication that the Chicago leader was spending untoward amounts of money. Since the Lorimer scandal this kind of thing had become an especially sensitive issue. Now the Robins campaign, to which Vrooman attached himself despite being Assistant Secretary of Agriculture in the Wilson administration, and the Popular Government League, a national reform body also supporting Robins, began the same line of attack in the obvious hope of exposing what they saw as Sullivan's progressive pretensions. "Spontaneously" letters from concerned citizens in the downstate, one of whom at least was a Progressive Party operative, were sent to Republican Senator George Norris of Nebraska (a close ally of Senator Robert Owen, a Robins' supporter) demanding the Senate Committee on Privileges and Elections look into the matter. Norris and Owen soon backed a resolution calling for an inquiry. On September 30, Sullivan received an open telegram from Robins citing the supposed "popular belief that great sums were spent in your interest," and the more substantial contention that all the other candidates were for "an immediate investigation."[59]

Sullivan counterattacked with a public letter to Senator John Kern (Bryan's 1908 running mate, who was a major force in the final Lorimer investigation), who also on the Committee, expressing his outrage that the Senate would tolerate this "grossly unfair maneuver." He went on to explain that the charges were based upon legitimate expenses for "circularizing, mailings, printing, and the like expenditures," that he had "strictly followed the law," and that all of this was just an attempt "to make political capital for the benefit of those running against me." If an investigation were necessary, let it be after the election, when it could be conducted objectively.[60]

Towards Robins, Sullivan was caustic and even more direct. It was his belief, he wrote in an open letter, that the Progressive knew full well raising this issue was political, and there was "as much truth in that charge as there is in the story that your fortune was accumulated in gold mining operations in Alaska" (the Robins camp was promoting this

legend during the campaign). Moreover, "to join you in asking the committee to investigate this charge or in fact to join you in anything, would impart to you and your wild
statements an air of truth and respectability to which in my judgment you are not entitled."
He followed up his refusal to be a victim in a partisan witch hunt with an extended letter
to Joseph Tumulty, Wilson's political secretary, explicating in depth the political motivations and machinations at the root of the attacks and asking for help stifling any senate
action. Soon an announcement was made that any inquiry, should one be conducted,
would take place following the November balloting. Robins claimed a victory of sorts in
making Sullivan "squirm."[61]

As both of his major opponents had declared the other irrelevant and himself as
their principal opponent, Sullivan became the chief target for most of the mudslinging.
Theodore Roosevelt, during both of his visits concentrated upon Roger, linking him with
the Republican Sherman in a mythical bipartisan machine. More importantly, the former
president dredged up the Ogden scandal, identifying it as the "foundation of his [Sulli-
van's] political and commercial career." Roger responded in kind, portraying Roosevelt
as a talker not a doer: "We cannot find," he proclaimed, doubtless well-aware of his exaggeration, "that he ever did a single thing except talk about the evils of which he is still
complaining!"[62]

He was no more passive in the face of the verbal assaults from the other Progressive
luminaries who came to the state. The most prominent of these was Senator Robert
Owen, who toured the downstate characterizing Sullivan as a machine politician and an
enemy of reform. He was joined by Congressman James Manahan of Oklahoma, and, of
course, Carl Vrooman. Sullivan in turn sent in "flying squads" of speakers that included
Governor Dunne (in a limited itinerary of seven downstate appearances followed by a
few in Cook County in which he continued to make only the most general of endorsements), Senator Lewis (in an even more limited role), Congressman Rainey, Senator
Thomas Gore of Oklahoma, and, most importantly, Postmaster Albert Burleson, who
came with the permission of the president to lend credibility to Sullivan's contention of
being Wilson's man.[63]

Burleson arrived in late October. At a major rally in Peoria, the postmaster argued
that the logic of the situation made self-evident both the administration's desire to see
Sullivan elected, and the need for those who supported the president to back his party's
candidate. What were the options? Sherman was a conservative, and it was absurd to
think of him voting with Wilson. Robins? He was too much under the influence of "his
leader, the great hunter! [Roosevelt]" No, the only way "of upholding the president," the
only certain means to assure that his programs would be enacted, and his position
strengthen as he dealt with the perils of a world that was now in the second month of
the worst war in history, was to vote for Roger Charles Sullivan.[64]

Just days before the election, Sullivan, with the other candidates, was provided with
an opportunity by the *Chicago Tribune* to make his final case in writing to the people of
the state. The resulting article closely echoed his most recent themes. He wanted it made
clear that he had deliberately waited to seek election to the senate until after the Seventeenth Amendment made it the people's choice; Roger Sullivan by taking his case to the
voters was not, therefore, playing politics as usual, but was acting as a progressive—
meaning that his "boss" status, whether true or not, was irrelevant. Moreover, as he saw
it the outbreak of a world war was a challenge that transcended party lines; it was now
the responsibility of all Americans "to support the peace policy of the president of the

United States," and to back his economic program "so that during the crisis" the country could remain on "a sound financial basis" and "improve our business and economic conditions." He further urged the voters not to let exaggerations about his past enter into their decision. After all Ogden Gas had *lowered* prices, and had *thwarted* in its time the gas monopoly, and he was certain that his record would "bear the searchlight of investigation."[65]

The times were too perilous for name calling, he argued, even as he now pointed out with pride that he had not attacked Robins as a "single-taxer" (which is to say, a follower of Henry George, whose economic theories were considered by many as "cranky"), nor Sherman as a "reactionary." However, it was a fact, not hyperbole, that neither Robins nor Sherman was supportive of the president. Indeed, the Republican was premising his campaign upon criticism of Wilson and more specifically of the tariff reform brought by the president's New Freedom. In this context, he, Sullivan, was the only choice for those who wished Wilson and the country well, those who were not "partisans but patriots."[66]

Sullivan had in fact done his best to keep his themes positive where possible. He responded to attacks, but he never sought to besmirch Robins' character. Sherman had no such qualms and continuously dismissed the Progressive as someone who was little more than an eccentric amateur. This eventually brought out Jane Addams to deny that Robins had been a "faddist" or "dreamer" during their service together on the Dunne school board. On the other hand, Sherman and Sullivan generally ignored each other or kept to the high ground of simply agreeing to disagree about national policy. Both were targeting Progressive voters, with the Democrats hoping to sway those committed to reform who might see in Wilson the most realistic hope for continued positive change, and the Republicans seeking to woo back into the fold those who had bolted four years earlier. The choice between Sullivan and Sherman was otherwise entirely self-evident for the Republicans, and required little elaboration.

The election was not a foregone conclusion, as late as the day of the election the *Washington Post* prognosticated that Roger Sullivan could very well win. Illinois newspapers, on the other hand, tended to be optimistic for whichever candidate they endorsed, and all the campaigns profusely proclaimed their professions of confidence. However, Republican, Lawrence Y. Sherman prevailed. Sullivan took 373,403 votes or 36.76 percent to Sherman's 390,611 or 38.46 percent, and Robins' 203,027 or 19.99 percent. The Democrats at least had the satisfaction of carrying Cook County with 159,372 ballots, with Sherman receiving 103,808 and Robins, 88,487.[67]

Sullivan was gracious in defeat, proud that he conducted a "clean campaign" and for having won the nomination by the vote of the people against the opposition of "all the political machines and payrolls," by which he meant Harrison, Dunne, and Bryan. Still, it was "extremely regrettable" that the voters were unwilling to give the national administration all the support it needed. It was even more regrettable that some would "penalize a man for his religious beliefs that he got from his mother," something he was sure was abetted "by high personages in the Democratic officialdom." Ironically, just as this concession speech was being published, William Jennings Bryan arrived in Chicago. This was his first trip to the Windy City since the beginning of the contest. His presence, for once, was largely ignored by the press.[68]

In truth, Roger Sullivan did well. Despite the reluctance of some leading Democrats, despite his reputation as a "boss," and despite his Catholicism, he nearly equaled Dunne's 1912 total of 38.11 percent. Had the Progressives come closer to their own 26.09 percent of four years earlier, he would have been elected. Indeed, the most significant aspect of the 1914 elections was as the swan song of the Progressive Party, which lost virtually everywhere. Even Theodore Roosevelt privately conceded after the election that "I don't think they can much longer be kept as a party." It would limp along, sustained by a diminishing corps of true believers, until Roosevelt mercifully committed infanticide in 1916. Well before that point, however, the weakness of the Progressive showing in the 1914 elections demonstrated beyond doubt the restoration of the Republicans as the majority party in Illinois.[69]

Sullivan could find solace from the fact that defeat worked to strengthen significantly his position among state Democrats. Not only did the campaign facilitate the unity and perfection of his organization, but in Cook County there was an almost universal sweep of Sullivan-men into office. The ballots were hardly counted and the concessions and congratulations hardly made, before Sullivan and his men began the preparations for revenge and the political destruction of Carter Harrison and his faction.

7

The Triumph of the
Chicago Democratic Machine
(1915–1916)

"The game's up"—Mayor Carter Harrison

Nearly twenty years after the fact Carter Harrison would write of his apprehensions about the 1915 mayoral primary. "Way down inside of me," he recalled, "I recognized that, barring an unexpected reversal of fortune, my days as mayor were numbered." When first elected as the city's chief executive back in 1897, Carter Harrison was viewed with askance by the reform-minded of the city, who believed him to be just another organizational politician like his father—which in fact he was. His credibility among them improved in 1898 when he stood up to Charles Yerkes' attempts to use state law, and the greed of individual aldermen, to purchase at a discount an indefinite monopoly of public transportation in the city. However, Harrison's subsequent refusal to embrace the calls for immediate municipal ownership of the traction systems dimmed his reformist halo. This resulted in his replacement in 1905 by the darling of the city's social reformers, Edward F. Dunne, who two years later was defeated by Republican Fred Busse. In 1911, Harrison only just managed to regain his party's mayoral nomination against Dunne, whose resurgence as a chief advocate of reform in the state and city Democratic Party was in 1912 to propel him into the governor's chair. After six years in exile, Harrison again became mayor, but only after a hard-fought struggle against the powerful reformist candidacy of Republican Charles Merriam.[1]

Facing a far more potent Sullivan Democracy than when he left office in 1905, the mayor sought to reinvent himself as a progressive. It appeared a reasonable strategy with the demands for liberal change in ascendancy. Moreover, as there was among many of the city and state's reformers a long-standing antipathy to Sullivan and the type of politics he was believed to represent, it was a worthwhile strategy for Harrison to build an anti–Sullivan coalition conjoining reformers with his own cadres to seize control of the party apparatus. His alliance with William Randolph Hearst, who was able to lend local press support and money, was a significant advantage. In remarkably short order what appeared to be a formidable alliance comprised of the mayor of Chicago, the state governor, the lone Democratic senator, the United States Secretary of State, William Jennings Bryan, and the powerful Hearst emerged to challenge Roger Sullivan's paramountcy.

However, the juggernaut proved to be a paper tiger. Neither Governor Dunne nor

Senator J. Hamilton Lewis were inclined to risk their own political careers unduly in crusading against the powerful Chicago leader, while William Jennings Bryan, whose hostility towards Sullivan knew no bounds, found himself fettered by President Woodrow Wilson. In the end, Carter Harrison and Hearst were largely left to their own devices, and these proved inadequate for overpowering Roger Sullivan, who, with the senatorial nomination, was becoming something like unassailable.

And Harrison's new progressivism also alienated much of his traditional base. In 1914, he initiated a conspicuous campaign to purify Chicago of its historical vice, ordering raids upon the "red light district," while also harassing saloons by enforcing Sunday closing laws and other heretofore generally ignored regulations. Leaders like the First Ward's "Bathhouse John" Coughlin and Michael "Hinky Dink" Kenna, abandoned the Harrison organization to become loosely affiliated with Sullivan. They and others of their ilk had been original components of the mayor's faction, and his apparently conscious choice to exchange them for reformist support would not pay off. Also adding to a general dissatisfaction with Harrison was the perception that it was he who was the aggressor in the factional wars. Democratic regulars had long hoped for an end to the antagonisms of the type that had resulted in the embarrassing seizure by the mayor's men of the 1912 Cook County Convention site. In contrast to city hall's intransient hostility (except under duress) towards all accommodation or compromise, Sullivan and his allies stood as champions of order and harmony.[2]

Mayor Harrison's clumsy efforts at playing boss were another source of disaffection. As early as March 1912, a rebellion within his own faction over city hall diktats was only narrowly headed off in one stormy meeting. Nine months later, the mayor took revenge against one of the leading dissenters, the prodigal Robert "Bobby" Burke. Burke's personal following was headquartered at the office of the County Democracy (the party's famed marching club), which he had run for decades. On Harrison's behalf, Miles J. Devine, formerly Burke's man and formally president of the organization, on December 8, 1912, led a party of sixteen that used a fire escape to break into and seize possession of the organization's offices at 167 West Randolph Street. Once inside, they replaced the front door to which only Burke had a key, and stationed guards to restrict access. The justification for this high-handedness was an allegation that a sum just over six thousand dollars was missing from the monies raised at picnics and other social affairs. Burke controlled the fund, and even admitted to appropriating the cash, but claimed that it was owed to him for expenses out-of-pocket. Once again, The County Democracy marching club divided, as Burke, who kept most of the records at home, quickly reorganized his followers, while the Devine/Harrison men retained the headquarters and began recruiting. In January 1913, Burke was indicted, in a typical political use of the judicial system, by a grand jury for the missing money. The issue never came to trial, nor did a lengthy civil suit that followed. By March 1913, Burke was fully realigned with Sullivan, though always in an outer orbit.[3]

Others of even greater standing were also leaving the city hall crowd. In March 1914, Anton Cermak left, supposedly because of the mayor's refusal to pledge support for every primary victor regardless of faction. However, there were probably larger issues, most likely those centered upon "Tough Tony's" demands for greater rewards, abetted, perhaps, by a sense that the "H-H" faction was beginning to falter. Regardless, Cermak left to resume his independence until later events mandated his reaffiliation with the Sullivan Democracy.[4]

Of even more immediate moment for the mayor was the loss of the Hearst newspapers as a reliable source of supportive propaganda. In the coming campaign, the usual vituperation towards Sullivan would be missing from the *Examiner* and the *American*, even as both went through the motions of supporting Harrison. Probably even more distressing was the apparent withdrawal of Hearst money. The formal demise of the "H-H" faction is not recorded, but it had much of its origins in the general antipathy towards the New York publisher that was always present among Harrison's local legions. The alliance appears to have begun unraveling with Hearst's refusal to back Wilson in 1912, and in May 1913, the Harrison version of the County Democracy voted to repudiate the publisher. By late 1915, the press had begun describing the alliance as the "old Hearst-Harrison" crowd (or some variation)., and by 1916 all references had ceased entirely.[5]

As the mayor's position declined, so Roger Sullivan's improved. Over the course of eighteen months in 1915 and 1916, his Sullivan Democracy, now increasingly referenced simply as the "Machine," would reduce its challengers to effective irrelevancy. All the many years of maneuver and factional battles would at last find a triumphant fruition that belonged not just to Sullivan, but also to the idea, first born decades before in the nineteenth century among city's businessmen politicians, of a consolidated and coordinated power structure within the Chicago, Cook County, and Illinois Democratic Party.

Despite his defeat in the general election Roger C. Sullivan's 1914 senate run proved to be an important enabler of his ultimate intraparty victory. Securing his nomination by such a substantial margin against his seemingly daunting opposition substantially enhanced and underscored his prestige, while also providing a convincing demonstration of his organization's claims to universal predominance within the state. In addition, Sullivan became a state-wide political celebrity. His intense speaking schedule exposed thousands of Illinois citizens to his personality, providing myriad opportunities to charm farmers with stories about his brief stint as a homesteader in North Dakota, and workers with remembrances of his days in the car machine shops.[6]

The national coverage also helped. *Collier's*, with its extensive circulation, for example, featured an in-depth article in the fall of 1914, centering on the question: "Is Roger Sullivan a Boss?" While answering in the positive, the author did emphasize Roger's "gentility" as a leader, his honesty, his insistence upon always keeping his word, his tolerance of dissent, and his forgiving nature. This piece and others also dutifully recited some of Roger's stump hyperbole with the inclusion of politically convenient exaggerations about the supposed desperate poverty from which he emerged as a child. The piece was part of a growing tendency to present him sympathetically that went far towards countering Sullivan's caricaturizing by his opposition.[7]

Soon there was a growing chorus calling upon Roger to seek the mayoral nomination, but this only evoked at least three public statements of disinterest. He was unwilling to take on another tough campaign, especially for a job as contentious as the mayor's office (that he might not win in the general election). However, the question remained, if not Sullivan then who? Following Democratic victories in 1912, there was a considerable number willing to make the sacrifice. Among these were City Clerk Frank D. Connery (who was an uncle of Boetius Sullivan's wife Loretta) and the Circuit Court Clerk John W. Rainey, but it was County Clerk Robert M. Sweitzer who attracted the most interest.[8]

Sweitzer was born in Chicago on May 10, 1868, as the son of a German father and Irish mother. He attended the local grammar schools and then St. Patrick's Academy. Unusually at the time for someone not destined for an academic career, he subsequently procured a master's of arts degree from the Christian Brothers' College in St. Louis, Missouri. Following his graduation, he returned to Chicago and worked successively at the W.F. McLaughlin Tea and Coffee Company and J.H. Walker Dry Goods, before beginning a long tenure with the John V. Farwell Company (also a food supplier). At some point, he became friends with John P. Hopkins, who was also in the food service industry, and Roger Sullivan, with whom he shared a passion for yachting on Lake Michigan. In 1910, he was Sullivan's successful candidate for County Clerk. As he and Roger's brother Mark had married sisters, he was also a distant in-law. He was well-liked throughout the city, and he would remain a popular figure and an important Democratic leader into the 1930s. He was known as intelligent, well-spoken, and a good campaigner. Not the least of his assets at the moment was his German name.[9]

Since beginning in August 1914, World War I's influence was increasingly felt even in the distant reaches of the American Midwest, where the German-American community became ever more defensive as so many of their fellow-citizens began to side with the British and the French. Germany's unrestricted use of submarine warfare (in response to a British blockade that brought starvation to the young and the elderly) and the impact of British propaganda in publicizing the harsh German occupation of Belgium and northeastern France had their effect. In Chicago, however, those who were born in Germany and their immediate descendants made up almost thirty percent of the population. This provided Sweitzer with an apparent natural constituency against Carter H. Harrison, a man of British ancestry.

Reflective of the increasingly sophisticated leadership structure of the Sullivan organization, which always embodied a degree of democratic centralism, Roger and his "cabinet" of leaders did not simply dictate the final choice of the candidate. Instead, Sweitzer was selected by two lively caucuses of eighty ward bosses who met with Sullivan and his sachems in late December 1914 at the famous People's Gas Building at 122 South Michigan (designed by Daniel Burnham, and opened in 1910). It was there that Sullivan maintained an office in room #823, which he retained as part of his Ogden Gas/Cosmopolitan Electric divestment deal of 1913. The local German-American press responded enthusiastically. The candidate was formally presented to the rank-and-file at the grand New Year's Eve party of the Burke version of the Cook County Democracy marching club where Roger, led the "grand march."[10]

In 1911, Roger Sullivan had dominated the campaign of the failed candidacy of Andrew J. Graham, speaking extensively. However, Sweitzer was vastly more politically experienced, and his friend and leader purposely kept himself in the background to avoid, or at least to minimize, making himself an issue during the primary. However, Sweitzer's campaign committee would be headed by Sullivan, and included such stalwarts as Bobby Burke, Patrick Nash, Frank Ryan, County Treasurer Henry Stuckart, and City Clerk Francis D. Connery.[11]

It was decided to emphasize the candidate's record of competence while focusing upon Harrison's foibles. The mayor was soon being accused of running the city into the red, of being a weak administrator, and for bearing the responsibility for the continuing poor service of the street cars. "Efficiency in government," became Sweitzer's principal theme. Issues of party loyalty, inevitable in a primary battle, also took a central place as the Harrison was scorned for helping by omission to defeat Sullivan in the senate race. Even worse, the mayor was painted as anti–Irish, anti–Catholic, and as being an "aristocrat" (not a trivial charge for the many recent immigrants from Europe, who did not recall the nobility fondly). Harrison would complain privately about a circular, the provenance of which is unclear, that urged Catholic voters to back his opponent and that included the "intimation that my opposition to Sullivan [for the senate] was based upon his race and his religion." Bitterly, he was to recount, without any evidence that the "Un-American Placard distributed throughout Illinois to defeat Roger Sullivan," was actually concocted by Sullivan himself.[12]

Carter Harrison fought back with an unrestrained, "Red Pepper" race. He brought every possible ally into his campaign committee including Chief Bailiff Anton Cermak (apparently now convinced to participate by promises of considerable recompense), Congressman Adolph Sabath, Sheriff John Traeger, City Controller Michael Zimmer, City Treasurer Michael J. Flynn, and Chief Clerk Michael Danisch. It was recognized that the survival of the Harrison faction was at stake, and they desperately attempted to make Sullivan the issue as a "menace" to the city. This did not resound especially well among party rank-and-file who just months before voted by a substantial margin to make Roger their senatorial nominee. Sweitzer's appeal to the German-American vote was another target. Harrison delighted in challenging his opponent to make a speech in German, knowing that he was not bilingual, all the while bragging about his own mastery of the language that dated back to his years as a student in the *Vaterland*. The mayor also sought to link Sweitzer with the "vice vote," as the candidate of the "overlords and captains of the underworld," in part because he counted among his backers many of the men Harrison had scorned. This meant little as everyone knew that for decades the mayor had treated with these men in disregard of their notorious reputations.[13]

In fact, this theme was probably an important source of the growing number of politicos jumping the Harrison ship. In an attempt to balance these losses with the presumed strength of the sentiments for reform within the party, Harrison appealed to Governor Edward F. Dunne, who wrote a note, and then traveled briefly to the city to speak on his behalf. The Governor's endorsement was, however, lukewarm as he almost grudgingly explained that despite past differences with Harrison, he now felt that the mayor was "by training, education, experience, and ability" the superior candidate. Harrison also lined up a number of state legislators to add their voices including Dunne-ally, Michael Igoe, while also trotting out a few defectors from the Sullivan faction. The most important of these were Thomas Little, once Sullivan's alderman from the Fourteenth Ward (who would be rewarded for his pains with consignment to political oblivion), and Thomas F. Flynn, Andrew Graham's campaign manager of record in the 1911 primary.[14]

Nor was Mayor Harrison above using the powers of his office to punish defectors. Immediately before the primary election on February 23, he ordered the closing of four saloons in the Eighteenth Ward, all of which were owned or operated by men who had switched sides. The most important of these was that of Barney Grogan at 1160 Van Buren. All were alleged to be havens for "thugs and disorderly women." This may well have been true, but Grogan and the others had been protected in 1910 during the mayor's well-publicized anti-vice campaign, and the timing of the current raids was clearly designed to send a message to others who might be wavering. Grogan defied the intent of the order by keeping his establishment open as a dispenser of soft drinks—and as a local Sweitzer headquarters. The mayor showed no greater restraint in directing the police to stop the mass and "disgraceful" posting of election posters—now a favorite tactic of the Sullivan Democracy. He was less successful in convincing County Judge (and Sullivanite) Thomas F. Scully to have every voter in the primary challenged. Scully dismissed the idea as voter suppression.[15]

Violence too played its part. The aforementioned Barney Grogan was physically assaulted in City Hall by Joe Gordon, a Harrison man and jewelry store owner, who blindsided the saloon owner as he was speaking to friends on the street. Days later, the resentment from this incident nearly precipitated a gun fight outside a saloon on Canal Street when Gordon was confronted by Tom Gary, Grogan's friend and a "Sweitzer worker." Both men held drawn pistols as they exchanged challenges and insults, and only the timely arrival of the police and their arrest with two others prevented bloodshed. Days later John Ryan, a teaming contractor and another defector, was jumped by several men and struck with a lead pipe outside of a Sweitzer rally. Earlier he had been threatened if he did not return to the Harrison fold. At about the same time, some Harrison supporters were beaten outside of a dance hall.[16]

Contrasting sharply with this street violence was the refined, if uncertain, wooing of the female vote—now a factor because of the enactment in 1913 of woman's statutory suffrage (women could vote in all elections except for those in the state constitution, including the selection of presidential electors, which referenced "male elector"). These hard-boiled male politicians were at something of a loss about how to appeal to the distaff part of humanity. Harrison made much of his supposed deference to his "better half" by reciting a story of having petitioned his wife's permission to run. When he became ill late in the campaign, Edith Ogden Harrison proved to be an able substitute speaker at rallies and meetings, and her husband's equal in the ferocity of her flagitious assaults upon Sweitzer and Sullivan. Meanwhile, the Harrison campaign also created special female committees to canvass the city's women block by block.

The Sweitzer camp was no less ardent in their courting of the "petticoat vote"; a women's auxiliary was organized, speakers were designated, and the theme that Sweitzer was the stronger advocate of women's rights was recited at every meeting. However, the response of those women who were habitually socially and politically active revealed much the same diversity of loyalties as those found among the men. Grace Wilbur Trout, president of the Illinois Equal Suffrage Association, declined to become involved. Similarly, Harriet Taylor Treadwell, head of the Chicago Political Equality League, publicly refused to endorse any candidate. On the other hand, Joanna E. Downes, president of the Illinois' Women's Democratic League, and representative of female "regulars," did not hesitate in offering her strong endorsement of Sweitzer, while the influential Margaret Haley of the Chicago Federation of Teacher's was equally supportive of Harrison. For the most part, however, most progressive women, including Jane Addams, were flocking to the standard of Judge Harry Olson, who was running in the Republican primary.[17]

Another important element to which both Sweitzer and Harrison hoped to appeal was the "liquor vote." Chicago was a city largely peopled by immigrants from places like Germany, Ireland, and Italy, for whom the use of alcoholic beverages was a part of daily life. They, with the liquor industry, were becoming apprehensive about the growing strength of the national forces demanding complete prohibition; no man could hope to become mayor if perceived as unwilling to defend the right to drink. Harrison's recent war on vice now made him vulnerable on the issue. He was successful, however, in obtaining (as he had been unable to do in 1911) the endorsement of the United Societies for Local Self-Government (the chief liquor lobbying group), thanks to the purchase of the presence in his campaign of the organization's influential secretary, Anton Cermak.

Sweitzer countered with an announcement of support by the unknown and probably contrived "Personal Liberty League."[18]

As the primary election neared, all sides, as usual, predicted imminent victory, and there were some signs that it might be close. But it was not to be. As one newspaper phrased it: "Harrison [was] Beaten Out of His Boots!" Sweitzer won handily by a total of 183,249 votes to Harrison's 104,063. The mayor only carried three of the thirty-five wards. He conceded and refused to countenance an independent candidacy. However, Harrison was not especially gracious, snidely asserting that "the sentiment was with me, but the sediment was with Sweitzer." He also would later admit having "held his nose" when subsequently voting for Sweitzer in the general election. His bitterness against Sullivan would never truly mellow. Although, The Harrison faction was to limp along into 1916, it began to rapidly wither without the sustenance of city patronage. In the end, it became little more than a mostly powerless refuge for those out of favor with Roger Sullivan. There was still to be guerrilla-style resistance, but the factional wars that had plagued the party for decades were, for all intents and purposes, at last concluded.[19]

Just as Harrison's defeat marked the end of an epoch in Chicago's political history, the emergence of Sweitzer's Republican opponent, William Hale Thompson, was to signal the beginning of another. Born on May 14, 1869, in Boston as the son and namesake of a multi-millionaire father, he moved with his family to Chicago at the age of nine days. He was initially educated at the exclusive Fessenden Preparatory School, and it was intended that he should attend the even more exclusive Exeter School back east to be followed by Yale. However, a youthful indiscretion involving the use of the State Street Bridge for a game of Indians convinced his father that immediate employment as a grocery clerk was indicated. Ever resourceful, young William soon saved enough to move west to Cheyenne, Wyoming where he worked as a hand herding cattle. In 1888, he convinced his father to purchase a 3,800-acre ranch where he successfully played cowboy for the next three years, amassing the impressive sum of $30,000 in profits. When his father died in 1891, he returned to Chicago. With no special need to work, he became prominent as a member of the Chicago Athletic Club, and coached their football team in 1896 to a national championship. In 1900, reportedly on a dare from one of his players, he ran as a Republican for the city council from the Second Ward, home of many of the city's bordellos and saloons. With the quiet backing of the First Ward's Democratic aldermen, "Bathhouse John" Coughlin and Michael "Hinky Dink" Kenna, he won even as he proclaimed the virtues of the Municipal Voters League (which withheld an endorsement).[20]

In office, he became an advocate of playgrounds for the city's children, then an important urban cause, but more importantly, he attracted the attention of William Lorimer, whose man he became. After leaving the city council because of changes in the boundary line of his ward (for which he unthinkingly voted), he was elected in 1902 as Lorimer's candidate for Cook County Commissioner, a position he held for the next two years. After leaving this office, he focused upon his hobbies of yachting and athletics, but also took the time for a failed bid in 1912 for the Cook County Board of Review. Meanwhile as Lorimer's position was being weakened by the events associated with his expulsion from the United State Senate, Thompson hooked up with Fred "Poor Swede" Lundin, an ambitious Republican operative. It was at Lundin's suggestion that Thompson ran in the 1915 mayoral primary, which he won over the Judge Harry Olson, broadly considered the most progressive candidate in either party since Charles Merriam in 1911.[21]

The immediate challenge for both Sweitzer and Thompson following their nominations was to secure the unified support of their parties. Both men won hard-fought battles against determined, even bitter opposition, but the will to win within the G.O.P. overruled factional discord. Soon the Republican candidate's prospects were boosted by endorsements from the likes of former Governor Charles Deneen, and even Judge Harry Olson. Doubtless much to his relief, a movement to induce Merriam to enter as an independent went nowhere, and even the Progressive Party mayoral nominee, Charles M. Thompson, withdrew in his favor.

Though perhaps with less sincerity, the Democrats, too, made an effort to put on a show of unity for their candidate. The Harrison faction, despite their leader's personal antipathy towards Sweitzer, lined up, and such factional luminaries (though not the former mayor himself) as Congressman Adolph Sabath, former County Judge John E. Owens, and John J. Sloan, (Harrison's primary manager), would all campaign. Senator Ham Lewis and Governor Edward F. Dunne came and spoke, but the effect was colored somewhat by the governor's description of William Hale Thompson in the course of his speech as "a true gentleman" (Edward F. Dunne liked just about everybody personally, including Roger Sullivan). Not all hopped on the bandwagon. George Schilling, a former Socialist and now a radical Democratic reformer currently occupying the office of president of the Board of Local Improvement, organized something called the Anti-Sweitzer Democratic League. It, however, was insignificant.[22]

While issues were to be discussed in passing, the race was mostly defined by invective, innuendo, and occasional thuggery. Thompson set the tone by imitating Carter Harrison in denouncing Sweitzer as one of Roger Sullivan's "good soldiers." The real question, Thompson assured the city was "whether Roger Sullivan will be the next mayor of Chicago by his proxy, Robert M. Sweitzer." Perhaps inevitably, the Republican resurrected the ancient Ogden Gas scandal, claiming correctly that Sullivan made a substantial profit with the company's 1913 sale to the local utility monopoly. A variation soon appeared in G.O.P. oratory that stressed Sullivan and Sweitzer's supposed representation of "vice" interests and the "flophouse gang." The Democratic camp retaliated in kind by revealing a $5,000 contribution to their opponent from James A. Patterson, a managing director of the People's Gas and Electric Company, while also linking Thompson to Lorimer.[23]

Adding further ugliness was the emergence late in the campaign of the religious issue. As in the senatorial race the previous year, anti–Catholic circulars appeared in Protestant neighborhoods, something for which both sides blamed the other. The Republicans claimed it was just a clever ploy by the Democrats to draw Catholic votes. Roger Sullivan in response labeled Thompson's charges as the ravings of a "habitual liar," even as he openly accused Republican leader (and future state attorney general) Edward J. Brundage of being the source of both the recent circulars and of the anti–Catholic flyer, "The Menace," the "foul sheet" that was circulated downstate during his bid for the senate. Brundage denied everything, claiming to have "thousands of Catholic friends," while labeling Roger as a "habitual falsifier."[24]

The religious issue was just one expression of the larger concern shared by both Sweitzer and Thompson about the votes of Chicago's diverse ethnic communities. Because of the Great War (the press coverage of which was crowding out even the campaign news in this closely followed contest) ethnic identifications were strengthened, and especially among German Americans. During the primary campaign, Thompson was profuse with his praise of Germans and German *Kultur,* and dismissed the atrocity stories reported and associated with the German occupation of Belgium as mere British propaganda (Thompson would conveniently evoke Anglophobia throughout his subsequent public career). Sweitzer also courted the German vote by stressing his German heritage. There were, of course, dangers in pursuing this tactic too vigorously as other ethnic groups, most notably the Poles, who were a substantial component of the electorate, and whose nation had been occupied (with a short respite under Napoleon) by the Russians, Germans, and Austrians since 1796, were resentful of any glorification of the German Empire. Thompson wisely moved on after the primary, and Sweitzer did his best to reach out to the other ethnic populations. It seemed to many that it was he who enjoyed the advantage among Chicago's ethnics based upon endorsements from German, Polish, Bohemian, and Jewish newspapers. Thompson could only cite backing from the Norwegian and Italian press. Another aspect of this scrambling for ethnic support was the desperate contest to obtain the nod from the United Societies for Local Self-Government. Significantly, despite the backing of Sweitzer by Anton Cermak, its secretary, the organization remained neutral.[25]

As the campaign progressed, Thompson, it became clear, was winning. Days before the election, the odds at Jim O'Leary's stockyard saloon put Sweitzer at one to three and Thompson at two to one. Such forecasts, however, did little to dim the determination and enthusiasm of the candidates or their supporters. These, strengthened by simmering ethnic and religious tensions, exploded in street battles on the afternoon of April 3, or three days before the polls opened. The *Chicago Tribune* described it best as a day and night of "Red fire, calliopes, auto sirens, elephants, riots [and] dozens of broken heads," while the *Chicago Herald* wrote more simply of "Bedlam" in the loop. Worse, the appearance of concerted action by both the Sweitzer and Thompson "mobs" suggested strongly some degree of coordination and planning.[26]

Whether because of the threats of strong police action, or because of general exhaustion, Election Day, April 6, 1915, was unexpectedly calm and peaceful. Everyone was optimistic about the outcome, but no one—in public anyway—anticipated the Republican landslide. Thompson was elected by a margin of 398,538 votes to Sweitzer's 251,061, the highest majority yet seen in a Chicago mayoral election. Of the thirty-eight aldermanic seats (the usual thirty-five or half of the seventy-member city council, plus three vacancies), the Republicans won twenty-six, the Democrats eleven, and the Socialists one. Barney Grogan was defeated for a seat, much to the joy of the city's reformers, but to their dismay, one of their targets of long standing, Edward "Sly Ed" Cullerton, was returned to the council after an absence of several years. The Republicans also were victorious by substantial margins in the races for city treasurer, city clerk, and municipal judge.[27]

Roger Sullivan did not expect to win. Sweitzer would reveal in 1920 that his friend correctly predicted his nomination but also warned him that victory in the election was highly unlikely after years of Harrison and with the shifting political tides. Significantly, the Democrat failed to appeal to women, who turned out in as large numbers as the men for the Republican. Thompson also successfully drew strong returns from most of the city's ethnic communities, including the Germans, Swedes, Bohemians, Jews, and African Americans. His victory was a tribute to the effectiveness of his campaign, but was also an indicator of the continued diminution of Democratic electoral strength in the city as the Progressive Party phenomenon disappeared and the appeal of Woodrow Wilson faded. Moreover, as the defeat of the incumbent Carter Harrison in his party's primary had already suggested, Chicagoans were ready for a change. Further undercutting the

Democrats was an economic downturn created by a disruption of trade brought by the onset of world war. Prosperity would return with increased sales of foodstuffs and manufactured items to the combatants, but only after the election.[28]

The conflagration in Europe and around the world may have played its part in the diminishing fortunes of the Illinois Democratic Party, but it also handed Roger Sullivan an unexpected gift when William Jennings Bryan announced his resignation on June 8, 1915, as secretary of state. At issue was the Wilson administration's written response to the sinking of the British liner RMS *Lusitania* by the U-20, a German submarine, resulting in the deaths of 1,198 including 128 Americans. Bryan, who was a pacifist and worked hard to negotiate nearly thirty arbitration treaties in his first year in office, felt Wilson's note was too harsh and could lead to war. In contrast, others, like Theodore Roosevelt, believed the president's repeated reliance on protests against what many saw as clear violations of international law, and even as acts "of piracy," to be pusillanimous and weak.[29]

Bryan was Sullivan's leading national enemy within the Democratic Party, and he had long been an important enabler of the shifting coalitions that made up the Chicago leader's state and local opposition. Now with Harrison out of the mayor's office, and with Bryan out of the national administration, never again to exert the same degree of influence, only Governor Edward F. Dunne and Senator J. Hamilton Lewis remained of the once apparently formidable "reform wing" of the party, and both were facing reelection within the next three years.

For the moment, the men of the Sullivan organization, secure in their strength, declined to cooperate with the dwindling Harrison faction's ever more desperate attempts to reach some kind of agreement about the upcoming Cook county judicial nominations. The elections proved to be another disappointment, but the nominees were chosen by the Sullivan Democracy, and electoral defeat did nothing to discourage its plans for the complete conquest of the Cook County Party. Reflective of Sullivan's increasing tendency of distancing himself from daily oversight with the delegation of authority, the strategy session at the Hotel Sherman was led by George Brennan, John McGillen, and Timothy Crowe—while Roger was taking time off in San Diego, California visiting the Panama Exposition. It was they who devised the strategy to win control of the county committee in the primaries of the coming April. Extensive arrangements to perfect ward organizations were made, representing another step towards an increasingly formal structure. Responsibility for financing would now come from the bottom rather than the top, and precinct captains were mandated to be reliable and disciplined "regulars." It was also decided to support the current county committee chair, Henry Stuckart (who was also County Treasurer) for reelection—a clear signal of his shift of allegiance to Sullivan.[30]

Roger's absence from such an important meeting illustrated the now well-ordered and self-sustaining nature of Sullivan Democracy. Never a personal following (despite a recent proclivity towards the public glorification of its leader), the organization was evolving into the de facto governing structure of Democratic politics in Chicago and Illinois— one that was to endure long after the death of Roger C. Sullivan. With the defeat of Carter Harrison in the 1915 primary, augmented by overwhelming intraparty victories the following year, the organization become virtually omnipotent.

Accepting the new realities, increasing numbers of Harrison men continued to cross over. The now former mayor could no longer offer much in the way of patronage, and all that remained outside Sullivan's aegis were a few remaining state jobs controlled by Governor Dunne. Significantly among the latest defectors were such major Harrison leaders as Michael Zimmer, former Sheriff and city controller, and Miles J. Devine, president of the Harrison version of the Cook County Democracy marching club.[31]

Still, with an ardor born of desperation, Harrison and his dwindling band of loyalists fought on. At a meeting of his ward workers held on January 16, 1916, at the Morrison Hotel, he with his second-in-command, Congressman Adolph Sabath, issued clarion calls for battle, explaining: "What we particularly want is to keep him [Sullivan] from getting control of the [Cook] county central committee," while promising also to front an opposition slate for the delegates-at-large for the upcoming national convention. A number of Dunne men also attended and eventually, much of his considerable personal following began working with Harrison.[32]

The Sullivan Democracy remained unimpressed. On February 6, 1916, a Sullivan city convention was held at the First Regimental Armory. Ostensibly, it was called to greet Roger on his return from a brief vacation at Palm Beach, Florida. Somewhere between five and six thousand people were in attendance, with another thousand outside. All of the leaders were there including Robert M. Sweitzer, and George Brennan. Thomas Webb of the county board of review presided. The highlight was a Sullivan speech. Everything was so precisely planned that just as he rose from his chair on the platform, the band struck up "America," and the curtains parted to reveal his oversized portrait, evoking stormy applause and cheers (and to the modern reader, a scene from the motion picture *Citizen Kane*). His talk was constructed with his usual craft. It deliberately excluded any reference to Governor Dunne or former-Mayor Harrison, but within its pithy sentences were disparaging asides about those lacking loyalty to the party (presumably a reference to Harrison's lukewarm backing of Sweitzer). He expended most his time praising President Woodrow Wilson, whom Sullivan likened to Abraham Lincoln. While admitting that he "had not always agreed with Mr. Wilson" (perhaps an oblique reference to his disappointment over the distribution of federal patronage, a conflict that had yet to be entirely resolved), he assured his listeners that the president's certain reelection would be a "guarantee of justice, right, peace, and prosperity."[33]

But even at this moment of ascendancy, Roger Sullivan characteristically sought harmony. Carter Harrison and some of his leaders were invited to serve as delegates to the national convention, a move subsequently endorsed by Governor Edward F. Dunne, and Senator Lewis, who, it was believed, were channeling the will of the national administration. However, the former mayor balked at a proposed division that gave Sullivan fifty of the fifty-eight total delegates (which was not unreasonable given the relative strengths of the two factions), and in particular, he objected to the inclusion of Michael Zimmer, whom he now distained as a traitor. Refusing further discussion, Harrison declared war by promising to "beat Roger Sullivan out of his boots in the popular vote in Cook County."[34]

In fact, "The Sullivan regulars "cleaned up the town," winning practically all of the primaries. In the elections, the Democrats would pick up three council seats. However, making the campaign especially interesting was an incident that nearly brought the careers and lives of Roger Sullivan as well as those of many of the city's leading lights to an abrupt end. While the source of their peril was political, it had nothing to do with the selection of candidates or the factional wars. On February 10, 1916, a grand banquet was organized for Archbishop George Mundelein (and future Cardinal), who was consecrated the previous December by Pope Pius X as Archbishop of Chicago. The elaborate dinner was held at the well-appointed University Club. Nearly 300 notables attended, including Governor Edward F. Dunne, former Governor Charles Deneen, Roger Sullivan, Judge Thomas Scully, and Andrew J. Graham as well as a collection of bishops, judges, and business leaders. Twenty minutes after the serving of the chicken bouillon, some guests began making quick egresses, while others collapsed in their seats suffering from "vertigo, fainting, nausea, and vomiting." The physicians present quickly organized treatment for the over 100 people affected. Fortunately, those at the head table, including the good Archbishop and Roger Sullivan, were unaffected, though Governor Dunne was reported as turning pale. It emerged later that a supervisor in the kitchen threw out four-fifths of the deadly brew because of its poor appearance. With the sick dispatched to hospitals, the program continued, and it was initially assumed that the source of the problem was ptomaine poisoning because of the improper storage of the chicken soup facilitated by the "exceedingly insanitary conditions" of the kitchen.[35]

However, when the broth was tested, it was found to contain arsenic. The immediate suspect was a chef using the name of Jean Crones, who was an anarchist apparently acting out his hatred for the Church and American society. One of his associates in the kitchen, John Allegrini, also an anarchist, was questioned closely, and provided details about Crones' plot. Allegrini was not charged due to insufficient evidence, but Crones was indicted for attempted murder. Meanwhile, the accused made his escape. Several weeks after the incident, a note was found floating in a bottle in the lake in Jackson Park, in which Crones, or someone writing for him, claimed to have ended his life because he was tired of being hunted. Helping to keep the story alive were missives allegedly written by Crones that were periodically sent to the newspapers admitting his guilt and taunting the police, and in April some of the guests created a $10,000 reward for his capture. Although for years sightings were reported (at one point he was supposed to be in Pittsburg disguised as a nun), he was never captured.[36]

For Roger, the relief at his near escape was soon mitigated by personal tragedy when his friend and ally, Andrew J. Graham, passed away on May 1, 1916. Graham had been battling illness characterized by heart pains long before partaking of the poison (his physician initially claimed there was no relationship, but it was later reported that the poisoning was a factor in his death). He had long been close to Sullivan, who was his neighbor on Washington Boulevard, and had run as his candidate for the mayoral nomination in 1911 against Carter Harrison. He was just fifty-five years of age. Two others also ultimately died as a result of the poisoning, Father John O'Hara of Brooklyn and Richard Burke, chief judge of the criminal court.[37]

But even the near murder of so much of the city and state's leadership did little to inhibit the inexorable forward movement of local politics. Harrison's Last Stand came with the primaries of April 10, 1916. Both ward and district party committeemen, and therefore control of the party machinery, were to be decided. Among Sullivan's local candidates were such familiar names as George Brennan, Patrick Nash, Michael "Hinky Dink" Kenna, and, of course, Roger himself, while Harrison's slate (composed in cooperation with Dunne and William O'Connell) was generally less distinguished but included state's attorney Maclay Hoyne, O'Connell, and former sheriff John E. Traeger. The vote proved to be the final death knell of the Harrison faction as an independent force of significance. In Chicago, Roger Sullivan's men won in twenty-eight of the thirty-five wards, as well as in all six of the outlying county districts. The machine was to command a four to one advantage in delegates in the coming county convention.[38]

Downstate the results were equally one-sided and assured Sullivan's retention of the state committee. In the race for the delegates-at-large, Robert Sweitzer, Governor Dunne, Sullivan, and Henry T. Rainey, were, in that order, the most popular. Harrison was elected, but only as the sixth of eight. The wild card on the list of victors was Bobby Burke who, unlike anyone else, was elected as uncommitted to Wilson. Though not on anyone's slate, he was unofficially backed by Sullivan, and ran well ahead of the former mayor. District delegates downstate were also overwhelmingly pro–Sullivan, but did include among their numbers a few long-standing opponents like Millard Fillmore Dunlap.[39]

The immediate effect of the primary was the suspension by the Harrison faction of all plans for further combat. Even the former mayor had to concede, in his later words, that "the game's up." "With his defeat, Harrison's faction was finished as a significant force." Adolph Sabath, chair of the Cook County Managing Committee since 1914 and Harrison stalwart, admitted that "the bombardments are over," and meekly agreed to issue the call for the County Convention where a new Cook Country chair, Sullivan-ally John M. Daily together with a Sullivan dominated committee was certain to be selected. All was sweetness and light at the meeting, with Sullivan sitting with his arm literally around the shoulders of Sabath. Nine of the eleven local endorsements by the conventions for the relatively minor county nominations (e.g. Assessor, Recorder, Circuit Court Clerk etc.) to be decided in a September primary were Sullivan's men, while the popular Maclay Hoyne, having temporary made his peace, was given the nod for the nomination for state's attorney.[40]

The state convention in Springfield was yet another Sullivan Democracy's victory party. Chairing was Attorney General Patrick Lucey, whose keynote was a panegyric for Roger Sullivan, which extolling the Chicago leader's role in nominating of Woodrow Wilson. This inspired rapturous cheering and applause. Governor Dunne was cordially received, and spoke of unity, but the climax was Sullivan's address calling for harmony in support of the president. During the passionate demonstration that followed, a dove was released to symbolize party peace. For the remainder of the session, the pigeon hovered distractingly over the assembled delegates—but without reported misadventure. Meanwhile, with but a lone dissenting voice, Sullivan was elected chair of the state delegation going to St. Louis, and his entire package of resolutions, including those backing

Archbishop George Mundelein (Library of Congress, LC-DOG-ggbain-20977).

Dunne and Wilson, were approved. Also without significant dissent, Charles Boeschen-stein was endorsed for reelection as national committeeman, while the state committee, with its heavy Sullivan majority, chose Arthur Charles to be once again its chair. Roger C. Sullivan had controlled state conventions in the past, but never before had a party gathering been so obviously his. He was now not just the leader, but also indisputably the living embodiment of the regular Democracy in Illinois.[41]

Such was the current enthusiasm of his friends that they decided, with his agreement, to work for his nomination for the vice presidency of the United States (resurrecting an idea that first appeared in 1908). This was not as bizarre as it might have at first appeared. Of the nine twice-elected presidents to this point, all but two had chosen, or at least had acquiesced to, a change of vice presidents for their second term. Most recently, William McKinley in 1900 had agreed to the replacement of Garret Hobart by the upstart governor of New York, Theodore Roosevelt. Vice presidents had long been disposable commodities whose selection and/or retention could depend upon shifting political tides. In this spirit Thomas Marshall, the sitting second man of state, had received the nomination in 1912 to placate Indiana's Democratic boss Thomas Taggart. Now Marshall appeared vulnerable as calls for his replacement came from such party luminaries like Henry Morgenthau (who was close to Wilson and treasurer of the Democratic national campaign in 1912 as he was to be again in 1916), who felt that he was "not strong enough" for the difficult campaign ahead. Even worse for the Hoosier, rumors emerged in the fall of 1915 that President Wilson thought it "unlucky" to have the same running mate twice—rumors denied by the White House.[42]

And Roger Sullivan brought with him some impressive assets. Certainly his presence on the ticket might boost the president's chances to secure Illinois' electoral votes. In addition, he would appeal, so it was felt, to Irish Americans, and even to a significant body of German Americans, who were understandably alienated from the president's growing rigidity towards Germany in that nation's increasingly desperate fight against Great Britain, France, and their allies. Moreover, Sullivan enjoyed good working relations with members of the administration, including most especially presidential secretary Joseph Tumulty. There were also many who felt that he deserved this honor for having secured the presidential nomination for Wilson in 1912, and for having remained loyal despite being compelled to compete for federal patronage with Governor Dunne and Senator Lewis.[43]

Sullivan's possible candidacy went largely unreported in the national press. However, in Illinois it evoked the alarm of Governor Dunne and Senator Lewis. Nonetheless, the Sullivan-for-Vice-President campaign moved forward. Two days before the convention was to convene, 1,000 members of the (once again combined) County Democracy, wear-ing their designated outfits of light gray summer suits, brown Oxford shoes, and leghorn straw hats, arrived in Missouri's first city with placards in their headbands proclaiming support for Roger. Their numbers were bolstered during the trip by the addition at Spring-field of an additional 300 downstate boosters wearing white suits. This mixed contingent, now temporarily renamed the Roger Sullivan for Vice President Marchers, staged a street demonstration on the second day of the convention, parading noisily from the Missouri River front to the hall.[44]

Meanwhile, a headquarters was established at the Jefferson Hotel, where a formal campaign committee that included Robert Sweitzer, Thomas Scully, and others began to operate. Alliances with New York's Charles Murphy, Indiana's Tom Taggart (now a United

States' senator), and other organizational leaders were brokered, and when Roger Sullivan himself arrived, he was greeted by crowd of over one hundred vociferous Chicago Democrats. Cheers included such poetic constructions as "Who's the man? He's the man. Sull-i-van!" The object of their affections began to personally canvass for support with meetings with Ambassador Morgenthau and others. However, Sullivan was also making clear that he would not allow his name to be placed into nomination unless there was a reasonable assurance of victory, and this was not possible without at least the tacit neutrality of the White House.[45]

And this Dunne and Lewis were making every effort to prevent. They were currently seething because Sullivan, as "leader of the Illinois Democrats," had successfully blocked their choice for the postmastership of Chicago—an office controlling massive patronage. Instead, Roger's man, Dixon C. Williams, a native of Arkansas who was president of the Southern Club of Chicago, got the job. Lewis went on the offensive and labeled the idea of "such a boss as Roger Sullivan" becoming the vice presidential nominee as "shameful." Dunne announced his support for Marshall, and should he fail, for Lewis. Carter Harrison added his now relatively feeble voice to the chorus. He already had spurned Sullivan's placating offer of an appointment to one of the delegation's committees, maintaining that he was simply "not in sympathy" with either the majority of the delegates or their leader. The Sullivan men were soon "frothing" with anger, feeling that as Roger had made every reasonable effort to bring harmony, including allowing Harrison, Dunne, and Lewis to come to the convention as delegates-at-large, and with tolerating the presence of his old enemy, M. F. Dunlap, the least his opponents could do was to remain silent.[46]

Roger Sullivan campaign ribbon (Sullivan family collection).

Sullivan's hopes began to wane as it became clear that he was not attracting anything like the necessary interest. Now, in a classic bit of political doublespeak, he began assuring the press that he "knew nothing about" any intention to introduce his name for the nomination for the vice presidency. He discounted any candidacy further by pointing out the numerous others who were attracting speculation including former Governor Joseph Folk of Missouri (said to be the choice of William Jennings Bryan), Mayor Newton Baker of Cleveland, and Senator Robert Owen of Oklahoma. At last, the president, certainly mindful that Sullivan on the ticket would be a lightning rod for progressive antipathy, let it be known that he found the renomination of Marshall acceptable.[47]

Accordingly, the Illinois caucus took only a symbolic vote on the issue. However, this revealed that forty-seven (forty-eight if one had not been absent) of the fifty-eight delegates were still for a Wilson-Sullivan ticket. Dunne, Harrison, Millard Fillmore Dunlap, and seven others absented themselves in protest. Immediately afterwards, at the direction of the "Biscuit Maker" (a moniker he was encouraging these days based upon his association with the Sawyer Biscuit Company) another vote was taken, and this predictably came out for Marshall. Afterwards, Sullivan claimed that he was never in any case serious about the second spot on the ticket. He did take the time, however, to thank his friends.[48]

In the end, Sullivan's candidacy had little apparent impact upon the course of the convention, beyond aggravating the still-fresh factional wounds of the Democratic Party of Illinois. However, there was probably more at work than was reported at the time. Dennis Egan, a man high in his leader counsels, backed up by George Brennan, Robert Sweitzer, and others would insist years later that the nomination was Roger's "if he had just said the word." Claiming to have had "enough votes pledged in St. Louis to nominate Roger Sullivan on the first ballot," it was Sullivan, himself, who "put his foot down" out of loyalty to the Democratic Party and a desire not to sow discord. Wilson was not "aggressive in his suggestion" that Marshall be retained, and the eastern urban leaders like Murphy and Taggart were on board, ready to be joined by "other states." Whether accurate or not, a serious Sullivan bid might well have changed history; it being difficult to imagine a man so much more dynamic than Marshall responding, as he did, with inaction in face of Wilson's eventual disability. On the other hand, whether the president would have secured reelection in such a close contest with a running mate so often vilified as a big city boss remains questionable. Still, there is little doubt that Roger Sullivan, if given the opportunity, would have fulfilled his function as the second man of state with dignity and competence.[49]

For all of the angst generated within the Illinois delegation by the vice presidential nomination, the Democratic national convention of 1916 was a generally restrained, even dull, affair. For one thing, there was no doubt that Woodrow Wilson would be renominated, and such suspense as the press attempted to create over the second spot on the ticket failed to inject much excitement. For another, William Jennings Bryan, now almost powerless, was for once relatively quiet. Though not an elected delegate, he was present as a reporter, and he was invited to speak, a move that pleased many on the floor. His brief (by his standards) address focused upon the supposed inadequacies of the Republicans, and emphasized "a united party," ready to do "battle" for Woodrow Wilson.[50]

Nor can the impact of the shadow of war be discounted in the understanding the relatively somber mood of the delegates. Just six weeks before, on March 15, General John "Blackjack" Pershing and his troops crossed the nation's southern border in response to outrages against Americans on American soil by Mexican "revolutionaries." Probably only the chaotic situation in Mexico brought by a state of perpetual revolution that had begun in 1910, kept a formal war from developing. Nonetheless, just over a week following the convention's adjournment, the lives of three American troops were lost in a skirmish at San Ignacio, Texas, and scattered fights would continue. It would not be until the fall that the tensions finally eased.[51]

The only real break in the restraint of the convention came with the presentation of the platform. Included was a recommendation to the states to recognize the right of women to vote, something Roger Sullivan strongly supported. However, the language was a compromise that came after a hard fight in the platform committee, and it matched the similarly luke-warm plank already in place in the Republican platform.[52]

A little more excitement was created by Illinois' own Robert Emmett "Bobby" Burke. Alone among the state's delegates, he was elected as uncommitted. Before the convention, he announced that he would "not vote for Woodrow Wilson under any circumstances," and that "Mr. Sullivan and all his forces" could not make him change his mind. He was, however, willing to back the Chicago leader for the vice presidential nomination. It was speculated that he might register his vote for Speaker Champ Clark, but he confessed he had no alternative candidate in mind. At the evening session of the second day of the convention, June 15, 1916, nominating and seconding speeches were delivered for the president, and at their conclusion, William Hughes of New Jersey introduced a resolution to make his nomination by acclamation. Burke immediately rose to protest and to demand a roll call. When this was denied, and the resolution to nominate was presented for a voice vote, he alone demurred, making the tally 1,092 votes to one.

Burke never spoke about his motivations. However, it was reported that his acting out a form of protest against the Wilson administration's recent dealings with Germany and Austria-Hungary, as well as its supposed favoritism towards the British and the French. This was substantiated when Chicago's German-American Alliance publicly sent their congratulations, which must have been embarrassing for Roger Sullivan. However, Burke was a valued ally, and his protest meant little, so his dissent was tolerated for the moment (besides it was a reminder to the Wilson administration of their need for Sullivan to control the Illinois party). Sanctions for this breach of political etiquette would have to wait until 1920.[53]

After the convention, the "humiliation" of Roger Sullivan (for so it was perceived by some of his men) over the vice presidential nomination was neither forgotten nor forgiven. What appeared to have been primarily a favorite son candidacy to allow his friends to honor him, while bringing a measure of national recognition as well, was transformed, in part through the actions of Governor Dunne and Senator Lewis, into a personal affront. Soon there emerged, apparently from within the Sullivan organization, a plan that would facilitate a measure of revenge, and perhaps also strengthen the state ticket. The exact provenance of the idea to replace Dunne as the gubernatorial nominee with Raymond Robins is unclear. Given the positive response with which it was greeted by the national administration, it is possible that the president, in keeping with his life-long proclivity of putting his own self-interest over those of his supporters, friends, and advisors conceived the scheme. On the other hand, there were earlier reports of discussions in Illinois almost immediately after the national convention of running some "regular" candidate against Dunne in the upcoming September primary, and names mentioned included former sheriff John E. Traeger and county clerk Robert M. Sweitzer. It was only later that Robins name began to be discussed, and Sullivan's cohort George Brennan was reported as the most enthusiastic about the idea.[54]

Robins was the Illinois Progressive candidate for Senator in 1914, and then the party's state chair. He was a longstanding opponent of Sullivan, and his reformist credentials were impeccable. Should he receive the Democratic nomination for governor, he would, or so it was presumed, draw much of the former Progressive vote, and therefore would stand a good chance of election. Of course, too, electing Robins or even running him for governor would go far towards fulfilling Sullivan's desire "to accumulate a certain amount of respectability in his remaining years."[55]

A bemused Robins was soon being importuned by letters and telegrams from Democrats eager to put him at the head of the state ticket, including one from a Danville man who promised that "the Democratic men here especially Sullivans [sic] main man of the local Daily [sic] paper," were going to do anything necessary "down this way" to secure his nomination. Even some Democrats who might not necessarily have followed Sullivan's lead could see the merit in replacing Dunne, who many felt "had not got the punch" and had "not" been "a successful executive." Nationally, Vance C. McCormick, the new chair of the Democratic national committee also looked with favor upon the scheme, believing that a Robins candidacy would help Wilson in Illinois. Vague promises of appointing Dunne to the federal farm board if he agreed to withdraw were made directly to the governor by McCormick during a visit to Chicago in early July. Later McCormick asked the Secretary of the Navy Josephus Daniels to use his influence with William Jennings Bryan to convince Dunne to go along (a suggestion the Commoner chose to ignore).[56]

However, for all the apparent support for the scheme, it died a quick death. For one thing, while there was considerable anger against Dunne among the Chicago Sullivanites, downstate was a different story. State Chair (and currently a candidate for the nomination for state treasurer) Arthur Charles made this point by saying to the press: "I am for Roger Sullivan when it comes to matters of personal friendship, but it looks to the downstate men as if it would be very foolish to start a Sullivan candidate against Dunne in the primaries.... I can't find any general sentiment out in the state for a fight on Dunne in the Democratic ranks." In the second place, the governor was determined to fight for the nomination even if it meant alienating the Wilson administration, and the primary could become divisive and bitter. In the third place, Raymond Robins, refused even the blandishments of Roger Sullivan himself, and declined to become involved for fear that, should he be elected, he would be the "bosses" creature. In early August, Robins announced he was behind the Republican ticket in Illinois as well as nationally.[57]

Subsequently, the Sullivan organization decided to forego naming a gubernatorial candidate. This was effectively an endorsement of the governor, and Dunne only faced two minor opponents. This happy state of affairs was maintained until just before the September 9, 1916, primary when the Cook County Democratic managing committee suddenly and unexpectedly endorsed one of these, William Brinton of Dixon. Brinton, to this point, was not an especially serious contender; he entered the contest "just to see how many votes he'd get," and he never had criticized Governor Dunne. At the heart of the Cook County regulars' sudden and emotional abandonment of Dunne was a particularly scathing pamphlet written by Philip J. McKenna, a follower of Carter Harrison and formerly president of the Chicago Sanitary District Board, and Joseph P. Gibbons, whom Dunne had appointed as state grain inspector. Titled "Save the Honor of Chicago," its chapters said it all: "Roger Sullivan has Never Been A [sic] Democrat," "Roger Sullivan Repudiated by President Wilson" and "A Public Office is Deemed a Private Snap." Sullivan was also characterized (once again) as a "menace" to the party.[58]

The revolt against Dunne appeared to be genuinely spontaneous and emotion-driven; Sullivan, who was in New York and other points east for most of this time, made no comment. However, this movement for Brinton was confined to Cook County, and was nowhere to be found downstate. Consequently, the governor easily won renomination by a margin of 151,763 to Brinton's 65,639, and 21,105 for James Traynor. But in Cook County, Brinton's numbers were unquestionably enhanced, and he was given 29,732 votes to 84,987 for Dunne, in a contest that would have been otherwise virtually unanimous for the governor.[59]

Aside from the Robins matter and the Dunne mutiny, the primaries proceeded smoothly. The remnants of the Harrison forces working with Dunne's personal following in Cook County managed to front a slate of candidates for the considerable number of county positions, but their weakness was apparent. Nonetheless, Roger Sullivan enjoyed himself rallying the troops and warning against overconfidence in a number of speeches, including one delivered at the First Regimental Armory before an audience of over 5,000. He explained that he was speaking as fulfillments of a pledge made during the senate race to "henceforth give my time and effort to helping you [the organization's candidates] who have so generously helped me." At his side on the platform were Maclay Hoyne, until recently a major pillar of the Harrison faction, Attorney General Patrick Lucey, and Robert Sweitzer. Roger's appearance rocked the hall as he praised the president, the support of whom he labeled every Democrat's "highest duty." He went on to credit Wilson for continued peace and "prosperity without financial debauchery."[60]

As it proved, any worries about "overconfidence" were unjustified. Sullivan's county candidates won by substantial margins in every contest including those for state's attorney, recorder, president of the sanitary board, clerk of the superior court, the board of assessors, the board of review, surveyor, and municipal court judges. His choices also carried the state primary, defeating along the way Barratt O'Hara for renomination as lieutenant-governor and securing the selection of state chair Arthur W. Charles as the party's nominee for state treasurer.[61]

As was his usual practice when in a position of strength, Roger Sullivan began reaching out to those lately his opposition by issuing a statement promising Governor Dunne that he could "rest assured that there will be a united Democracy behind him in the November election." He made light of the defection from Dunne in the primary, explaining that "our decision to run Mr. Brinton as a candidate for governor was an eleventh hour one." An agreement was reached permitting the governor to oversee the downstate campaign, where Dunne still enjoyed considerable personal popularity, while Sullivan and his lieutenants were to be in charge in Cook County. Further, Dunne was to compose the state platform. However, in a conference in Chicago between Sullivan, Vance McCormick, chair of the Democratic National Committee, and feminist leaders like Antoinette Funk, it was agreed that a plank calling for full woman's suffrage must be included.[62]

The state convention, held in Springfield on September 25, ran smoothly. Sullivan allowed the governor to deliver the keynote address and to present a platform that returned to the strident progressivism of 1913. Planks included calls for woman's suffrage, closer regulation of corporations and banks, a corrupt practices law, and the eight-hour day for men and women.[63]

The strength of the Republican state ticket, thanks to the return of most Progressives did not go unnoticed by the Wilson administration, which insisted that Sullivan and the Illinois leadership concentrate upon securing Illinois' electoral votes for the president, leaving the county and state candidates largely to their own devices. Even Governor Dunne received little assistance, financial or otherwise, from either the state or the national committee. Only William Jennings Bryan came to help and to speak for his old friend and ally. Otherwise Dunne's campaign mainly consisted of a few self-financed auto tours.

This stood in sharp contrast with the circus-like atmosphere of the Lowden appearances with the Republican nominee traveling the state in a train in company of an elephant and a fife and drum corps. No clowns were hired, but local politicians were asked to join and speak as the show moved through their areas. As Lowden was in sympathy with much of what Dunne accomplished, he either attacked the governor for supposed deficiencies in governmental economy and efficiency, or he focused upon Woodrow Wilson. Roger Sullivan's sole public venture into the local campaign came just days before the elections when he issued a signed statement exhorting Democrats and the voters to reelect Maclay Hoyne as state's attorney. Failure to return him to office, Sullivan argued, "would be to place a premium on crime and to give free reign to criminals." Since Hoyne had been in the past an important factional opponent, Sullivan's missive can be best understood as a necessary restatement of his organization's endorsement.[64]

However, the center ring in the state, as in the nation, remained the president's reelection campaign. The western headquarters opened at the Karpen Building on Michigan Avenue. Senator Thomas Walsh of Montana was placed in charge. Roger Sullivan cooperated closely, and was present (and cheered by the crowd) to greet the president during his visit in late October. Later, he even appeared at a meeting with Senator Lewis and Governor Dunne to speak in praise of Wilson.[65]

Although the Democratic campaign did its best to emphasize the accomplishments of the president's New Freedom domestic program, it was foreign affairs—for the first time in any national election since 1900—that dominated the rhetoric. "He kept us out of war," was the slogan used to convince the American people, and especially American women (who were believed to be more pacifistic than their menfolk), that but for the restraint and wisdom of Woodrow Wilson, America's sons would be even now fighting and dying on battlefields overseas. As time went on this theme was presented in ever more negative terms. Eventually it was reduced to the simple but effective argument that a vote for Hughes was a vote for war. It was a powerful point that resonated well with a public that mostly believed that no American interest was involved in the European war.

The Republican response was predictably heated as they denigrated (correctly as it proved) the fruits of the president's diplomacy as a "false peace." Theodore Roosevelt, who was campaigning for Hughes, mocked Wilson for "speaking bombastically" and creating "dishonor" by doing nothing of substance about the outrages on the high seas. Charles Evans Hughes went even further and blamed the president in part for the deaths of Americans on the torpedoed British liner *Lusitania* in 1915, arguing that a stronger policy earlier would have convinced the Germans to forego unrestricted submarine warfare completely.[66]

On election night, Hughes lead began to build as returns were reported from the eastern states, and his lead appeared so formidable that the president, and the country, went to bed convinced of a Republican victory. However, gains in the West began first to equalize the count, and then to put Wilson ahead. It was not to be until the evening of November 9, when California, contrary to general expectations, came in for the Democrat that the outcome became certain. This inspired a minor celebratory riot in the Chicago loop by two hundred or so younger Wilson's supporters requiring a police intervention.[67]

The Democrats were less successful in the Illinois; Hughes won the state by the substantial margin of 52.27 percent to 43.33 percent for Wilson. Even in Cook County, though their majority was less, the Republicans prevailed easily, sweeping all of the Cook County offices except for state's attorney, where Maclay Hoyne's positive reputation and Sullivan's endorsement made him the exception among the Democratic candidates. The Republicans also took all of the state offices on the ballot from Governor down to the Trustees of the University of Illinois. Sullivan and the state Democrats could take cheer at Wilson's narrow victory, but that could neither disguise the fact that the Republicans had returned as the majority party in Illinois, nor quell a growing but quietly stated suspicion that the interests of the state Democracy had been sacrificed for the president's ambitions.[68]

8

"Grand Dukes and Bolsheviki"
(1917–1919)

"Roger Sullivan's gas and traction Democracy"—Maclay Hoyne, state's attorney

The victory in 1915 of Roger C. Sullivan's candidate in the mayoral primary over Carter Harrison, conjoined to the defeat in 1916 of Edward F. Dunne as governor, solidified his supremacy in the state and local Democratic Party. Only Senator J. Hamilton Lewis remained of the once touted reformist coalition cobbled together for the purpose of opposing Sullivan's leadership, and the senator, facing a difficult reelection in 1918, was too weak to muster further challenges. Tellingly, he soon endorsed Roger's candidate, Dixon Williams, as Chicago postmaster, a man who just months before he had vehemently opposed.[1]

However, victory carried a double-edge. It was all well and good that Harrison and Dunne with their dwindling cadres of loyalists were now largely consigned to the margins of party politics, but the loss of both the mayor's and governor's offices reduced the party to an enduring minority status in the state. While this was a reflection of both state and national trends and had little to do with Sullivan, or his leadership, it also meant that, with the Republicans routinely winning most important state-wide elections, any hopes Roger may have harbored for further political advancement were now highly problematic. He would have to content himself with a heading a truncated state and local Democracy, based upon the largely distributed federal plums, those of Cook County, and such jobs and patronage as were available by law and custom to the minority party in Chicago and Illinois.

Still, within the Democratic Party, Sullivan remained ascendant. In the February 1917 aldermanic primaries as well as in those for the few administrative positions up for grabs (which historically had belonged to Harrison), such opposition as remained was scattered and featured Florence E. Sullivan, a Dunne man, filing for city treasurer against Roger's Clayton Smith, and John J. McLaughlin, once a major member of the Sullivan organization, running for city clerk against the regular James T. Igoe. There were also lively aldermanic fights in some of the wards. But it was no contest as the Sullivan Democracy continued its relentless advance. Indeed, Roger had become so complacent that he spent most of the campaign in Palm Beach with his family.[2]

On the Republican side, the outcome was somewhat more dramatic, as there, too, organizational politics prevailed. Charles Merriam, once the reformist champion of his party, and now a major opponent of Mayor William Hale Thompson, was defeated (losing by five votes) for renomination as alderman of the Seventh Ward by Thompson's choice, Leo Flanagan. Crying fraud, Merriam mounted a doomed independent candidacy. Other Republicans were also divided about Thompson, and this undercut GOP unity as the election approached. Whether because of Republican discord or, as was more likely, because of a growing dissatisfaction with the mayor, the Democrats easily won the elections. Most importantly, they regained the control of the city council lost in 1915, raising their totals from thirty-two to forty-two of the seventy seats.[3]

However, the drama of Chicago factional politics seemed trivial in face of the sobering onset of war. On the day following the primary election, the United States Senate voted by a margin of 82 to 6 to enter the conflict against Germany, a decision ratified a day later by the House of Representatives by 373 to 50.[4]

After securing reelection (November 7, 1916) based on the slogan, "He kept us out of war!" President Woodrow Wilson sought to implement his self-defined role as peacemaker by fronting a German peace proposal to France, Great Britain, and their allies. The offer held the promise for a cession of hostilities based upon the *status quo antebellum*. This was unacceptable to the allied powers, which insisted upon restitution and reparations. Germany responded with a massive offensive on the Western Front in France planned to begin on March 21, 1917. It was felt that this attack would bring victory if augmented by a resumption of unrestricted submarine warfare to starve out Great Britain. On January 31, 1917, the Imperial Government notified the United States of its decision to rescind its earlier pledges concerning its use of the undersea weapon. Three days later, Wilson broke diplomatic relations with both Germany and its partner, the Austrian-Hungarian Empire. Several weeks later, on February 28, a note from Germany's foreign minister Arthur Zimmermann, intercepted by the British, was released to the American people. The offer to exchange American territory for Mexican support in the event of war outraged the American people.

On March 2, Wilson asked Congress for the authority to arm American merchant carriers, which was granted, but only after a filibuster led by Wisconsin's Robert La Follette was overridden by a cloture vote in the senate. Even as the Congress debated, Britain and France's ally, the Russian czar, was overthrown and a provisional government that seemed to promise a liberal democratic future was established. Russia's repudiation of the most oppressive regime in Europe helped transform the war in the minds of Wilson and others from the imperialistic struggle that it was, into a moral battle between autocracy and democracy, one in which the destiny of mankind hung in the balance. Calling for a crusade to make the "world safe for democracy," the president, on April 2, 1917, appeared before Congress to ask for a declaration of the existence of a state of war with Germany.[5].

Since January 1917, there had been a rising clamor for American entry; flags began to appear on newspaper mastheads and lively discussions about the nation's military potential began filling the pages of the press. Now all official focus was upon preparing for total war. For two and half years Americans had read of the carnage on the battlefields, and there was every expectation that further bloody years would be necessary before Germany would yield. Added to this was a pervasive insecurity, akin to that felt by the new kid in school, which fueled a determination to prove that the United States could match its new allies in manly fortitude and combat prowess. Moreover, because the country did not habitually maintain a substantial war establishment, special sacrifice and service for accelerated armament was demanded. Some bought Liberty Bonds, or donated money to the Red Cross, the YMCA, the Salvation Army, the War Recreational Board, and other such organizations; Chicago would be proud of the almost 1.65 billion dollars its citizens would ultimately contribute. Others enlisted, volunteered for a government job, or flocked to the factories for war work. The political establishment, with some notable exceptions, enthusiastically embraced the war effort. Carter Harrison signed up with the Red Cross and served as a lieutenant in France. Most conspicuously representing the Sullivan faction was John P. Hopkins as a member of the Illinois State Council of Defense. This was created by the legislature, at the request of the Wilson administration, to be one of forty-eight such state boards operating under the newly configured National Council of Defense.[6]

Its responsibilities were to coordinate all civilian war activities including:

> Producing, collecting, and conserving food and other essential commodities; making inventories of human and material resources; selling bonds, sustaining morale; arranging for patriotic meetings; providing recreation and amusement for men in uniform; educating youths in the skills needed on the home front; and encouraging the saving of records essential to the preparation of a war history.[7]

Its chair was Samuel Insull, the electrical and gas utility magnate and Sullivan's close friend. Hopkins served as secretary, as chair of the Committee on Industrial Survey, and as a member of the auditing committee. The others on the council represented a cross section of the state's economic and political elite and included Lieutenant Governor John Oglesby (whose office in Springfield was the official headquarters, although most meetings were actually held at the Edison building belonging to Insull at 120 West Adams Street in Chicago), the former speaker of the state house, David Shanahan, meatpacking millionaires J. Ogden Armour, and John A. Spoor, banker B. F. Harris, Charles H. Wacker of the Chicago Plan Commission, union leaders Victor Olander and John H. Walker, Republican operative Fred W. Upham, corporate lawyer Levy Mayer, and noted Chicago physician Dr. Frank Billings. Hopkins rarely missed a meeting, and when he did, Roger Sullivan usually stood in as his proxy.

In 1918, Roger accepted an appointment to the Special Citizen's Committee of Chicago for the War Exposition and, with John Hopkins, was a member of the Ways and Means Committee of the Chicago Liberty Loan Committee. Mrs. Roger Sullivan also did some local work through the Catholic Woman's League in Chicago, and joined her husband and former governor Edward F. Dunne in late 1917 on the Cook County Auxiliary Committee. This was designed to facilitate the recruitment into war work of the county's various ethnic communities (the committee included three African Americans). As the state legislature did not meet after the summer of 1917 until the fighting ended, the State Council of Defense with Governor Lowden and his cabinet effectively became the state's war-time government.[8]

Not all Americans would so easily stand-to. Some immigrants from Germany and their children and grandchildren found it difficult to accept the depiction of their cousins and relatives in Europe as "Huns" and enemies of civilization. The mother of Illinois' future senator, Everett Dirksen, for example, refused to remove a revered photograph of Kaiser Wilhelm II from the family wall. Many others also were not comfortable with the characterization of the German emperor—a man they had been taught to venerate since childhood—as a war criminal. A considerable portion of the Irish-American community found it equally challenging to identify the cause of democracy with the British, who for

Women making ordnance in Chicago (Library of Congress, DIG-ppmsca-40774).

centuries denied—and continued to deny–Ireland self-rule and independence. The socialist community (with some important exceptions), centered in the Socialist Party of America, the Socialist Labor Party, and the Industrial Workers of the World, were ideologically
bound to an interpretation of the Great War as an imperialist conflict between ruling
classes in which the working man was cannon fodder. There were also considerable numbers who, for either religious or philosophical reasons, simply opposed the idea of all
war despite the ridicule and persecution their beliefs inspired. Lastly there was a body
of Americans, especially in the Midwest, who clung to the nation's traditional policy of
avoiding foreign entanglements.

Mayor William Hale Thompson, already a controversial figure, saw political capital
in all of this. His much publicized comment that Chicago was the "sixth largest German
city in the world," despite its truth, occasioned much anger, as did his refusal formally
to invite a French diplomatic mission, headed by French minister of justice, Rene Viviani,
and Marshal Joseph Joffre, for a visit. The city council quickly responded with its own
official welcome, and the French celebrities were met with three days of ecstatic ceremony.
Roger Sullivan and John Hopkins were members of the greeting committee.[9]

In September 1917, Thompson, now running unsuccessfully for the Republican senatorial nomination, provoked still greater anger when he permitted something called the
People's Council of America for Democracy and Peace to hold its meeting in Chicago.

The group, which was hardly subversive but rather pacifistic (Illinois congressman William E. Mason was to be the featured speaker), had been denied permission to gather in Minnesota, North Dakota, and Wisconsin, but managed to rent the West Side Auditorium for the first day of September. However, Governor Lowden took charge on the grounds that the group was bent upon creating "disorder and rioting" and ordered Chicago's police to prevent the gathering. Thompson, furious, disputed the governor's right to intervene, and directed police superintendent Herman F. Schusettler not only to allow the meeting, but to protect it as well. It, accordingly, convened on the second day of September. Lowden sent several regiments of the Illinois National Guard from Springfield to break it up, but the meeting adjourned before they arrived. The situation was a national scandal, and an embarrassment for much of the city, and created considerable antipathy towards "Burgomeister Bill." The city council overwhelmingly voted its condemnation.[10]

The anger with Thompson proved to be but a tepid foreshadowing of the hysteria that would arise in face of actual resistance to the war effort—whether constitutionally protected or not. The early passage of a draft in May—the first since the Civil War—served as an initial focal point, and opponents of conscription soon made themselves conspicuous with anti-war speeches and meetings in Chicago and across the nation. In Toledo, Ohio a riot, involving over 2,000 men, broke out in response to a street meeting called to protest the new measure. Descriptions of the president as "Kaiser Wilson" brought a violent response from the police, who were joined by newly enlisted soldiers, and other bystanders. Days later, twelve socialists were arrested in Cincinnati for distributing pamphlets questioning the constitutionality of the draft. In June, a mob surrounded a New York City jailhouse demanding the release of several men arrested for speaking at an anti-draft gathering, and elements of the National Guard were called. At their annual picnic that summer, the Socialists of Chicago openly dedicated themselves to identifying strategies to undermine the draft, the president, and the war. And so it went. Making the activities of the American Left all the more sinister were events in Russia, where that summer the radical Bolsheviks first threatened the Provisional Government, and then, in November, succeeded in its overthrow. This, with their subsequent negotiations to withdraw from the war, helped to further brand all socialists with the mark of treason as enablers of "German Peace Plots."[11]

Retribution was not long in coming as those dedicated to making the world safe for democracy strove to prevent dissent. In June 1917, the Espionage Act was enacted, and this, augmented by a Sedition Act the following year, essentially empowered the federal government to repress any and all criticism. Draft resisters faced well-publicized arrests and indictments, and socialists of all stripes, being the most active and the most easily despised of the war's opponents, were made a special target as the Great War to transform the world based upon American values (or so it was being promoted) became increasingly anti–Marxist in tenor.

Chicago as the site of the headquarters of the Socialist Party of America and the Industrial Workers of the World was an obvious focal point for repression. Raids by justice department agents were conducted in September 1917 upon both the Socialists and IWW. Much of their leadership, including revered socialist leader Eugene Debs (who had once served in the Indiana General Assembly as a Democrat), would be convicted of sedition. Nor were German Americans excused from the patriotic scrutiny and excess. The offices and printing plants of numerous German language newspapers like Chicago's

Arbeitzer Zeitung and the *Social Demokratin* were raided and thoroughly looted, as was the Radical Book Store. It also became fashionable to disparage all things German; schools dropped the language from their curricula, and sauerkraut became liberty cabbage. Entering the fray to neutralize all internal enemies were members of private organizations like the American Protective League, who eagerly made "prompt and reliable reports" about their fellow citizens. Personal assaults were not uncommon.[12]

All of this was not without effect upon local Chicago politics. In September, a conference was held by representatives of the Democratic and Republican parties, where it was agreed to front a fusion ticket in the judicial elections to counter what was expected to be an unusually large Socialist vote. This meant that all twelve of the Democratic and Republican incumbent jurists ran without major party opposition, while two seats that were recently made vacant through the deaths of their occupants would be split. As it proved, the Socialists did increase their return, but hardly decisively, in the November elections.[13]

However, Roger Sullivan was sufficiently impressed with the results, and with the possibility of some kind of Socialist electoral victory as an anti-war statement, that he now proposed more fusion tickets in the coming year. Noting that the Socialists had polled about one third of the vote, he explained: "Chicago cannot afford, from any point of view, to have its next mayor developed by the elements coalesced by the anti-war ticket for judges," nor could it risk the embarrassment of a disloyal United States Senator (both clear references to Mayor Thompson's expected candidacy for his party's nomination to the senate in the fall, and, if that failed, for reelection as mayor in the spring of 1919). Accordingly, Sullivan publicly proposed "agreed upon" candidates for senator in 1918 and mayor in 1919, in collusion with the Republicans as well as "for all intervening city and county offices in accord with these fundamentals." The plan, which was consistent with his long-standing policy of seeking consensus over conflict, attracted considerable attention for a time. However, some wondered whether it was all a ploy to get himself elected senator, while others, like former Governor Edward F. Dunne (loyal to his ally Senator Ham Lewis), felt it would evolve into a simple—and unfair—trade with the Republicans of the mayor's office for Lewis' ouster from the Senate. No formal agreement was reached, but in the aldermanic elections the following spring a single candidate in the Twenty-Third Ward (a Republican) was run with the apparent backing of both major parties.[14]

Despite some sharp fights put up by the increasingly insignificant Harrison faction, the aldermanic primaries of 1918 were another set of victories for the Sullivan machine. Every incumbent Democratic alderman (almost all of whom had made their peace with Sullivan) was renominated and "the Sullivan regulars were as a rule in easy control of the Democratic nominations all over the city." Even better, the actual elections in April increased the number of Democrats on the city council to forty-five, or a gain of two. The Socialists lost two of their seats, but did pick up the Fifteenth Ward, bringing their new total to just two. Chicago's honor and patriotism were vindicated.[15]

Next up was the question of the senatorial and county nominations to be decided by primary in September 1918. Ham Lewis, the state's sitting Democratic senator, had the advantage of incumbency, but he also had stood with former governor Dunne and former mayor Harrison in the factional wars. Consequently, there was some discussion among the regulars about finding another candidate. However, with the prevailing Republican strength making a major intraparty fight inadvisable and, more importantly, with the Wilson administration's clear signals that it wanted Lewis back in the Senate, where he was serving as Democratic whip, Sullivan and his sachems decided to extend the olive branch. It was agreed that Sullivan's men on the state committee would oversee the senator's campaign. This had the added advantage of assuring that neither Lewis nor his campaign manager, William O'Connell, would join with Dunne and others in formal opposition over the Cook County nominations.[16]

Although they were probably not very hopeful for success, Sullivan's dwindling collection of disparate party foes organized themselves into something called the "Allied Democracy"—a name obviously inspired by the nation's wartime "Allies," Britain, France, Italy, and Japan. A meeting of the "antis," or "anti–Sullivan" men, was held at the Brevoort Hotel in Chicago at the end of May, and a committee that included Dunne, Harrison, Sheriff John A. Traeger, State's Attorney Maclay Hoyne, Congressman Adolph Sabath, and others was appointed to draw up an opposition slate. A platform was composed that, among other things, demanded a "local government under which the people will not be compelled to wear gas masks," and in slaps at both Mayor William Hale Thompson and Sullivan, also called for greater public utility reform and regulation, elected officials not beholden to the public utilities, increased gas prices "to reimburse the gas corporation for 'holdups' by the Ogden gas company and similar corporations," and clean, honest registration and elections.[17]

Dunne was the group's featured speaker, joined eventually by Carter Harrison, back from France. The former governor generally avoided naming names, but recited his favorite theme of the evils of the utility corporations and Sullivan's friend, the utility baron, Samuel Insull. Harrison was less restrained and broadened his attacks to include Boetius Sullivan ("son of the leader of the self-styled regular Democracy") for representing the gas monopoly as an attorney before the state utility commission, where, it was carefully pointed out, Sullivan man and now commission member, former attorney general Patrick Lucey, voted for an increase in prices.[18]

Sullivan got in his own licks. At the pre-primary county convention (which was actually just a rally of the regulars), at the Coliseum on August 26, he was introduced as "Illinois' great Democratic leader," and delivered a passionate keynote speech to the 12,000 assembled partisans in which he likened the leaders of the Allied Democracy to "Grand Dukes and Bolsheviki" (a remarkable oxymoronic analogy), "actuated by personal selfishness." He expanded his theme to include condemnations of those "office holders and public men who have shown a tendency to embarrass the government in time of war," meaning Mayor Thompson, and those "who have sought to array class against class," meaning the socialists. This provoked a scathing retort from Carter Harrison, who found it bad form for "a millionaire capitalist" to dub "every citizen of moderate means who dares to lift his voice against barefaced public robbery as an I.W.W. and a Bolshevik." Moreover, or so the former mayor maintained, the actual grand dukes and Bolsheviki were those "who planned and put over the gas steal," a reference to the now ancient and mostly forgotten, but endlessly revived, Ogden Gas scandal.[19]

The Allied Democrats were hopelessly outgunned and outnumbered, and concentrated their fight upon only a few positions. Incumbent county judge and Sullivan candidate Thomas Scully was opposed by the Allies' John E. Owen, once county judge and sheriff, and one of the leading actors in the great battle for control of the 1912 county convention. For the sheriff's office, the Sullivan men were backing Anton Cermak, once a pillar of the Harrison faction but now with the machine. The primary elections, held on September 11, 1918, returned the usual Sullivan majorities of over two to one in Cook

County, as well as equally substantial results in the state contests, where Lewis won easily against token opposition.

Sullivan took the occasion of his victory to once again seek consensus; "our opponents at the primary polls put up a fair, clean fight," he soothed, "and now that our own ticket has won, the hand of friendship is being extended to every Democrat." This time his plea found some success; an agreement reached with Edward F. Dunne (though not with Harrison) to unite behind the candidacy of Lewis. This signaled the demise of the Allied Democracy. At the state convention, held in Springfield on September 20, the machine was, as was now usual, in control. Lewis was renominated upon a very liberal platform that proclaimed its concern about the "record of disloyalty" of Mayor Thompson, as well as its support of Wilson and, most especially, of women's suffrage with an endorsement of what would become the Nineteenth Amendment, then pending in many state legislatures. A new state chair, Ernest Hoover from Taylorville, Illinois, long a Sullivan-ally, was chosen.[20]

Lewis' Republican opponent was Medill McCormick. He had won a tough primary battle against Mayor Thompson. But for the adverse response to the meeting of the People's Council for Democracy and Peace in Chicago, the mayor might well have secured his party's nomination as well as subsequent election (which would have, no doubt, created some interesting moments for future histories of the United States Senate). McCormick was the grandson of Joseph Medill, the founder of the powerful and generally progressive *Chicago Tribune*. He briefly ran the paper between 1903 and 1907. However, unknown to the public at large, he was tormented by personal demons (he would commit suicide in 1925), and for a period he abandoned the paper for therapy from the famed Swiss psychiatrist, Carl Jung. By 1912, he was well-enough to accept an appointment as vice chair of the national committee of the Progressive Party. Under this banner, he was elected to the Illinois House of Representatives, and then, in 1914, to Congress. He soon followed Roosevelt back into the Republican Party, where he was a leading celebrity of the reformist wing as a known and vehement opponent of William Hale Thompson.[21]

Lewis and the state committee planned their campaign based upon an appeal for nonpartisan war-time support for Wilson. Recognizing that the Democrats were now a minority in the state, it made sense to emphasize Lewis' incumbency while evoking the aura of patriotic majesty associated with the commander-in-chief. Roger Sullivan actively helped. In late September, he spoke for the senator and the Democratic ticket at the Iroquois Club, urging loyalty to the war effort. Subsequently, he traveled to Washington, D.C., in a vain attempt to line up important administration speakers to come to Illinois. However, before the campaign could truly begin, a tragedy intruded that, for a time, overshadowed even the slaughter in Europe—and it would help break the heart of Roger C. Sullivan.[22]

On June 1, 1918, a small article appeared in the *New York Times* reporting the appearance of a "queer epidemic" that "resembled influenza" raging across northern China, killing thousands in its wake. The story attracted little interest. There was a war on, and besides, many Americans were even now recovering from an outbreak of the usual flu, or "grip," circulating since the previous winter. Within a couple of weeks, however, the American press began noting the reports of a particularly viral strain of influenza raging within the German lines, all the while assuring the public that no cases were to be found among the Allied soldiery. Indeed, there was a certain satisfaction evident at what appeared to be a fitting divine retribution against the evil Huns and their Kaiser, who became seriously ill from the disease.[23]

It soon become apparent, however, that God was not a recognizer of persons after all; the infection spread, acquiring along the way the moniker of the "Spanish Flu," as Spain was one of the first areas in the "civilized world" to report openly its ravages. His Catholic Majesty, King Alphonso, XIII, would nearly succumb, even as one third of the population of his capital of Madrid took to their beds. And Spain was not exceptional. The influenza epidemic of 1918 was to prove to be the most sweeping and persistent in modern history, attacking in three waves. The first, and milder, came in the spring, the more deadly in the fall, followed by a last and sporadic appearance in early 1919. Its cold-like symptoms initially masked lethal effects founded in the virus' rare ability to reproduce itself in the lung (as was only discovered in 2008). Mortality was twenty-five times higher than usual. It was made particularly frightening because it tended to strike the young and strong. Moreover, it could kill within a day, transforming in a matter of hours, a healthy young adult into a feverish and helpless mass of wretched humanity choking its life out in great drowning gasps as lungs filled inexorably with blood-tinged fluids. The death toll would exceed even that of the Great War, and estimates of its world-wide mortality range between twenty and one hundred million.[24]

The first American cases began to appear in the early weeks of July 1918 in the great port of New York City; but through early August, the authorities there were assuring the public that the epidemic brought "no necessity for alarm," as it was of a "mild form." However, passengers from recently arrived ocean liners began dying, joined by fatalities in the many new army camps around the nation. The thousands of recently drafted young men crowded together in relatively primitive conditions provided an ideal spawning ground for the disease. Soon cities like Boston, Philadelphia, and Baltimore began counting their dead, as even important men, like the Assistant Secretary of the Navy Franklin Delano Roosevelt, were unable to escape its ghastly grasp. By late September, the flu was found in twenty-four states, by December into all forty-eight. It was to eventually sicken a quarter of the American people.[25]

Chicago watched the westward spread of the disease with morbid fascination. Like the press everywhere, Chicago's journalists sought to sooth their readers with assurances from public health officials that there was "no cause for alarm." As September ended, however, as the infection rate rose in the city to between 40,000 to 60,000 cases, and as growing numbers of deaths were reported at the nearby Great Lakes Naval Training Facility and elsewhere, all such pretense faded. On September 26, all public funerals were banned in the state. Two days later, the State Council of Defense appointed the Illinois Influenza Commission to maintain records and help coordinate the fight against the disease. On September 30, all street cars and elevated cars were ordered cleaned by the City Health Department, which began distributing literature with advice on prevention (which chiefly consisted of avoiding crowds and sleeping in fresh air). At the beginning of October, afflicted persons were ordered quarantined, and public expectoration was forbidden. All churches that were found to be poorly ventilated were directed to be closed, while pastors elsewhere were urged to ask those with obvious signs of illness to vacate their services. On October 14, theatres were shut down, and four days later, virtually all public gatherings including conventions, banquets, lectures, debates, lodge and union meetings, and athletic contests (but not all churches or any of the schools) were ordered cancelled. Meanwhile, state party leaders met to discuss suspending the fall campaign. Eventually, even the saloons ceased operation.[26]

In early November, things began improving, no thanks, however, to several purported "vaccines" that were hurriedly introduced. The military draft, which had been suspended, as well as most public activities such as football games and the like were resumed. However, the deaths would continue well into the spring of the New Year. In all, about 550,000 Americans, or five times the number of those who killed in the war, died in the epidemic, while those succumbing in Chicago from the flu or flu-related pneumonia were officially numbered at 14,759 between August 1918 and May 1919. Despite these high numbers, Chicago fared well with an infection rate of no more than 63 in 1,000 when contrasted to Philadelphia's 156, Baltimore's 147, and Pittsburgh's' 99. There also would be some small compensation. For example, smoking was permanently banned on streetcars and other forms of public transportation.[27]

For Roger Sullivan, the flu epidemic's immediate importance was its interference with a Liberty Loan drive that fall in which he was closely involved. Ceremonies on October 7, 1918, in fact, despite all fears and precautions, came off without a hitch, and featured massive parades and Theodore Roosevelt. The city eventually was able to exceed its quota. Nonetheless, the cruelty of the epidemic was soon to touch Sullivan closely. On the evening of October 13, 1918, Roger's business and political partner, dearest friend, and the former mayor of Chicago, John P. Hopkins died from effects of influenza. Roger sat at the bedside. Two weeks earlier, John developed difficulty swallowing. This was a recurring pathology, dating as far back as 1895, when he spent time at a German spa seeking a cure for what he described as a "chronic" throat affliction. Despite illness, he continued working long hours for the State Council of Defense. But he soon weakened, attending his last meeting in Chicago on October 4. Still, he might have survived but for the strain upon his apparently weak heart. He was just fifty-nine years old.[28]

His funeral two days late in keeping with wartime conditions and the continuing peril of the epidemic, was relatively restrained. Among his pallbearers were Patrick Nash, Francis S. Peabody, William J. Graham, John J. Corbett, John McGillen and William G. Legner. Scores of other political figures attended. These included Mayor Thompson, Edward Brundage, Medill McCormick, Ham Lewis, Ernest Hoover, Arthur Charles, Charles Boeschenstein, Tom Taggart, Norman Mack, and Urey Woodson. Samuel Insull with the entire membership of the State Council of Defense was also present. Others, like Governor Frank Lowden (who was listed as an honorary pallbearer) sent telegrams. Services were held at St. James Church at Wabash Avenue and Twenty-Sixth Street, and featured a military and naval escort. The Very Reverend John Cavanaugh, president of Notre Dame University, preached the funeral sermon, and Archbishop George W. Mundelein pronounced absolution. Both the county board and city council passed resolutions, and the county building, city hall, and many courts were closed. He was buried at Calvary Cemetery in Evanston, Illinois.[29]

Roger was named executor of John's sizable estate estimated to be worth in the neighborhood of seven million dollars (or perhaps eighty million dollars as valued at the beginning of the twenty-first century). The contents of his portfolio were concentrated in the utility business, with sizable holdings of Commonwealth Edison, the Public Service Company of Northern Illinois, the Midwest Utility Company, and the People's Gas and Coke Company stocks. He also held large investments in the Great Lakes Dredge and Dock Company, Union Carbide and Carbon, as well as smaller, but still substantial interests in such concerns as the Pullman Company, Swift and Company, Peabody Coal, American Can, Standard Oil of California, and the Congress Hotel. There was about three hundred thousand dollars in cash and Liberty Bonds in three banks. Hopkins, like Sullivan, was always an important player in the business world of Chicago.[30]

On October 25, Sullivan was named to the State Council of Defense, vowing to do as well as "our lamented and dear friend, John P. Hopkins." He, too, would be secretary, and he replaced John as chair of the Industrial Survey, and on the Auditing Committee, the Special Committee to Investigate the Naval Great Lake Training Center, the Special Committee to Investigate Rumors of the Abandonment of Fort Sheridan, and the Non-War Construction Bureau. In truth, as Sullivan's selection came just as the active phase of the war was ending, his activity was limited. The Council, however, continued its technical existence until November 21, 1919, the date of its last meeting.[31]

John P. Hopkins was the most prominent and beloved citizen in Chicago and Illinois to succumb to the influenza. However, even the news of his death and the epidemic itself were buried by the reports of unexpected peace that began circulating in late October. On November 11, 1918, the fighting ended as joyous chaos broke out on Chicago's streets. Naturally, the November elections were also largely overshadowed as this crowded year closed. In face of the flu and peace, the most newsworthy moment came when President Wilson, on October 25, issued an appeal (in part composed for the benefit of Ham Lewis' candidacy) for the election of a Democratic Congress as necessary for the war effort. As Wilson had called for a suspension of partisan politics following American entry into the conflict, this was seen by the Republicans as a betrayal. Wilson's appeal inadvertently undercut Lewis' hopes to present himself as the nonpartisan candidate.[32]

The president's ill-conceived intrusion probably helped the opposition. Lewis lost to McCormick, though he carried Chicago and Cook County, where the Democrats reelected Thomas Scully as county judge, Henry Horner as probate judge, Robert Sweitzer as county clerk, and Edward Tobin as superintendent of schools. The voters also selected Patrick Nash for the board of review, while maintaining the Democracy's control of the county board. Probably most disappointing was the defeat of the popular Anton Cermak for sheriff. Given the extent of G.O.P. success across the nation, however, the Democrats of Cook County under the leadership of Sullivan could count their blessings.[33]

Predictably, despite the worst pandemic in American history, despite the dramatic ending of the most sanguinary war in modern history to that point, and despite the death of a man of the stature of John P. Hopkins, there would be no respite as the political cycle brought yet another set of elections. These would be marked by the last reformist crusade in the city during the Progressive Era. The outcome would determine the political survival of "Big Bill" Thompson and the character of the subsequent era of Chicago's political history. Adding drama were the fears of impending world revolution in wake of the forcible imposition of Bolshevik rule in Russia and the collapse of Europe's empires.

Mayor Thompson was controversial and unpopular among the city's traditional elites. Charges of corruption in his administration, and especially in his police force, his courting of anti-war and German-American opinion, and his generally confrontational attitude contributed to a growing sense of distain and embarrassment. By the logic of the situation, the Democrats were being presented a golden opportunity to check the growing Republican ascendency in Illinois. But who should they run?

The days when Roger would retreat to the Sherman hotel with a few paladins and then announce a slate were long gone. What had begun as the Sullivan faction had evolved into the regular organization, and there were growing habits of collective leadership— or at least of customs of consultation. As in 1915, there was some suggestion that Sullivan might run. And as in 1915, he vigorously quashed the idea. Similarly, the party's last standard-bearer, Robert Sweitzer, appeared before the Cook County executive committee to make clear his own disinclination. About the only man initially willing to promote himself was Tom Carey. Once chair of the county committee under Carter Harrison, whom he had served loyally, Carey now sought to rally the remaining elements of the former mayor's following. Harrison was also importuned to make a bid, but, at his post in France with the Red Cross, the best he would do was to promise not to challenge Carey as an independent should his friend become the nominee.[34]

Roger Sullivan's focus, as always, was upon unifying the party. He and George Brennan lobbied the executive committee and key members of the Harrison-Dunne grouping for a consensus candidate. At last, a compromise seemed to have been reached in Congressman James McAndrews. However, Sullivan's own regulars balked, and refused even his strongest pleas. Exasperated, he complained to the press: "I don't suppose people will believe this, but this was one time when the committee tossed me out the window. This is the first time this has happened [apparently forgetting how in 1908, he was reelected to the national committeeman despite his protests]. I did everything in my power to name a man who would be mutually agreeable to the Harrison-Dunne faction and our men." Bemused, he further exclaimed: "I have been accused of being a political boss, but I'll have to say I have the least to say of any boss in the world!"[35]

Of course, as he well knew, this was not a rejection of his leadership, but simply a tactical disagreement in which the majority prevailed. That Sullivan could be overruled by his lieutenants spoke to the nature of his leadership and the organization he built. He also could not have been too displeased that Sweitzer finally agreed to run again. Highly respected, The County Clerk was the most personally popular Democrat in the city. He would retain office in face of several Republican sweeps until 1934, when scandal rather

unfairly ended his career (future mayor and "boss," Richard J. Daley began his climb working for "Beaming Bob"). He was also an excellent campaigner, a strong leader, and Roger Sullivan's close and reliable friend.[36]

The platform was written by former governor Dunne (another outcome of Sullivan's harmony offensive), and committed the party to home rule in utility matters that would bring freedom from the capricious whims of the state legislature, lower gas prices, and greater scrutiny of the traction companies. The Harrison and Dunne leaders naturally approved the platform, but were openly disappointed by the selection of Sweitzer. However, they ultimately accepted his candidacy, or at least declined to back Carey.[37]

Sweitzer showed his usual vigor during the primary in his speeches at numerous rallies. His campaign theme was: "I

Robert Sweitzer (Library of Congress, LC-dig-ggbain-018608).

will!" Carey's initial strategy was to present himself as a stalking horse for Carter Harrison, something he soon replaced with claims to be Harrison's actual preference for the nomination. This was undoubtedly true, but the fact that the former mayor declined even a formal statement of support, rendered this ploy rather ineffective. Carey was also hampered by the sad death of his wife at the end of January from appendicitis. Sweitzer easily won with a margin of 111,497 to Carey's 48,182, or the "regular's" usual more than two to one majority among Democratic voters.[38]

Mayor William Hale Thompson was also renominated, but only after a lively contest that was virtually a rerun of that four years before. Once again, the chief justice of the municipal court, Harry Olson, entered as a more respectable alternative to the now infamous mayor. However, the contest was enlivened still further by the entry of Charles Merriam. His candidacy attracted some criticism by those sympathetic to reform in the party, as it was felt, probably correctly, that he was undermining Olson. Merriam argued that he was the only man with a real chance of defeating Thompson. The contest was otherwise predictable, with the usual charges of corruption and incompetence being flung like confetti.

The most interesting and heated moment came during a debate between Thompson and Merriam. Held before a crowd of several thousand on January 6, 1915, at a Masonic Temple, at first it went well. The mayor spoke to a generally respectful crowd that was divided roughly evenly between his and his opponent's backers. Thompson then left the hall to general applause. However, when Merriam rose to speak he was greeted by a maelstrom of hissing, catcalling, and other rude noises. As it proved, many present were city hall officers planted by the Thompson campaign. Soon even the ladies and young girls joined in, and fistfights broke out. "Kid Merriam" (as one newspaper sarcastically labeled him) distinguished himself with impressive roundhouse swings against assailants. Eventually order was restored. Thompson's vote was 124,194 to Olson's 84,252, and Merriam's 17,690; proving that the mayor's machine still ruled in the Republican Party of Chicago.[39]

After the primaries, the race became further complicated by the emergence of two other candidacies. Inspired by the Bolshevik revolution in Russia, (the full intrinsic horror of which was not as yet recognized despite constant press reports about ongoing civil war, terrorism, atrocity, famine, and even cannibalism), union men in Chicago organized the Independent Labor Party of Cook County. John Fitzpatrick, the widely respected president of the Chicago Federation of Labor was nominated for mayor. According to his own account, the immediate issue was frustration that a deal with Mayor Thompson in November 1918, to appoint two union men to the school board was rejected by the city council "acting under the lash of Roger Sullivan." Following the recruitment of an executive committee, a convention of about 400 delegates was held. Among those participating were the Chicago Federation of Teacher's Margaret Haley and at least a few disaffected Socialists including a former alderman. Beyond selecting a local ticket, the new party planned to create (in direct emulation of the Russian Bolsheviks) a soldiers and sailors council to promote the advancement of "political and industrial democracy at home."[40]

Much more worrisome to both Thompson and Sweitzer, however, was the entry into the race of Maclay Hoyne. He had long been a loose political cannon, and Sullivan backed his last reelection as a Democrat in 1918 as state's attorney only to appease the Harrison men. Hoyne had made a name for himself as a law and order prosecutor, but also as someone fully willing to use his office transparently for personal ends. Although he had originally worked closely with the Thompson administration, he soon was making headlines investigating the police department and its chief Charles Healey. In October 1916, he staged a raid upon various offices of city hall—a move that helped assure his reelection that November. This was followed by indictments of Healey and others. The chief resigned, but was intelligent enough to secure the services of Clarence Darrow, who won his acquittal in January 1918.[41]

Had Hoyne successfully convicted Healey, it might have been a mortal blow to the Thompson administration, and it would have unquestionably improved his chances for the Democratic mayoral nomination. Instead, his candidacy was embraced only by those still committed to the ideals of reform and progressivism, and who, therefore, found the nominees of both major parties unacceptable. For many, the nominations of Thompson and Sweitzer seemed to reduce the election to a choice between two political bosses, the mayor or Roger Sullivan—and thanks to Thompson's antics, the boss business was becoming more disreputable than usual. These antipathies had spurred renewed attempts to convince Carter Harrison to enter (although the former mayor had been as much of a political boss as Sullivan, albeit somewhat less skilled and more motivated by personal ambition), and unauthorized petitions to place his name on the ballot circulated. However, he remained firm in his refusal. Hoyne by this point was already known to be interested, and some of the remaining Harrison forces together with many of the Merriam men coalesced around Hoyne's now formidable independent candidacy. It was to be the last reform crusade in Chicago during the Progressive Era.[42]

Predictably, Maclay Hoyne's first public statement featured a scathing attack upon Roger Sullivan, his organization, and the state and local political culture in general. As it summarizes well the nature of the progressive antipathy towards the Democratic leader and his organization (and his status as paramount leader), it is worth quoting extensively. The Democratic Party, Hoyne asserted, was nothing but: "Roger Sullivan's gas and traction Democracy" (the traction reference being unfair as Sullivan was never an investor in the streetcar companies or in any way closely tied with the long-departed traction baron Charles Yerkes), created solely for his own benefit and that of "a few cronies." Its primary goal, according to Hoyne, was to control the Cook county organization with the election of city and county officials being only of secondary interest. By controlling the county party, it could create a currency in the form of the votes of city council members and legislators, with which it could then exchange favors with the dominant Republicans. "They neither believe in nor support the Jeffersonian doctrine of equal rights to all, nor special privileges for none." Instead they were "out for spoils … and fat contracts through which they can make money," and in this they had been eminently successful. As Hoyne explained to the city:

> Their extravagant administration of the drainage board enriched many of them. Some of the "small fry" derive profit from "fixing" taxes in the county treasurer's office. Others collect change through contracts let by the board of elections commissioners. Still others obtain wealth though operations in and about the board of assessors and board of review.

Most recently, he noted, the late John Hopkins' Great Lakes Dredge and Dock Company, of which Roger Sullivan was now president, received the "largest contract of its kind" ever awarded by Chicago. Moreover, Sullivan and company in pursuit of their own nefarious interests "treacherously slaughtered" Edward F. Dunne at the polls in 1907, and then sold out to the subsequent administration of Fred Busse "for thirty pieces of silver in city appointments."[43]

Hoyne, it is important to note, was careful to avoid characterizing the activities of Sullivan and his men as "criminal." He thus shielded himself not just from a lawsuit that he could not have won, but also from the obvious question as to why, as state's attorney, he had not pursued legal remedies against the very practices he was now condemning so vigorously. Nor did he try to explain accepting, just three years previously, the backing of a notorious character like Roger Sullivan. Finally, as the state's attorney was doubtlessly aware, the motives and methods of the Sullivan's "gas and traction Democracy" were identical to those practiced by Hoyne's mentor and friend, Carter Harrison, when he in was in power, as well as by just about every other political figure or alliance in the city's history .[44]

Although framed with the "base metal of hypocrisy," the tactic seemed to have been effective; sizable numbers of Republicans and Democrats joined up as foot soldiers for this latest assault against "bossism." Representing the traditional progressive circles were Jane Addams, and Clarence Darrow. Representing disaffected Democrats were some of the supporters of Tom Carey from the primary, even as Charles Merriam and his crew brought in disaffected Republicans. Throughout, Hoyne focused upon Sweitzer and his connection to Sullivan, deriding Sweitzer's claims of independence from the "gasocracy" and its leader. Thompson also attracted his share of the state's attorney's excoriation, but it was Sullivan who Hoyne riddled and ridiculed.[45]

Sweitzer responded energetically, while Sullivan kept a lower profile than usual. The County Clerk enjoyed an early tactical success in soliciting the support of most of his party's luminaries. The leaders of Tom Carey's primary race signed on, as did most of the Harrison upper echelons including Adolph Sabath. Even Edward F. Dunne dutifully offered his endorsement, and he and Michael Igoe, once the former governor's floor leader in the Illinois House, actively campaigned for their party's nominee. Carter Harrison, on the other hand, came out for Hoyne late in the contest, calling him Chicago's "only hope." Sweitzer, for his part, concentrated his barrages upon Thompson, promising efficient honest government that would not embarrass the city. However, relations between the Thompson and Sweitzer campaigns were—at least until the last days of the campaign—generally cordial. At a joint debate between the mayor and county clerk, the audience conducted themselves appropriately and with apparent good feeling.[46]

Throughout Mayor Thompson was in top form. Generally dodging the issues raised by Sweitzer and Hoyne, he instead extolled his own virtues as a patriotic American dedicated to protecting the constitutional rights of the citizenry. His appeal was particularly effective among the growing African American community. Not burdened with an excess of modesty, he found no difficulty in comparing himself to Abraham Lincoln. Ethnic appeals to the Germans and other groups were also common themes. The press, which was unrestrained in its antipathy towards the mayor, was another special target; Thompson, at one point, initiated a short-lived lawsuit against the *Chicago Tribune*, claiming distortions of his records and statements.[47]

As tensions heightened, violence became more common. Just days before the election, Chicago's downtown was treated to a Thompson parade. The heckling by Sweitzer, Hoyne, and Fitzpatrick supporters was unrelenting and fistfights soon broke out. Meanwhile, the candidates were dashing around the city in cars and limousines to speak at successive rallies, creating a "whirlwind, wild west, knock-'em dead finish." All sides, of course, predicted victory, but it was the Hoyne candidacy that determined the outcome.[48]

Thompson won with 259,828, or but 36.88 percent of the vote. Sweitzer took 238,206 votes or 34.48 percent, while Hoyne took 110,851 or 16 percent, and Fitzpatrick, 55,990 or just 8 percent of the total (underscoring the relative insignificance of the political clout of organized labor in Chicago). Thompson's small plurality made it clear that but for Hoyne, Robert Sweitzer would have won the election (it being not unreasonable to assume that most, or at least a sufficient percentage, of Hoyne's vote would have fallen otherwise into the Democratic column). In pursuit of their own brand of ideological purity, the reform-minded only managed to reelect the man considered by most Chicagoans (and the historians) as the city's most disreputable mayor ever.[49]

Maclay Hoyne was not forgiven. Not long after the election, Thomas Scully, the Cook County Judge (in charge of elections) appeared before Superior Court Judge Henry Guerin asking for the appointment of a special grand jury and prosecutor to investigate Hoyne's alleged failure as state's attorney to fully probe election fraud allegations. Hoyne correctly interpreted this as politically motivated. Hearings were held, and Roger Sullivan testified. He did not add much, but he did reveal that although he "did not regard [Hoyne] as a friend," he had attempted to work out an arrangement with the prosecutor to keep him out of the contest. Guerin eventually decided to deny Scully's motion, but in the primaries of 1920, Hoyne would be defeated for renomination as state's attorney by the candidate of the regulars, Michael Igoe.[50]

Hoyne's independent run may have been one decisive factor in Thompson's reelection, but Chicago's growing African American community was also important. In the decade after 1910, the city's black population expanded from 44,103 or 2 percent of the total to 109,458 or 4 percent, thanks to the Great Migration north by people of African descent from a South that offered limited opportunity and the daily humiliations of a Jim Crow culture. Adding to the power of their numbers was their concentration in the Second Ward, where 47,647 African American's (or 70 percent of the ward's population of 68,572) resided in the home base of Mayor Thompson. The GOP was still broadly regarded as the party of liberation (a not inconsiderable asset among a people for whom enslavement was a living memory), and the mayor used this to buttress his pose as the champion of equal rights. In all, he won 73 percent of the vote in the Second Ward. Shortly after the election, he expressed his gratitude for his renomination and reelection in a special statement to "that element of American citizens composing a great majority of the citizenship of the second ward," in which he publicized his belief that the Declaration of Independence and the Constitution should be applied "without any distinction of race, creed or color." He was also careful to praise black servicemen who demonstrated during the war "as great a degree of bravery and heroism as any other element in the American armies."[51]

For some Chicagoans, however, the African-American contribution to the reelection of a man so widely despised only added momentum to growing racial resentments. For years white working class and immigrant neighborhoods strove to ward off settlement of people of color into their community through devices like the Hyde Park Improvement Association (now reorganized as the Hyde Park-Kenwood Improvement Association), and the use of terror and intimidation. Much of this anger was founded in competition for jobs now aggravated by the cancellation of major war contracts.

Already between January and June 1919, there had been fourteen bombings of the homes of African Americans (one of which killed a child), in self-designated white areas. These tensions soon began to manifest themselves at places of common recreational usage including the public beaches where informal but strict rules of segregation prevailed.

It was at one of these that on August 27, 1919, Eugene Williams, a black youth, inadvertently drifted into a white area of Lake Michigan bringing retaliation from rock throwers. Williams was hit and drowned. Soon horrific rumors (often involving a mythical black or white pregnant woman) raged within both the white and black communities. Shortly, random attacks and organized search-and-destroy missions by thugs in automobiles escalated into full scale rioting by white mobs burning, looting, and murdering. It raged until August 3, when Governor Frank Lowden deployed 6,000 troops of the Illinois National Guard. Mayor Thompson, much to the disappointment of his African-American constituencies, delayed responding. Officially, 38 were killed (23 blacks and 15 whites), and 537 were injured.[52]

As the child of Irish-American immigrants, and as a politician with strong roots in the urban ethnic communities where so much of the resentment towards migrating African Americans simmered, Roger Sullivan might have been expected to have shared, or at least silently acquiesced, in the antagonisms of his constituencies. However, hatred was not his style, and he was a generous and tolerant spirit—even his chief lieutenant and successor, George Brennan, felt his friend was sometimes "too soft" in his relations with people. Within the context of the prevailing racism of the period, Sullivan appears to have been exceptionally sympathetic and tolerant towards Chicago's growing black population.

A major basis for this conclusion comes from Julius Taylor, a brilliant African-American journalist and businessman. Turner began publishing his *The Broad Ax* in Salt Lake City, Utah in August 1895, and moved his operation to Chicago in the summer of 1899. A confirmed "race man," he filled his pages with the promotion of "equal rights of all men before the law," and unstinting attacks upon the hypocrisy and injustice of Jim Crow, then coloring the nation's psyche. A maverick in a time when black Americans generally clung to the "party of Lincoln," he advocated instead "the grand and glorious principles of Democracy, which have been handed down to us from the illustrious Thomas Jefferson."[53]

The Broad Ax published consistently into the 1920s. With usually four pages, but sometimes as many as eight, it editor, publisher, and chief employee, Julius Taylor, usually gave over his front page to politics, particularly of the Democratic variety. No factional myrmidon, in 1911, he vigorously boomed Carter H. Harrison II's return to the mayor's office, while endorsing Roger Sullivan in 1914 during the senatorial primary and election. Along the way, Taylor managed to cultivate relationships with much of the local party leadership including Sullivan, whom he characterized as "one of his warm friends," as well as "a true friend of the colored race," willing to extend favors regardless of ethnicity.[54]

Julius Taylor would particularly cite Roger's appointment, during his tenure as clerk of the probate court, of William G. Anderson as his private secretary;. "Friends and associates would upbraid him for placing a colored man in such an important position in his office." "Mr. Sullivan would bristle and retort," Taylor wrote, "that he did not care one thing for the color of the skin of Mr. Anderson … but that as long as he discharged his duties properly that he would continue to employ him in that capacity and Mr. Anderson retained that position until Mr. Sullivan's term expired in December 1894." Taylor also credited Sullivan and John Hopkins, "boiling over with rage and indignation," for the tabling at the 1904 Democratic national convention of a platform plank calling for the repeal of the Fourteenth and Fifteen Amendments. Two years later, Roger conspicuously refused to attend a Chicago meeting featuring South Carolina Senator Ben Tillman, a vicious advocate of lynching.[55]

Sullivan was traveling out west when chaos broke out on the streets of Chicago. However, shortly after his return, he agreed to an interview by Taylor. Expressing disappointment at the "rough and lawless element," the "boss" made clear his conviction that "Chicago was plenty large enough for the white and colored people to dwell together without resorting to violence." While hardly a ringing call for justice, it was for an urban Democratic leader and organizational politician in this time and place an enlightened attitude—especially as so many of those participating in the attacks were working-class Democrats. It was also one that stood in marked contrast to the hypocrisy of Republican Mayor William Hale Thomson, who just weeks before the disorder won reelection in large part because of the African-American vote, but stood pat for days as the tragedy unfolded.[56]

The riots, and their implications, illustrated the volatility that had always been the defining element of the political environment of Chicago ever since its massive growth spurt began after the Civil War. For decades, Sullivan's success in acquiring power in politics and wealth in business was based upon his mastery of the challenges of change. However, by 1919, as his health deteriorated and the gratifications of wealth and political influence began to fade, he was becoming weary.

9

"Time for younger men"
(1919–1920)

"Whatever Mr. Sullivan says around here goes."—*Chicago Evening Post*,
April 17, 1920

By any standard, Roger C. Sullivan's life was inordinately strenuous and challenging. As a political leader, as a businessman, and as a pater familias with a self-assumed responsibility for a massive and growing clan, there was little time for rest. In his later years, he increasingly sought refuge in travel, but even this carried its weight of stress. His wife, Helen, had been urging retirement since at least 1912, and intermittently, he had made noises about obeying her blandishments.

While the evidence is sparse, it suggests that he may have been burdened by growing health issues, quite possibly heart disease. Certainly his near-obesity and packed schedule would have been contributory factors. Moreover, there was a history of some early death in his family. Roger's father and four of his eight siblings died before the age of 50; his mother and older brother died before the age of 60, and at least three of these family deaths were heart-related. Of course, as life expectancy in 1920 was 56.3 years (although this figure was skewed by the relatively high infant mortality rates), the patterns of the Sullivans were not that unusual. Still, in 1919, as Roger celebrated his fifty-ninth birthday, he was feeling (and showing) his years.[1]

Amidst the growing number of passing friends and family, life must have begun losing some of its savor. Certainly, the loss of John P. Hopkins in October of 1918 was a major blow. John was his best friend, political partner, traveling companion, and certainly as a close as a brother. He could not be replaced. But this was just the beginning. During the eighteen months that followed, it must have seemed that he was being stalked by death In early March 1919, Helen Sullivan McEvoy, Roger's second eldest daughter, age 29, died of infection following the birth of her third child (the most common cause of death for young women before modern obstetrics). Then at the end of June, John J. Corbett, a long-standing political ally passed, followed in September by Judge Thomas Scully of the County Court. In January 1920, an even closer friend, William "Smiley" Corbett, John's brother, expired. He had been ill for much of 1919, and in June was compelled to close his famous Lambs Café, due to the impending imposition of Prohibition. Each of these losses would have been painful, but collectively they must have been devastating.[2]

Accordingly, being prudent and far-sighted, Roger Sullivan began to put his affairs in order. His stated goal, according to newspaper reports, was to leave at least one million dollars each to his wife and his children. As his worth at this point was generally judged to be about ten million, this would not pose a great challenge. Sullivan's estate planning included trust funds to benefit family members, and to assist (as he had for years) with the educational expenses of deserving youths. "He stated frequently that he did not believe in charity which began after death." During his lifetime, he made generous distributions of cash, securities, and property to charities, institutions, and friends. In his final years, his generosity only escalated.[3]

The transfer of assets was also astute business as it probably eliminated some estate taxes and preempted the need for family conferences to discuss the distributions. Dedicated father that he was, Roger nurtured his children's business instincts. He encouraged them "to select the stocks and bonds which he was to give them and then commented jokingly upon the selection later ... the younger Sullivans often traded stocks with their father and if he gained by the transactions he would be immensely pleased." Another favorite practice was to turn over some of the real property investments he had accumulated over the years, as he did with a valuable property on Washington Boulevard given to his son.[4]

Boetius was also the beneficiary of a more interesting deal that involved the construction of new residences for himself and his sister Mary. In the summer of 1917, he purchased two prime lots in a "silk stocking" area on the North Side (the corner of Sheridan Road and Wellington Avenue). At the time, this raised some concern among some of Roger's West Side neighbors that he was abandoning them. For decades Sullivan had run the Democratic Party in and from the Fourteenth Ward, and his presence was unquestionably an asset in obtaining city services and other benefits. Boetius denied any such intention concerning his father, claiming that he and his sister, Mary Sullivan Wolf, were simply looking to construct "plain residences" to provide more room for their growing families.

The two "plain residences" were quickly constructed (a considerable achievement given war time restrictions on building materials). They were rectangular buildings of four stories, mirror images of each other, built contiguously and connected by a basement tunnel. Each featured 22 rooms, five baths, and two kitchens. By the summer of 1919, Roger, by his own account, was staying "a great deal" at his daughter's new house on Wellington Avenue, but he also insisted that his residence remained on Washington Boulevard. However, later in the fall of 1919, he formally transferred his own 24-room home to his daughter Frances Sullivan Cummings, who explained that her father (and her mother as well, apparently), was dividing his time roughly equally between herself and her sister. The source of this seemingly awkward arrangement is not clear, but it may have been simply reflective of a gradual move shaped by Sullivan's desire to remain close to his children. What is certain is that by the end of 1919, the Wellington Avenue home had become Roger's principal abode.[5]

Sullivan reputation as a family man was one important source of the wide familiarity and affection with which he was increasingly held. Just three months before his death, for instance, the *Chicago Tribune* ran a huge photograph of Roger, his wife, and his grandchildren accompanied by an article (headlined: "Roger Victim of Boss Rule in Own Home") emphasizing his subornation to Helen's domestic authority and his dedication to his growing clan. In comparison to Mayor Thompson, the other local "machine" leader, who by this point was an object of contempt for much Chicago's establishment and citizenry, Sullivan appeared as a paragon of family values and virtues.[6]

A Chicago Dynasty and Its Founders
Democratic Leader in Illinois, His Wife and Their Grandchildren.

Front row, left to right—Catherine Cummings, Josephine Cummings, Mrs. Roger Sullivan, Virginia Wolf, William McEvoy Jr., Helen McEvoy, Mary McEvoy, Thomas Brennan Jr., Roger Sullivan, Jean Wolf, and Mary Wolf.
Back row, left to right—Roger Sullivan II., Adam Wolf II., Mary Sullivan, Jane Sullivan, and Virginia Cummings.

"A Chicago Dynasty and Its Founders," *Chicago Tribune,* **January 23, 1920 (Sullivan family collection).**

With the end of the previously intense factional warfare, and with the fading of reformist passions as the Progressive Era was drawing to a close, Sullivan was also becoming less and less the subject of imprecation and flagitious sarcasm as an obvious symbol for those unhappy with Chicago and Illinois' political culture. Instead, he was growing into being something of an endearing fixture in the city and state. Since at least 1912, his celebrity had developed to the point where a simple headline reporting that "Roger" or "Roger C." had done or said something was sufficient for public recognition. Increasingly, the press enjoyed exploiting any irony or humor they could find in his statements or activities.

In April 1919, for example, the newspapers eagerly reported his decision to have a room in the County Building converted into a miniature grocery in which supplies from his Sawyer Biscuit Company were sold to public employees at a substantial discount. *Crispo Ginger Snaps* were ten cents less than elsewhere, while *Crispo* crackers were fifty-nine cents instead of the usual seventy-five, and bagged coffee was even proportionately cheaper. On the door of Room #225 the sign read "Coffee, Cakes, and Crackers," and the "store" was soon vying for "customers" with the nearby offices of the sheriff and county clerk. A permit had been issued, but no fee exacted. Roger wanted to help out county workers, most of whom he knew by name, with the high cost of living (a growing issue at the time). No one in the building questioned the idea, because after all, "whatever Mr. Sullivan says around here goes."[7]

Later in the year, he inspired more affectionate jocularity with complaints about worn shoes. It seems that in support of the war effort and as a protest against the high cost of footwear occasioned, so he said, by the unions making unreasonable demands, he had decided to forgo buying a new pair for two years. Other prominent men were questioned by reporters, and it emerged that there was an epidemic of edema and painful dogs among the Windy City's rich and powerful. Julius Rosenwald, head of Sears and Roebuck, proudly confirmed that he, too, had not purchased new footwear in two years, while J. Ogden Amour, of the Amour Company, topped this with claims of it having been three or four years. What else could he do with prices so unreasonable? Others like Ernest K. Hamill, president of the Corn Exchange National Bank told similar stories. The idea of these "hard luck millionaires" hobbling along on sore feet because of the expensiveness of shoes was one that must have evoked reluctant smiles even among the city's most humorless anti-capitalists.[8]

On January 14, 1920, Sullivan announced his retirement. This time he seemed to mean it. He explained:

> It is time for younger men to take on the responsibility of leadership.... It is a personal satisfaction to quit the active game with a clean slate and a clear conscience and with the Democratic organization in Cook County and in Illinois occupying the excellent position in which it now stands.

For the first time since he arrived in Chicago over forty years earlier, his party was at peace; in the last judicial primaries, the Sullivan organization won handily and without much opposition. Now the plan was to turn over most daily affairs of the organization to a triumvirate of George Brennan, Dennis Egan, and John F. O'Malley. Sullivan was to retire formally following the national convention in San Francisco that summer. He specifically disqualified himself from any part in the campaign for the fall elections, and probably foresaw for himself a role, not unlike that which the late former mayor John P. Hopkins' had played for years, i.e., to remain as an elder statesman to be honored and consulted on important matters. However, he made no reference to letting go of his business interests, the growth of which he cited as one reason for his decision.[9]

Just shortly before his announcement, Sullivan achieved a political and personal miracle in managing (somehow) to become (almost) friends with William Jennings Bryan. In early January the two met amicably in Chicago. The pair then traveled together by rail to Washington, D.C., to attend a meeting of the national committee, where arrangements for the upcoming convention were to be discussed. Along the way, Roger and Will reached a meeting of minds about the composition of the Illinois delegation, which Sullivan was to chair. Also discussed was the upcoming state presidential primary. Bryan promised neither to run nor to interfere. For his part, Sullivan agreed to keep Robert Emmett "Bobby" Burke, the lone dissenter opposing the renomination of President Woodrow Wilson in 1916 (and once Bryan's point man in Illinois), off his list of delegates. Following arrival in the nation's capital, the two aging political warriors were seen walking the streets in friendly conversation.[10]

One important reason for Sullivan's presence in Washington was to secure the Democratic convention for Chicago. He was joined in appearing before the relevant committee on the city's behalf by J. Hamilton Lewis and Carter H. Harrison. Members were astonished to see Roger and Carter entering the room arm in arm, smiling and chatting, in apparent good fellowship. However, Harrison was not entirely prepared to forget the past. He would only affirm a détente on the issue at hand (however, in the end San Francisco won). Still it was a remarkable moment. Most of the specifics of these reconciliations with Bryan and Harrison are not clear, but it seems reasonable to assume that it was Sullivan who took the initiative. What would have been more natural than to seek to mend fences in the sunset of a long career—especially for a person like Roger Sullivan who was so possessed by an affinity for his fellow man? Harmony, or at least the satisfaction of having reached out to those who had so long conceived themselves as his enemies, was for the most part achieved. But there still remained other political issues to be addressed by the retiring leader.[11]

Like all of the state's political elite, and in his role Roger Sullivan, as the "recognized head of Democratic politics," was highly supportive of a new state charter to replace the existing constitution that dated back to 1870, and which many believed was awkward and antiquated. As a Chicago politician, he was very much dedicated to achieving a greater degree of home rule for the metropolis. After years of discussions and failed attempts to induce the legislature to call a constitutional convention, in 1919, this was at last accomplished. However, as the meeting date of January 6, 1920, approached, Sullivan became concerned about proposals to eliminate cumulative voting, which guaranteed a greater measure of representation in the legislature for minority parties (like the Democrats). His efforts to protect his party's interest eventually extended to a proposal to forego party labels in legislative elections entirely. This did not excite much enthusiasm. However, Roger, as the state's leading Democrat, with Governor Frank Lowden, the state's leading Republican, helped prepare the convention's rules to provide that "controversial articles" in the proposed state charter would be voted upon separately. The work of the constitutional convention went on until the summer of 1922, but, as it proved, in vain. In December of that year, the voters overwhelmingly defeated the fruit of their labor by a margin of 921,398 to 185,298.[12]

However, of far greater immediate importance was the question of who Illinois would back in the national convention. In the fall of 1919, Sullivan began calling for the renomination of the president, arguing that Western Democrats would have "nothing but Wilson." Like most of them, Roger was at this point a fervent advocate of the president's Paris Peace Treaty. However, over the next months as the American people began to turn against the Versailles agreement and its principal author, and as the president's incapacity after a series of strokes that fall became more apparent, Sullivan began to look elsewhere. Woodrow Wilson, through his own naiveté and arrogance in addressing the not completely solvable problems of a post-war world, began a precipitous fall in the public's estimation. Once he had stood on Olympic heights as the world's perceived savior. Now less than a year later, having proved to be merely human after all, he lurked in the hadean depths, a sick, wheelchair-bound, and tragic figure isolated in the White House, increasingly repudiated by an American people disappointed and fatigued with his, and all, progressive crusades.

However, the Democrats could not simply turn their backs upon an incumbent president as they had Grover Cleveland back in 1896. But to embrace Wilson and his implacable opposition to any modification of his treaty was to invite certain defeat. In this context, none of the leading candidates for the presidential nomination was ideal. William G.

McAdoo, until November 15, 1919, the secretary of the treasury, was an able, brilliant man, who unfortunately for his prospects, was married to one of President Wilson's daughters, identifying him too closely with the unpopular administration. Moreover, he was strongly associated with the "dry" or pro-prohibition elements of the party. Like virtually all mainstream politicians and a clear majority of the citizenry in Chicago, Roger Sullivan was no fan of the Eighteenth Amendment.

Also among those being highly touted for the White House was A. Mitchell Palmer, the attorney general, who was less linked to Wilson. However, as he had been a vigorous facilitator of the ongoing raids and deportation of radicals (which he justified with a doom-laden prediction of a Bolshevik revolution breaking out in May 1920), and because he stood on the side of management during recent labor troubles in the coal fields, he was despised by union leaders. Another alternative was the moderately progressive governor of Ohio, James Cox, who owned a national chain of newspapers. He had always backed Wilson, but was not handicapped by any direct affiliations. However, Cox was relatively unknown, had no foreign policy record, and was unexciting. Roger Sullivan, as was usually his custom, hedged his bets, and refused to commit to anyone. In late March, however, the Palmer men claimed Roger's support; something he neither denied nor affirmed. A few weeks later, the *New York Times* reported that he now was moving into the camp of Cox, and it is likely that Roger Sullivan, like most of the old regulars of the party, would have eventually come around to the governor, the eventual nominee.[13]

Not all of Roger Sullivan's attention that fall and spring was given over to settling his affairs, preparing to retire, or fulfilling his final political responsibilities; he also managed to find time to travel extensively, combining business with pleasure. In August 1919, he traveled to California in the private railway car of Cornelius K. G. Billings, sportsman, utilities magnate, and a fellow member of the board of the Union Carbide & Carbon Company. The lengthy sojourn, which included most of the Western states and time at a conference of governors in Salt Lake City, climaxed with a visit to attorney A.S. Trude's Idaho ranch, where Dr. Frank S. Billings (C.K.G.'s brother, and Roger's old friend and physician) demonstrated his skill with a rife by dropping a bear from an automobile speeding full tilt over rough terrain (killing animals unable to defend themselves with high-powered firearms being considered a manly pursuit during this era).[14]

Following his retirement announcement in January 1920, Sullivan was off again, vacationing for several weeks in Palm Beach with his wife, two of his daughters, and three of his grandchildren. He was back in Chicago for only a few days before departing for Hot Springs, Arkansas by a most indirect route through Washington, D.C., where he participated in discussions about the upcoming national convention. Afterwards at the Arkansas resort, a cold that had been plaguing him for months (perhaps since the Idaho trip) escalated into an infection of the throat and lungs. He returned home on March 22, 1920. News stories soon reported that he was "seriously ill." However, Billings and his other physician, Dr. Charles Mix, assured the city that "it was just Mr. Sullivan's annual cold—a slight touch of bronchitis." As "his temperature and pulse are normal," they maintained, there was no real cause for worry; "all he needs is a rest." He was met at the station by his son Boetius and several of his men, but his condition was such that he not permitted to speak.[15]

He was confined to bed at the 342 Wellington Avenue house, and daily bulletins began to be issued. His condition deteriorated; his respiration, pulse, and temperature were abnormal and becoming worse. There was a danger of an abscess in one lung. But

Roger C. Sullivan with grandchildren Mary Wolf, Roger Sullivan II and Helen McEvoy at Palm Beach (Sullivan family collection).

he rallied. By the first week of April, Billings and Mix found reason for optimism in their patient's "marked improvement." On April 3, 1920, Sullivan was feeling sufficiently well to meet with his old friends, Urey Woodson, Kentucky newspaper publisher and former secretary of the Democratic national committee, and Fred B. Lynch, national committeeman from Minnesota. Throughout the meeting, Sullivan was reportedly cheerful and full of "pep." Tellingly, however, it was announced afterwards that he would not be leading the Illinois delegation to San Francisco after all. Three days later, he was able to spend the day listening to bulletins read to him by his secretary, Edward Heffernan, about the aldermanic elections. On Sunday, April 11, George Brennan paid a visit and was impressed with his improvement. Details about the Illinois delegation were discussed.[16]

Over the next days, all went well, and recovery began to seem assured. However, on the afternoon of April 14, 1920, at about 3 o'clock, he suffered a myocardial infarction or heart attack. His wife, Helen, immediately summoned his four remaining children. Also called was his cousin, Frank T. Sullivan, who, following his immigration from Ireland, had once lived with the family while attending law school. Father Kelly of Our Lady of Mt. Carmel parish also soon arrived. By about 3:30 p.m., it was becoming apparent to the attending physicians that the end was near. The family was told to prepare itself.

Prayers for the dying were recited and last rites administered as Roger lay surrounded by his family dressed in his pajamas and bathrobe, propped up in bed by pillows to ease his breathing. Helen asked quietly if he were feeling any better. "No, I am not any easier." he replied in a choked voice. These were to be his last words. At about 3:50 p.m. he slipped into a coma, and at 4:30 p.m., he died. The official cause of death as listed on his death certificate (which showed him as "retired") was "putrescent bronchial pneumonia," complicated by "myocarditis" (an inflammation of the muscles of the heart). He had lived 59 years, two months, and eleven days.[17]

The first reactions were of surprise. Everyone had assumed that Roger was improving and that the crisis had passed; the press had long ceased running stories. Sullivan's chief lieutenant, George Brennan explained:

> John O'Malley and Dennis Egan came into the office this morning and asked me if I had called to find out how the boss was. I told them not to worry the family, that everything was all right. I was knocked speechless when the message came this afternoon…. We tried to keep from exciting him or bothering him, and kept his friends from the house as much as we could. The doctors told me two weeks ago they thought he was safely out of danger.[18]

The second reaction was an outpouring of grief and praise so completely at odds with the habits of criticism by the press and the civic leadership towards Roger Sullivan that it inspired at least one ironic editorial observation. The *Urbana Courier*, a downstate newspaper, bemusedly wrote: "we have been taught to think of Roger Sullivan as a villain of deepest dye, one who would hamstring a friend without reluctance, or torture thru [sic] a lingering death any ill-fated enemy to be unfortunate enough to get within his power." Now that he had passed, "Roger Sullivan, the modern bluebeard, becomes a typical and much-loved American citizen," who "as a poor, unknown, friendless boy fought his way to the top."[19]

Once the heart-felt obsequies, highlighted by the largest funeral in the city's history, were completed, press attention focused upon his estate. Roger Sullivan had succeeded in distributing most of his assets to his children and his wife, apparently reaching his reputed goal of a million dollars for each as his final estate (once estimated to be as much as $10,000,000) was valued at only $2,017,000 with outstanding debts of $583,000. Of this, Helen Sullivan, his wife received about $500,000, while his children and the estate of his deceased daughter, Helen, shared in a trust fund of $156, 930. His remaining holdings included interests in the Congress Hotel valued at $15,000, Sawyer Biscuit Company stock, valued at $207,402, Union Carbide and Carbon stock, valued at $13,376, and a number of personal notes to friends and relatives."[20]

Each of Roger's children was important to him, but it was his son, in these times of virtually unchallenged domestic patriarchy, who was his pride and embodied his father's notions of gentility and grace. As a gentleman of means, who was also very conscious of the responsibilities of his position and of his heritage, Boetius was delegated to use both his own money and his inheritance to honor his father's memory. On the first anniversary Roger's death, he announced his funding of a number of Sullivan scholarships, in addition to one in the name of John P. Hopkins, to Andover Academy, which Boetius attended as a boy. An annual award of $500 also was to be granted to one professor at the institute. This was soon followed by the creation of four full Roger C. Sullivan scholarships for any college "provided it was not socialistic or atheistic," to be distributed based upon a competition among deserving Chicago high school students (one each for freshmen, sophomore, junior, and senior students) in both the public and parochial educational

Chicago Daily Tribune.

FINAL EDITION

ROGER SULLIVAN DEAD OF HEART SEIZURE

DUBLIN HUNGER STRIKERS FREE; WALKOUT ENDS

Resignation of Lord French Is Seen.

$800 TO $3,000 FOR GOLD COAST HOME, G.O.P. WEEK

High Rents for Visitors Who Want the Best

"AMERICA IS HATED ABROAD"—News Item

SUDDEN ATTACK STRIKES CHIEF OF DEMOCRATS

Family at Bedside; Mourned by Many.

325 School Engineers to Strike

RUSSIAN REDS FOMENTED RAIL STRIKE, CHARGE

Palmer Gives Data to Wilson, Cabinet

CHICAGO TROOPS ENTRAIN FOR RIOT DUTY IN STRIKE

THE WEATHER

CHARITY BALL CLOSES HOUSE OF DEVONSHIRES

NEVADA READY FOR PICKFORD CASE CONTEST

Roger Sullivan's death reported, *Chicago Tribune*, April 15, 1920 (Sullivan family collection).

systems. He was also generous to the University of Illinois, to which he donated in 1925, in his father's name, $100,000 for the creation of radio station (that was to receive the call letters WILL), with an additional grant of $8,000 a year to each. Originally a fifty watt station, among its original featured programming was "Turning Cream into Gold." Boetius also donated $100, 000 to the University of Notre Dame for a five thousand kilowatt station to be permanently funded by an endowment. Three Roger C. Sullivan scholarships of $250 were also established.[21]

For most of his life, Boetius Sullivan would exercise only a limited political involvement (although he was clearly respected within the Democratic Party). Instead, he focused upon his careers as a lawyer with the firm of Cooke, Sullivan & Ricks, and as a businessman. He served on the board of the Sawyer Biscuit Company, where he remained after it was merged with the United Biscuit Company (eventually it was to become part of the Kellogg's). He also was a director for the Fire Insurance Company of Chicago, and the Central Wax Paper Company. On February 14, 1961, he died at the age of 75 years. However, the family tradition of political involvement was maintained in a limited fashion by his son, Boetius H. Sullivan Jr., who was an active supporter of Mayor Richard J. Daley.[22]

Like his son, Roger Sullivan's wife and daughters also led prosperous lives, each representing in their own way a fruition of the American dream as embraced by their husband and father. Helen Sullivan used much of her inheritance from her husband for scholarships and charity. She died on December 5, 1929, leaving an estate worth 1.1 million, of which one seventh was donated to charity with the remainder distributed among her children and grandchildren. She was 69 years of age, and like her Roger, she died at the house on 342 Wellington Avenue. Also like her husband, she was honored with a high church funeral. Services were held at Our Lady of Mt. Carmel, and were presided over by the Rt. Rev. Edward F. Hoban, Bishop of Rockford. Many important figures including Patrick Nash, Samuel Insull, Edward J. Kelly, Michael L. McKinley, and Cook County Sheriff John Traeger, attended.[23]

Eldest daughter Mary Sullivan's husband Robert Wolf, served as president of the Sawyer Biscuit Company and as an insurance executive. He died in 1935. Mary survived until 1949, when she passed leaving four sons (including a set of twins, one named Roger Charles, and the other Charles Roger), and two daughters. Frances Sullivan's husband, Leo Cummings (after an early career as a dentist) was vice president of the Union Bank. The couple had twelve children (one named Roger). Leo died in 1930, but she lived on until 1958. Frances was the most politically active of Sullivan's daughters. She went to the 1936 national Democratic Convention as an alternate, and beginning in 1933, she served as an arbitrator for the Illinois Industrial Commission, until 1951, amidst accusations of favoritism towards workers (though she was thanked by Governor Adlai Stevenson for eighteen years "of long, conscientious and enlightened service"), she resigned. She also remained an advocate within the party of her father's values of "party organization, unity, and above all competent leadership." Virginia Sullivan Brennan died at the age of 40 on April 3, 1937. She left a son and two daughters. Her husband Thomas Brennan, who headed a business machine company that bore his name, remarried but there were to be no more offspring. In all, Roger Sullivan's progeny, by the second decade of the twenty-first century, had blessed his memory with thirty-one grandchildren and over one hundred great grandchildren, something that would have pleased him immensely.[24]

Nearly as gratifying would have been the new Roger C. Sullivan junior high school with the capacity for 2,300 students and 65 teachers that opened in the fall of 1926. Located at 6631 North Bosworth Avenue in Chicago, and costing the then impressive sum of 1.5 million dollars, it represented an educational innovation as junior high schools were something relatively new at the time, the first being opened in 1909 in Indianapolis. A dedication ceremony was held on November 16, 1928, "to pay respects to the memory of the man for whom the school is named." Among the speakers was William Bogan, superintendent of Chicago's school system, who praised Sullivan for always refusing to interfere with the operation of the Board of Education, or with the promotion and hiring of teachers because he believed that "the schools are sacred." The keynote address was delivered by Samuel Insull, who spoke of Roger's life, character, and career. The utility baron (who in just a few years would be unfairly reviled after his utility empire collapsed in wake of the Depression) portrayed his "personal friend" as an American success story, rising from the bottom [here he recited the enduring myth that the Democratic leader had quit school because of the death of his father], to becoming a success "in both the business world and the public life of this city, and of the State of Illinois." However, for all of his prominence, Sullivan's most memorable character trait was "his kindliness and helpfulness ... he was never unmindful of the other fellow." It was this human quality that made him so deserving of this honor as a man who was "a kindly friend, an extraordinary man in politics and government, a man of ideal family ties, a towering figure in national, state and municipal affairs, a man loved and respected by those who knew him best." An elaborate plaque in memory of Roger C. Sullivan was unveiled to grace the entranceway. In 1933, due to the effects of the Depression, the school was briefly closed, but reopened as a senior high school. For a man so genuinely possessed by an "intense love of education," it was an honor he would have greatly relished.[25]

Although it remains in operation, the identity and character of the great man for whom their school was named is now only recalled there in the vaguest terms. Even among his descendants, the memories of Roger C. Sullivan have now degraded into a mere image devoid of human qualities, one chiefly defined by the barest outlines of his political and business careers. Moreover, the Cook County Democratic Party, which recognizes him as the founder of the "organization," retains little understanding of his character or the full scope of his accomplishments. In the histories, he became merely a figure to be referenced in passing, often in error. Such perhaps is the fate of the legacies of all but the most extremely prominent men and women—to be forgotten and made irrelevant as living recollections die away. In this Roger has been no exception.

But fate sometimes takes a kindly twist. In 1968, one of his granddaughters was inspired by old photographs to travel to Ireland to see the ancestral villages and to seek lost relations. Inquiring after the O'Sullivan family at the Kenmare post office, she was told to see the Rogers family. Protesting that she was looking for O'Sullivans, the reply was that in an area where everyone was named O'Sullivan, families were distinguished by branch-names—in this case the "O'Sullivan Rogers"—after the first name of an original ancestor. Thus enlightened, the traveler located Dromneavane townland where the O'Sullivan Roger family farmed fifty-seven hillside acres overlooking the Kenmare River "with views that are the finest in the district."

She knocked on the door, and was greeted by a heretofore unknown cousin named Rose O'Sullivan McCarthy, a granddaughter of Roger's maternal uncle, Cornelius "Connie" Roger O'Sullivan. After a warm welcome, tea, and conversation, they toured the property that, as Rose explained, Roger helped his Uncle Con purchase decades before.

Inside, she pointed out "the furniture your grandmother picked out." Other members of the clan still lived and raised dairy cows on the property, and the reception was warm as the American visitor was invited to tour the area. Then in one of the several cottages nearby, completely unexpectedly, and in a place of honor on the dining room wall, was found a large photograph of Roger C. Sullivan, the generous and successful cousin from across the ocean who never forgot his kin or his friends. In this place at least, he remained and would remain a living presence, and for a man who so loved his family that he purchased a burial plot large enough to accommodate a hundred other Sullivans as his companions in rest and resurrection, it would have been enough.[26]

Afterword:
The House Sullivan Built
(1920–1955)

"Leaders are not made ... they just grow."—Robert M. Sweitzer, county treasurer

Even as the living memories of Roger C. Sullivan were fading, his legacy continued in the vitality and growth of his remarkable political organization. By his "retirement," the association of Democratic political operatives that he had so patiently and laboriously worked to construct had come to exercise an unprecedented hegemony in the parties of his city, county, and state. His title as "boss of the Illinois Democrats" was both accurate and well-deserved. However, making the coalition's tensile strength and permanence all the clearer was the ease of the transfer of leadership following Sullivan's death.

Roger prepared well for his abdication by appointing a troika meant to inspire confidence among the leaders and the rank and file Dennis Egan, a former election commissioner, alderman, and legislator enjoyed a strong reputation and would be briefly considered as a candidate for mayor; John F. O'Malley, once a saloon owner (who took Sullivan's seat in the Illinois delegation to the national convention in San Francisco in 1920), had long been the "boss" of the "near north side," and represented politicos of the old school, while George Brennan had served as Sullivan's chief lieutenant and " no man" for well over a decade.[1]

Understanding the dynamics of party politics as he did, there is little doubt that Roger Sullivan expected that one of the three, and Brennan in particular, would emerge as paramount leader in his place. So it was to be. Within months of Roger's death, Brennan's ascendency became universally acknowledged without any public hint of factional discord.

George E. Brennan had been second only to Sullivan in the organization since early in the century. His skill as a political tactician would excite even the admiration of Carter Harrison, who later wrote of Brennan's "uncanny ability" and "political finesse." He was born on 20 May 1865 at Fort Byron, New York, as the son of Patrick and Anastasia Hines Brennan, both recent Irish immigrants. When he was a child, his family moved to Illinois. As a boy in Braidwood, Illinois, he went to work in a mine, and at the age of thirteen tragically lost a leg while chocking cars. Such was the nature of the injury that to save his life, his limb had to be amputated on the spot without anesthetic. The injury would remain painful and plague him for the rest of his life. It would, however, motivate him to resume his education, and he became a country schoolteacher.

He soon achieved a promotion to the position of assistant superintendent of the Joliet, Illinois schools. It was during this time that he became active in politics, and this helped secure him an appointment as chief clerk (1893–97) for Governor John P. Altgeld's secretary of state and sometimes ally/sometimes enemy, William H. "Buck" Hinrichsen. Brennan was also elected a member of the Sangamon (Springfield) Democratic County Committee, and it was here that he first came into contact with Chicago's political elites. About 1897, he relocated to the Windy City, and was chosen by Tom Gahan to manage his unsuccessful bid for the office of County Treasurer. From this point on, he was an important player in municipal Democratic politics, and he soon joined with Hopkins and Sullivan. In 1901, Hopkins, as chair of the state Democratic Committee, appointed him to be that body's secretary. He excelled in serving as an important liaison between Sullivan and Hopkins and downstate Democrats. Like so many politicians in this time and place, he also became a millionaire as the Chicago manager of a branch of the United States Fidelity and Guaranty Company, which did a booming business bonding for the city. He was devoted to his wife, Jessie Fogarty Brennan (who always preferred to be known as Mrs. George E. Brennan, even after her husband's death in 1928, when she became politically active herself). The two had one daughter, Mary W. Brennan.[2]

Brennan "won full title as the "Big Boss'" by leading the opposition to the nomination of William McAdoo at the 1920 Democratic convention to the benefit of the eventual nominee, James Cox of Ohio. The Chicago organization had long held a grudge against McAdoo, Woodrow Wilson's son-in-law, who, as secretary of the treasury, had thwarted some of their requests for federal patronage. By September 1920, George Brennan's possession as leader was secure.[3]

From the beginning, Brennan sought a complete unity within the state and local Democratic Party. He liked to cite what he claimed was Roger Sullivan's deathbed expression of regret that elements of the Harrison and Dunne men as yet remained outside the organization. Brennan did his best, even offering to back Carter Harrison for the governorship in 1920 (the former mayor wisely declined the honor of certain defeat). In the end, the new boss was "largely successful." The Harrison-Dunne group would no longer stand in opposition, and, while petty squabbles, unavoidable among an association of so many ambitious men, were inevitable, the total wars of earlier factional struggles were never renewed. Brennan also made an effort to accommodate the interests of the non–Irish urban ethnics of the city. Those of Irish descent had enjoyed predominance for decades within the Democratic Party, although never one that was absolute, and in the 1920s, other groups and their leaders, if only by the force of their growing numbers, began to demand and play a larger role. The Irish, never a single unified political group, continued in their hegemony into the late twentieth century, but under Brennan there would be a growing consciousness of the need for greater diversity in terms of candidates and perquisites.[4]

In 1923, George Brennan surpassed Sullivan in electing a mayor. William E. Dever had been Mayor Edward F. Dunne's city council floor leader, and enjoyed a solid reputation as a progressive and honest judge. That he was willing to run as Brennan's candidate was evidence of the organization's growing respectability, which by now contrasted favorably as against the reputation of the sitting Republican mayor, the notorious and frequently risible, William Hale Thompson. Thompson was compelled to withdraw from the Republican primary, and his party's nominee, the relatively unknown Arthur C. Leuder, was easily defeated by Dever running on a reform platform.

Mayor Dever ran a clean administration, fought the growing local gangster subculture, while focusing upon major infrastructure improvements. He worked in tandem with Brennan, who exercised a decisive voice over city patronage while backing almost all of the mayor's initiatives. The boss' reputation soared nationally when he once again led the fight against McAdoo at the 1924 national convention, and in 1926, he used this and his association with the mayor as the basis for a bid for the United States Senate. Hampered by illness, he narrowly lost a hard-fought contest.[5]

The following year, Dever was defeated for reelection by a resurgent Thompson, whose campaign was a spectacle featuring attacks upon the supposed influence of "British imperialism" upon the textbooks of Chicago's schools. Where Brennan might have led the organization further will never be known. In July 1928, he began suffering the agonies of an impacted tooth. The trip to the dentist, even in those days of comparative dental horror, was routine, and an operation was performed successfully. However, an infection developed and spread, requiring the lancing of an abscess in his neck. The physicians were optimistic that his health was sufficiently "vital" for a full recovery. However, Brennan was an amputee. In 1922, he nearly died from an inflammation, and in 1926, while campaigning for the senate, he fell from a platform and permanently injured the tendon of his other leg. Moreover, as only now was revealed, he suffered from diabetes. In face of these latest assaults, his body began to fail and he was rushed to John B. Murphy hospital. There, he endured three more surgeries, and for over a week he fought for his life. But on August 7, 1928, he slipped into a "diabetic coma," and shortly after 8:00 a.m. the following day, he died. He was 63 years of age[6]

For all of his known health challenges, his death came as an unexpected shock; he had always been so energetic and in-charge that no one anticipated his sudden removal from the political scene. As there was no obvious successor at hand, consternation for a time ruled. But in the words of Robert M. Sweitzer, long-standing County Treasurer who had been Sullivan's candidate for mayor, and who was a major insider in the organization, "leaders are not made, but like Topsy, they have not father or mother; they just grow." "Such a man" Sweitzer assured, "will appear sooner or later, and when he does, the Democratic Party will have a leader." By the time Sweitzer's Social Darwinist musings were made public that Christmas of 1928, such a man was in fact already making his presence apparent. This was Anton Cermak.[7]

Cermak was a singular force within the Chicago Democratic Party. Through intelligence, tenacity, and the sheer power of his personality, he had built a sizable following and an impressive measure of power. He was born of Czech or Bohemian descent on May 9,1873 in the town of Kladno, 16 miles northwest of Prague in the Austrian section of the Austrian-Hungarian Empire. His family arrived in America in 1874, and following a short stay in Chicago, settled in Braidwood, Illinois where his father worked in the coal mines. Anton attended the local public school, where his teacher for several years was a young George E. Brennan, the future "boss."

At the age of sixteen, the young Cermak briefly tried his luck in the Windy City, where he found a job in a mill. He endured a miserable winter, and returned to Braidwood to work in the mines. Already a natural leader, he was delegated to approach management about possible raises, and was summarily terminated. Walking to Chicago, he found work towing streetcars. He managed to save enough to start a business peddling waste wood purchased at a discount from the International Harvester Company. In the fertile entrepreneurial field that was Chicago, his venture began to grow, and he branched out into a building and loan company as well as several real estate ventures.

He was also becoming involved in the local Democratic Party. Beginning as a precinct worker, he rapidly rose to become a ward captain. In 1902, he was endorsed by his former teacher, Brennan, for the support of what was then the Hopkins/Sullivan organization as a candidate for the state legislature. He was handily elected, and reelected in 1904, 1906, and 1908. At first ignored by the progressive Legislative Voters League, he eventually earned their endorsement. During this period, he became the secretary of an organization that would provide him with a strong city-wide base. This was the United Societies for Local Self-Government, a "dry" organization in part funded by the liquor interests to fight the Anti-Saloon League and other groups dedicated to the elimination of the drug alcohol. It was especially reflective of and effective among Chicago's Bohemian and German communities. "Tough Tony" maintained his control among the various ethnic factions, sometimes through the use of his fists.[8]

In 1909, he left the legislature to serve on the city council, where he established a considerable presence. In 1912, he began a six-year term as bailiff of the Municipal Court, and was mentioned as a possible mayoral candidate for 1915. In 1917, he became involved in a fight over control of patronage with some the judges of the Court, and was accused of misconduct and graft. However, he was cleared in well-publicized hearings where he was ultimately characterized as a "conscientious, pain-staking hard-working, and efficient." His reputation soared, and in 1918, he ran a nearly successful campaign for Sheriff. The following year he returned to the city council, this time with an endorsement from the Municipal Voters League, which had in the past not been friendly.[9]

Following the death of Sullivan, who he had only fully joined in 1918, Cermak's star continued to ascend. With a strong base in the Bohemian community, he also cultivated the support of other non–Irish urban ethnics. This paid off with his election as president of the Cook County Board of Commissioners in 1922, and then in 1928, with a spirited, but vain, run for the United States Senate. By this point, Anton Cermak was one of the most powerful men in Chicago as the chair of the Cook Country Democratic Party Central Committee, able to call upon a massive network of friends held together by the broad patronage at his command.

However, after George Brennan's passing, there were others with aspirations. Press reports appeared claiming that Brennan at some point during his last days had appointed Michael Igoe as his successor. Igoe was a politico of long-standing. He had been associated with reform mayor and governor, Edward F. Dunne, and he was a hero of the "South Side Irish" (as opposed to the "West Side Irish"). However, this "revelation" failed to excite a movement on his behalf. Igoe never confirmed the story (although his brother-in-law swore it was true), stating only that Brennan had asked him at the 1928 National Democratic convention to take charge of some unspecified matters.[10]

Over the next two years, Cermak moved with almost Stalinist precision towards securing the leadership—claiming, until his goal was in sight, not to be harboring any such ambition. Martin O'Brien, chair of the Cook Country Party managing committee was replaced by Cermak loyalist and County Recorder, Clayton Smith. To propitiate Igoe, Cermak helped arrange for his elevation to national committeeman (a post Brennan had held) to replace state chair Thomas Donovan, who had been given the job after Brennan's death precisely because he was a downstater with no municipal following, and was, therefore, not a contender. During the fall of 1928, Cermak arranged for a reorganization of the Cook County party structure that included his factional rivals but which effectively guaranteed his control. Indeed his move was so ruthless that it inspired criticism from Robert Sweitzer as encouraging "factionalism."[11]

By March 1930, it was widely conceded that Anton Cermak was the "successor to the late George Brennan as 'boss' of the local Democracy." The showdown with Igoe came later in the year over the mayoral nomination the following spring. Cermak easily out-maneuvered Igoe and was unanimously endorsed for the job by the central committee. He easily won the subsequent primary and election. In the spring of 1932, Cermak thwarted Igoe's gubernatorial aspirations with his own candidate, Henry Horner. Horner's electoral success finalized "Tough Tony's" position as paramount leader. Igoe was at the same time defeated for reelection for his party office as a ward committeeman, and in June, he lost his seat on the national committee. He was replaced by Anton Cermak.[12]

Much sometimes has been made of the fact that Cermak was of Bohemian descent, and therefore the first (and only) "boss" who was not a descendant of immigrants from the Emerald Isle. However, as the historian Paul Michael Green has convincingly argued, Cermak, while undoubtedly enjoying the support he had built up over time among non–Irish Democrats, also worked to build a close coalition with many "new–Breed Irish," and in effect, enabled continued Irish predominance into the late twentieth century. Ironically, just about the only public accusations at the time against Cermak of engaging in any kind of political ethnic cleansing came from Republicans.[13]

For example, as early as October 1929, in the run-up to judicial elections, Republican operative Edward J. Brundage made a play for votes by claiming that Cermak in removing O'Brien from the chairmanship of the managing committee of the Cook County Democrat Party was "driving out the Irish." This prompted an immediate statement of denial from Boetius Sullivan, Roger's son, who had become close to Cermak. "Bo" also pointed out that Brundage, having managed Lawrence Sherman's senatorial campaign in 1914 against Roger, was probably responsible for its anti–Catholic and anti–Irish tenor. However, the best evidence of Cermak's intent was his selection upon becoming mayor of Patrick Nash as his replacement as head of the Cook Country Central Committee. "P.A." learned politics "under the tutelage of Roger Sullivan" and was his next door neighbor on Washington Boulevard. He had become a leader of the "West Side Irish," as well as a longstanding ally of Cermak. The significance of Nash's appointment was well-appreciated and understood at the time as representative of the fact that "as now constituted, the party organization embraces all the Democratic factional groups on a harmonious basis."[14]

However, Cermak's political judgment was not always infallible. In the 1932 contest for the Democratic presidential nomination, he chose Al Smith. Cermak became a dutiful soldier for the eventual nominee, Franklin Delano Roosevelt, in the election campaign, but he felt the need to mend fences. Accordingly, a meeting was scheduled in Miami on February 15, 1932, where the now President-elect was to conclude a short vacation on a friend's yacht. The Mayor of Chicago was among the dignitaries gathered to greet their new leader at Biscayne Park on the Miami waterfront. Among the milling multitudes was Giuseppe Zangara, a sickly and half-mad anarchist armed with a small pistol. The little man intended to shoot Roosevelt, but his arm was jostled by an alert elderly woman. In all, five others were hit, including Anton Cermak as he was speaking to the President-elect. Emergency surgery was performed to remove the bullet that had entered on the right side and lodged beneath the eleventh rib. Initially pessimistic, the physicians soon pronounced the crisis as passed. The Mayor quickly developed pneumonia, and, wracked by intestinal pain from ulcerative colitis, lingered for days before expiring at 5:57 p.m. (Chicago time) on March 6.[15]

Patrick Nash was almost immediately elevated by a unanimous consensus into the leadership position, adding to his post as chair of the Cook County Committee that of national committeeman. Part of his "legitimacy" was rooted in the fact that he was "one of the old chiefs who followed Roger Sullivan for years." The mayor's seat was his for the taking, but being 70 years old and disinclined to take on the daily administrative tasks of the city, he, instead, chose Edward J. Kelly. Kelly was an engineer who had been associated with the sanitary district for years, and became and remained a South Park Commissioner after 1922. He was a Cermak loyalist and was selected by the city council as acting mayor, and subsequently would win election in his own right[16]

"'Boss' Sullivan," *Chicago Examiner,* **March 26, 1912.**

The pair, "took over a powerful political organization, built earlier by Roger Sullivan," and refined and expanded by Brennan and Cermak. Controlling ever-widening federal patronage during the New Deal, as well as that of the city, country, and much of the state, the "machine" became the most powerful and efficient of its type. After Nash's death in 1943, Kelly became the single leader. When his reign ended in 1947, Richard J. Daley was already on the rise, and would become mayor and "boss" in 1955. He perfected the organizational politics in Chicago into a high art. He would become one of the great figures in American political history. Such were his singular skills and legendary status, and such was the changing political culture in Chicago, that he had no comparable successor.[17]

But it is to Roger C. Sullivan (who Daley resembled superficially in appearance) that the primary credit must be accorded for the conception and implementation of the great idea of a coalizing the disperse elements of the Chicago and Illinois Democratic Party into a single and enduring organization. After 1916 and into the latter part of the twentieth century, thanks in large measure to Roger's achievements, the Chicago

George Dunne, 1976-1982.

Edward R. Vrdolyak, 1982-

Richard J. Daley, 1953-1976.

Jacob Arvey, 1946-1950.

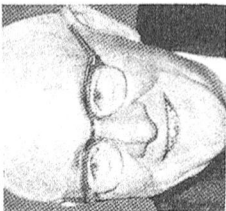

Joseph L. Gill, 1950-1953.

DEMOCRATIC PARTY OF COOK COUNTY

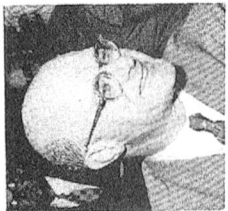

Patrick Nash, 1931-1943.

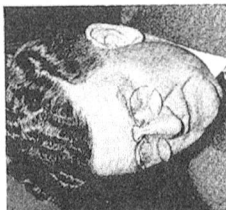

Anton J. Cermak, 1928-1931.

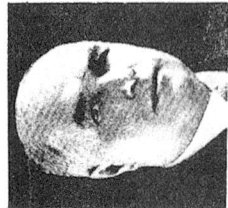

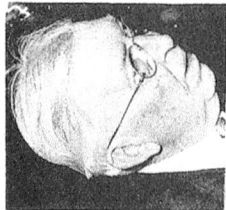

Roger C. Sullivan, 1915-1920.

Edward Kelly, 1943-1946.

George E. Brennan, 1920-1928.

Chairman Patrick Nash accompanies Mayor Cermak and other party leaders to Springfield for the inauguration of Governor Horner, 1933.

Democratic Machine would endure and shape the history of one the major metropolitan centers of the world, while also exercising a significant influence upon national affairs. To be sure, the great political edifice would be expanded and remodeled as it was adapted to changing times and shifting personalities, but at its core, it remained the house Sullivan built.

Opposite: **Bosses and leaders, from the 70th anniversary program of the Cook County Democratic Party celebration, 1985 (courtesy Cook Country Democratic Committee).**

Chapter Notes

Introduction

1. Chicago Tribune, 15 April 1920, p. 3; 16 April 1920, p. 6.

2. *Chicago Herald-Examiner*, 16 April 1920, p. 4; *Chicago Evening Post*, 15 April 1920, p. 10; *Chicago Daily News*, 16 April 1920, p. 8.

3. *Baltimore Sun*, 16 April 1920, p. 6; *Boston Globe*, 15 April 1920, p. 13; *Cincinnati Enquirer*, 21 April 1920, p. 6; *Detroit Free Press*, 16 April 1920, p. 1; *Washington Post*, 15 April 1920, p. 2; *Los Angeles Times*, 15 April 1920, p. 13; *New York Tribune*, 15 April 1920, p. 10; *Post-Dispatch* (St. Louis) 15 April 1920, p. 3; *New York Times*, 15 April 1920, p. 11. The term "businessman-politician" referencing Sullivan and Hopkins in this context appears in Melvin G. Holli and Peter D'A Jones, *Ethnic Chicago* (Eerdmans, 1984), p. 421.

4. *Chicago Tribune*, 15 April 1920, p. 3; 16 April 1920, p. 7; 28 January 1936, p. BR6; *Chicago Evening Post*. 16 April 1920, p. 5; Lowden to Roger C. Sullivan, 26 December 1918, Frank O. Lowden Papers, Special Collections Research Center, the University of Chicago Library, Chicago, Illinois; William S. Gray, John S. Dryer, and Rodney H. Brandon, *Proceedings of the Constitutional Convention of the State of Illinois, Convened January 6, 1920*, 3 vols. (Springfield: Illinois State Journal, 1922), p. I: 984–85.

5. Sullivan Family Collection.

6. *Chicago Daily News*, 15 April 1920, p. 1; *Chicago Evening Post*, 17 April 1920, p. 1.

7. *Chicago Tribune*, 17 April 1920, p. 5; 26 October 1922, p. 1721; October 1937, p. 3; 3 September 1949, p. 5; *San Francisco Chronicle*, 18 April 1920, p. 2; Born in New York State, B. J. Mullaney first came to Chicago to become advertising director for Amour & Company. He then went to work as an editor of the *Chicago Herald*. Between 1907 and 1910, he was secretary to Republican Mayor Fred Busse. In 1910, he accepted a two year appointment as commissioner of public works. In 1917, he became vice president of the People's Gas and Coke Company, controlled by his friend Samuel Insull. It was this connection that probably brought him close to Roger Sullivan, who also counted Insull as a friend.

8. *Chicago Tribune*, 18 April 1920, p. 5; *Chicago Record-Herald*, 17 April 1920, p. 2; *Chicago Evening Post*, 17 April 1920, pp. 1, 2; *Chicago Daily News*, 17 April 1920, pp. 1, 3.

9. *Chicago Tribune*, 18 April 1920, p. 5.

10. *Chicago Tribune*, 18 April 1920, p. 5; *Chicago Herald-Examiner*, 16 April 19120, pp. 1, 2; *Chicago Evening Post*, 17 April 1920, pp. 1, 2; *Chicago Daily News*, 17 April 1920, pp. 1, 3. "Roger Sullivan's Funeral Film," Chicago Historical Society, Video Archives, Chicago Illinois; "In Memoriam Roger C. Sullivan (funeral bulletin including sermon)," Sullivan Family Collection.

Chapter 1

1. A detailed account of Sullivan's career and the political culture in Illinois and Chicago during this period may be found in Richard Allen Morton, *Roger C. Sullivan and the Making of the Chicago Democratic Machine, 1881–1908* (Jefferson, NC: McFarland, 2016).

2. James Langland, *The Chicago Daily News Almanac and Year-Book of 1911* (Chicago: Chicago Daily News, 1910), p. 586.

3. Charles E. Merriam, *Chicago: A More Intimate View of Urban Government* (New York: Macmillan, 1929), p. 253.

4. *Chicago Times*, 11 December 1892, p. 2; *Chicago Sunday Post*, 11 December 1892, p. 3.

5. See Richard Allen Morton, "A Victorian Tragedy, the Strange Deaths of Mayor Carter H. Harrison and Patrick Eugene Prendergast," *Journal of the Illinois State Historical Society* 96, no. 1 (Spring 2003): 6–36.

6. *Chicago Times-Herald*, 31 March 1897, p. 3; *Chicago Tribune*, 30 July 1921, pp. 3, 11; 14 July 1899, p. 2. By this point, Burke was a senior politician, feared and hated by many, to be sure, but also widely respected. Born in Chicago in 1858, he never moved from the North Side neighborhood where he spent his childhood. His family was relatively poor and he began his career as a printer working for the *Chicago Times* and as a union activist. By 1885, he was the chief clerk for the city attorney, and in 1891, he became bailiff and the secretary of the Cook County Democratic Committee. He was a close friend and supporter of Carter Harrison, Sr., and managed his patron's successful mayoral campaign in 1893. As a reward, he became city sealer. In 1896 and early 1897, he initially backed Judge John Barton Payne for mayor, but soon shifted to become the leading force behind the nomination of Harrison, Jr. Following the election, he accepted an appointment as Chief oil inspector, a minor but very lucrative post. He also was once again chosen as secretary of the Cook County Committee. He was

described as "caring for the small potatoes in the pile," and as a "polite and adroit ... roly-poly, red-faced, little stout man." His skill, however, as a politician was not matched by his business acumen; his personal wealth always suffered by comparison to the young businessman politicians becoming so omnipresent in Chicago politics. Despite this, during the early years of the junior Harrison's administration there was no more powerful figure in the party.

7. Carter H. Harrison, *Stormy Years: The Autobiography of Carter H. Harrison, Five Times Mayor of Chicago* (Indianapolis: Bobbs-Merrill, 1935), p. 232; Walter A. Townsend, *Illinois Democracy: A History of the Party and Its Representative Members—Past and Present*, 5 vols. (Springfield: Democratic Historical Association, 1935), II: 34. Carter H. Harrison, Jr. (he was actually the fourth in succession of that name in his family) had been hovering on the fringes of power in the Chicago Democratic Party since his father's death in 1893. Born on 23 April 1853 in Chicago (he would be the first mayor of the city to be actually born there), at the age of 13 he went with his mother to the German Confederation, where he was educated at Altenburg, then in the Duchy of Saxe-Altenburg. Following his mother's death in 1876, he returned to Chicago and attended St. Ignatius College (now Loyola University), and then Yale University, where he obtained a degree in law. He practiced in the Windy City until 1888, when with his brother, William Preston Harrison, he took charge of his father's newspaper, the *Chicago Times*. For financial reasons this had to be sold in 1895 to Adolf Kraus, previously the editor and his father's ally of long standing. Harrison the younger, more urbane and personable than his father, was known for being an avid cyclist in an era when a bicycle race could outdraw a major league baseball game (in early campaigns he distributed photographs of himself posed with his safety bike and doing his best to appear athletic). He was also imbued with much of his father's political ambition and ability. These qualities, however, were to emerge slowly. During the Hopkins administration, Harrison sought some political consideration, but nothing came of this; however, in 1896, he was selected as an alternate to the Democratic national convention, where he managed to secure appointment as an assistant sergeant-at-arms. During the 1896 campaign, he supported Bryan, but was not prominent, and tellingly in the fall of that year the Harrison Club, founded by his father as a base for a political machine and in mothballs since his death, was reformed. Bright, charismatic, and with a magical name, he began attracting the support of a number of political operatives as a possible mayoral candidate in 1897.

8. *Chicago Tribune*, 8 August 1928, p. 1; *New York Times*, 8 August 1928, p. 19. George E. Brennan was born on 20 May 1865 at Fort Byron, New York, as the son of Patrick and Anastasia Hines Brennan, both recent Irish immigrants. When he was a child, his family moved to Illinois. As a boy in the burg of Braidwood, he went to work in a mine, and at the age of thirteen tragically lost a leg while chocking cars. Such was the nature of the injury that to save his life, his limb was amputated on the spot without anesthesia. The injury would remain painful and would plague him for the rest of his life (the complications would eventually kill him). However, it provided a motivation to resume his education, and he became a country school-teacher—among his students was Anton Cermak, who would be Brennan's eventual successor as boss. His intelligence and common sense soon brought him a promotion to assistant superintendent of the Joliet, Illinois, schools. It was during this period that he became active in politics, and he secured an appointment as chief clerk (1893–97) for Governor John P. Altgeld's secretary of state and sometimes ally/sometimes enemy, William H. "Buck" Hinrichsen. Brennan was also soon elected a member of the Sangamon (Springfield) Democratic County Committee, and it was in this position that he first encountered Chicago's political leaders. About 1897, he relocated to the metropolis on Lake Michigan to manage Tom Gahan's unsuccessful bid for the office of County Treasurer. From this point on, he was an important player in municipal Democratic politics, and he soon joined with Hopkins and Sullivan, becoming eventually their heir at Sullivan's death in 1920. In 1901, Hopkins, as chair, appointed him as the state committee's secretary to serve as an important liaison for Sullivan and Hopkins with downstate Democrats. Like so many politicians in this time and place, he also became a business millionaire. He rose to become the Chicago manager of a branch of United States Fidelity and Guaranty Company, which did a booming business bonding for the city. He was devoted to his wife, Jessie Fogarty Brennan (who always preferred to be known as Mrs. George E. Brennan, even after her husband's death in 1928, when she dabbled in politics herself). The two had one daughter, Mary W. Brennan.

Chapter 2

1. *Chicago Tribune*, 23 April 1907, p. 2; 8 June 1907, p. 16; 25 November 1907, p. 11; 6 December 1907, p. 4.

2. *Chicago Tribune*, 12 November 1907, p. 1; 15 November 1907, p. 2; Paolo E. Coletta, *William Jennings Bryan, Political Evangelist* (Lincoln: University of Nebraska Press, 1964), pp. 398–99.

3. *Chicago Tribune*, 3 January 1908, p. 8; 18 January 1908, p. 7; 21 January 1908, p. 2; 22 January 1908, p. 8; 24 January 1908, p. 4; *Chicago Record-Herald*, 21 January 1908, p. 4.

4. *Chicago Tribune*, 9 April 1908, p. 4; *Chicago Record-Herald*, 13 April 1908, p. 8.

5. *Chicago Tribune*, 22 February 1908, p. 3; *Chicago Record-Herald*, 22 February 1908, p. 2.

6. *Chicago Tribune*, 22 February 1908, p. 3; *Chicago Record-Herald*, 22 February 1908, p. 2.

7. *Chicago Tribune*, 18 March 1908, p. 2.

8. *Chicago Tribune*, 9 April 1908, p. 4; 13 April 1908, p. 3; 14 April 1908, p. 5; 19 April 1908, p. 1; 20 April 1908, p. 2; 27 April 1908, p. 5; Carter H. Harrison, *Stormy Years, The Autobiography of Carter H. Harrison, Five Times Mayor of Chicago* (Indianapolis: Bobbs-Merrill, 1935), pp. 260–61.

9. *Chicago Tribune*, 5 February 1908, p. 7; 11 February 1908, p. 7; 21 April 1908, p. 2; though he was made the butt of the joke, it was admitted that Roger Sullivan "was not what you might call obese either."

10. *Chicago Tribune*, 7 March 1933, pp. 4, 10; Alex Gottfried, *Boss Cermak of Chicago: A Study in Political Leadership* (Seattle: University of Washington Press, 1962), pp. 15–24, 67, 80.

11. *Chicago Tribune*, 22 February 1908, p. 3; *Chicago Record-Herald*, 22 February 1908, p. 2.

12. *Chicago Tribune,* 22 February 1908, p. 3; *Chicago Record-Herald,* 22 February 1908, p. 2.
13. *Chicago Tribune,* 26 April 1908, p. 5; 27 April 1908, p. 5.
14. *Chicago Tribune,* 19 April 1908, p. 1; *New York Times,* 23 April 1908, p. 1; 28 April 1908, p. 6.
15. *Chicago Tribune,* 5 May 1908, p. 6.
16. *Chicago Tribune,* 21 June 1908, p. 4; 27 June 1908, p. 2; 28 June 1908, p. 2; 29 June 1908, p. 2; 3 July 1908, p. 3; 4 July 1908, p. 3; *Chicago Record-Herald,* 21 June 1908, p. 1; 24 June 1908, p. 5; 28 June 1908, p. 2; 6 July 1908, p. 3; *New York Times,* 4 July 1908, p. 3; 7 July 1908, p. 3; *Atlanta Constitution,* 27 June 1908, p. 7; *Denver Post,* 5 July 1908, p. 6.
17. *Chicago Record-Herald,* 6 July 1908, p. 1.
18. *Chicago Record-Herald,* 6 July 1908, p. 6; *Chicago Tribune,* 3 July 1908. pp. 2, 4; *Chicago Record-Herald,* 22 June 1908, p. 2.
19. *Chicago Record-Herald,* 4 July 1908, p. 4; *Denver Post,* 2 July 1908, p. 2; 4 July 1908, p. 3; 5 July 1908, pp. 1, 5.
20. *Chicago Tribune,* 24 April 1908, p. 1.
21. *Chicago Tribune,* 7 July 1908, p. 3.
22. *Ibid.*
23. *Ibid.*
24. *Ibid.*
25. Chicago Tribune, 28 June 1908, p. 4; 6 July 1908, p. 4; 7 July 1908, p. 3; *Chicago Record-Herald,* 1 July 1908, p. 1; Milton W. Blumenberg, *Official Report of the Proceedings of the Democratic National Convention Held in Denver, Colorado, July 7, 8, 9 and 10, 1908, Resulting in the Nomination of Hon. William Jennings Bryan (of Nebraska) for President and Hon. John Worth Kern (of Indiana) for Vice-President* (Chicago: Press of Western Newspaper Union, 1908), p. 4 (hereafter cited as *Official Proceedings,* 1908). Paolo Coletta, *William Jennings Bryan,* part I, p. 405; *Arthur F. Mullen, Western Democrat* (New York: Wilfred Funk, 1940), p. 161. Bryan also did not ask for a plank favoring the initiative and referendum as he had originally planned.
26. *Official Proceedings, 1908,* pp. 33–5; *Chicago Tribune,* 3 July 1908, p. 3; 5 July 1908, p. 3; 6 July 1908 (convention edition), p. A1; 8 July 1908 (convention edition), p. A3; *Chicago Record-Herald,* 4 July 1908, p. 4; 8 July 1908, p. 3; *New York Times,* 7 July 1908, p. 2; 8 July 1908, p. 1; 9 July 1908, p. 3; *Denver Post,* 5 July 1908, p. 1; 7 July 1908, p. 2; *Denver Post,* 5 July 1908, p. I:1; 6 July 1908, pp. 1, 3.
27. *Chicago Tribune,* 4 July 1908, p. 4; *Chicago Record-Herald,* 6 July 1908, pp. 1, 5; 7 July 1908, p. 3.
28. *Official Proceedings, 1908,* pp. 50–2; *Chicago Tribune,* 7 July 1908 (convention edition), p. A2; 7 July 1908, p. 1; *Chicago Record-Herald,* 6 July 1908, p. 1; 7 July 1908, p. 3; 9 July 1908, p. 5.
29. *Official Proceedings, 1908,* pp. 244–48; *Denver Post,* 10 July 1908, pp. I:1, 2, 5.
30. *Chicago Tribune,* 14 February 1914, p. 7; 27 February 1908, p. 5; 11 April 1908, p. 8; 17 May 1908, p. 5; 22 June 1908, p. 4; 1 July 1908, p. 5; 6 July 1908 (convention edition), p. A3; 10 July 1908, p. 8; *Chicago Record-Herald,* 11 July 1908, pp. 1, 3.
31. *Chicago Tribune,* 18 August 1917, p. 7; *New York Times,* 18 August 1917, p. 7; *Chicago Record-Herald,* 2 July 1908, p. 2; 11 July 1908, pp. 1, 4; *Official Proceedings, 1908,* pp. 251–53, 280–81; Claude G. Bowers, *The Life of John Worth Kern* (Indianapolis: Hollenbeck Press, 1918), pp. 156–166.

32. *Chicago Tribune,* 4 July 1908, p. 3.
33. *Chicago Tribune,* 11 July 1908, p. 2; *Chicago Record-Herald,* 13 July 1908, p. 1; *Fort Worth Star-Telegram,* 28 June 1908; *Denver Post,* 7 July 1908, p. 5; 11 July 1908, p. 4.
34. *Chicago Tribune,* 11 July 1908, p. 2; *Chicago Record-Herald,* 13 July 1908, p. 1; *Fort Worth Star-Telegram,* 28 June 1908; *Denver Post,* 7 July 1908, p. 5; 11 July 1908, p. 4.
35. Richard F. Pettigrew, *Imperial Washington: The Story of American Public Life from 1870–1929* (New York: Arno and The New York Times, 1970), p. 257.
36. *Chicago Tribune,* 23 September 1908, p. 8.
37. *Chicago Tribune,* 26 July 1908, p. 27; July 1908, p. 1; 28 July 1908, p. 1; *Chicago Record-Herald,* 28 July 1908, p. 1; *Denver Post,* 5 July 1908, p. 2.
38. *Chicago Tribune,* 24 July 1908, p. 2; 4 August 1908, 6 August 1908, p. 2; 24 August 1908, p. 6.
39. *Chicago Tribune,* 3 August 1908, p. 4; 10 April 1939, pp. 1–2; Lewis was born in Danville, Virginia, on 13 May 1863, and in 1866 his family moved to Savannah, Georgia. He was educated in the law, and went on in 1885 to practice in Seattle, Washington. He served in the territorial legislature and then in Congress before being defeated in 1898 for reelection. He was subsequently appointed inspector general with the rank of colonel (he would cling to the title of "colonel" for the remainder of his life) for Puerto Rico during and immediately after the Spanish-American War. He was then appointed by President William McKinley as a member of a delegation to mediate duty collections on the Canadian border in the Northwest. This was followed by service on the Alaskan boundary commission. He moved to Chicago in 1903, where he practiced law while becoming involved in Democratic politics. He was an excellent speaker and a charismatic man known for his impressive pink whiskers.
40. *Chicago Tribune,* 8 August 1908, p. 2; 2 October 1939, p. 17; Eugene F. Lyle Jr., "Taft: A Career of Big Tasks," *World's Work,* 14 (July 1907): 9135–44.
41. Walter Clyde Jones, "The Direct Primary in Illinois," *Proceedings of the American Political Science Association,* vol. 7 (1910): 138–62; *Daily News Almanac* (1909), pp. 425–31; (1921), p. 1014.
42. *Chicago Tribune,* 9 August 1908, p. 1; 10 August 1908, p. 5; 11 August 1908, p. 3; 13 August 1908, p. 3; 18 August 1908, p. 4; 20 August 1908, p. 3; 7 October 1943, p. 1; *Chicago Record-Herald,* 8 August 1908, pp. 1, 2; 9 August 1908, pp. 1, 2; 10 August 1908, pp. 1–6. Nash was born in 1863 the son of a sewer contractor in Chicago. He benefited from the fact that he was Sullivan's next door neighbor on Washington Boulevard. This connection, together with a talented political mind and great energy, won Roger's attention (of whom he was "an ardent follower"), who promoted him through the ranks. Between 1915 and 1918, he served on the Chicago Board of Assessors, and between 1918 and 1924, upon the elected Board of Review (both taxing agencies). By Sullivan's death in 1920, Nash was his point man for their home ward, and was, therefore, counted as among the more powerful local political figures. This would be the base for his eventual rise in 1931 to the position of Cook County chair, and then in 1933 to national committeeman. Thereafter until his death in 1943, he, with Mayor Kelly, built upon the foundations laid by in succession by Sullivan, George Brennan, and Anton Cermak to maintain and

expand the Chicago Democratic machine. Partnered with his brother, Dick, Nash also made a fortune in the sewer business, and did much to promote the modernization of Chicago's West Side.

43. *Chicago Tribune*, 10 September 1908, p. 4; *Chicago Record-Herald*, 10 September 1908, pp. 1–3.

44. *Chicago Tribune*, 9 September 1908, p. 5.

45. *Ibid.*, 13 September 1908, p. 5; 3 October 1908, p. 5; 4 October 1908, p. 4; 16 October 1908, p. 5; *Chicago Record-Herald*, 3 October 1908, p. 3.

46. *Chicago Tribune*, 1 September 1908, p. 7.

47. *Chicago Tribune*, 14 September 1908, p. 6; 27 September, p. 4; 25 October 1908, p. 4.

48. *Chicago Tribune*, 10 October 1908, p. 4; 15 October 1908, p. 5; 29 October 1908, p. 2; 20 October 1908, p. 4.

49. *Chicago Tribune*, 1 November 1908, pp. 1, 2; 2 November 1908, p. 3; *Chicago Record-Herald*, 1 November 1908, pp. 1, 2.

50. *Daily News Almanac* (1908), pp. 298–301; (1909), pp. 345, 421; *Los Angeles Times*, 5 November 1908, p. 14.

51. *Chicago Tribune*, 4 November 1908, p. 11.

Chapter 3

1. "A Short Measure of What President Roosevelt Has Done," *World's Work*, 17 (March 1909): 11311; James Langland, comp. *Daily News Almanac and Year-Book for 1920* (Chicago: Chicago Daily News, 1920), p. 115 (hereafter cited as *Daily News Almanac*): see Kathleen Dalton, *Theodore Roosevelt: A Strenuous Life* (New York, Knopf, 2002); Lewis L. Gould, *The Presidency of Theodore Roosevelt* (Lawrence: University Press of Kansas, 1992).

2. *Chicago Tribune*, 29 December 1908, p. 5; 3 January 1908, p. 6.

3. *Chicago Tribune*, 15 April 1909, p. 2; 16 April 1909, p. 10; 23 April 1909, p. 1.

4. *Chicago Tribune*, 9 August 1908, p. 1; 11 August 1908, pp. 1, 2; United States Congress, Senate, *Election of William Lorimer: Hearings before a Committee of the Senate Pursuant to Senate Resolution No. 60 Directing a Committee of the Senate to Investigate Whether Corrupt Methods and Practices Were Used or Employed in the Election of William Lorimer as a Senator of the United States from the State of Illinois*, Senate Doc. 484, 62nd Cong., 2nd Sess., 9 vols. (Washington, D.C.: Government Printing Office, 1912): V:4403 (hereafter cited as *Dillingham Committee Hearings*); Joel Tarr, *A Study in Boss Politics, William Lorimer of Chicago* (Urbana: University of Illinois Press: 1971), pp. 199–200.

5. Tarr, *Lorimer*, 291; *Dillingham Committee Hearings*, pp. V: 4243–46; VIII: 7800; *Bluebook, 1909* (Danville: Illinois Printing, 1909), pp. 234, 240, Browne was born in Earlville, Illinois, on 30 January 1866, and educated at the State Normal School and the Wesleyan University Law School, both in Bloomington, Illinois. He was first elected to the Illinois House in 1900. Thomas Tippet was born in Richland County, Illinois, in 1851, was a farmer by profession, and was public school educated, and taught for a number of years. He had also edited the *Olney Times*, and was the proprietor of the Oakwood Stock Farm in Olney. He was first elected to the House in 1894.

6. *Dillingham Committee Hearings*, III: 2280–86,

2288–89, 2303, V: 4373–74, 4383–85, 4388; *Chicago Tribune* 28 July 1909, p. 1; 29 October 1911, p. 1.

7. *Chicago Tribune*, 21 January 1909, pp. 1–2. Tarr, *Lorimer* Like Sullivan and so many of the other dominant political figures in Chicago and Illinois, Lorimer was a self-made millionaire. Like them, he swam the murky channels of partisan power with the same ease and finesse as he had the shark-infested waters of business. Unlike Roger and most other leaders, however, he was not of Irish descent, but was born in England on 27 April 1861. His family moved first to Michigan in 1866, and then in 1870 to Chicago. His earliest employment was at the age of ten as a sign painter, followed by time working in the packing houses and on the street railways. Later he built a fortune in real estate development and brick manufacturing. His political career began during the 1884 presidential election as a Republican worker in Chicago's Sixth Ward, which eventually became his political base. He was a superb organizer and mediator, and he chose his alliances well. In 1895, he was elected to Congress from the city's Second Congressional district, and in the same year he became the chair of the Republican Cook County Central Committee. He served in Congress until 1901, when he was defeated for reelection. During this time, he had become a leading "boss" in the local party, though his power significantly diminished as a result of factional setbacks and his involuntary retirement from the House of Representatives. In 1904, he returned to Congress, this time from the Sixth District on the West Side, and his influence and power was once again on the rise. By 1909, he was counted among the most powerful and popular men in his party.

8. *Chicago Tribune*, 1 February 1909, p. 5; 30 June 1917, p. 1; 24 June 1919, p. 14; *Dillingham Committee*, V:4400, 4403, 4368, 4382 VIII: 7585, 7639–40, 7731. These kinds of family affiliations were not uncommon. For instance, Lorimer's daughter, Ethel, was married to Ralph Graham, son of Andrew Graham, Sullivan's mayoral candidate in the 1911 Democratic primaries.

9. *Dillingham Committee*, IV:1264; *Chicago Tribune*, 19 January 1909, p. 4; 25 March 1909, pp. 1–2; for a full account of Lorimer's activities see Tarr, *Lorimer*.

10. *Chicago Tribune*, 20 May 1909, p. 1; 16 May 1909, p. 1.

11. *Chicago Tribune*, 13 May 1909, p. 4; 14 May 1909, p. 2; 16 May 1909, p. 4; 23 May 1909, p. 2; 25 May 1909, p. 1; 26 May 1909, p. 1; 27 May 1909, p. 4.

12. *Chicago Tribune*, 12 May 1909, p. 3; 25 May 1909, p. 1; 27 October 1911, p. 1; *Dillingham Committee Report*, V:4375–82; 4385; VIII:7476, 7729, 7731.

13. *Chicago Tribune*, 5 September 1909, p. 7; 10 September 1909, p. 8.

14. *Chicago Tribune*, 1 June 1909, p. 4; 23 October 1909, p. 1; 11 November 1909, p. 5; 23 December 1909, p. 10; *Los Angeles Times*, 30 May 1909, p. 16; *Belvidere Daily-Republican*, 1 June 1909.

15. *Chicago Tribune*, 30 October 1909, p. 5; 11 November 1909, p. 5; 23 November 1909, p. 7; 24 November 1909, p. 2; 29 November 1909, p. 10.

16. *Chicago Tribune*, 7 October 1908, p. 5; Carter H. Harrison, *Stormy Years: The Autobiography of Carter H. Harrison, Five-Times Mayor of Chicago* (Indianapolis: Bobbs-Merrill, 1935), p. 262.

17. *Chicago Tribune*, 5 January 1906, p. 8; 17 April 1908, p. 6; 29 September 1909, p. 10; 9 January 1953, p. 9; *New York Times*, 9 January 1953, p. 21; *Daily News*

Almanac (1910), p. 471; Barry Dean Karl, *Charles E. Merriam and the Study of Politics* (Chicago: University of Chicago Press, 1974). Merriam was born in 1874 as the son of a postmaster in Hopkinton, Iowa. He attended Lenox College in his home town before moving on to Iowa State University. He graduated with a law degree, but declined to practice. Instead, he went on to Columbia University where he obtained a master's degree and a doctorate of philosophy in the young field of political science. He then pursued further study at the Universities of Paris and Berlin. In 1900, he joined the faculty of the new University of Chicago (it had been founded just eight years before as the second school of higher education of this name), where he became known for his advocacy of an "efficient" democratic process that centered upon a more powerful and active executive. A positivist in the sense that he believed that practice should follow theory, his services were secured in 1905 by the City Club to investigate Chicago's tax structure. In 1908, he was secretary to a special harbor commission appointed by Mayor Fred Busse to investigate improving the Lake Michigan waterfront. In 1909, he successfully ran as a Republican for alderman from the Seventh Ward.

18. *Chicago Tribune*, 5 May 1907, p. 1; 17 November 1909, p. 4; 8 December 1909, p. 1; 17 December 1909, p. 1; 24 December 1909, p. 1; 16 January 1910, p. 1; 23 January 1909, p. 7; 21 March 1910, p. 1; 28 March 1910, p. 2; 13 April 1910, p. 1; 23 April 1910, p. 1; 30 April 1910, p. 3; 7 May 1910, p. 7; 3 June 1910, p. 7; 6 July 1910, p. 10; 1 September 1910, p. 9; 10 January 1911, p. 6; *Daily News Almanac* (1911), p. 532; William Bayard Hale, "Chicago, Its Struggle and Its Dream," *World's Work* 19 (April 1910): 12, 792–805; perhaps surprisingly, the police department emerged as a relative model of efficiency in its accountancy. Fisher would serve until March 1911, when he was appointed by President William Howard Taft as secretary of the interior.

19. *Chicago Tribune*, 22 October 1950, pp. 1, 2, 3.

20. *Chicago Tribune*, 30 April 1910, p. 1; 8 May 1910, pp. 1, 2; 28 May 1910, p. 1; 29 May 1910; 31 May 1910, p. 1; 8 June 1910, pp. 1, 2; 28 June 1910, p. 1; 29 June 1910, p. 1; 30 June 1910, pp. 1, 2; 2 August 1910, p. 2; 10 September 1910, pp. 1, 4; *Dillingham Committee Report*, III: 2404–826; 2469–73, 2594; V: 5752–57; 5799–804: Tarr, *Lorimer*, pp. 233–38.

21. *Chicago Tribune*, 21 June 1910, p. 2; 13 December 1910, pp. 1, 2; United States Congress, Senate, *Proceedings Before the Committee on Privileges and Elections and a Subcommittee Thereof in the Matter of the Investigation of Certain Charges Against William Lorimer, United States Senator from Illinois*, Senate Doc. 942, pt. 2, 61st Congress, 3rd Session (Washington, D.C.: Government Printing Office, 1910).

22. *Chicago Tribune*, 3 February 1910, p. 2; 15 February 1910, p. 2; 18 February 1910, p. 1; *Daily News Almanac* (1911), p. 47.

23. *Daily News Almanac* (1911), p. 483; *Chicago Record-Herald*, 14 April 1910, pp. 1, 4; *Chicago Tribune*, 3 April 1907, p. 1; 8 April 1908, p. 1.

24. *Chicago Tribune*, 14 April 1910, p. 2.

25. *Chicago Tribune*, 30 June 1910, p. 2; 12 July 1910, p. 2; 13 July 1910, p. 1.

26. *Chicago Tribune*, 14 July 1910, p. 1; Harrison, *Stormy Years*, pp. 262–65.

27. *Chicago Tribune*, 14 July 1910, p. 1; Harrison, *Stormy Years*, pp. 262–65.

28. *Chicago Tribune*, 21 July 1910, pp. 1, 2.

29. *Chicago Tribune*, 20 July 1910, p. 5; 21 July 1910, p. 4; 22 July 1910, pp. 1, 2; *Chicago Record-Herald*, 16 July 1910, p. 1; *Belvidere Daily Republican*, 23 July 1910, p. 1.

30. *Chicago Tribune*, 26 July 1910, pp. C1, 2; *Chicago Record-Herald*, 26 July 1910, pp. 1, 2; *Chicago Daily News*, 25 August 1910, pp. 1, 2; 26 June 1910, p. 8; *Chicago Evening Post*, 25 June 1910, p. 1.

31. *Chicago Tribune*, 26 July 1910, pp. C1, 2; *Chicago Record-Herald*, 26 July 1910, pp. 1, 2; *Chicago Daily News*, 25 August 1910, pp. 1, 2; 26 June 1910, p. 8; *Chicago Evening Post*, 25 June 1910, p. 1.

32. *Chicago Tribune*, 26 July 1910, pp. C1, 2; *Chicago Record-Herald*, 26 July 1910, pp. 1, 2; *Chicago Daily News*, 25 August 1910, pp. 1, 2; 26 June 1910, p. 8; *Chicago Evening Post*, 25 June 1910, p. 1.

33. *Chicago Tribune*, 26 July 1910, pp. C1, 2; *Chicago Record-Herald*, 26 July 1910, pp. 1, 2; *Chicago Daily News*, 25 August 1910, pp. 1, 2; 26 June 1910, p. 8; *Chicago Evening Post*, 25 June 1910, p. 1.

34. *Chicago Tribune*, 26 July 1910, pp. C1, 2; *Chicago Record-Herald*, 26 July 1910, pp. 1, 2; *Chicago Daily News*, 25 August 1910, pp. 1, 2; 26 June 1910, p. 8; *Chicago Evening Post*, 25 June 1910, p. 1.

35. *Chicago Tribune*, 26 July 1910, pp. C1, 2; *Chicago Record-Herald*, 26 July 1910, pp. 1, 2; *Chicago Daily News*, 25 August 1910, pp. 1, 2; 26 June 1910, p. 8; *Chicago Evening Post*, 25 June 1910, p. 1.

36. *Chicago Tribune*, 26 July 1910, pp. C1, 2; *Chicago Record-Herald*, 26 July 1910, pp. 1, 2; *Chicago Daily News*, 25 August 1910, pp. 1, 2; 26 June 1910, p. 8; *Chicago Evening Post*, 25 June 1910, p. 1.

37. *Chicago Tribune*, 2 August 1910, p. 3.

38. *Chicago Tribune*, 6 August 1910, p. 3; 21 August 1910, p. 1; 15 September 1910, p. 2.

39. "The Civil Service Throughout the Country," *Good Government, the Official Journal of the Civil Service Reform League* XXVII no. 9 (September 1910): 68.

40. *Chicago Tribune*, 16 September 1910, p. 3; 17 September 1910, p. 4; 20 September 1910, p. 5; *Chicago Record-Herald*, 17 September 1910, p. 3; 19 September 1910, p. 2; 20 September 1910, p. 4.

41. *Chicago Tribune*, 21 September p. 2; *Chicago Record-Herald*, 17 September 1910, p. 3.

42. *Chicago Tribune*, 23 September 1910, p. 6; 24 September 1910, pp. 1, 2; *Chicago Record-Herald*, 22 September 1910, pp. 1, 2.

43. *Chicago Tribune*, 24 September 1910, p. 2; *Chicago Record-Herald*, 24 September 1910, pp. 1, 2.

44. *Chicago Tribune*, 13 September 1910, p. 5; 16 September 1910, p. 3; 25 September 1910, p. 5; 6 November 1910, p. 5; 8 November 1910, p. 3.

45. *Daily News Almanac* (1911), p. 32.

Chapter 4

1. *Chicago Tribune*, 13 June 1904, p. 1; 14 June 1904, pp. 1, 2; 15 June 1904, pp. 1, 2; *Chicago Record-Herald*, 13 June, pp. 1, 2; 14 June 1904, pp. 1, 2; 15 June 1904, pp. 1, 2; *New York Times*, 15 June 1904, p. 1. Robert, L. Duffus, "The Tragedy of Hearst," *World's Work* 44 (October 1922): 623–30; W.A. Swanberg, *Citizen Hearst, A Biography of William Randolph Hearst* (New York: Charles Scribner's Sons, 1961), pp. 56–7, 61–5; John K. Winkler, *William Randolph Hearst, A New Appraisal* (New York: Hastings, 1955), pp. 97–117.

2. *Chicago Tribune,* 5 May 1905, p. 4; 12 August 1906, p. 4; *Chicago Record-Herald,* 5 May 1905, p. 312; August 1906, p. 3; *New York Times,* 14 August 1906, p. 3.

3. *Chicago Tribune,* 26 July 1908, p. 27; July 1908, p. 1; 28 July 1908, p. 1; *Chicago Record-Herald,* 28 July 1908, p. 1; *Denver Post,* 5 July 1908, p. 2; *New York Times,* 29 July 1908, p. 1.

4. *Chicago Tribune,* 30 June 1917, p. 2; 9 December 1910, p. 9.

5. *Chicago Tribune,* 10 December 1910, p. 4; 8 January 1911, p. 5; 13 January 1911, p. 4.

6. *Chicago Inter-Ocean,* 2 January 1908, p. 2.

7. *Chicago Tribune,* 15 December 1910, p. 6; 17 January 1911, p. 2; 22 January 1911, p. 2.

8. *Chicago Examiner,* 20 January 1911, p. 5; 31 January 1911, p. 11; 11 February 1911, p. 2.

9. *Chicago Examiner,* 19 January 1911, p. 9; 30 January 1911, p. 7; 6 February 1911, p. 9; *Chicago Record-Herald,* 30 January 1911, p. 2; 11 February 1911, p. 1.

10. *Chicago Tribune,* 30 December 1910, p. 7; 12 January 1911, p. 3; 18 January 1911, p. 1; 19 January 1911, p. 9; 21 January 1911, p. 4; 4 February 1911, p. 4; 6 February 1911, p. 7; 8 February 1911, p. 4; 10 February 1911, p. 4; *Chicago Record-Herald,* 18 January 1911, p. 3.

11. *Chicago Tribune,* 6 January 1911, p. 2; 31 January 1911, p. 2; *Chicago Record-Herald,* 17 January 1911, p. 10.

12. *Chicago Record Herald,* 6 February 1911, p. 7.

13. *Chicago Tribune,* 3 April 1907, p. 1; 23 December 1910, p. 10; 30 January 1911, p. 3; 1 February 1911, p. 4; 2 February 1911, p. 7; 15 February 1911, p. 7; 16 February 1911, p. 4; *Chicago Record-Herald,* 27 January 1911, p. 7; 30 January 1911, p. 2; 8 February 1911, p. 7; 21 February 1911, p. 15; Dunne's criticism was not entirely fair, as Sullivan had returned a strong vote for him in 1907 in his Fourteenth Ward.

14. *Chicago Record-Herald,* 5 February 1911, p. 5; 13 February 1911, p. 4; 19 February 1911, p. 2; 17 February 1911, p. 9; 20 February 1911, p. 2; in between, the odds on Dunne fell to 3 to 1.

15. *Chicago Tribune,* 27 February 1911, p. 4; Harrison, *Stormy Years,* 269–70.

16. James Langland, comp., *The Chicago Daily News Almanac and Year-Book for 1912* (Chicago: Chicago Daily News, 1911), p. 461 (hereafter cited as *Daily News Almanac).*

17. *Chicago Tribune,* 8 March 1910, p. 1; 10 March 1911, p. 3; 16 March 1911, p. 4; 18 March 1911, p. 1; *Chicago Record-Herald,* 6 March 1911, p. 7; 7 March 1911, p. 2; 30 March 1911, p. 2.

18. *Chicago Tribune,* 1 March 1911, p. 1; 10 March 1911, p. 1; 12 March 1911, p. 4; 15 March 1911, p. 1; 17 March 1911, p. 2; 19 March 1911, p. 2; 21 March 1911, p. 3; 26 March 1911, p. 1; *Chicago Record-Herald,* 10 March 1911, p. 2; 13 March 1911, p. 1; 16 March 1911, p. 2; 17 March 1911, p. 2; 20 March 1911, p. 1; 21 March 1911, p. 2. 27 March 1911, p. 2; Michael P. McCarthy, "Prelude to Armageddon, Charles E. Merriam and the Chicago Mayoral Election of 1911," *Journal of the Illinois State Historical Society* 67 (November 1974): 505–11.

19. "Merriam and the Hyde Park Association," undated flyer in the Charles E. Merriam Papers, Special Collections Research Center, University of Chicago Library, Chicago, Illinois; *Chicago Tribune,* 26 March 1911, p. 5.

20. *Chicago Tribune,* 11 March 1911, p. 4; 19 March 1911, p. 2; 25 March 1911, p. 5; Harrison, *Stormy Years,* pp. 278–80.

21. *Chicago Tribune,* 16 March 1911, p. 5; April 1911, p. 4.

22. *Chicago Record-Herald,* 33 March 1911, p. 2.

23. *Ibid.*

24. *Chicago Tribune,* 30 March 1911, p. 4; 3 April 1911, p. 2; *Chicago Record-Herald,* 5 April 1911, pp. 1, 2; *Daily News Almanac* (1912), pp. 456–60; McCarthy, "Prelude to Armageddon," 513–14.

25. Harrison, *Stormy Years,* pp. 291–95; Charles E. Merriam, *Chicago: A More Intimate View of Urban Politics* (New York: Macmillan, 1929), pp. 281–87; Barry D. Karl, *Charles E. Merriam and the Study of Politics* (Chicago: University of Chicago Press, 1974), p. 72.

26. *Chicago Tribune,* 22 August 1909, p. 2; 23 March 1911, p. 4; 18 March 1911, p. 2; 17 February 1912, p. 1; 16 March 1912, p. 3; *Chicago Defender,* 18 March 1911, p. 1; 8 April 1911, p. 1; 24 February 1912, pp. 1, 8; *Chicago Record-Herald,* 17 March 1911, p. 4; Allan H. Spear, *Black Chicago: The Making of a Negro Ghetto, 1890–1920* (Chicago: University of Chicago Press, 19670, pp. 12, 21–2.

27. *Chicago Tribune,* 5 April 1911, pp. 1, 5; 18 June 1911, p. 4; 26 April 1911, p. 7; *Chicago Examiner,* 7 May 1911, p. 4.

28. *Chicago Tribune,* 8 September 1911, pp. 1, 4; *Chicago Record-Herald,* 8 September 1911, pp. 1, 2.

29. *Chicago Tribune,* 5 October 1911, pp. 1, 4; *Chicago Record Herald,* 5 October 1911, pp. 1, 2.

30. *Chicago Tribune,* 5 October 1911, p. 4.

31. United States Congress, Senate, *Election of William Lorimer, Hearings Before a Committee of the Senate Pursuant to Senate Resolution No. 60 Directing a Committee of the Senate to Investigate Whether Corrupt Methods and Practices Were Used or Employed in the Election of William Lorimer as a Senator of the United States from the State of Illinois,* Senate Doc. 484, 62nd Cong., 2nd Sess., 9 vols. (Washington, D.C.: Government Printing Office, 1912): V:4367–41; *Chicago Tribune,* 27 October 1911, pp. 1, 4, 11; 4 November 1911, pp. 1, 4; New York Times, 27 October 1911, p. 15; *Daily News Almanac* (1911), p. 404; (1912), pp. 410–12; Joel Tarr, *A Study in Boss Politics, William Lorimer of Chicago* (Urbana: University of Illinois Press, 1971), pp. 268–92.

32. Tarr, *A Study in Boss Politics,* pp. 293–307; *Daily News Almanac* (1913), pp. 156–67.

33. *Daily News Almanac* (1911), pp. 399–400; (1912), pp. 462–64; *Chicago Tribune,* 6 October 1911; p. 5; 8 November 1911, p. 3.

34. *Who's Who,* 1926; *Chicago Inter-Ocean,* 31 December 1911, p. 12; interview with Frank Sullivan (grandnephew), 21 March 2008.

35. *Chicago Tribune,* 28 December 1911, p. 6; *Chicago Daily Journal,* 28 December 1911, p. 4; *Chicago West Side Reporter,* 29 December, 1911.

36. *Chicago Tribune,* 17 April 1012, p. 11; 27 November 1912, p. 13; 1 May 1913, p. 11; 18 April 1918, p. 15; 21 April 1918, p. C4. *Illinois Republican Northwestern* (Belvidere), 2 April 1912.

37. Gottfried, Alex. *Boss Cermak of Chicago: A Study in Political Leadership* (Seattle: University of Washington Press, 1962); *Chicago Tribune,* 6 March 1933, p. 10; 7 March 1933, p. 4; *Chicago Examiner,* 9 March 1912, p. 5; Anton Cermak was born on 9 May 1873 in Kladno, then in the Austrian-Hungarian Em-

pire, and now in the Czech Republic. He was brought to America by his parents at a very young age, and the family settled in Braidwood, Illinois, a rough coal-mining community located about sixty miles south of Chicago. His youth and adolescence were troubled. However, it was during this period that he made the acquaintance of George Brennan, who taught him in the local schools. This would eventually prove to be a profitable association. An early attempt to escape to the Windy City was frustrated by the inability to find stable work, and he returned to Braidwood to work in the mines. Always a powerful personality, he was delegated by his peers to present a petition to their employer demanding improvements in conditions and wages. He was fired, and moved back to Chicago in 1890. "Tough Tony" (he was good with his fists and always willing to use them) found work in odd jobs in saloons and elsewhere, but his intelligence and initiative soon revealed themselves in his creation of a scrap wood business. This evolved into a growing concern, and he branched out into real estate and investment, becoming wealthy. He also became involved in local Democratic politics, beginning as a precinct captain and rising to ward leader. Sponsored by George Brennan, now a major lieutenant in what was then the Sullivan-Hopkins faction, Cermak was elected in 1902 to the first of four terms as a state legislator. Although always careful not to thwart or offend the Chicago leaders, he refused to be their myrmidon, rejecting, for instance, instructions on how to vote during the legislative senatorial election of 1911. Despite this, he was never endorsed by the reformist Legislative Voters League, which classified him as a professional politician. In 1907, his political strength was immeasurably enhanced by his election as the secretary of the United Societies for Local Self-Government, a "dry" lobbying group recently created by the liquor and beer interests. This helped solidify his following among the city's Bohemian community. He soon revealed real executive talent as well as a capacity for ruthlessness in holding together the Bohemians and Germans who made up the two largest components of the organization. In the years ahead, he became a public fixture in the fight against any restriction on the consumption of alcoholic beverages. In 1909, with Sullivan's blessing, he was elected to the city council, where he built a reputation as a dynamic alderman—though never becoming a favorite of the reformist Municipal Voters' League. In the primary of 1912, he dutifully endorsed Graham, but then, with his finger to the winds, he joined up with Harrison.

38. *Chicago Tribune*, 2 January 1912; 22 January 1912, p. 1; 29 January 1912, p. 4; 18 February 1912, p. 4; Carter H. Harrison, *Stormy Years: The Autobiography of Carter H. Harrison, Five Times Mayor of Chicago* (Chicago: Bobbs-Merrill, 1935), p. 316.

39. *Chicago Examiner*, 3 April 1912, p. 1.

40. *Chicago Tribune*, 28 February 1912, pp. 1, 2; *Chicago Record-Herald*, 28 February 1912, pp. 1, 2; *Daily News Almanac* (1813), pp. 481–82.

41. United States Congress, Senate, Campaign Contributions, Testimony Before a Subcommittee of the Committee on Privileges and Elections, 63rd Congress, 3rd Session, Vol. 1 (Washington, D.C.: Government Printing Office, 1913), pp. 921–22; *Chicago Tribune*, 15 February 1912, p. 5; 25 February 1912, p. 4.

42. *Chicago Examiner*, 11 March 1912, p. 2; 26 March 1912, p. 18; 4 April 1912, p. 20.

43. *Chicago Examiner*, 11 April 1912, p. 5; 12 April 1912, p. 7; *Chicago Record-Herald*, 10 April 1912, p. 3; 11 April 1912, p. 2; 13 April 1912, p. 4; *Chicago Evening Post*, 13 April 1912, p. 2.

44. *Chicago Tribune*, 13 April 1912, p. 5; 9 May 1912, p. 5; *Chicago Record-Herald*, 13 April 1912, p. 4; 14 April 1912, p. 4; James Langland, comp., *The Chicago Daily News Almanac and Year-Book for 1912* (Chicago: Chicago Daily News, 1911), p. 526 (hereafter cited as *Daily News Almanac*).

45. *Chicago Tribune*, 14 April 1912, p. 1; *Chicago Record-Herald*, 15 April 1912, pp. 1, 5; 16 April 1912, p. 11.

46. *Chicago Tribune*, 14 April 1912, p. 1; *Chicago Record-Herald*, 15 April 1912, pp. 1, 5; 16 April 1912, p. 11.

47. *Chicago Tribune*, 16 April 1912, p. 1, *Chicago Record Herald*, 16 April 1912, p. 1; *Chicago Evening Post*, 15 April 1912, pp. 1, 3; 16 April 1912, p. 10; *Chicago Daily News*, 15 April 1912, pp. 1, 2.

48. *Chicago Tribune*, 16 April 1912, p. 1, *Chicago Record Herald*, 16 April 1912, p. 1; *Chicago Evening Post*, 15 April 1912, pp. 1, 3; 16 April 1912, p. 10; *Chicago Daily News*, 15 April 1912, pp. 1, 2.

49. *Chicago Tribune*, 16 April 1912, p. 1, *Chicago Record Herald*, 16 April 1912, p. 1; *Chicago Evening Post*, 15 April 1912, pp. 1, 3; 16 April 1912, p. 10; *Chicago Daily News*, 15 April 1912, pp. 1, 2.

50. *Chicago Tribune*, 16 April 1912, p. 1, *Chicago Record Herald*, 16 April 1912, p. 1; *Chicago Evening Post*, 15 April 1912, pp. 1, 3; 16 April 1912, p. 10; *Chicago Daily News*, 15 April 1912, pp. 1, 2. The "H-H" convention included delegates from all the wards save the Third, Fourth, Fifth, Sixth, Seventh, Thirteenth, Fourteenth, Twenty-third, Twenty-seventh, and Thirty-first, while the Sullivan or "regular" version of the convention claimed full representation except for the First, Seventh, Eighth, Twelfth Nineteenth, Twenty-fifth, and Twenty-sixth Wards.

51. *Chicago Tribune*, 16 April 1912, p. 1, *Chicago Record Herald*, 16 April 1912, p. 1; *Chicago Evening Post*, 15 April 1912, pp. 1, 3; 16 April 1912, p. 10; *Chicago Daily News*, 16 April 1912, p. 10; Harrison, *Stormy Years*, p. 323.

52. *Chicago Tribune*, 24 April 1912, p. 4; 29 April 1912, p. 5; 30 April 1912, p. 11; 1 May 1912, p. 3; 2 May 1912, p. 4; 3 May 1912, p. 5; 5 May 1912, p. 2; 9 May 1912, p. 5; 10 May 1912, p. 1; 11 May 1912, p. 1; 18 May 1912, p. 2; 19 June 1913, p. 2; *Chicago Record-Herald*, 17 April 1912, p 1, 6. James Langland, comp., *Daily News Almanac*, 1913, p. 522.

53. *Chicago Tribune*, 19 April 1912, p. 7; *Chicago Record-Herald*, 19 April 1912, p. 12; *Chicago Evening Post*, 16 April 1912, p. 10.

54. *Chicago Tribune*, 20 April 1912, p. 7; Harrison, *New York Times*, 20 April 1912, p. 24; *Stormy Years*, p. 324.

55. *Chicago Tribune*, 3 May 1912, p. 5.

56. Walter A. Townsend, author, Charles Boeschenstein, supervising editor, *Illinois Democracy: A History of the Party, Its Representative Members—Past and Present*, 4 vols. (Springfield, Democratic Historical Association, 1935): 1:285–6, 2:59.

57. *Daily News Almanac* (1913), p. 485.

58. Chicago Tribune, 3 May 1912, p. 5.

Chapter 5

1. *Chicago Tribune*, 5 April 1912, p. 5; 10 April 1912, pp. 1, 4; 11 April 1912, p. 2.

2. Stockbridge, "Champ Clark of Pike County"; Lafayette Pence, "Why the Democratic Party Should Nominate Champ Clark for President," *Editorial Review* VI, no. 4 (April 1912): 305–12; *New York Times*, 10 March 1912, p. 4; some of Clark's campaign buttons featured the slogan: "You've gotta quit kickin my dawg around," based upon a traditional rural ditty, one variation of which ran: "Every time I go to town, the boys start kickin' my dawg around. I don't care if he is a hound; you've gotta quit kickin' my dawg around." It is not to be wondered that Clark was broadly acclaimed among America's more bucolic citizenry.

3. William McCombs, Louis Jay Lang, ed. *Making Woodrow Wilson President* (New York, Fairview, 1921), pp. 99–104; Arthur Link, *Wilson: The Road to the White House* (Princeton: Princeton University Press, 1947), p. 430; Congressional Quarterly, *Presidential Elections, 1789-1996* (Washington, D.C., 1996), pp. 149–50.

4. Robert M. Dittey, "Judson Harmon of Ohio—A Man of Deeds, Not Words," *Editorial Review* VI, no. 4 (April 1912): 316–24; William Bayard Hale, "Judson Harmon and the Presidency," *World's Work* XXII no. 2 (June 1911): pp. 14446–59; William Jennings Bryan, and Mary Baird Bryan, *The Memoirs of William Jennings Bryan* (n.p.: Mary Baird Bryan, 1925), p. 159; John H. Bankhead, "Why Oscar Underwood Should Be Elected President," *Editorial Review* VI, no. 4 (April 1912): 342–46; Evans C. Johnson, *Oscar W. Underwood, A Political Biography* (Baton Rouge: Louisiana University Press, 1980), pp. 1–35, 190–91.

5. Edward N. Hurley, *The Bridge to France*, reprint (New York: Kessinger, 2004), pp. 9–12; William Edward Dodd, *Woodrow Wilson and His Work* (New York: P. Smith, 1932), p. 85; *Good Government, the Official Journal of the National Civil Service League*, XXVII no. 9 (September 1910): 68; *Washington Post*, 14 March 1910, p. 6; 26 March 1910, p. 3; 18 July 1910, p. 4; *Chicago Tribune*, 14 November 1910, p. 2; 15 November 1933, pp. 1, 2; see Richard Allen Morton, *Justice and Humanity, Edward F. Dunne, Illinois Progressive* (Carbondale: Southern Illinois University Press, 1998); Sullivan was not exceptional in being a political boss while supporting reform. See David R. Colburn and George E. Pozzetta, "Bosses and Machines," *The History Teacher* 9 no. 3 (May 1976), pp. 445–463; *Washington Post*, 14 March 1910, p. 6; 26 March 1910, p. 3; 18 July 1910, p. 4; *Chicago Tribune*, 14 November 1910, p. 2; 15 November 1933, pp. 1, 2.

6. *New York Tribune*, January 6, 1912; January 7, 1912; *Los Angeles Times*, January 6, 1912; *San Francisco Chronicle*, April 4, 1912.

7. *New York Tribune*, 1 March 1912, p. 3; *Los Angeles Times*, 7 April 1912: III:23.

8. Bryan, *Memoirs*, 185; Champ Clark, *My Quarter Century of American Politics* (New York: Harper, 1920), 424; McCombs, *Making Woodrow Wilson President*, 162; *Boston Daily Globe*, May 24, 1912; *Washington Post*, October 25, 1927; June 29, 1912; *New York Times*, September 21, 1912; *Chicago Evening Post*, June 27, 1912; June 28, 1912; *Chicago Daily News*, June 25, 1912; *New York Tribune*, April 25, 1912; May 13, 1912; July 1, 1912; *St. Louis Post-Dispatch*, May 11, 1912; *San Francisco Chronicle*, May 26, 1912.

9. Bryan, *Memoirs*, p. 185; Champ Clark, *My Quarter Century of American Politics* (New York: Harper, 1920), p. 424; McCombs, *Making Woodrow Wilson President*, p. 162; *Boston Daily Globe*, 24 May 1912, p. 2; James Kearney. "How Wilson Was Shown to the Nation," *Washington Post*, 25 October 1927, pp. 1, 7; 29 June 1912, pp. 1, 5; Charles M. Rosser, "Bryan and Wilson at Baltimore in 1912," *New York Times*, 21 September 1921, p. 11; *Chicago Evening Post*, 27 June 1912, p. 1; 28 June 1912, p. 1; *Chicago Daily News*, 25 June 1912, p. 3; *New York Tribune*, 25 April 1912, p. 413; May 1912, p. 5; 1 July 1912, p. 2; *St. Louis Post-Dispatch*, 11 May 1912, p. 6; *San Francisco Chronicle*, 26 May 1912, p. 34.

10. *Cincinnati Inquirer*, 8 May 1912, p. 1; 14 May 1912, p. 4; 27 June 1912, p. 1; *New York Tribune*, 12 February 1912, p. 1; 4 February 1912, p. 6; 18 May 1912, p. 623 June 1912, p. 6.

11. Dixon, Wecter, *The Hero in America: A Chronicle of Hero Worship* (New York: Charles Scribner's Sons, 1972), p. 373, quoted in Gerald Leinwand, *William Jennings Bryan, An Uncertain Trumpet* (Lanham: Rowman & Littlefield Publishers, Inc., 2007), p. 98; Genevieve Forbes Herrick and John Origen Herrick, *The Life of William Jennings Bryan* (Chicago: John R. Stanton Company, 1925), p. 273; Wayne C. Williams, *William Jennings Bryan* (New York: G.O. Putnam's Sons, 1936), p. 330.

12. David D. Anderson, *William Jennings Bryan* (Boston: Twayne, 1981), p. 168; Louis W. Koenig, *Bryan, A Political Biography of William Jennings Bryan* (New York: G. P. Putnam's Sons, 1971), p. 496; Michael Kazin, *A Godly Hero: The Life of William Jennings Bryan* (New York: Alfred A. Knopf, 2006), pp. 187, 190.

13. Paol E. Colletta, *William Jennings Bryan, II Progressive Politician and Moral Statesman, 1909-1915* (Lincoln: University of Nebraska Press, 1969), pp. 61, 70–74.

14. Arthur S. Link, *Wilson: The Road to the White House*, p. 459.

15. *Chicago Daily News*, 26 June 1912, p. 3; *Baltimore Sun*, 27 June 1912, p. 12; 21 June 1912, p. 11; 30 June 1912, p. 4; Chicago *Tribune*, 24 June 1912, p. 7; *Chicago American*, 27 June 1912, third edition, p. 2; *Chicago Evening Post*, 27 June 1912, p. 2.

16. *Washington Post*, 26 June 1912, p. 3; *Chicago Tribune*, 24 June 1912, p. 7; 29 June 1912, p. 1; *Baltimore Sun*, 22 June 1912, p. 11; *Chicago Evening Post*, 27 June 1912, p. 2; *Chicago Daily News*, 5 o'clock edition, 29 June 1912, p. 1; H.L. Mencken, *Thirty-Five Years of Newspaper Work: A Memoir by H. L. Mencken* (Baltimore: Johns Hopkins University Press, 1994), 47–48. Apparently the janitorial services were no better. The famous satirist and correspondent for the *Baltimore Evening Sun*, H. L. Mencken, recalled "a necessary visit" late in the convention "to the filthy toilet under the stand," which left him "with a case of pediculus pubis [pubic lice]." On the other hand, smoking, at least, was banned in the hall. Mencken, like probably most of those who were there, believed "Bryan really hoped that he might get the nomination himself."

17. *Convention Proceedings, 1912*, pp. 3–20, 36, 59–78; Bryan, *Memoirs*, 170–171; *Baltimore Sun*, 20 June 1912, p. 16; 25 June 1912, pp. 1, 2, 11; *Chicago Evening Post*, 24 June 1912, p. 1; 25 June 1912, p. 1.

18. Milton W. Blumenberg, Urey Woodson, *Official Report of the Proceedings of the Democratic National*

Convention held in Baltimore, Maryland June 25, 26, 27, 28, 29, and July 1 and 2, Resulting in the Nomination of Hon. Woodrow Wilson (of New Jersey) for President and Hon. Thomas Riley Marshall (of Indiana) for Vice President* (Chicago: Petersen Linotype, 1912), pp. 100–01; *Washington Post,* 24 June 1912, pp. 2, 3, *Chicago Tribune,* 17 April 1912, p. 10; 25 June 1912, p. 3; *Chicago American,* 25 June 1912, home edition, pp. 1, 3; *Baltimore Sun* 26 June 1912, p. 12; 28 June 1912, p. 17; *Chicago Daily News,* 26 June 1912, pp. 1, 3, 27 June 1912, p. 1; Carter H. Harrison, *Stormy Years: The Autobiography of Carter H. Harrison, Five Times Mayor of Chicago* (Indianapolis: Bobbs-Merrill, 1935), p. 317; Harrison had vainly sought Clark's help before the Peoria state convention.

19. *Convention Proceedings,* pp. 100–01; *Washington Post,* 24 June 1912, pp. 2, 3, *Chicago Tribune,* 17 April 1912, p. 10; 25 June 1912, p. 3; *Chicago American,* 25 June 1912, home edition, pp. 1, 3; *Baltimore Sun* 26 June 1912, p. 12; 28 June 1912, p. 17; *Chicago Daily News,* 26 June 1912, pp. 1, 3; 27 June 1912, p. 1; Carter H. Harrison, *Stormy Years: The Autobiography of Carter H. Harrison, Five Times Mayor of Chicago* (Indianapolis: Bobbs-Merrill, 1935), p. 317.

20. *Convention Proceedings, 1912,* pp. 128–39; Bryan, *Memoirs,* 175–79; *Baltimore Sun,* 23 June 1912, p. 12; 30 June 1912, p. 2; *Chicago American,* 27 June 1912, third edition, p. 2; *Indianapolis Star,* 29 June 1912, p. 2; Gustavus Myers, *History of the Great American Fortunes,* volume 3, *Great Fortunes From Railroad (continued)* (Chicago: Charles H. Kerr, 1911), pp. 54, 66, 81, 91, 146, 222, 272, 276–77, 306, 396, 409; Paolo Coletta, *William Jennings Bryan, II, Progressive Politician and Moral Statesman, 1909–1915* (Lincoln: University of Nebraska Press, 1969), p. 65.

21. *Convention Proceedings, 1912,* pp. 197–98.

22. *Convention Proceedings, 1912,* 199–229; *Chicago Tribune,* 29 June 1912, pp. 1, 2.

23. Joseph P. Tumulty, *Woodrow Wilson As I Know Him* (Garden City, NY: Garden City, 1921), p. 121; Frank Parker Stockbridge, "How Woodrow Wilson Won His Nomination," *Current History* 20 (24 July 1924): 571; McCombs, *Making Woodrow Wilson President,* pp. 143–45; McCombs presents a "strangely distorted" (Tumulty's words) version of events. He makes no reference to Sullivan, and attributes to himself the hero's role of deflecting Wilson's despair-driven desire to withdraw that Friday night. His book was published posthumously from scattered notes and prose well after his break with Wilson, and while generally accurate, it always tends to present himself as the leading actor at every point.

24. Arthur Link, "A Letter from One of Wilson's Managers," *American Historical Review* 50, no. 4 (July 1945): 774.

25. *Convention Proceedings, 1912,* pp. 233–40; Dodd, *Woodrow Wilson and His Work,* p. 168.

26. Maurice Lyons, *William F. McCombs, President Maker* (Cincinnati: Bancroft, 1922), pp. 90–2.

27. Link, p. 464.

28. LeRoy Ashby, *William Jennings Bryan: Champion of Democracy* (Boston: Twayne, 1987), p. 140.

29. *Convention Proceedings, 1912,* pp. 263–64; 272; *Chicago American,* 29 June 1912, 9 o'clock edition, p. 1; *Washington Post,* 30 June 1912, pp. 1, 3.

30. Lyons, *President Maker,* p. 94; McCombs, *Making Woodrow Wilson President,* p. 157.

31. Clark, *Quarter Century of American Politics,* pp. 407–10, 420–8; Bryan, *Memoirs,* p. 181; *Washington Post,* 2 July 1912, pp. 1–2; *Chicago Tribune* 1 July 1912, p. 1; *Baltimore Sun,* 1 July 1912, pp. 1, 2; Charles M. Thomas, *Thomas Riley Marshall, Hoosier Statesman* (Oxford, OH: Mississippi Valley, 1939), pp. 123–24; Link, *Road to the White House,* pp. 460–61.

32. *Chicago Tribune,* 1 July 1912, p. 3; *New York Times,* 2 July 1912, p. 1; *Baltimore Sun,* 1 July 1912, pp. 10, 12; *Chicago Examiner,* 3 July 1912, p. 3.

33. *Chicago Tribune,* 1 July 1912, p. 3; *New York Times,* 2 July 1912, p. 1; *Baltimore Sun,* 1 July 1912, pp. 10, 12; *Chicago Examiner,* 3 July 1912, p. 3; Lyons, *President Maker,* p. 88; Stanley Cohen, *A. Mitchell Palmer: Politician* (New York: Columbia University Press, 1963); James William Madden, *Charles Allen Culberson* (Austin: Gammel's Bookstore, 1929).

34. *New York Tribune,* 1 July 1912, p. 1; Koenig, p. 496.

35. Link, Road to the White House, pp. 455–59.

36. *Madden, Culberson,* p. 147; Link, p. 454.

37. *New York Times,* 1 July 1912, pp. 1–2; Lyons, *President Maker,* p. 94; James Kerney, *Political Education of Woodrow Wilson* (New York: Century, 1926), p. 229; McCombs, *Making Woodrow Wilson President,* p. 166; Thomas, *Thomas Riley Marshall,* pp. 123–24; *Chicago Tribune,* 3 July 1912, p. 3; Johnson, *Oscar W. Underwood,* p. 187.

38. Bryan, *Memoirs,* p. 335; Koenig, *Bryan,* p. 495.

39. Johnson, *Oscar W. Underwood,* pp. 279–305; *Baltimore Sun,* 2 July 1912, pp. 2, 9.

40. *Baltimore Sun,* 24 June 1912, p. 2; *Chicago Tribune,* 1 July 1912, p. 1; 2 July 1912, p. 2; *Chicago Evening Post,* 28 June 1912, p. 3; *Baltimore Sun,* 2 July 1912, pp. 9, 10; Bryan, *Memoirs,* p. 184; *Daily News Almanac* (1913), p. 132; *Convention Proceedings,* 309–10.

41. *Chicago Tribune,* 1 July 1912, p. 1; 2 July 1912, p. 1; *New York Times,* 1 July 1912, p. 1; Thomas, *Thomas Riley Marshall,* p. 126; Williams, *William Jennings Bryan,* p. 330.

42. *Convention Proceedings, 1912,* pp. 323–32; *Chicago Tribune* 2 July 1912, p. 1.

43. *Chicago Tribune,* 2 July 1912, p. 3; *New York Times,* 2 July 1912 p. 1; Lyons, *President Maker,* pp. 97, 101.

44. *New York Times,* 2 July 1912, p. 1; *Washington Post,* 3 July 1912, p. 1: William Bayard Hale, "Thomas Riley Marshall," *World's Work,* 24 (October 1912): 630–38.

45. *Convention Proceedings, 1912,* pp. 336–53; Lyons, *President Maker,* pp. 101–02; McCombs, *Making Woodrow Wilson President,* p. 173; *Baltimore Sun,* 2 July 1912, p. 1; 3 July 1912, pp. 1, 2, 5, 10; *Chicago Tribune,* 3 July 1912, p. 3; *Chicago Daily News,* 2 July 1912, p. 3; *New York Tribune,* 3 July 1912, p. 3; Kerney, *Political Education of Woodrow Wilson,* p. 230, Link, "A Letter from One of Wilson's Managers": 774–5 Lawrence B. Stringer to J. Hamilton Lewis, 1913?, Box 1, *Stringer Papers,* Abraham Lincoln Presidential Papers, Springfield, Il.; quoted in Ashby, *William Jennings Bryan,* p. 141; McCombs desperation was not feigned; he would later admit that "There never was a time when I did not know that the next ballot might not be our end"; *Presidential Elections,* p. 232, in 1852, also at Baltimore, it took 49 ballots to nominate Franklin Pierce, and in 1860 in Charleston, South Carolina, the Democratic convention adjourned after 57 ballots without nominating anyone.

46. *Convention Proceedings*, 1912, pp. 336–53; Lyons, *President Maker*, pp. 101–02; McCombs, *Making Woodrow Wilson President*, p. 173; *Baltimore Sun*, 2 July 1912, p. 1; 3 July 1912, pp. 1, 2, 5, 10; *Chicago Tribune*, 3 July 1912, p. 3; *Chicago Daily News*, 2 July 1912, p. 3; *New York Tribune*, 3 July 1912, p. 3.

47. *Convention Proceedings*, 1912, pp. 365–76; *Baltimore Sun*, 3 July 1912, p. 11.

48. *Chicago Tribune*, 3 July 1912, pp. 2, 3; *Chicago Examiner*, 3 July, 1912, p. 3; *Chicago Daily News*, 1 July 1912, p. 3; *Washington Post*, 3 July 1912, p. 1.

49. *Washington Post*, 6 July 1912, p. 1; Tumulty, *Woodrow Wilson As I Know Him*, p. 99.

50. *Chicago Tribune*, 3 July 1912, p. 3; *Chicago Examiner*, 3 July 1912, p. 3; Link, "A Letter from One of Wilson's Managers": 774; Arthur Link, ed., *The Papers of Woodrow Wilson, vol. 18, 1908–1909* (Princeton: Princeton University Press, 1966, 1992), pp. 53–59.

51. Kerney, *Political Education of Woodrow Wilson*, p. 234. In the motion picture *Wilson* (1944) produced by Twentieth Century Fox, and produced while the convention was still a living memory for many, a somewhat contradictory account of the governor of New Jersey's nomination is presented. On one hand, Bryan is depicted as playing off Wilson and Clark using the deadlock to secure his own nomination. On the other, Bryan's withdrawal of support for Clark is falsely presented as the decisive moment in breaking the impasse and creating a stampede for Wilson. The actual sequence of events and Roger C. Sullivan's role are ignored.

Chapter 6

1. *Baltimore Sun*, 15 June 1912, p. 10; 5 July 1912, pp. 1, 2; *New York Times*, 5 July 1912, p. 1; 6 July 1912, pp. 1, 2; *Chicago Tribune*, 15 July 1912, p. 2; 29 July 1912, p. 4; 6 August 1912, p. 7; *Chicago Evening Post*, 3 July 1912, p. 2; *Chicago Daily News*, 3 July 1912, p. 1.

2. *Chicago Tribune*, 26 July 1912, p. 4; *Chicago American*, 25 July 1912, p. 1.

3. *Chicago Tribune*, 6 August 1912, p. 7; 2 August 1912, p. 5; 25 August 1912, p. 5; 2 September 1912, p. 4.

4. *Chicago Tribune*, 19 July 1912, p. 5; 24 July 1912, p. 2; 31 July 1912, p. 5; 14 September 1912, p. 7; 9 August 1908, p. 1; 2 October 1939, p. 14; 6 November 1952, p. 1; James Langland, comp., *The Chicago Daily News Almanac and Year-Book for 1910* (Chicago: Daily News, 1911), p. 273 (hereafter cited as *Daily News Almanac*); United States, Congress, *Biographical Directory of the United States Congress, 1774–1989*, bicentennial edition (Washington, D.C.: Government Printing Office, 1989), p. 1758. Adolph Joachim Sabath was an immigrant success story and an embodiment of the American Dream as then defined. He was born on 4 April 1866 of Bohemian stock in Zabori in the Austrian-Hungarian Empire (now the Czech Republic). In 1881, he paid his own way to Chicago where he immediately went to work to finance the passage of his parents and his ten siblings (a common arrangement among European immigrants). He continued his labor in stores as a salesman and clerk, while attending business school at night. In 1881, he completed a course of study at the Chicago College of Law, and he was admitted to the bar the following year. Sabath practiced as an attorney, but also made a fortune in real estate. By the time he was admitted to the bar, he was already promi-

nent in local Democratic politics, and he was chosen a ward committeeman just as he was finishing law school. Before the Harrison faction came into being in 1897, he sometimes worked with Hopkins and Sullivan, and he was frequently associated with Bohemian-born Anton J. Cermak. In 1895, Sabath was chosen to be a justice of the peace by Governor John P. Altgeld at the request of the local Bohemian community. Two years later, he was appointed by Mayor Carter Harrison as a police magistrate, a position in which he served until 1906, when he successfully ran for the United States House of Representatives. He remained in Congress until his death in 1952. In 1909, he was elected as an H-H man to the Cook County Democratic Committee, and by 1910, he was counted as among the faction's leaders. At the H-H version of the 1912 Cook County Democratic convention, he was elected chair of their executive committee. Where Sabath's life was a classic story of rags to riches, Maclay Hoyne's was privileged from birth. He was a native Chicagoan, born on 12 October 1872 as the son of Thomas Maclay Hoyne, a prominent attorney. In 1895, he graduated from Williams College in Massachusetts, and in 1897, from the Union College of Law. He then became a partner in his father's firm, now renamed Hoyne, O'Connor, and Hoyne. In July 1903, he was appointed by Mayor Harrison as an assistant corporation counsel, and in 1906, he made an unsuccessful bid as a Democrat for county judge. Between 1902 and 1908, he also attended to the lucrative trade of representing the city in all telephone litigation. For two years during Mayor Fred Busse's tenure, he served as a special counsel for the Board of Aldermen's committee on gas, oil, and electric lights. In 1908, he lost the Democratic primary for the nomination for state's attorney, but four years later he won, and he was now, therefore, one of the leading candidates in this years' county election cycle.

5. *Chicago Tribune*, 14 September 1912, p. 4.

6. *Ibid.*, 20 September 1912, p. 5.

7. *Ibid.*, 8 October 1912, p. 5; 10 October 1912, p. 5; 11 October 1912, pp. 1, 2; *Chicago Record-Herald*, 11 October 1912, pp. 1. 2.

8. *Chicago Tribune*, 12 October 1912, p. 5.

9. *Ibid.*

10. *Daily News Almanac* (1913), pp. 436–37; 478–80.

11. *Chicago Tribune*, 10 November 1912, p. 5; William Bayard Hale, "Mr. Bryan," *World's Work*, 26 (June 1913): 154–71.

12. *Chicago Tribune*, 28 January 1913, p. 2; *Illinois State Register*, 30 January 1913, p. 2; Charles Karch to Woodrow Wilson, 22 January 1913, *Thomas Woodrow Wilson Papers* (microfilm ed. Series 2, reel 41); Illinois General Assembly, House, *Journal of the House of Representatives of the 48th General Assembly of the State of Illinois* (Springfield: Illinois State Journal Company, 1914), pp. 5, 25 (hereafter cited as *House Journal*).

13. *Chicago Tribune*, 12 May 1913, p. 4; 19 May 1913, p. 5.

14. *Chicago Tribune*, 14 May 1913, p. 4; 18 May 1913, p. 1; 30 August 1913, p. 7; *New York Times*, 18 May 1913, p. 11; *Chicago Evening Post*, 15 April 1920, p. 2.

15. *Chicago Tribune*, 10 August 1913, p. A1; 17 May 1944, pp. 1, 10; information on the walking stick provided by Frank Sullivan (grandnephew), 2 July 2008.

16. *Chicago Tribune*, 10 August 1913, p. A1; 3 Sep-

tember 1913, p. 7; *New York Times*, 29 August 1913, p. 9; 30 August 1913, p. 7; *Chicago Tribune* 30 August 1913, p. 1; 3 September 1913, p. 7; 19 December 1912, p. 2. It is an illustrative list worth reproducing: George E. Brennan, James T. Brady (State Auditor of Public Accounts), Francis D. Connery (City Clerk), Joseph. F. Connery (Recorder of Cook County), James M. Dailey (Sanitary District Trustee), John J. Gaynor (Sanitary District Comptroller), Stephen J. Griffin (Chief Clerk of the Board of Review), George L. LeClaire, Patrick. J. Lucey (State Attorney General), John F. O'Malley (State Senator), Chief George L. McConnell (Chief Clerk of the County Clerk's office), John McGillen (Sanitary District Clerk), Michael. L. McKinley (Superior Court Judge), R. M. Mitchell (former state senator), Patrick A. Nash, Thomas J. O'Hare (Assistant State Attorney General), John W. Rainey (Clerk of the Circuit Court), Frank S. Ryan (County Controller) W. K. Sheridan (Member of the Country Board of Assessors), Denis E. Sullivan (Superior Court Judge), Thomas M. Sullivan (Sanitary District Trustee), Robert M. Sweitzer (County Clerk), and Frank. J. Walsh (Clerk of the Criminal Court). One, who asked to remain anonymous, explained to the press: "All of us are political friends of Mr. Sullivan, and most of us are more-or-less indebted to him for our offices. I don't think it is strange that a bunch of men who are filling $10,000, $12,000, and $15,000 jobs should want to come this far to greet the man responsible." Of course, most were also successful businessmen in their own right. They were obviously doing very well indeed as many could afford to stay at the exclusive and expensive Waldorf Astoria, with only a few consigned to the only slightly less prestigious Knickerbocker.

17. *Chicago Tribune*, 2 September 1913, p. 9; Stephane Lauzanne, "Will French Women Ever Vote?" *World's Work* 48 (August 1924): 398–402.

18. *Chicago Tribune*, 3 September 1913, p. 7; 7 September 1913, p. 4.

19. *Chicago Evening Post*, 15 April 1920, p. 2.

20. Daniel Hudson Burnham, *Plan of Chicago Prepared under the Direction of the Commercial Club during the years MCMVI, MCMVII, and MCMVIII* (Chicago: Commercial Club, 1909), p. xviii; *Good Government, the Official Journal of the National Civil Service League*, XXVII, no. 9 (September 1910): 68.

21. *Chicago Tribune*, 4 October 1913, p. 13; 22 October 1913, p. 9; 24 November 1913, p. 7; 2 January 1914, p. 3.

22. *Chicago Tribune*, 18 January 1914, p. 2.

23. *Ibid*.

24. *Ibid*.

25. *Ibid*.

26. *Ibid.*, 25 September 1913, p. 5; 22 October 1913, pp. 9, 18; 23 June 1920, p. 17; 27 May 1937, p. 27; 18 January 1941, p. 7; *Belvidere Daily Republican*, 13 October 1913, p. 1; Samuel Insull, *The Memoirs of Samuel Insull: An Autobiography* (Polo, IL: Transportation Trails, 1992), p. 149; Insull was also close to Helen Sullivan, and was an active pallbearer during her funeral.

27. *Chicago Tribune*, 19 October 1913, p. 8.

28. *Ibid.*, 24 December 1913, p. 7; 7 February 1914, p. 5; 8 February 1914, p. 6; *New York Times*, 10 April 1966, p. 75; Helen M. Cavanagh, *Carl Schurz Vrooman, Self-Styled "Constructive Conservative,"* (Chicago: Lakeside, 1977), pp. 133–35; Ross E. Paulson, *Radicalism and Reform, The Vrooman Family and American*

Social Thought, 1837–1937 (Lexington: University of Kentucky Press, 1968), pp. 211–16.

29. *Chicago Tribune*, 20 January 1914, p. 3; 13 February 1914, p. 2; 20 February 1914, pp. 1, 8.

30. *The Commoner*, February 1914, p. 2.

31. *Chicago Tribune*, 17 February 1914, pp. 1, 2; 20 February 1914, pp. 1, 8; 26 February 1914, p. 5; 27 February 1914, p. 4.

32. Carter H. Harrison to William Jennings Bryan, 11 May 1914; Newberry Library, Chicago, Illinois; Edward F. Dunne to William Jennings Bryan, 25 May 1914, William Jennings Bryan Papers, Manuscript Division, Library of Congress, Washington, D.C.; Carter H. Harrison to William Jennings Bryan, 15 June 1914, Bryan Papers; *Illinois State Register*, 1 March 1914, p. 6; 13 April 1914, p. 1.

33. Carter H. Harrison to William Jennings Bryan, 15 June 1914, Bryan Papers, Chicago *Tribune*, 6 December 1942, p. B10.

34. *Chicago Tribune*, 16 July 1914, p. 13; 17 July 1914, p. 8; 22 July 1914, p. 8; *Illinois State Register*, 16 July 1914, p. 1; 19 July 1914, pp. 1, 2; 20 July 1914, p. 1; 30 July 1914, p. 1; "The Appointer General," *World's Work*, 26 (October 1913): 616.

35. *Chicago Tribune*, 26 April 1914, p. I:7; 27 April 1914, p. 8; 29 April 1914, p. 10.

36. *Chicago Tribune*, 23 July 1913, p. 12; 21 September 1913, p. 4; 28 September 1913, p. 4; 1 October 1913, p. 4; 2 October 1913, p. 7; 12 December 1913, p. 12; 13 December 1913, p. 5; 12 May 1914, p. 2; *Illinois State Register*, 13 May 1914, p. 1; *Chicago Record-Herald and Inter-Ocean*, 13 May 1914, p. 4; 14 May 1914, p. 5; 15 May 1914, p. 5; 17 May 1914, p. 4; Flyer, "Roger C. Sullivan, Candidate for the United States Senate," Lawrence Y. Sherman Papers, Abraham Lincoln Presidential Papers, Springfield, Illinois.

37. *Chicago Tribune*, 12 May 1914, p. 2. *Chicago Record-Herald and Inter-Ocean*, 16 May 1914, p. 4.

38. *Chicago Tribune*, 14 May 1914, p. 4; 15 May 1914, p. 9; 19 May 1914, pp. 1, 2; 21 May 1914, p. 15; 22 May 1914, p. 4.

39. *Chicago Tribune*, 21 May 1914, p. 15; *Carlinville Democrat*, 29 May 1914, p. 4, *Chicago Record-Herald and Inter-Ocean*, 15 May 1914, p. 5. This was a common name for downstaters resulting from the fact that southern Illinois became known as Little Egypt sometime in the 1830s when settlers from northern Illinois went there to buy corn during years of poor harvests. This practice evoked comparisons to biblical accounts of ancient people traveling to Egypt to buy grain, and it was the source of Southern Illinois towns acquiring the monikers of Cairo, Thebes, and Karnak.

40. *Chicago Tribune*, 11 February 1914, p. 6; 15 February 1914, p. I:5; 15 March 1914, p. I:6; 10 July 1914, p. 13; 19 July 1914, p. I:2; Corinthians 6:15, Belial was another name for Satan. In Milton's *Paradise Lost*, he became a separate fallen angel, one Satan's lieutenants.

41. *Chicago Tribune*, 17 February 1914, p. 1; 16 July 1914, p. 13; 30 July 1914, p. 7; 13 August 1914, p. 9; 23 August 1914, pp. II:1. II:2; 6 September 1914, p. 10.

42. Lawrence B. Stringer to J. Hamilton Lewis, undated, 1914(?), Lawrence B. Stringer Papers, Abraham Lincoln Presidential Papers, Springfield, Illinois.

43. *Chicago Tribune*, 26 August 1914, p. 8; 29 August 1914, p. 13.

44. 29 August 1914, p. 13; 31 August 1914, p. 8; 3 September 1914 p. 9; *Illinois State Register*, 4 September

1914, p. 6; *Chicago Record-Herald and Inter-Ocean*, 19 May 1914, p. 4; *Chicago Herald*, 28 August 1914, p. 7; 29 August 1914, p. 7.

45. *Chicago Tribune*, 15 July 1914, p. 7; *Chicago Herald*, 19 August 1914, p. 11.

46. Charles Karch to Edward F. Dunne, Open Letter, 3 September 1914, Stringer Papers.

47. *Chicago Herald*, 29 August 1914, p. 7; Roger C. Sullivan, campaign letter, 4 September 1914, Sherman Papers.

48. *Chicago Record-Herald and Inter-Ocean*, 20 May 1914, p. 4; James Langland, comp. *The Daily News Almanac and Year-Book for 1915* (Chicago: Daily News, 1914), pp. 421–22.

49. *Chicago Herald*, 19 September 1914, p. 5.

50. *Ibid.*

51. Lawrence B. Stringer to J. Hamilton Lewis, 1914 (?), Stringer Papers.

52. Neil V. Salzman, *Reform and Revolution, The Life and Times of Raymond Robins* (Kent: Kent State University Press, 1991).

53. *Chicago Tribune*, 14 August 1914, p. 7; 19 September 1914, p. 5; 23 September 1914, pp. 1, 4; 20 October 1914, p. 4; 21 October 1914, p. 7; 23 October 1914, p. 5.

54. *Chicago Tribune*, 8 October 1914, p. 9; 19 October 1914, p. 4; 22 October 1914, p. 5; Carter H. Harrison, *Stormy Years, The Autobiography of Carter H. Harrison, Five Times Mayor of Chicago* (Indianapolis: Bobbs-Merrill, 1935), pp. 329–30.

55. *Chicago Tribune*, 27 October 1914, p. 9; Henry T. Rainey to Joseph P. Tumulty, 23 October 1914; Rainey to Tumulty, 25 October 1914; Dixon B. William to Tumulty, 26 October 1914; H.N. Wheeler to Tumulty, 27 October 1914; J.M. Page to Tumulty, 28 October 1914, Henry T. Rainey Papers, Manuscript Division, Library of Congress, Washington, D.C.

56. Joseph Tumulty, *Woodrow Wilson as I Know Him* (Garden City, NY: Garden City, c. 1921), p. 103; Harry M. Fisher to Tumulty, 15 October 1914, Tumulty Papers. Wilson also declined to endorse publicly Adolph Sabath, a Harrison leader, who was running for reelection to Congress.

57. *Daily News Almanac* (1916), p. 264; *Washington Post*, 21 January 1914, p. 1.

58. Primary Handbill, 1915; Primary campaign letter, 20 February 1915, Carter H. Harrison IV Papers, Newberry Library, Chicago Illinois; Reverend John R. Vance to D.C. Williams, 30 October 1914, Tumulty Papers.

59. Richard L, Boggs to Arthur W. Charles, 30 September 1914; Robins to Sullivan, telegram received 30 September 1914, Tumulty Papers; *Washington Post*, 6 October 1914, p. 3; *Chicago Herald*, 4 September 1914, p. 7; 17 September 1914, p. 7.

60. Sullivan to Kern, telegram, 18 September 1914; telegram 28 September 1914, Tumulty Papers; *Chicago Herald*, 19 September 1914, p. 5; 26 September 1914, p. 7.

61. Sullivan to Robins, telegram, 30 September 1914m Tumulty Papers; *Chicago Tribune*, 1 October 1914, p. 7; 2 October 1914, p. 5; *Washington Post*, 6 October 1914, p. 11; 10 October 1914, p. 11.

62. *Chicago Tribune*, 14 October 1920, p. 9; 15 October 1914, p. 5; 20 October 1914, p. 1.

63. *Chicago Tribune*, 15 October 1914, p. 5; 27 October 1914, p. 9.

64. *Chicago Tribune*, 25 October 1914, p. 5.

65. *Chicago Tribune*, 28 October 1914, p. 1.

66. *Chicago Tribune*, 28 October 1914, p. 1; *News Gleaner* (Shawneetown, Illinois), 18 September 1914, p. 4.

67. *Washington Post*, 1 November 1914, p. 15; *Chicago Tribune*, 3 November 1914, p. 5; Walter S. Rogers, "The Embarrassing Mr. Sullivan," Harper's Weekly 59 (October 1914), pp. 394–95; William W. Allen and Vincent A. Lacey, *Illinois Elections 1818–1900: Candidates and County Returns for President, Governor, Senator, and House of Representatives* (Carbondale: Southern Illinois University Press, 1992), pp. 277–79. *Daily News Almanac* (1915), p. 641.

68. *Chicago Tribune*, 8 November 1914, p. A3.

69. Joseph L. Gardner, *Departing Glory, Theodore Roosevelt as Ex-President* (New York: Charles Scribner's Sons, 1973), p. 328.

Chapter 7

1. Carter H. Harrison, *Stormy Years, The Autobiography of Carter H. Harrison, Five Times Mayor of Chicago* (Indianapolis: Bobbs-Merrill, 1925), p. 340.

2. *Ibid.*, pp. 339–340. According to Harrison, the specific cause of his estrangement from Coughlin and Kenna was their refusal to support County Judge John E. Owens for renomination. However, their unhappiness with the mayor's decision to "clean up" Chicago was well known.

3. *Chicago Tribune*, 4 March 1912, p. 3; 30 June 1912, p. 3; 12 December 1912, p. 2; 26 January 1912, p. 6; 3 February 1913, p. 4; 5 March 1912, p. 7.

4. *Chicago Tribune*, 22, March 1914, p. 8; 23, March 1914, p. 13; 12 April 1916, p. 2.

5. *Chicago Tribune*, May 5, 1913, p. 5; 11 November 1915, p. 3.

6. *Chicago Herald*, 28 September 1914, p. 4; *Chicago Tribune*, 28 October 1914, pp. 1, 8.

7. Peter Clark Macfarlane, "Is Roger Sullivan a Boss?" *Collier's* 53 (6 August 1914): 5–6; "The Farm Boy Who Became Illinois' 'Benevolent Boss,'" *Literary Digest* 65 (15 May 1920): 87–94; *Chicago Herald*, 28 September 1914, p. 4; *Chicago Tribune*, 6 January 1920, p. 3. However, for all Macfarlane's claimed expertise, he failed to uncover (or reveal) the importance during this period of the lunchtime "clubhouse" of Sullivan's inner circle, a bar and grill run by an old friend and prominent "sportsman" named William "Smiley" Corbett (who owned a racehorse with the same name). The Lambs' Café was located in the basement of the Ashland Block building at the northeast corner of Clark and Randolph and replaced the Sherman Hotel after 1910 (when it was being rebuilt) as the site of regular lunches for Sullivan, Hopkins, Brennan, and others to discuss politics and to meet with supplicants.

8. *Chicago Tribune*, 18 December 1914, p. 17; 22 December 1914, p. 13; 30 December 1914, p. 11.

9. *Chicago Tribune*, 7 April 1938, p. 1; *Daily News Almanac* (1915), p. 567; Harrison, *Stormy Years*, p. 346.

10. *Chicago Tribune*, 28 December 1914, p. 11; 30 December 1914, p. 11; Reuben Donnelley, comp., *Lakeside Annual Directory of the City of Chicago 1915* (Chicago: Chicago Directory, 1915), p. 1596.

11. *Chicago Tribune*, 30 December 1914, p. 11; 7 January 1915, p. 7.

12. *Chicago Tribune*, 3 January 1915, p. 4; 23 January

1915, p. 7; Handwritten note by Harrison on Sweitzer campaign handbill, Harrison to Edward J. Sweeney, 12 April 1915, Carter H. Harrison IV Papers, Newberry Library, Chicago, Illinois.

13. *Chicago Tribune*, 9 February 1915, p. 3; 16 February 1915, p. 9; 22 February 1915, p. 4; *Chicago Herald*, 23 January 1915, p. 5; 11 February 1915, p. 4.

14. *Chicago Tribune*, 21 January 1915, p. 3; 5 February 1915, p. 7; 9 February 1915, p. 7; 11 February 1915, p. 7; 14 February 1915, p. 7; 20 February 1915, p. 9; *Chicago Herald*, 30 January 1915, p. 4; 20 February 1915, p. 4. Violence of this type could assume a more lethal expression during elections and primaries. In August 1914, the offices of the West Side Benevolent Association were bombed. It was the campaign headquarters for Fred Bruder, a member of the "H-H" faction, who was running for the Board of County Commissioners, and opposed by the circle of the same said Grogan, was bombed. Nobody was seriously hurt, but apparently a "message" of one sort or another was being delivered.

15. *Chicago Tribune*, August 13, 1914, p. 13; 20 February 1915, p. 14; 23 February 1915, p. 8; 24 February 1915, p. 5; 31 January 1915, p. 5; *Chicago Herald*, 21 February 1915, p. 7.

16. *Chicago Tribune,* 13 February 1915, pp. 1, 4; 22 February 1915, p. 4.

17. *Chicago Herald*, 2 January 1915, pp. 1, 3; 4 January 1915, p. 11; 7 January 1915, p. 7; 14 January 1915, p. 4; 14 February 1915, p. 7; 22 February 1915, p. 4; *Chicago Herald*, 20 January 1915, p. 6; 9 February 1915, p. 4; 12 February 1915, p. 4.

18. *Chicago Herald*, 16 February 1915, p. 9; 17 February 1915, p. 8.

19. *Chicago Herald*, 24 February 1915, p. 1; 7 April 1915, p. 2; *Daily News Almanac* (1916), pp. 560–61; *Chicago Herald*, 24 February 1915, p. 1; Harrison, *Stormy Years*, p. 348.

20. Douglas Bukowski, *Big Bill Thompson, Chicago, and the Politics of Image* (Urbana: University of Illinois Press, 1998), pp. 22–24.

21. *Ibid.*, pp. 19–23; *Chicago Tribune*, 20 March 1944, p. 14; *New York Times*, 20 March 1944, p. 17.

22. *Chicago Tribune*, 23 February 1915, p. 8; 9 March 1915, p. 4; 17 March 1915, p. 7; 31 March 1915, pp. 1, 2; 2 April 1915, p. 9; *Chicago Herald*, 28 February 1915, p. 8; 3 March 1915, p. 8; 8 March 1915, p. 6; 14 March 1915, p. 4; 28 March 1915, p. 7.

23. *Chicago Tribune*, 9 March 1915, p. 4; 13 March 1915, p. 4; 19 March 1915, p. 6; 22 March 1915, p. 7; 26 March 1915, p. 5; 27 March 1915, p. 8; 29 March 1915, p. 8; *Chicago Herald*, 23 March 1915, p. 5.

24. *Chicago Tribune*, 2 April 1915, p. 9; 3 April 1915 pp. 1, 4; 3 April 1915, pp, 1, 2, 3; *Chicago Herald*, 3 April 1915, p. 3.

25. *Chicago Tribune*, 16 February 1915, p. 2; 18 February 1915, p. 4; 19 February 1915, p. 4; *Chicago Herald*, 27 March 1915, p. 5; 24 March 1915, p. 6. The newspapers endorsing Sweitzer included: the German: *Der Abendpost*, *Der Illinois Staats-Zeitung*, *Der Chicago Presse* (the latter two were usually Republican), The Bohemian: *DenniHasated*, Narod, *Suornost* (usually Republican), the *Jewish Record*, Jewish *Sentinel*, the *Reform Advocate*, the Polish: *Dzienik Chicagoski*, and the *Polish Telegraph*; among those endorsing Thompson were the Norwegian *Skandinaven*, the *Swedish Courier*, the *Swedish Messenger*, and *L'Itlalia*.

26. *Chicago Tribune*, 3 April 1915, p. 5; 4 April 1915, pp. 1, 3; *Chicago Herald*, 4 April 1915, p. 1.

27. James Langland, comp. *The Daily News Almanac and Year-Book for 1916* (Chicago: Daily News, 1915), pp. 567–68 (hereafter cited as *Daily News Almanac*).

28. *Chicago Daily News*, 15 April 1920, p. 2; John M. Allswang, *A House for All Peoples: Ethnic Politics in Chicago, 1890–1936* (Lexington: University of Kentucky Press, 1971), p. 34; David A. Moss, *Socializing Security, Progressive-Era Economists and the Origins of American Social Policy* (Cambridge: Harvard University Press, 1995), p. 133.

29. *New York Times*, 5 May 1915, p. 1; 8 June 1915, p. 1; William Jennings Bryan and Mary Baird Bryan, *The Memoirs of William Jennings Bryan* (Mary Baird Bryan, 1925), pp. 415–28.

30. *Chicago Tribune*, 4 August 1915, p. 7; *Chicago Herald*, 18 February 1916, p. 3.

31. *Chicago Tribune*, 20 December 1915, p. 10; the press no longer referenced the "H-H" faction after late 1915.

32. *Chicago Tribune*, 5 January 1916, p. 13; 16 January 1916, p. 10; 17 January 1916, p. 9. This year the unit rule did not apply to Illinois as the latest formulation of the primary law, reenacted again to satisfy the Illinois Supreme Court, allowed ward and district conventions that chose the national delegates, to also issue binding instructions regarding candidates.

33. *Chicago Tribune*, 7 February 1916, p. 3. *Miami Herald*, 11 February 1915, p. 12.

34. *Chicago Tribune*, 16 February 1916, p. 11; 18 February 1916, p. 4; 20 February 1916, p. 7; *Chicago Herald*; 19 February 1916, p. 3.

35. *Chicago Tribune*, 3 February 1916, p. 5; 9 February 1916, pp. 1, 2; 11 February 1916, pp. 1, 2; 23 February 1916, p. 13; 29 February 1916, p. 4; 1 March 1916, p. 2; *Chicago Herald*, 11 February 1916, p. 1; 1 March 1916, p. 5.

36. *Chicago Tribune*, 12 February 1916, p. 13; 13 February 1916, p. 4; 17 February 1916, pp. 1, 4; 10 March 1916, p. 11; 14 March 1916, p. 10; 16 March 1916, p. 1; 18 April 1916, p. 123; July 1916, p. A3; 24 November 1916, p. 2; 27; 28 June 1918, p. 13; 22 March 1920, p. 1.

37. *Chicago Tribune*, 2 May 1916, p. 9; 11 June 1916, p. A8; 13 June 1916, p. 19.

38. *Chicago Tribune,* 5 March 1916, pp. 9; 5 April 1915, pp. 1, 2; 9 April 1916, p. 512; April 1916, pp. 1, 4; *Chicago Herald*, 5 April 1916, p. 1.

39. *Chicago Tribune*, 5 March 1916, pp. 9; 5 April 1915, pp. 1, 2; 9 April 1916, p. 5; 12 April 1916, pp. 1, 4; Chicago Herald, 5 April 1916, p. 1.

40. Carter H. Harrison, *Stormy Years: The Autobiography of Carter H. Harrison, Five Times Mayor of Chicago* (Indianapolis: Bobbs-Merrill, 1935), p. 331; Michael F. Funchion, "The More Things Change: Chicago's Pol Legacy," *Crain's Chicago Business* (27 April 1987): 71; *Chicago Tribune*, 14 April 1916, p. 10; 18 April 1916, p. 7; *Chicago Herald*, 12 April 1916, p. 2; 18 April 1916, p. 4; *Washington Post*, 22 April 1916, p. 2.

41. *Chicago Tribune,* 22 April 1916, p. 8; *Chicago Herald*, 14 April 1916, p. 6; 15 April 1916, p. 3; 18 April 1916, p. 5.

42. *Chicago Tribune*, 9 May 1916, p. 12; *New York Times*, 23 October 1915, p. 8; 13 June 1916, p. 7; Charles M. Thomas, *Thomas Riley Marshall, Hoosier States-*

man (Oxford, OH: Mississippi Valley, 1939), pp. 222–23.

43. *Chicago Tribune*, 9 May 1916, p. 12.

44. *Chicago Herald*, 7 June 1916, p. 3; 12 June 1916, p. 2.

45. *Chicago Tribune*, 12 June 1916, p. 3; 13 June 1916, p. 3; 14 June 1916, p. 2; *New York Times*, 15 June 1916, p. 3; *Chicago Herald*, 13 June 1916, p. 3; 14 June 1916, p. 2.

46. *Chicago Tribune*, 13 April 1916, p. 8; 23 April 1916, pp. 1, 8; 14 June 1916, p. 4.

47. *St. Louis Post-Dispatch*, 14 June 1916, p. 2; 16 June 1916, p. 3.

48. *Chicago Tribune*, 13 June 1916, p. 3; 15 June 1916, pp. 1, 2, 4; 16 June 1916, p. 6; *Chicago Herald*, 15 June 1916, pp. 2, 3.

49. *Chicago Daily News*, 15 April 1920, p. 2.

50. *Convention Proceedings*, 1916, pp. 91, 94–101; *Chicago Herald*, 14 June 1916, p. 1.

51. James Langland, comp. *The Daily News Almanac and Year-Book for 1917* (Chicago: Daily News, 1916), pp. 538–39 (hereafter cited as *Daily News Almanac*).

52. *Daily News Almanac* (1917), pp. 554–55; *St. Louis Post-Dispatch*, 16 June 1916, pp. 1, 2; the lobbyists for women's suffrage did their best for a plank endorsing a federal constitutional amendment, but this was voted down by a margin of forty to four, while by the vote of twenty-six to seventeen an alternative plank was turned back that would simply recognize state sovereignty in the matter. Instead it was decided by a count of twenty-five to twenty to settle for a simple recommendation to the states.

53. *Convention Proceedings*, 1916, pp. 106–07; *Chicago Tribune*, 16 May 1916, p. 9; 12 June 1916, p. 2; 17 June 1916, p. 3.

54. *Chicago Tribune*, 18 June 1916, p. 4.

55. Norman Harper to Raymond Robins, 8 July 1916, Raymond Robins Papers, Wisconsin Historical Society, Madison, Wisconsin.

56. Jesse Heylin to Raymond Robins, 21 July 1 1916; Unsigned to Carl Vrooman, 17 July 1916; William H. Stevens to Raymond Robins, 3 July 1916; Raymond Robins Papers; *Illinois State Register*, 11 July 1916, p. 1. Josephus Daniels to William Jennings Bryan, 17 July 1916, Josephus Daniels Papers, Library of Congress, Manuscript Division, Washington, D.C.

57. *Chicago Tribune*, 9 July 1916, p. 5; 6 August 1916, p. 6; *Chicago Herald*, 6 August 1916, p. A5; Raymond Robins to George Perkins, 13 July 1916, Raymond Robins Papers.

58. *Illinois State Register*, 30 July 1916, p. 2; *Chicago Tribune*, 6 September 1916, p. 5; 10 September 1916, p. 1; 12 September 1916, p. 1; Chicago Herald, 3 September 1916, p. 8.

59. *Daily News Almanac* (1917), pp. 581, 598.

60. *Chicago Tribune*, 3 September 1916, p. 8; 4 September 1916, p. 4; *Chicago Herald*, 2 August 1916, p. 5; 6 September 1916, p. 7.

61. *Daily News Almanac* (1917), pp. 581, 598; *Chicago Tribune*, 14 September 1916, p. 3.

62. *Chicago Tribune*, 14 September 1916, p. 2; 16 September 1916, p. 4; 25 September 1916, p. 6.

63. *Chicago Tribune*, 27 September 1916, p. 4.

64. *Illinois State Register*, 29 October 1916, pp. 1, 2; 4 October 1916, p. 4; 6 November 1916, p. 1; *Chicago Tribune*, 6 October 1916, p. 10; 14 October 1916, p. 5;

20 October 1916, p. 9; 29 October 1916, p. 9; Walker to Dunne, 9 May 1916, John Hunter Walker Papers, Illinois Historical Survey, University of Illinois Library, Urbana-Champaign; William T. Hutchinson, *Lowden of Illinois, The Life of Frank O. Lowden, City and State* (Chicago: University of Chicago Press, 1957), pp. 286–87.

65. *Chicago Tribune*, 20 October 1916, pp. 1, 2; 25 October 1916, p. 8; Theodore H. Price and Richard Spillane, "Stalking for Nine Million Votes," *World's Work*, 32 (October 1916): 663–77; J. Leonard Bates, *Senator Thomas J. Walsh of Montana, Law and Public Affairs from TR to FDR* (Urbana: University of Illinois Press, 1997), pp. 135–39.

66. *Chicago Tribune*, 1 October 1916, pp. 1, 2; 2 October 1916, p. 8; 13 October 1916, p. 7; 21 October 1916, p. 3.

67. *Chicago Tribune*, 10 November 1916, p. 3; *New York Times*, 17 October 1916, p. 4. *Daily News Almanac* (1917), p. 426.

68. *Daily News Almanac* (1917), pp. 432, 591–94, 597.

Chapter 8

1. *Chicago Tribune*, 24 January 1917, p. 1.

2. *Chicago Tribune*, 30 January 1917, p. 3; 23 January 1917, p. 13; 25 February 1917, pp. 1, 10; *Washington Post*, 31 January 1917, p. 6; Humbert Nelli, "John Powers and the Italians: Politics in a Chicago Ward, 1896–1921," *Journal of American History* 57 (June 1970): 67–84.

3. *Chicago Tribune*, 28 February 1917, pp. 1, 8.

4. *Chicago Tribune*, 31 March 1917, p. 8; 4 April 1917, pp. 1, 5; *Chicago Herald*, 4 April 1917, p. 1; James Langland, comp., *The Daily News Almanac and Year-Book for 1918* (Chicago: Chicago Daily News, 1917), pp. 623–24 (hereafter cited as *Daily News Almanac*).

5. *New York Times*, 12 December 1916, p. 2; 13 December 1916, pp. 1, 3; 30 December 1916, p. 1; 1 February 1917, p. 1; 4 February 1917, p. 2; 1 March 1917, pp. 1, 2; 2 March 1917, pp. 1, 2; 3 March 1917, pp. 1, 2; 5 March 1917, pp. 1, 2; 9 March 1917, pp. 1, 2; 16 March 1917, p. 2; 3 April 1917, pp. 1, 2; *Daily News Almanac* (1918), p. 392.

6. *Daily News Almanac* (1918), pp. 487, 518–21; (1921), p. 381; *Chicago Tribune*, 9 May 1917, p. 9. See Joseph R. Ornig, *My Last Chance To Be a Boy: Theodore Roosevelt's South American Expedition of 1913–1914* (Baton Rouge: Louisiana State University Press, 1994).

7. *Chicago Tribune*, 13 May 1917, pp. 1, 2; "What the Council of National Defense is Doing," *World's Work*, 33 (April 1917): 629–36; William T. Hutchinson, *Lowden of Illinois: The Life of Frank O. Lowden, Vol. I, City and State* (Urbana, University of Illinois Press, 1957), p. 330.

8. *Chicago Tribune*, 18 September 1917, p. 15; 7 November 1917, pp. 1, 2; *Daily News Almanac* (1918), pp. 624–26.

9. *Daily News Almanac* (1918), pp. 570–71; *Chicago Tribune*, 5 May 1917, pp. 1, 2; *Chicago Herald*, 4 May 1917, pp. 1, 2; 5 May 1917, p. 2; 6 May 1917, p. 6; James Middleton, "Are Americans More German Than English?" *World's Work*, 31 (Dec. 1915): 141–47; Bernard Dernberg, "II. The Ties that Bind America and Germany," *World's Work* 29 (December 1914): 186–

89; Edward G. Lowry, "The War in the Middle West," *World's Work*, 33 (March 1917): 510–15; Douglas Bukowski, *Big Bill Thompson, Chicago, and the Politics of Image* (Urbana: University of Illinois Press, 1998), pp. 62–3.

10. *Chicago Tribune*,1 September 1917, pp. 1, 2; 2 September 1917, pp. 1, 2; 3 September 1917, pp. 1, 2. 3; 4 September 1917, pp. 1, 2; 5 September 1917, p. 2; 6 September 1917, pp. 1, 2; *Chicago Herald*, 3 September 1917, p. 1; 4 September 1917, p. 1; 5 August 1919, p. 7; Hutchinson, *Lowden of Illinois, Vol. I, City and State*, pp. 378–80; Bukowski, *Big Bill Thompson*, pp. 62–3.

11. *Chicago Tribune*, 30 May 1917, pp. 1, 2; 2 June 1917, p. 2; 18 June 1917, p. 7; 12 September 1917, p. 1.

12. *Chicago Tribune*, 11 August 1917, p. 1; 6 September 1917, pp. 1, 2; 7 September 1917, pp. 1, 2; 12 September 1917, p. 1; *Daily News Almanac* (1918), pp. 409–415; H.C. Petersen and Gilbert C. Fite, *Opponents of the War, 1917–1918* (Seattle: University of Washington Press, 1968); "Fighting Germany's Spies," pt. VIII, *World's Work* 36 (August 1918): 393–401.

13. *Chicago Tribune*, 18 September 1917, p. 15; 7 November 1917, pp. 1, 2; *Daily News Almanac* (1918), pp. 624–26.

14. *Chicago Tribune*, 8 November 1917, p. 7; 9 November 1917, p. 11; 13 November 1917, p. 17; 23 February 1918, p. 12.

15. *Chicago Tribune*, 27 February 1918, pp. 1, 2; *Chicago Herald*, 27 February 1918, pp. 1, 2.

16. *Chicago Tribune*, 19 July 1918, p. 7; 21 July 1918, p. 9; 23 July 1918, p. 9; 12 August 1918, p. 7.

17. *Chicago Tribune*, 30 May 1918, p. 8; 27 July 1918, p. 7; 7 August 1918, p. 7; 10 August 1918, p. 8.

18. *Chicago Tribune*, 10 August 1918, p. 8.

19. *Chicago Tribune*, 26 August 1918, p. 8; 31 August 1918, p. 7; *Chicago Herald-Examiner*, 26 August 1918, p. 5; 31 August 1918, p. 5.

20. *Chicago Tribune*, 8 September 1913, p. 13; 12 September 1918, pp. 1, 4; 14 September 1918, p. 7; 18 September 1918, p. 10; 21 September 1918, p. 5; *Chicago Herald-Examiner*, 17 September 1918, p. 5; *Daily News Almanac* (1919), pp. 801, 804–07. Ernest Hoover was born in Taylorville in 1872. On 24 December 1907, he married Minnie Lantz. By 1900, he was working as a druggist, and in 1910, he was a real estate agent. By 1920, he was a mortgage broker, and he subsequently went into banking. In the late 1940s, he served on the Illinois Civil Service Commission. 1880 U.S. Federal Census, Taylorville, Christian County, Illinois, ED 76, National Archives microfilm publication roll T9_181, page 752.1000, image 0244; 1900 U.S. Federal Census, Taylorville, ward 4, Christian County, Illinois, ED 23, National Archives microfilm publication roll T623_242, page 35A, image 70; 1910 U.S. Federal Census, Taylorville Ward 4, Christian County, Illinois, ED 32, National Archives microfilm publication roll T624_235, page 10A, image 190; 1920 U.S. Federal Census, Taylorville Ward 3, Christian County, Illinois, ED 32, National Archives microfilm publication roll T625_299, page 4A, image 1102; 1930 U.S. Federal Census, Taylorville, Christian County, Illinois, ED 36, National Archives microfilm publication roll 411, page 6B, image 452.0.

21. Kristie Miller, *Ruth Hannah McCormick, A Life in Politics, 1880–1944* (Albuquerque: University of New Mexico Press, 1992).

22. *Chicago Tribune*, 29 October 1918, p. 11; 4 November 1918, p. 17; *Chicago Herald-Examiner*, 21 September 1918, p. 1; 24 September 1918, p. 7; 28 September 1918, p. 9.

23. *New York Times*, 1 June 1918, p. 3; 27 June 1918, p. 1; 28 June 1918, p. 2; 11 July 1918, p. 2; 14 July 1918 p. 4.

24. Tokiko Wantanabe, et al, "Viral RNA Polymerase Complex Promotes Optimal Growth of 1918 Virus in the Lower Respiratory Tract of Ferrets," *Proceedings of the National Academy of Sciences* 105 (51) (29 December 2008); Leigh Dayton, "Cracked: Flu Pandemic's Deadly Code" *The Australian*, 30 December 2008, p. 5; Gina Kolata, *Flu: The Story of the Great Influenza Epidemic of 1918 and the Search for the Virus that Caused It* (New York: Farrah, Straus, and Giroux, 1999), pp. 7–9.

25. *New York Times*, 16 August 1918, p. 6; 20 August 1918, p. 20; 13 September p. 7; 26 September 1918, p. 24; Kolata, *The Great Influenza Epidemic*, p. 7.

26. *Chicago Tribune*, 20 September 1918, p. 13; 1 October 1918, p. 1; 6 October 1918, p. 1; 13 October 1918, p. 13; 17 October 1918, p. 13; 18 October 1918, p. 14; Paul A. Buelow, "Chicago" in Fred R. van Hartesveldt, *The 1918–1919 Pandemic of Influenza, The Urban Impact in the Western World* (Lewiston: Edwin Mellen, 1992), pp. 134–36.

27. *New York Times*, 3 November 1918, p. 18; *Chicago Tribune*, 8 October 1918, p. 13; 1 November 1918, p. 17; 5 November 1918, p. 13; *Daily News Almanac* (1920), p. 377; Buelow, "Chicago," pp. 127–28, 140.

28. *Chicago Tribune*, 6 May 1895, p. 1; 7 July 1895, p. 1; 16 September 1895, p. 2; 14 October 1918, p. 13; *Chicago Herald*, 14 October 1918, p. 1; 4 October 1918; 12 October 1918, *State Council Minutes*.

29. *Chicago Tribune*, 15 October 1918, p. 11; 16 October 1918, p. 9.

30. *Chicago Tribune*, 26 November 1918, p. 17.

31. 25 October 1918, *State Council Minutes*; Roger C. Sullivan to Lowden, 22 October 1918, Frank O. Lowden Papers, Special Collections Research Center, The University of Chicago Library, Chicago, Illinois. *Daily News Almanac* (1920), p. 807.

32. *Chicago Tribune*, 26 October 1918, p. 4; *New York Times*, 26 October 1918, p. 1.

33. *Daily News Almanac* (1919), 807–16.

34. *Chicago Tribune*, 12 January 1919, p. 12; 24 February 1919, p. 10; *Chicago Herald and Examiner*, 1 February 1919, p. 4.

35. *Chicago Tribune*, 17 January 1919, pp. 1, 8; Chicago *Herald and Examiner*, 17 January 1919, p. 1; Other candidates who were considered were former Senator Lewis, McAndrews, John E. Traeger, Clayton Smith, and Joseph Sabath. *Chicago Tribune*, 28 January 1919 p. 4; 30 January 1919, p. 10; 22 February 1919, p. 3.

36. *Chicago Tribune*, 17 January 1919, pp. 1, 8; Chicago *Herald and Examiner*, 17 January 1919, p. 1; Other candidates who were considered were former Senator Lewis, McAndrews, John E. Traeger, Clayton Smith, and Joseph Sabath.

37. *Chicago Tribune*, 28 January 1919 p. 4; 30 January 1919, p. 10; 22 February 1919, p. 3.

38. *Chicago Tribune*, 19 January 1919, p. 15; 20 January 1919, p. 12; 2 February 1919, p. 10; 24 February 1919, p. 10; *Daily News Almanac* (1920), p. 846.

39. *Chicago Tribune*, 23 January 1919, p. 10; 7 February 1919, p. 8; 12 February 1919, pp. 1, 8; *Daily News Almanac*, p. 807.

40. *Chicago Tribune*, 5 January 1919, p. A2; 13 January 1919, p. 12; 7 February 1919, p. 8.

41. Chicago Tribune, 21 December 1915, p. 1; 11 October 1916, p. 1; 12 December 1916, p. 1; 13 January 1918, p. 1; Douglas Bukowski, *Big Bill Thompson, Chicago, and the Politics of Image* (Urbana: University of Illinois Press, 1998), pp. 53–54.

42. *Chicago Tribune*, 26 February 1919, p. 1; 27 February 1919, p. 1; *Chicago Herald and Examiner*, 26 February 1919, pp. 1, 2.

43. *Chicago Tribune*, 28 February 1919, p. 5; *Chicago Herald and Examiner*, 18 January 1919, p. 3.

44. *Chicago Tribune*, 28 February 1919, p. 5; *Chicago Herald and Examiner*, 28 February 1919, p. 6.

45. *Chicago Tribune*, 18 March 1919, p. 5; 20 March 1919, p. 11; *Chicago Herald and Examiner*, 16 March 1919, p. 6; 18 March 1919, p. 3; 22 March 1919, p. 4.

46. *Chicago Tribune*, 22 February 1919, p. 5; 7 March 1919, p. 9; 14 March 1919, p. 7; 22 March 1919, p. 7; 24 March 1919, p. 7; 25 March 1919, p. 7; 28 March 1919, p. 9; 30 March 1919, p. 4; *Chicago Herald and Examiner*, 18 March 1919, p. 3.

47. *Chicago Herald and Examiner*, 25 March 1919, p. 7; 27 March 1919, p. 6; *Chicago Herald and Examiner*, 26 March 1919, p. 4; 29 March 1919, p. 4.

48. *Chicago Herald and Examiner*, 29 March 1919, pp. 1, 6; 30 March 1919, pp. 1, 2; *Chicago Herald and Examiner*, 1 April 1919, p. 1.

49. *Daily News Almanac* (1920), pp. 847–57; *Chicago Herald and Examiner*, 2 April 1919, pp. 1, 2; *Chicago Tribune*, 19 April 1919, p. 14; on the other hand, the Democrats retained control of the city council. Anton Cermak elected to represent the Twelfth Ward.

50. *Chicago Tribune*, 12 April 1919, p. 17; 20 April 1919, p. A7; 27 April 1919, p. 13; 29 April 1919, p. 11; 2 May 1919, p. 10; 7 May 1919, pp. 1, 6; 10 May 1919, p. 14; 14 May 1919, p. 10; *Daily News Almanac* (1921), p. 791.

51. *Daily News Almanac* (1920), p. 847; (1921), pp. 654, 807; (1922), pp. 654, 782; *Chicago Defender*, 5 April 1919, p. 1.

52. Rollin Lynde Hartt, "When the Negro Comes North: II, Future Results of the Migration," *World's Work*, 48 (July 1924): 318–23; William M. Tuttle, Jr., *Race Riot, Chicago in the Red Summer of 1919* (New York: Athenaeum, 1970), pp. 32–66, 176; Elliot M. Rudwick, Race Riot at East St. Louis, July 2, 1917 (New York: World, 1966); Roberta Senechal de la Roche, *In Lincoln's Shadow: The 1908 Race Riot in Springfield, Illinois* (Carbondale: Southern Illinois University Press, 1980). However, for all of its horrors, the Chicago Race Riot of 1919 was not without precedent in the state. In 1908, the capital city of Springfield was the scene of roving white mobs attacking African Americans, and in 1917, Illinois witnessed a grisly race riot in East St. Louis. The same divisive factors of competition for employment and housing were present in both. However, events in Chicago in 1919 were much more directly reflective of a national trend. Days before the outbreak in the Windy City, Washington, D.C., experienced racial unrest that resulted in the death of five. In late September, similar mob action broke out in Omaha, Nebraska, and then in October in the small town of Elaine, Arkansas, where 11 blacks and "four or five" white men died.

53. *Tulsa Daily World*, 10 July 1920, p. 4; *The Broadax*, 31 August 1895; 15 July 1899, p. 1; Allan H. Spear, *Black Chicago: the Making of a Negro Ghetto, 1890–*

1912 (Chicago: University of Chicago Press, 1967), pp. 82–3, 114.

54. *The Broad Ax*, 25 March 1911, p. 1; 23 April 1911, p. 1; 23 September 1911, p. 13; 1 October 1914, p. 1; 17 April 1920, p. 1; 24 April 1920, p. 1.

55. *The Broad Ax*, 25 March 1911, p. 1; 23 April 1911, p. 1; 23 September 1911, p. 13; 1 October 1914, p. 1; 17 April 1920, p. 1; 24 April 1920, p. 1.

56. *The Broad Ax*, 6 September 1919, p. 2; 24 April 1920, p. 1.

Chapter 9

1. Sullivan Family Collection; James Langland, comp. *The Daily News Almanac and Year-Book for 1921* (Chicago: Daily News, 1920), pp. 59–60 (hereafter cited as *Daily News Almanac*); David Y. Kyvig, *Daily Life in the United States, 1920–1940: How Americans Lived Through the Roaring Twenties and the Great Depression* (New York: Ivan R. Dee, 2004), p. 218; On the other hand, Sister Mame lived until she was 84, Brother John J. until 77; Brother Frank until he was 66; and Roger's son, Boetius, did not pass until he was 75.

2. *Chicago Tribune*, 9 March 1919, p. 15; 10 March 1919, p. 15; 12 March 1919, p. 19; 18 March 1919, p. 1; 9 April 1919, p. 9; 15 June 1919, p. A10; 29 June 1919, p. 15; 12 September 1919, p. 7; 13 September 1919, p. 7; 14 September 1919, p. 14; 16 September 1919, p. 10; 12 October 1919, p. G32.

3. *Los Angeles Times*, 20, 1920, p. 14.

4. *Chicago Tribune*, 11 June 1917, p. 13; 18 May 1919, p. A12; 12 October 1919, p. G32; 14 June 1959, p. A9.

5. Sullivan Family Collection. Roger Sullivan spent his last days at his daughter's home at 342 Wellington Avenue. On the first floor were located an entrance hall and an entrance room featuring dramatic split staircases, playroom, kitchen, maids' rooms, maids' dining room, kitchen, and laundry. The second floor featured a music room, dining room, living room, powder room, solarium, a butler's pantry with a dumb waiter. The third floor was given over to bedrooms, and the fourth floor was a large attic for storage. For security purposes and so that the thirteen children could play together in the winter without going outside, a tunnel connected Mary's home with Boetius' next door.

6. *Chicago Tribune*, 10 August 1919, p. 1; 11 August 1919, p. 2; 17 August 1919, p. 7.

7. *Chicago Evening Post*, 17 April 1920, p. 2.

8. *Chicago Tribune*, 23 January 1920, p. 3.

9. *Chicago Tribune*, 14 January 1920, p. 7.

10. *Chicago Tribune*, 16 January 1920, p. 4; 28 January 1920, p. 10.

11. *Chicago Tribune*, 11 January 1920, p. 1; *Washington Post*, 9 January 1920, p. 4.

12. Silas H. Strawn to Lowden 24 October 1918; Lowden to Victor F. Lawson, telegram, 25 October 1918; Walter H. Wilson to Lowden, 29 October 1918, Frank O. Lowden Papers, Special Collections Research Center, Library of the University of Chicago, Chicago, Illinois; *Chicago Tribune*, 23 June 1919, p. 19; 27 December 1919, p. 14; *Daily News Almanac* (1920), pp. 815–16; (1923), pp. 676, 760–76; Elizabeth Cady Stanton, et al., *A History of the Woman's Suffrage Movement*, 2nd ed. (Rochester, NY: Mann, 1922), p. 162; William H. Stuart, *The Twenty Incredible Years* (Chicago:

M.A. Donohue, 1935), p. 81; For more on the ratification fight see Richard Allen Morton, *Justice and Humanity, the Politics of Edward F. Dunne* (Carbondale: Southern Illinois University Press, 1998), pp. 121–22.

13. *Chicago Tribune*, 3 March 1920, p. 1; 27 March 1920, p. 7; *New York Times*, 12 April 1920, p. 17; *Washington Post*, 26 March 1920, p. 6.

14. *Chicago Tribune*, 5 August 1919, p. 7; 10 August 1919, p. 1; 11 August 1919, p. 2; 6 September 1919, pp. 1, 3.

15. *Chicago Tribune*, 23 March 1920, p. 6.

16. *Chicago Tribune*, 2 April 1920, p. 1; 3 April 1920, p. 1; 4 April 1920, p. 1; 15 April 1920, p. 1; *Los Angeles Times*, 5 April 1920, p. 13; *Daily News Almanac* (1921), pp. 771–72. This was an election for those ten wards in which no candidate received a majority in the regular balloting on 14 February 1920. The majority requirement was a function of a change in the charter voted by the city council in 1919 by which aldermanic elections were to be bipartisan and held in February. Despite the dearth of party labels, the Democrats retained control.

17. *Los Angeles Times*, 15 April 1920, pp. 1, 3; *New York Times*, 15 April 1920, p. 11; *Washington Post*, 15 April 1915, p. 2; *Belleville News-Democrat*, 15 April 1920, p. 1; *Grand Forks Herald* (North Dakota), 14 April 1920, p. 1. *Official Death Certificate*, Sullivan Family Collection.

18. *Chicago Tribune*, 15 April 1920, p. 1.

19. *Urbana Daily Courier*, 20 April 1920, p. 4.

20. *Chicago Tribune*, 20 July 1922, p. 6.

21. *Chicago Tribune*, 23 May 1921, p. 3; *Daily Illini* (Urbana-Champaign), 14 April 1925, p. 1; 18 April 1925, pp. 1, 4; *Morning Oregonian*, 23 October 1921, p. 4; *The Notre Dame Scholastic*, 53 (1924–25): 714; 54 (12 November 1926): 236. Arthur J. Hope, *Notre Dame, One Hundred Years* (South Bend, IN: Icarus, 1979), Notre Dame website, accessed 15 November 2009. http://www.archives.nd.edu/hope/hope27.htm. Hope erroneously reports that Boetius declined further support for the upkeep of the Notre Dame station.

22. *Chicago Tribune*, 20 March 1959, p. B5; 15 February 1961, p. 11.

23. *Chicago Tribune*, 8 December 1929, p. 16; 21 December 1929, p. 22.

24. *Chicago Tribune*, 10 February 1935, p. 18; 5 April 1936, p. 8; 26 June 1936, p. 42; 4 April 1937, p. 18; 12 May 1937, p. 18; 19 December 1949, p. B10; 2 February 1951; 19 February 1951, p. 5; 7 June 1952, p. B7; 28 July 1955, p. D6.

25. "Dedication Ceremony, Speeches," Sullivan Junior High School, October 1926, Samuel Insull Papers, University Archives, Loyola University, Chicago Illinois, pp. 1, 5, 9, 10, 15, 17, 19; *Chicago Tribune*, 2 October 1926, p. 3; 11 November 1928, p. J1; 17 November 1928, p. 7; 30 September 1932, p. 21; 11 March 1965, p. N1; Thomas H. Briggs, *The Junior High School*, (Boston: Houghton Mifflin, 1920); Leonard V. Coos, *The Junior High School* (Boston: Houghton Mifflin, 1920).

26. Interview with Frank Sullivan (grandnephew), 9 February 2009.

Afterword

1. *Chicago Tribune*, 26 April 1906, p. 13; 14 January 1920, p. 7; 6 May 1920, p. 4; 3 March 21 1921, p. 7; O'Malley died in April 1921; Egan in February 1928.

2. Carter H. Harrison, *Stormy Years: The Autobiography of Carter H. Harrison, Five Times Mayor of Chicago* (Indianapolis: Bobbs-Merrill, 1935), p. 232; Walter A. Townsend, *Illinois Democracy: A History of the Party and Its Representative Members—Past and Present*, 5 vols. (Springfield: Democratic Historical Association, 1935), II: 34; *Chicago Tribune*, 8 August 1928, p. 1; *New York Times*, 8 August 1928, p. 19.

3. *New York Times*, 7 July 1920, p. 3; *Chicago Tribune*, 7 July 1920, p. 2.

4. *Chicago Tribune*, 4 April 1922, p. 4; 3 March 1922, p. 11; 8 August 1929, p. 8.

5. John R. Schmidt, *The Mayor Who Cleaned Up Chicago: A Political Biography of William E. Dever* (DeKalb: Northern Illinois University Press, 1989); Carroll Hill Wooddy, *The Case of Frank L. Smith, A Study in Representative Government* (Chicago: University of Chicago, 1931).

6. *Chicago Tribune*, 1 August 1928, p. 1; 8 August 1928, pp. 1–2.

7. *Chicago Tribune*, 25 December 1928, p. 32.

8. *Chicago Tribune*, 26 May 1906, p. 5; 24 October 1906, p. 6; 25 May 1908, p. 3; 13 June 1908, p. 9.

9. *Chicago Tribune*, 1 April 1916, p. 7; 28 October 1917, p. 3; 29 December 1917, p. 13.

10. *Chicago Tribune*, 9 August 1928, p. 9; 10 August 1928, p. 2.

11. *Chicago Tribune*, 30 August 1929, p. 8; 6 September 1928, p. 9; 8 September 1929, p. 10; 30 September 1929, p. 8; 2 October 1929, p. 4.

12. *Chicago Tribune*, 16 March 1930, p. B1; 15 November 1930, p. 5; 11 December 1930, p. 11; 22 August 1967, p. A6. In 1934, Igoe was elected congressman-at-large, but resigned to accept an appointment as a United States Attorney. In 1938, after Cermak's death, he was the machine candidate for the United States Senate, but lost by a close margin. Subsequently, he served as a federal district judge between 1939 and 1965.

13. Paul Michael Green, "Irish Chicago: The Multi-Ethnic Road to Machine Success" in Melvin G. Holli and Peter D'A Jones, *Ethnic Chicago*, Rev ed. (Grand Rapids, MI: William B. Eerdmans, 1984), pp. 412–59.

14. *Chicago Tribune*, 29 October 1929, p. 6; 30 October 1929, p. 8; 11 April 1931, p. 2; 7 October 1943, p. 16.

15. *Chicago Tribune*, 16 February 1932, pp. 1–2; 17 February 1933, p. 1; 6 March 1933, p. 1.

16. *Chicago Tribune*, 3 March 1933, p. 3; 19 March 1933, p. 3; 21 March 1933, p. 5; 14 April 1933, p. 38; 25 October 1950, p. 4.

17. 7 October 1943, p. 15; 21 October 1950, p. 4.

Bibliography

Manuscript Collections

Addams, Jane. Papers (microfilm ed.). Manuscript Division, Library of Congress. Washington, D.C.

Alschuler, Samuel J. Papers. Abraham Lincoln Presidential Library. Springfield, Illinois.

Baker, Newton D. Papers. Western Reserve Historical Society. Cleveland, Ohio.

Bryan, William Jennings Papers. Manuscript Division, Library of Congress. Washington, D.C.

Bynum, William Dallas Papers. Manuscript Division, Library of Congress. Washington, D.C.

Cleveland, Grover S. Papers (microfilm ed.). Manuscript Division, Library of Congress. Washington, D.C.

Daniels, Josephus Papers. Manuscript Division, Library of Congress. Washington, D.C.

Darrow, Clarence S. Papers. Manuscript Division, Library of Congress. Washington, D.C.

_____. Papers. University of Chicago Library, Special Collections. Research Center, Chicago, Illinois.

Deneen, Charles S. Papers. Abraham Lincoln Presidential Library. Springfield, Illinois.

Dever, William E. Papers, Chicago Historical Museum. Chicago, Illinois.

Dunlap, Millard Fillmore Papers. Abraham Lincoln Presidential Library. Springfield, Illinois.

Dunne, Edward F. Collection. Abraham Lincoln Presidential Library. Springfield, Illinois.

_____. Scrapbooks and Papers. Illinois Historical Survey, University of Illinois Library. Urbana-Champaign.

Dunne, Robert Jerome Papers. Chicago Historical Museum. Chicago, Illinois.

Fisher, Walter L. Papers. Manuscript Division, Library of Congress. Washington, D.C.

Fitzpatrick, John J. Papers, Chicago Historical Museum. Chicago, Illinois.

Harrison IV, Carter H. Papers. Newberry Library. Chicago, Illinois.

Humphrey, Otis J. Papers. Abraham Lincoln Presidential Library. Springfield, Illinois.

Insull, Samuel Papers. Samuel Insull Collection, E.M. Cudahy Library. Loyola University, Chicago.

James, Edmund J. Papers. Archives, University of Illinois Library. Urbana-Champaign.

Johnson, Tom L. Papers. Western Reserve Historical Society. Cleveland, Ohio.

Jones, Samuel J. Papers (microfilm ed.). Toledo-Lucas County Public Library. Toledo, Ohio.

Lowden, Frank O. Papers. University of Chicago Library, Special Collections Research Center. Chicago, Illinois.

Merriam, Charles E. Papers. University of Chicago Library, Special Collections Research Center. Chicago, Illinois.

Municipal Voters League Papers. Chicago Historical Museum. Chicago, Illinois.

Palmer, John Mayo Papers. Abraham Lincoln Presidential Library, Springfield, Illinois.

Rainey, Henry T. Papers. Manuscript Division, Library of Congress. Washington, D.C.

Robins, Raymond Papers. Wisconsin Historical Society. Madison, Wisconsin.

Schilling, George S. Papers. Abraham Lincoln Presidential Library. Springfield, Illinois.

Schwartz, Ulysses Papers. Chicago Historical Museum. Chicago, Illinois.

Sherman, Lawrence Y. Papers. Abraham Lincoln Presidential Library. Springfield, Illinois.

Stringer, Lawrence B. Papers. Abraham Lincoln Presidential Library. Springfield, Illinois.

Thompson, Owen P. Papers. Abraham Lincoln Presidential Library. Springfield, Illinois.

Tree, Lambert Papers. Chicago Historical Museum. Chicago, Illinois.

Tumulty, Joseph P. Papers. Manuscript Division, Library of Congress. Washington, D.C.

Walker, John H. Papers. Abraham Lincoln Presidential Library. Springfield, Illinois.

Wilson, Thomas Woodrow Papers, Manuscript Division, Library of Congress. Washington, D.C.

Newspapers

Aberdeen Daily American (North Dakota)
Aberdeen Daily News (North Dakota)
Atlanta Constitution
Baltimore Sun
Belleville News-Democrat (Illinois)
Belvidere Daily Republican (Illinois)
Belvidere Recorder (Illinois)
Belvidere Republican Northwestern (Illinois)
Boston Globe
The Broad Axe (Chicago)
Carlinville Democrat (Illinois)
Champaign News-Gazette (Illinois)
Chicago American
Chicago Daily Journal
Chicago Daily News
Chicago Defender
Chicago Eagle
Chicago Evening Journal
Chicago Evening Post
Chicago Examiner
Chicago Herald
Chicago Herald-Examiner
Chicago Inter-Ocean
Chicago Record-Herald
Chicago Record-Herald and Inter-Ocean
Chicago Times
Chicago Times-Herald
Chicago Tribune
Chicago West Side Reporter
Cincinnati Inquirer
Cleveland Plain Dealer
Commoner (Lincoln, Nebraska)
Daily Illini (Urbana-Champaign, Illinois)
Daily Northwestern
Delavan Tri-County Times (Delavan, Illinois)
Denver Post
Detroit Free Press
Fort Worth Star-Telegram (Texas)
Grand Forks Herald (North Dakota)
Illinois Republican Northwestern (Belvidere)
Illinois State Journal
Illinois State Register
Indianapolis Star
Los Angeles Times
New York Times
New York Tribune
News-Gleaner (Shawneetown, Illinois)
St. Louis Post-Dispatch
Washington Post
Worcester Daily Spy

Books

Allen, Howard W., and Vincent A. Lacey, eds. *Illinois Elections, 1818–1920; Candidates and Returns for President, Governor, Senate, and House of Representatives.* Carbondale: Southern Illinois University Press, 1992.

Allswang, John. *Bosses, Machines, and Urban Voters: An American Symbiosis.* Port Washington, NY: Kennikat, 1977.

_____. *A House for All Peoples: Ethnic Politics in Chicago, 1890–1916.* Lexington: University of Kentucky Press, 1971.

_____. *The Political Behavior of Chicago's Ethnic Groups, 1918–1932.* New York: Ayer, 1980.

Anderson, David B. *William Jennings Bryan.* Boston: Twayne, 1981.

Anti-Saloon League of America. *Yearbook,* various dates. Westerville, Ohio: The League.

Ashby, Leroy. *William Jennings Bryan, Champion of Democracy.* Boston: Twayne, 1987.

Bacon, Edwin, and Morrill Wyman. *Direct Elections and the Law-Making by Popular Vote.* Boston: Houghton-Mifflin, 1912.

Bailey, Harry A., and Kate Ellis. *Ethnic Group Politics.* Columbus, Ohio: Charles E. Merrill, 1969.

Barnard, Harry. *Eagle Forgotten: The Life of John P. Altgeld.* New York: Bobbs-Merrill, 1938.

Bates, J. Leonard. *Senator Thomas J. Walsh of Montana: Law and Public Affairs from TR to FDR.* Urbana: University of Illinois Press, 1997.

Becker, Earl L. *A History of Labor Legislation in Illinois.* Chicago: University of Chicago Press, 1929.

Bennett, Fremont, comp. *Politics and Politicians of Chicago, Cook County, and Illinois.* Chicago: Blakely Printing, 1886.

Biles, Roger. *Big City Boss in Depression and War: Mayor Edward J. Kelly of Chicago.* DeKalb: Northern Illinois University Press, 1984.

_____. *Richard J. Daley: Politics, Race, and the Governing of Chicago.* DeKalb: Northern Illinois University Press, 1995.

Billington, Ray Allen. *Westward Expansion: A History of the American Frontier.* New York: Macmillan, 1949.

Blum, John M. *Joe Tumulty and the Wilson Era.* Boston: Houghton-Mifflin, 1951.

Bowers, Claude G. *The Life of John Worth Kern.* Indianapolis: Hollenbeck, 1918.

Boyle, Ohio D. *A History of Railroad Strikes.* Washington, D.C.: Brotherhood, 1935.

Bragdon, Henry Wilkinson. *Woodrow Wilson: The Academic Years.* Cambridge: Belknap Press of the Harvard University Press, 1967.

Brennan, John A. *Silver and the First New Deal.* Reno: University of Nevada Press, 1969.

Briggs, Thomas H. *The Junior High School.* Boston: Houghton Mifflin, 1920.

Bright, John. *Hizzoner Big Bill Thompson.* New York: Jonathan Caper and Harrison Smith, 1930.

Brownell, Blaine A., and Warren E. Stickle. *Bosses and Reformers: Urban Politics in America, 1880–1920.* Boston: Houghton Mifflin, 1973.

Bryan, William Jennings, and Mary Baird Bryan. *The Memoirs of William Jennings Bryan*. N.p., 1925.

Bryce, James. *The American Commonwealth*, revised edition. Philadelphia: J.D. Morris, 1906.

Buder, Stanley. *Pullman: An Experiment in Industrial Order and Community Planning, 1880–1930*. New York: Oxford University Press, 1967.

Buelow, Paul A. "Chicago." In Fred R. VanHartesveldt. *The 1918–1919 Pandemic of Influenza: The Urban Impact in the Western World*. Lewiston: Edwin Mellen, 1992.

Bukowski, Douglas. *Big Bill Thompson, Chicago and the Politics of Image*. Urbana: University of Illinois Press, 1998.

Burnham, Daniel Hudson. *Plan of Chicago Prepared Under the Direction of the Commercial Club*. Chicago: Commercial Club, 1909.

Carpenter, Kenneth, ed. *Gold and Silver in the Presidential Campaign of 1896*. New York: Arno, 1974.

Carwardine, William H. *The Pullman Strike*. Chicago: Charles Kerr and Co., 1894.

Catt, Carrie Chapman, and Nellie Rogers Shuler. *Woman's Suffrage and Politics: The Inner Side of the Suffrage Movement*. Seattle: University of Washington, 1969, and New York: Charles Scribner's Sons, 1926.

Cavanagh, Helen. *Carl Schurz Vrooman. Self-styled "Constructive Conservative."* Chicago: Lakeside/R.R. Donnelley and Sons, 1977.

Chamberlain, Eugene Tyler. *Early Life and Public Service of Hon. Grover Cleveland, The Fearless and Independent Governor of the Empire State, Also the Life of Hon. Thomas A. Hendricks*. Chicago: Caxton Publishing Co., 1884.

Champernowe, Henry. *The Boss: An Essay Upon the Art of Governing American Cities*. New York: Richmond & Co., 1894.

Chicago Directory Company. *Chicago Securities, 1898: A Digest of Information Relating to Stocks, Bonds, Banks, and Financial Institutions of Chicago*. Chicago: Chicago Directory Company, 1898.

Church, Charles A. *History of the Republican Party of Illinois, 1854–1912, with a Review of the Aggressions of the Slave-Power*. Rockford, IL: Wilson Brothers, 1912.

Civic Federation of Chicago. *Fifty Years on the Civic Front, 1893–1943: A Report on the Achievements of the Civic Federation, Chicago*. Chicago: n.p., 1943.

_____. *First Annual Report of the Central Council*. Chicago: R.R. Donnelley and Sons, 1895.

Clark, Champ. *My Quarter Century of American Politics*. 2 vols. New York: Harper and Bros., 1920.

Cleveland, Grover. *The Government in the Chicago Strike of 1894*. Princeton: Princeton University Press, 1913.

Coletta, Paola E. *William Jennings Bryan*. 3 vols. Lincoln: University of Nebraska Press, 1959, and 2 vols., Lincoln: University of Nebraska Press, 1964.

Comwell, Elmer E. "Bosses. Machines, and Ethnic Groups" in Sellin, Thorstein, ed. *The Annals of the American Academy of Political and Social Sciences*. Essay Index Reprint Series. Plainview, NY: Books for Library Press, 1964, 1975: 27–39.

Cook, Fred J. *American Political Bosses and Machines*. New York: Franklin Watts, 1973.

Coos, Leonard V. *The Junior High School*. Boston: Houghton Mifflin, 1920.

Counts, George S. *School and Society in Chicago*. New York: Harcourt Brace, 1928.

Croly, Herbert. *The Promise of American Life*. New York: Macmillan, 1909.

Dalton, Kathleen. *Theodore Roosevelt: A Strenuous Life*. New York: Knoft, 2002.

Darrow, Clarence S. *The Story of My Life*. New York: Scribner's 1932.

De la Roche, Roberta Senechal. *In Lincoln's Shadow: The 1908 Race Riot in Springfield, Illinois*. Carbondale: Southern Illinois University Press, 2008.

Destler, Chester McArthur. *Henry Demarest Lloyd and the Empire of Reform*. Philadelphia: University of Pennsylvania Press, 1963.

Dewey, Davis Rich. *Financial History of the United States*. 2nd ed. New York: Longmans, Green, 1903.

Dodd, William Edward. *Woodrow Wilson and His Work*. New York: P. Smith, 1932.

Donnelly, Reuben, comp. *Lakeside Annual Directory of the City of Chicago*. Chicago: Chicago City Directory Company, various dates.

Dorsett, Lyle W. *The Pendergast Machine*. New York: Oxford University Press, 1968.

Drake, St. Clark, and Horace Cayton. *Black Metropolis: A Study of Negro Life in a Northern City*. New York: Harcourt Brace, 1945.

DuBois, Ellen Carol. *Feminism and Suffrage: The Emergence of an Independent Women's Movement in America, 1848–1869*. Ithaca: Cornell University Press, 1978.

Duis, Perry R. *The Saloon: Public Drinking in Chicago and Boston, 1880–1920*. Champaign: University of Illinois Press, 1983.

Duncan, Otis Dudley, and Beverly Duncan. *The Negro Population of Chicago: A Study of Residential Succession*. Chicago: University of Chicago Press, 1957.

Dunn, Arthur W. *From Harrison to Harding: A Personal Narrative, Covering a Third of a Century, 1888–1921*, 2 vols. New York: G.P. Putnam's Sons, 1922.

Dunne, Edward F. *Illinois, the Heart of the Nation*. 5 vols. Chicago: Lewis, 1933.

_____. *Judge, Mayor, Governor*. Edited by William L. Sullivan. Chicago: Windermere, 1916.

Ebner, Michael H., and Eugene M. Tobin. The *Age of Urban Reform: New Perspectives on the Progressive Era*. Port Washington, NY: Kennikat, 1977.

Edwards, Richard. *Edwards' Chicago, Illinois Business Directory for 1873*. Chicago: Richard Edwards Publisher, 1873.

Ehrich, Louis R. *The Question of Silver*. 2nd ed. New York: G.P. Putnam's Sons/Knickerbocker Press, 1896.

Einhorn, Robin L. *Property Rules: Political Economy in Chicago, 1833–1872*. Chicago: University of Chicago Press, 1991.

Emery, Sarah E.V. *Seven Financial Conspiracies Which Have Enslaved the American People*. Lansing, MI: Lansing Review Co., 1896.

Fadely, James Philip. *Thomas Taggart: Public Servant, Political Boss, 1856–1929*. Indianapolis: Indiana Historical Society, 1997.

Flanagan, Maureen A. *Charter Reform in Chicago*. Carbondale: Southern Illinois University Press, 1987.

Flexner, Eleanor. *Century of Struggle: The Woman's Rights Movement in the United States*. Cambridge: Harvard University Press, 1975.

Franch, John. *Robber Baron, the Life of Charles Tyson Yerkes*. Urbana: University of Illinois Press, 2006.

Fremon, David C. *Chicago Politics, Ward by Ward: Bloomington*. Indiana University Press: 1988.

Funchion, Michael F. "The Political and Nationalist Dimensions." In *The Irish in Chicago*. Edited by Lawrence J. McCaffrey, et al. Urbana: University of Illinois Press, 1987.

Gardner, Joseph L. *Departing Glory: Theodore Roosevelt as Ex-President*. New York: Charles Scribner's Sons, 1973.

George, Alexander L., and Juliette L. George. *Woodrow Wilson and Colonel House: A Personality Study*. New York: Dover, 1964.

Ginger, Ray. *Altgeld's America: The Lincoln Idea Versus Changing Realities*. New York: Quadrangle, 1959.

Glad, Paul W. *McKinley, Bryan, and the People*. Philadelphia: J.B. Lippincott, 1964.

Gold and Silver in the Presidential Campaign of 1896. New York: Arno, 1974.

Goodspeede, Weston A., and Daniel B. Healy. *History of Cook County in Two Volumes Illustrated*. Chicago: Goodspeede Historical Association, c. 1909.

Gosnell, Harold F. *Machine Politics: Chicago Model*. Chicago: University of Chicago Press, 1937.

Gottfried, Alex. *Boss Cermak of Chicago: A Study in Political Leadership*. Seattle: University of Washington Press, 1962.

Gould, Lewis L. *The Presidency of Theodore Roosevelt*. Lawrence: University of Kansas Press, 1992.

Gradel, Thomas J., and Dick Simpson. *Corrupt Illinois: Patronage, Cronyism, and Criminality*. Urbana: University of Illinois Press, 2015.

Green, James R. *Death in the Haymarket: The Story of Chicago, the First Labor Movement, and the Bombing that Divided Gilded Age America*. New York: Pantheon, 2006.

Green, Paul M., and Melvin G. Holli, eds. *The Mayors: The Chicago Political Tradition*. Carbondale: Southern Illinois University Press, 1987.

Grossman, James R. *Land of Hope: Chicago, Black Southerners, and the Great Migration*. Chicago: University of Chicago Press, 1989.

Hachey, Thomas E. *Britain and Irish Separatism: From Fenians to the Irish Free State, 1867–1922*. Washington, D.C.: Catholic University of America Press, 1977.

Haley, Margaret. *Battleground: The Autobiography of Margaret A. Haley*. Edited by Robert Reid. Champaign: University of Illinois Press, 1982.

Harpine, William D. *From the Front Porch to the Front Page: McKinley and Bryan in the 1896 Presidential Campaign*. College Station: Texas A&M Press, 2005.

Harrison, Carter H., IV. *Stormy Years: The Autobiography of Carter H. Harrison, Five Times Mayor of Chicago*. Indianapolis: Bobbs-Merrill, 1935.

Hawes, George W., comp. *Illinois State Gazetteer and Business Directory for 1858–59*. Chicago: George W. Hawes, 1860.

Heddrick, Mary J. *The Chicago Schools: A Social and Political History*. Beverly Hills: Sage, 1971.

Herman, Charles H. *Recollections of Life and Doings from the Haymarket Riot to the End of World War I*. Chicago: Normandie House, 1945.

Herrick, Genevieve, and John O. Herrick. *The Life of William Jennings Bryan*. Whitefish, MT: Kessinger, 1970.

Historical Encyclopedia of Illinois. Chicago: Munsell, 1904.

Holli, Melvin G. *Reform in Detroit: Hazen S. Pingree and Urban Politics*. New York: Oxford University Press, 1969.

Holli, Melvin G., and Peter d'A Jones, eds. *Ethnic Chicago*, rev. Grand Rapids. MI: William B. Eerdmans, 1984.

Hurley, Edward N. *The Bridge to France*, reprint. New York: Kessinger, 2004.

Hutchinson, Thomas. *Lakeside Annual Directory of the City Chicago, 1879*. Chicago: Chicago Directory Company, 1879.

Hutchinson, William T. *Lowden of Illinois: The Life of Frank O. Lowden*. 2 vols. Chicago: University of Chicago Press, 1957.

Huthmacher, J. Joseph. *Massachusetts People and Politics, 1919–1933*. Cambridge: The Belknap Press of Harvard University Press, 1959.

Ickes, Harold L. *The Autobiography of a Curmudgeon*. New York: Reynard and Hitchcock, 1943.

Illinois Political Directory, with Portraits and Biographical Sketches. Chicago: W. L. Bodine, c. 1899.

Insull, Samuel, and Larry Plachno. *The Memoirs of Samuel Insull.* Polo, IL: Transportation, 1992.

Jensen, Richard. *The Winning of the Midwest: Social and Political Conflict, 1888–1896.* Chicago: University of Chicago Press, 1971.

Johnson, Claudius O. *Carter Henry Harrison I.* Chicago: University of Chicago Press, 1926.

Johnson, Evans C. *Oscar W. Underwood: A Political Biography.* Baton Rouge: Louisiana University Press, 1980.

Jones, Stanley. *The Presidential Election of 1896.* Madison: University of Wisconsin Press, 1964.

Karl, Barry D. *Charles S. Merriam and the Study of Politics.* Chicago: University of Chicago Press, 1974.

Katz, William Loren, ed. *The Negro in Chicago: A Study of Race Relations and a Race Riot in 1919.* New York: Arno, 1958.

Keating, Ann Durkin. *Building Chicago: Suburban Developers and the Creation of a Divided Metropolis.* DeKalb: Northern Illinois University Press, 2002.

Kent, Frank R. *The Great Game of Politics.* Buffalo: Economics, 1923, 1959.

Kerney, James. *The Political Education of Woodrow Wilson.* New York: Century, 1926.

King, Hoyt. *Citizen Cole of Chicago.* Chicago: Horder's, 1932.

Kleppner, Paul. *The Cross of Culture: A Social Analysis of Midwestern Politics, 1850–1900.* New York: Free, 1970.

Kolata, Gina. *The Story of the Great Influenza Epidemic of 1918 and the Search for the Virus That Caused It.* New York: Farrah, Straus, and Giroux, 1999.

Kraus, Adolf. *Reminiscences and Comments.* Chicago: Toby Rubovits, 1925.

Kyvig, David Y. *Daily Life in the United States, 1920–1940: How Americans Lived Through the Roaring Twenties and the Great Depression.* New York: Ivan R. Dee, 2004.

Lasch, Christopher. *Haven in a Heartless World: The Family Besieged.* New York: Basic, 1977.

Lear, Linda J. *Harold L. Ickes: The Aggressive Progressive.* New York: Garland, 1981.

Leidenberger, Georg. *Chicago's Progressive Alliance: Labor and the Bid for Public Streetcars.* DeKalb: Northern Illinois University Press, 2006.

Leonard, John W., ed. *The Book of Chicagoans, 1905.* Chicago: A.N. Marquis, 1905.

Lewis, Lloyd. *Chicago: The History of Its Reputation.* Pt. 1. New York: Harcourt, Brace, 1929.

Lind, Alan R. *Chicago Surface Lines: An Illustrated History.* Park Forest, IL: Transport History, 1974.

Lindberg, Richard C. *King of Clark Street: Michael C. McDonald and the Rise of Chicago's Democratic Machine.* Carbondale: Southern Illinois University Press, 2009.

Link, Arthur S., ed. *The Papers of Woodrow Wilson.* Princeton: Princeton University Press, 1966.

_____. *Wilson: The Road to the White House.* Princeton: Princeton University Press, 1953.

Lloyd, Caro. *Henry Demarest Lloyd, 1847–1903: A Biography.* New York: G.P. Putnam's Sons/Knickerbocker, 1912.

Lohr, Lenox R. *Fair Management: The Story of the Progress Exhibition.* Chicago: Cuneo, 1952.

Lyons, Maurice F. *William F. McCombs, President Maker.* Cincinnati: Bancroft, 1922.

Mahan, Alfred. *The Influence of Sea Power upon History, 1660–1793.* London: S. Low, Marston, 1890.

Martin, Ralph G. *The Bosses.* New York: G.P. Putnam's Sons, 1964.

Masters, Charles J. *Governor Henry Horner, Chicago Politics, and the Great Depression.* Carbondale: Southern Illinois University Press, 2007.

McCaffrey, Lawrence, et al. *The Irish in Chicago.* Urbana: University of Illinois Press, 1987.

McCombs, William F., and William James Lang, ed. *Making Woodrow Wilson President.* New York: Fairview, 1921.

McDonald, Forrest. *Insull.* Chicago: University of Chicago Press, 1962.

McMurry, Scott. *Meeting the Challenge: The History of Ross & Hardies, 1902–2002.* Chicago: Ross and Hardies, 2002.

Merriam, Charles S. *The Government of the Metropolitan Region.* Chicago: University of Chicago Press, 1933.

_____. *Chicago: A More Intimate View of Urban Politics.* New York: Macmillan, 1929.

Merrill, Horace S. *Bourbon Leaders: Grover Cleveland and the Democratic Party.* Boston: Little, Brown, 1957.

Merriner, James. *Grafters and Goos Goos: Corruption and Reform in Chicago.* Carbondale: Southern Illinois University Press, 2008.

Merton, Robert K. "The Latent Functions of the Machine," in Stave, Bruce M., ed. *Urban Bosses, Machines, and Progressive Reformers.* Lexington, MA: D.C. Heath, 1972.

Meyers, Gustavus. *History of the Great American Fortunes.* vol. 3 *Great Fortunes from Railroads (continued).* Chicago: Charles Kerr, 1911.

Meyers, Margaret G. *A Financial History of the United States.* New York: Columbia University Press, 1970.

Miller, Kristie. *Ruth Hannah McCormick: A Life in Politics.* Albuquerque: University of New Mexico Press, 1992.

Miller, Zane L. *Boss Cox's Cincinnati: Urban Politics in the Progressive Era.* New York: Oxford University Press, 1968.

Morton, Richard Allen. *Justice and Humanity: Edward F. Dunne, Illinois Progressive.* Carbondale: Southern Illinois University Press, 1998.

_____. *Roger C. Sullivan and the Making of the Chicago Democratic Machine, 1881–1908.* Jefferson, NC: McFarland, 2016.

Moss, David A. *Socializing Security: Progressive-Era Economists and the Origins of American Social Policy.* Cambridge: Harvard University Press, 1995.

Mullen, Arthur F. *Western Democrat.* New York: Wilfred Funk, 1949.

Munro, William Bennett. *Personality in Politics: A Study of Three Types in American Public Life.* New York: Macmillan, 1924.

Nevins, Allan. *Grover Cleveland: A Study in Courage.* New York: Dodd, Mead, 1934.

_____. *Letters of Grover Cleveland.* Boston: Houghton Mifflin, 1933.

Norton, Samuel Wilber. *Chicago Traction: A History of Legislative and Political.* Chicago: N.p., 1907.

Nowland, James D., ed. *Illinois Major Party Platforms, 1900–1964.* Institute of Government and Public Affairs. Champaign: University of Illinois Press, 1966.

Oberholtzer, Ellis Parson. *The Referendum in America: Together with Some Chapters on the Initiative and Recall.* New York: Scribner's, 1912.

Ornig, Joseph R. *My Last Chance to Be a Boy: Theodore Roosevelt's South American Expedition of 1913–1914.* Baton Rouge: Louisiana State University Press, 1994.

Ostrogorski, Moisei. *Democracy and the Organization of Political Parties,* vol. 2. New York: Macmillan, 1902.

Palmer, George T. *A Conscientious Turncoat: The Story of John M. Palmer, 1817–1900.* New Haven: Yale University Press, 1941.

Parker, George F. *Recollections of Grover Cleveland.* New York: Century, 1909.

Paulson, Ross E. *Radicalism & Reform: The Vrooman Family and American Social Thought, 1837–1937.* Lexington: University of Kentucky Press, 1968.

Peterson, H.C., and Gilbert C. Fite. *Opponents of the War, 1917–1918.* Seattle: University of Washington Press, 1968.

Pettigrew, Richard F. *Imperial Washington: The Story of American Public Life from 1870–1920.* New York: Arno, 1970 [1922].

Platt, Harold L. *The Electric City: Energy and the Growth of the Chicago Area, 1880–1930.* Chicago: University of Chicago Press, 1991.

Poor's Publishing Company. *Moody's Manual of Railroad and Corporation Securities, Twenty-Second Annual Number, 1921.* New York: Poor's, 1921.

Porter, Kirk H., and Donald Bruce Johnson. *National Party Platforms, 1840–1964.* Urbana: University of Illinois Press, 1966.

Pringle, Henry F. *The Life and Times of William Howard Taft.* 2 vols. New York: Farrar and Rinehart, 1939.

Proctor, Ben. *William Randolph Hearst: The Early Years, 1863–1910.* Oxford: Oxford University Press, 1998.

Reynolds, George M. *Machine Politics in New Orleans, 1897–1926.* New York: Columbia University Press, 1936.

Rice, Wallace. *75 Years of Gas Service in Chicago.* Chicago: The People's Gas Light and Coke Company, 1925.

Riordan, William L. *Plunkitt of Tammany Hall.* New York: E.P. Dutton, 1905.

Robinson, Doane. *History of South Dakota.* Logansport, IN: B.F. Bowen, 1904.

Roseboom, Eugene H. *A History of Presidential Elections: From George Washington to Richard M. Nixon.* New York: Macmillan, 1957, 1960.

Rothman, David. *Conscience and Convenience: The Asylums and Its Alternatives in Progressive America.* Boston: Little, Brown, 1980.

Rudwick, Elliot. *Race Riot at East St. Louis, July 2, 1917.* New York: World, 1966.

Salter, J.T. *Boss Rule: Portraits in City Politics.* New York: McGraw-Hill, 1935.

Salzman, Neil V. *Reform and Revolution: The Life and Times of Raymond Robins.* Kent, OH: Kent State University Press, 1991.

Sandberg, Carl. *Chicago Poems.* New York: Henry Holt, 1916.

Schmidt, John R. *"The Mayor Who Cleaned Up Chicago": A Political Biography of William E. Dever.* DeKalb: Northern Illinois University Press, 1989.

Shapiro, Ben. *Project President: Bad Hair and Botox on the Road to the White House.* Nashville: Thomas Nelson, 2008.

Skilnik, Bob. *Beer: A History of Brewing in Chicago.* Fort Lee, NJ: Barricade, 2006.

Snead, William T. *If Christ Came to Chicago!* Chicago: Laird and Lee, 1894.

Spear, Allan H. *Black Chicago: The Making of a Negro Ghetto, 1890–1920.* Chicago: University of Chicago Press, 1967.

Staley, William H. *History of the Illinois Federation of Labor.* Chicago: University of Chicago Press, 1930.

Stanton, Cady Elizabeth, et al. *A History of the Woman's Suffrage Movement,* 2d ed. Rochester, NY: Mann, 1922.

Stave, Bruce M. *The New Deal and the Last Hurrah: Pittsburgh Machine Politics.* Pittsburgh: University of Pittsburgh, 1970.

_____. *Urban Bosses, Machines, and Progressive Reformers.* Lexington, MA: D.C. Heath, 1972.

Steffens, Lincoln. *The Shame of the Cities.* New York: McClure, Phillips, 1904.

———. *The Struggle for Self-Government.* New York: McClure, Phillips, 1906.

Stein, C.A. *Resurgent Republicanism.* Ann Arbor, MI: Edwards Bros., 1963.

Steinberg. Alfred. *The Bosses.* New York: Macmillan, 1972.

Stone, Ralph. *The Irreconcilables: The Fight Against the League of Nations.* New York: W.W. Norton, 1973.

Strong, Josiah. *Our Country, Its Possible Future and Its Present Crisis.* New York: Baker and Taylor for the American Home Missionary Society, 1885.

Stuart, William H. *The Twenty Incredible Years.* Chicago: M.A. Donohue, 1935.

Studenski, Paul, and Herman E. Krooss. *Financial History of the United States.* New York: McGraw-Hil, 1952.

Swanberg, W.A. *Citizen Hearst: A Biography of William Randolph Hearst.* New York: Charles Scribner's Sons, 1961.

Tansill, Charles. *America and the Fight for Irish Freeman, 1866–1922.* New York: Devin-Adair, 1957.

Tarr, Joel Arthur. *A Study in Boss Politics: William Lorimer of Chicago.* Champaign: University of Illinois, 1971.

Thomas, Charles A. *Thomas Riley Marshal, Hoosier Statesman.* Oxford, OH: Mississippi Valley, 1939.

Thompson, Charles Willis. *Presidents I Have Known and Two Near Presidents.* Indianapolis: Bobbs-Merrill, 1929.

Timberlake, James S. *Prohibition and the Progressive Movement.* New York: Athenaeum, 1970.

Townsend, Walter A. *The Illinois Democracy: A History of the Party and Its Representative Members—Past and Present,* 5 vols. Springfield: Democratic Historical Association, 1935.

Trask, David F. *The War with Spain in 1898.* Lincoln: University of Nebraska Press, reprint, 1997.

Troesken, Werner. *Why Regulate Utilities? The New Institutional Economies and the Chicago Gas Industry, 1849–1924.* Ann Arbor: University of Michigan Press, 1996.

Tumulty, Joseph P. *Woodrow Wilson As I Know Him.* Garden City, NJ: Doubleday, 1921.

Tuttle, Charles R. *The Illinois Currency Convention.* Chicago: Charles H. Kerr, 1895.

Tuttle, William M., Jr. *Race Riot: Chicago in the Red Summer of 1919.* New York: Atheneum, 1971.

Van Devander, Charles W. *The Big Bosses.* New York: Ayer, 1974.

Walker, John K. *William Randolph Hearst, A New Appraisal.* New York: Hastings House, 1955.

Waller, Robert. *Rainey of Illinois: A Political Biography, 1903–1934.* Illinois Studies in Social Sci-

ences, no. 60. Champaign: University of Illinois Press, 1977.

Walworth, Arthur. *Wilson and His Peacemakers: American Diplomats at the Paris Peace Conference, 1919.* New York: W.W. Norton, 1986.

Webb, W.L. *Champ Clark.* New York: Neale, 1912.

Weber, Harry P. *Outline History of Chicago Traction.* Chicago: n.p., 1936.

Weiss, Nancy Joan. *Charles Francis Murphy, 1859–1924: Respectability and Responsibility in Tammany Politics.* Northampton, MA: Smith College, 1968.

Welch, Richard F. *Big Tim Sullivan, Tammany Hall, and New York City from the Gilded Age to the Progressive Era.* Madison, NJ: Farleigh Dickinson University Press, 2008.

Wendt, Lloyd, and Herman Kogan. *Big Bill of Chicago.* Indianapolis: Bobbs-Merrill, 1953.

Whicher, George F. *William Jennings Bryan and the Campaign of 1896.* Boston: D.C. Heath, 1953.

White, William Allen. *The Autobiography of William Allen White.* New York: Macmillan, 1946.

Wilson, Woodrow. *Congressional Government.* Boston: Houghton-Mifflin, 1885.

———. *Division and Reunion.* New York: Longmans, Green, 1893.

———. *A History of the American People.* 5 vols. New York: Harper and Bros., 1902.

Winkler, John K. *William Randolph Hearst: An American Phenomenon.* New York: Simon & Schuster, 1928.

Wooddy, Carroll Hill. *The Case of Frank L. Smith: A Study in Representative Government.* Chicago: University of Chicago Press, 1931.

Young, David. *Chicago Transit: An Illustrated History.* DeKalb: Northern Illinois University Press, 1998.

Zink, Harold. *City Bosses in the United States: A Study of Twenty Municipal Bosses.* Durham: Duke University Press, 1930.

Articles

Abbott, W. J. "The Carter Harrison Dynasty in Chicago." *Munsey* 24 (1898): 809–15.

Addams, Jane. "Why the Ward Boss Rules." *The Outlook* 58 (2 April 1898): 879–82.

"Appointer General." *World's Work* 26 (October 1913): 616.

Bankhead, John H. "Why Oscar Underwood Should Be Elected President." *Editorial Review* 6 (April 1912).

Barnes, James A. "The Gold Standard Democrats and the Party Conflict." *Mississippi Valley Historical Review* 17 (December 1930): 422–450.

Beito, David T., and Royster Beito. "Gold Democrats and the Decline of Classic Liberalism, 1896–1900." *Independent Review* 4 (Spring 2000): 555–75.

Block, Marvin W. "Henry T. Rainey of Illinois." *Journal of the Illinois State Historical Society* 65 (Summer 1972): 142–58.

Boxman, Burton A. "Adolph Joachim Sabath in Congress: The Early Years, 1907–1932." *Journal of the Illinois State Historical Society* 66 (1973): 327–40.

Bryan, William Jennings. "The Issue for 1900." *North American Review* 170 (June 1900): 753–71.

Buenker, John D. "City Ethics and the Politics of Accommodation." *Chicago History* 3 (Fall 1974): 92–100.

_____. "Dynamics of Chicago Ethnic Politics, 1900–1930." *Journal of the Illinois State Historical Society* 57 (1974): 175–99.

_____. "Edward F. Dunne: The Urban New Stock Democrat as Progressive." *Mid-America* 50 (1968): 3–21.

_____. "The Illinois Legislature and Prohibition, 1907–1919." *Journal of the Illinois State Historical Society* 62 (1969): 363–84.

_____. "The Urban Political Machine and the Seventeenth Amendment." *Journal of American History* 56 (September 1969): 305–22.

Cain, Louis P. "To Annex or Not? A Tale of Two Towns, Evanston and Hyde Park." *Explorations in Economic History* 29 (1983): 58–72.

Candeloro, Dominic. "The School Board Crisis of 1907." *Journal of the Illinois State Historical Society* 68 (1975): 396–406.

Darrow, Clarence S. "Chicago's Traction Question." *International* 12 (October 1905): 13–22.

Dernberg, Bernard. "The Ties That Bind America and Germany," pt. 2. *World's Work* 29 (December 1914): 186–89.

Dittey, Robert M. "Judson Harmon of Ohio—A Man of Deeds Not Words. *Editorial Review* 6 (April 1912): 316–24.

Duffus, Robert L. "The Tragedy of Hearst." *World's Work* 44 (October 1922): 623–31.

Dunne Edward F. "Chicago's Fight for Municipal Ownership." *Independent* 51 (18 October 1906): 927–30.

_____. "How Chicago Will Do It." *World's Work* 10 (June 1905): 6265–66.

"Exit the American Saloon." *World's Work* 37 (March 1919): 492–93.

Fairlie, John A. "The Illinois Legislation of 1923." *Journal of Political Economics* 21 (1913): 931–7.

_____. "Municipal Functions in the United States." *Annals of the American Academy of Political and Social Sciences* 25 (1905): 304–8.

"Fighting Germany's Spies," pt. 8. *World's Work* 38 (August 1918): 393–401.

Fitch, George. "The Noiseless Suffragette." *Collier's* 51 (9 August 1913): 4–6.

_____. "Politics in Illinois. *Collier's* 51 (9 August 1913): 21–2; 29.

Fite, Gilbert C. "Republican Strategy and the Farm Vote in the Presidential Campaign of 1896." *American Historical Review* 55 (1960): 794–803.

Giffen, Robert. "The Gresham Law." *Economic Journal* 1 (1891): 304–06.

Gould, Alan B. "Walter L. Fisher: Profile of an Urban Reformer." *Mid-America* 57–58 (1975): 151–72.

Green, Paul Michael. "Irish Chicago: Multi-Ethnic Road to Machine Success" in Melvin G. Holli, and d'A Jones, Peter. *Ethnic Chicago.* W.B. Eerdmans, 1995.

Grosser, Hugo S. "The Movement for Municipal Ownership in Chicago." *Annals of the American Academy of Political and Social Sciences* 27 (1906): 27–90.

Hale, William Bayard. "Chicago, Its Struggle and Its Dream." *World's Work* 19 (April 1910): 12792–805.

_____. "Judson Harmon and the Presidency." *World's Work* 22 (June 1911): 14446–59.

_____. "Thomas Riley Marshall." *World's Work* 24 (October 1912): 630–38.

Hart, Rollin Lynde. "When the Negro Comes North: II, Future Results of the Migration." *World's Work* 48 (July 1924): 318–23.

Havig, Alan R. "The Raymond Robins Case for Progressive Republicanisms." *Journal of the Illinois State Historical Society* 64 (1971): 401–18.

Hawthorne, Daniel. "Golf and Good Health." *World's Work* 40 (August 1912): 393–403.

Hayes, Samuel P. "The Politics of Reform in Municipal Government in the Progressive Era." *Pacific Northwest Quarterly* 55 (1964): 157–69.

Hendrick, Burton J. "The Recall of Justice Hughes." *World's Work* 32 (August 1915): 397–410.

Hoffman, Charles. "The Depression of the Nineties." *Journal of Economic History* 16 (June 1956): 137–64.

Hofstadter, Richard. "The Folklore of Populism." In *Anti-Semitism in the United States,* ed. Leonard Dinnerstein. New York: Holt, Rinehart, and Winston, 1957.

Huthmacher, J. Joseph. "Charles Evans Hughes and Charles Francis Murphy: The Metamorphosis of Progressivism." *New York History* 44 (January 1965): 28–34.

_____. "Urbana Liberalism and the Age of Reform." *Mississippi Valley Historical Review* 49 (September 1962: 231–41.

"Interview with Mr. Dalyrumple." *Street Railway Journal* 26 (August 1905): 22–4.

Jones, Walter Clyde. "The Direct Primary in Illinois." *Proceedings of the American Political Science Association* 7 (1910): 138–62.

Kearney, James. "How Wilson Was Shown to the Nation." *Washington Post* (25 October 1927): 1, 5.

Lauzanne, Stephane. "Will French Women Ever Vote?" *World's Work* 48 (August 1924): 398–402.

Lewis, Alfred Henry. "The Real Woodrow Wilson." *Hearst Magazine* 22 (May 1912): 2265–2274.

Lindstrom, Andrew F. "Lawrence Stringer: A Wilson Democrat." *Journal of the Illinois State Historical Society* 66 (1973): 20–40.

Link Arthur S. "The Baltimore Convention of 1912." *American Historical Review* 50 (July 1945): 691–713.

_____. "A Letter from One of Wilson's Managers." *American Historical Review* 50 (July 1945): 768–75.

Low, Theodore J. "Machine Politics—Old and New." *The Public Interest* 9 (Fall 1967): 83–97.

Lowry, Edward G. "The War in the Middle West." *World's Work* 33 (March 1917): 510–15.

Lyle, Eugene F. "Taft: A Career of Big Tasks." *World's Work* 14 (July 1907): 9135–44.

McCarthy, Michael P. "Prelude to Armageddon, Charles E. Merriam and the Chicago Mayoral Election of 1911." *Journal of the Illinois State Historical Society* 67 (November 1974): 5051–11.

McFarlane, Peter Clark. "Is Roger Sullivan a Boss?" *Collier's* 58 (8 August 1914): 5–6.

McKitrick, Eric L. "The Study of Corruption." *Political Science Quarterly* 72 (December 1957): 502–14.

Middleton, James. "Are Americans More German Than English?" *World's Work* 31 (December 1915): 141–47.

Miller, Kristie. "Ruth Hanna McCormick and the Election of 1930." Journal *of the Illinois State Historical Society* 63 (1968): 191–210.

Morton, Richard Allen. "Edward F. Dunne: Illinois' Most Progressive Governor." *Illinois Historical Journal* 83 (1990): 218–34.

_____. "'It was Bryan and Sullivan who did the trick': How William Jennings Bryan and Illinois' Roger C. Sullivan Brought the Nomination to Woodrow Wilson in 1912." *Journal of the Illinois State Historical Society* 108 (Summer 2015): 147–81.

_____. "'A Man of Belial': Roger C. Sullivan, the Progressive Democracy and Senatorial Elections of 1914." *Journal of the Illinois State Historical Society* 91 (Autumn 1991): 133–59.

_____. "A Victorian Tragedy: The Strange Deaths of Carter H. Harrison and Patrick Eugene Prendergast." *Journal of the Illinois State Historical Society* 96 (Spring 2003), 6–36.

Murphy, Majorie. "Taxation and Social Conflict: Teacher Unionism and Public School Finance in Chicago, 1889–1934." *Journal of the Illinois State Historical Society* 74 (1981): 242–60.

Nelli, Humbert. "John Powers and the Italians: Politics in a Chicago Ward, 1896–1921." *Journal of American History* 57 (June 1970): 67–84.

Pollack, Norman. "The Myth of Populist Anti-Semitism." *American Historical Review* 68 (October 1962): 76–80.

Powers, Stanley. "Chicago's Strike Ordeal." *World's Work* 10 (July 1905): 6378–84.

Price, Theodore H., and Richard Spillane. "Stalking for Nine Million Votes. *World's Work* 32 (October 1916): 663–77.

Roberts, Sidney I. "The Municipal Voters League and Chicago Boodlers." *Journal of the Illinois State Historical Society* 53 (1960): 117–40.

Rogers, Walter S. "The Embarrassing Mr. Sullivan." *Harper's Weekly* 59 (24 October 1914): 394–95.

"A Short Measure of What President Roosevelt Has Done." *World's Work* 17 (March 1909): 1311–12.

Smith, Herbert Knox. "Gifford Pinchot, Forester." *World's Work* 16 (July 1908): 10427–10430.

Stockbridge, Frank. "Champ Clark of Pike County." *World's Work* 23 (May 1912): 483–84.

_____. "How Woodrow Wilson Won His Nomination." *Current History* 20 (July 1924): 567–71.

Sullivan, Mark. "Why the West Dislikes New York." *World's Work* 51 (February 1926): 406–11.

Tarbell, Ida. "How Chicago Is Finding Itself." Pts. 1 and 2. *American Magazine* 667 (1908): 29–41, 124–38.

Tarr, Joel A. "The Urban Politician as Entrepreneur." *Mid-America* 59 (January 1967): 56–63.

"Theodore Roosevelt." *World's Work* 37 (February 1919): 371–72.

Trout, Grace Wilbur. "Sidelights on Illinois Suffrage History." *Journal of the Illinois State Historical Society* 12 (1920): 145–79.

Waller, Robert A. "The Illinois Waterway from Conception to Completion, 1908–1913." *Journal of the Illinois State Historical Society* 65 (1972): 125–41.

West, Roy O., and William C. Walton. "Charles Deneen, 1863–1940." *Journal of the Illinois State Historical Society* 34 (1941): 12–25.

"What the Council of National Defense Is Doing." *World's Work* 33 (April 1917): 629–36.

Wish, Harvey. "Governor Altgeld Pardons the Anarchists." *Journal of the Illinois State Historical Society* 31 (1938): 424–48.

Wrone, David R. "Illinois Pulls Out of the Mud." *Journal of the Illinois State Historical Society* 58 (1965): 54–75.

Unpublished Manuscripts and Theses

Beldon, Gertrude. "A History of the Woman Suffrage Movement in Illinois." Ph.D. diss., University of Chicago, 1971.

Callender, Richard W. "Walter L. Fisher, 1862–1935: The Regulation of Public Utilities." Master's thesis, University of Illinois, 1963.

Eisenstein, Sophia J. "The Elections of 1912 in Chicago." Master's thesis, University of Chicago, 1947.

Fisher, Walter L. "Autobiographical Sketch." Illinois Historical Survey, University of Illinois Library, Urbana-Champaign. [1932?]

Green, Paul M. "The Chicago Democratic Party, 1840–1920: From Factionalism to Political Organization." Ph.D. diss., University of Chicago, 1975.

Haupt, Richard Walter. "History of the French Lick Springs Hotel." Master's thesis, Indiana University, 1953.

Lilly, Samuel A. "The Political Career of Roger Sullivan." Master's thesis, Eastern Illinois University, 1964.

McCarthy, Michael. "Businessmen and Professionals in Municipal Reform: The Chicago Experience, 1867–1920." Ph.D. diss., Northwestern University, 1970.

Morrison, Geoffrey F. "A Political Biography of Champ Clark." Ph.D. diss., St. Louis University, 1971.

Philip, William B. "Chicago and the Downstate: The Story of Their Conflict, 1870–1934." Ph.D. diss., University of Chicago, 1940.

Post, Louis F. "Living a Long Life Over Again." Louis Freeland Post Papers, Manuscript Division, Library of Congress, Washington, D.C.

Straetz, Ralph Arthur. "The Progressive Movement in Illinois, 1910–1916." Ph.D. diss., University of Illinois, 1958.

Thurner, Arthur W. "The Impact of Ethnic Groups on the Democratic Party in Chicago, 1920–1928," Ph.D. diss., University of Chicago, 1966.

Tingley, Ralph R. "From Carter Harrison II to Fred Busse: A Study of Chicago Political Parties and Personages from 1896 to 1907." Ph.D. diss., University of Chicago, 1950.

Warner, Mildred C. "The History of the Deep Waterway in the State of Illinois." Master's thesis, University of Illinois, 1947.

Weber, Robert David. "Rationalizers and Reformers, Chicago Local Transportation in the Nineteenth Century" Ph.D. diss., University of Wisconsin, 1971.

Index

Numbers in *bold italics* indicate pages with illustrations

www.ingramcontent.com/pod-product-compliance
Lightning Source LLC
Chambersburg PA
CBHW080553270326
41929CB00019B/3290